SELECTED ESSAYS

T. S. ELIOT

SELECTED
ESSAYS

NEW EDITION

Harcourt, Brace & World, Inc.

New York

Fourteenth Printing

TO

Harriet Shaw Weaver

IN GRATITUDE,
AND IN RECOGNITION OF HER SERVICES
TO ENGLISH LETTERS

I HAVE EXPANDED the original volume of *Selected Essays: 1917-1932* by including a few essays from the now superfluous *Essays Ancient and Modern*. There remain several uncollected papers which I am disposed to preserve, as well as a number of unpublished lectures, on matters connected with the art of poetry, which await their final form. But *Selected Essays* is already bulky enough; and any literary essays which are not to be found in it must abide their collection into another book.

On reviewing the contents of this book, I find myself at times inclined to quarrel with my own opinions, and more often to criticise the way in which they were expressed. For myself, this book is a kind of historical record of my interests and opinions. As one grows older one may become less dogmatic and pragmatical; but there is no assurance that one becomes wiser; and it is even likely that one becomes less sensitive. And where I have adhered to the same opinions, many readers may prefer them in the form in which they were first expressed.

T. S. E.

London: July, 1950.

M Y ACKNOWLEDGMENTS are due to Messrs. Methuen & Co. Ltd. and Alfred A. Knopf, Inc. (for the parts of *The Sacred Wood*, reprinted); to Messrs. Doubleday, Doran & Co. (for essays reprinted from *For Lancelot Andrewes*); to The Hogarth Press (*Homage to John Dryden*); to The Haslewood Press (for *A Dialogue on Dramatic Poetry*); to Messrs. Constable & Co. Ltd. (for *Seneca in Elizabethan Translation*, originally printed as Introduction to the Tudor Translations Series edition of the *Tenne Tragedies*); to the Shakespeare Association and the Oxford University Press (*Shakespeare and the Senecan Tradition*); to Mr. Walter de la Mare and the Royal Society of Literature (*Arnold and Pater*); to The Blackamore Press (*Baudelaire*); to the English Association (*Charles Whibley*). Also to *The Egoist, The Athenaeum, The Times Literary Supplement, Art and Letters, The Hound and Horn, The Bookman*, and *The Criterion*, in which most of these papers originally appeared.

My thanks are also due to Mr. B. L. Richmond, without whose suggestions and encouragement the essays on Elizabethan dramatists would not have been written; and to Mr. F. V. Morley for his assistance in selecting the essays and in reading the proofs, and for his pertinacity in harrying me to do what work I have myself done in preparation of this volume.

T. S. E.

London: April, 1932.

CONTENTS

I

II

III

I

TRADITION AND
THE INDIVIDUAL TALENT

IN English writing we seldom speak of tradition,
though we occasionally apply its name in deploring its absence.
We cannot refer to "the tradition" or to "a tradition"; at most,
we employ the adjective in saying that the poetry of So-and-so is
"traditional" or even "too traditional." Seldom, perhaps, does
the word appear except in a phrase of censure. If otherwise, it is
vaguely approbative, with the implication, as to the work approved, of some pleasing archaeological reconstruction. You can
hardly make the word agreeable to English ears without this
comfortable reference to the reassuring science of archaeology.

Certainly the word is not likely to appear in our appreciations
of living or dead writers. Every nation, every race, has not only
its own creative, but its own critical turn of mind; and is even
more oblivious of the shortcomings and limitations of its critical
habits than of those of its creative genius. We know, or think
we know, from the enormous mass of critical writing that has
appeared in the French language the critical method or habit of
the French; we only conclude (we are such unconscious people)
that the French are "more critical" than we, and sometimes even
plume ourselves a little with the fact, as if the French were the
less spontaneous. Perhaps they are; but we might remind ourselves that criticism is as inevitable as breathing, and that we
should be none the worse for articulating what passes in our
minds when we read a book and feel an emotion about it, for
criticizing our own minds in their work of criticism. One of the
facts that might come to light in this process is our tendency to

3

insist, when we praise a poet, upon those aspects of his work in which he least resembles any one else. In these aspects or parts of his work we pretend to find what is individual, what is the peculiar essence of the man. We dwell with satisfaction upon the poet's difference from his predecessors, especially his immediate predecessors; we endeavour to find something that can be isolated in order to be enjoyed. Whereas if we approach a poet without this prejudice we shall often find that not only the best, but the most individual parts of his work may be those in which the dead poets, his ancestors, assert their immortality most vigorously. And I do not mean the impressionable period of adolescence, but the period of full maturity.

Yet if the only form of tradition, of handing down, consisted in following the ways of the immediate generation before us in a blind or timid adherence to its successes, "tradition" should positively be discouraged. We have seen many such simple currents soon lost in the sand; and novelty is better than repetition. Tradition is a matter of much wider significance. It cannot be inherited, and if you want it you must obtain it by great labour. It involves, in the first place, the historical sense, which we may call nearly indispensable to any one who would continue to be a poet beyond his twenty-fifth year; and the historical sense involves a perception, not only of the pastness of the past, but of its presence; the historical sense compels a man to write not merely with his own generation in his bones, but with a feeling that the whole of the literature of Europe from Homer and within it the whole of the literature of his own country has a simultaneous existence and composes a simultaneous order. This historical sense, which is a sense of the timeless as well as of the temporal and of the timeless and of the temporal together, is what makes a writer traditional. And it is at the same time what makes a writer most acutely conscious of his place in time, of his own contemporaneity.

No poet, no artist of any art, has his complete meaning alone. His significance, his appreciation is the appreciation of his relation to the dead poets and artists. You cannot value him alone; you must set him, for contrast and comparison, among the dead. I mean this as a principle of aesthetic, not merely historical, criticism. The necessity that he shall conform, that he shall cohere, is not onesided; what happens when a new work of art is created is something that happens simultaneously to all the works of art which preceded it. The existing monuments form an ideal order among themselves, which is modified by the introduction of the new (the really new) work of art among them. The existing order is complete before the new work arrives; for order to persist after the supervention of novelty, the *whole* existing order must be, if ever so slightly, altered; and so the relations, proportions, values of each work of art toward the whole are readjusted; and this is conformity between the old and the new. Whoever has approved this idea of order, of the form of European, of English literature will not find it preposterous that the past should be altered by the present as much as the present is directed by the past. And the poet who is aware of this will be aware of great difficulties and responsibilities.

In a peculiar sense he will be aware also that he must inevitably be judged by the standards of the past. I say judged, not amputated, by them; not judged to be as good as, or worse or better than, the dead; and certainly not judged by the canons of dead critics. It is a judgment, a comparison, in which two things are measured by each other. To conform merely would be for the new work not really to conform at all; it would not be new, and would therefore not be a work of art. And we do not quite say that the new is more valuable because it fits in; but its fitting in is a test of its value—a test, it is true, which can only be slowly and cautiously applied, for we are none of us infallible judges of conformity. We say: it appears to conform, and is perhaps individual, or it appears individual, and many conform; but we are hardly likely to find that it is one and not the other.

To proceed to a more intelligible exposition of the relation of the poet to the past: he can neither take the past as a lump, an indiscriminate bolus, nor can he form himself wholly on one or two private admirations, nor can he form himself wholly upon one preferred period. The first course is inadmissible, the second is an important experience of youth, and the third is a pleasant and highly desirable supplement. The poet must be very conscious of the main current, which does not at all flow invariably through the most distinguished reputations. He must be quite aware of the obvious fact that art never improves, but that the material of art is never quite the same. He must be aware that the mind of Europe—the mind of his own country—a mind which he learns in time to be much more important than his own private mind—is a mind which changes, and that this change is a development which abandons nothing *en route*, which does not superannuate either Shakespeare, or Homer, or the rock drawing of the Magdalenian draughtsmen. That this development, refinement perhaps, complication certainly, is not, from the point of view of the artist, any improvement. Perhaps not even an improvement from the point of view of the psychologist or not to the extent which we imagine; perhaps only in the end based upon a complication in economics and machinery. But the difference between the present and the past is that the conscious present is an awareness of the past in a way and to an extent which the past's awareness of itself cannot show.

Some one said: "The dead writers are remote from us because we *know* so much more than they did." Precisely, and they are that which we know.

I am alive to a usual objection to what is clearly part of my programme for the *métier* of poetry. The objection is that the doctrine requires a ridiculous amount of erudition (pedantry), a claim which can be rejected by appeal to the lives of poets in any pantheon. It will even be affirmed that much learning deadens or perverts poetic sensibility. While, however, we persist in believing that a poet ought to know as much as will not encroach upon his necessary receptivity and necessary laziness, it is not desirable to confine knowledge to whatever can be put into a useful shape for examinations, drawing-rooms, or the still more pretentious modes of publicity. Some can absorb knowledge, the more tardy must sweat for it. Shakespeare acquired more essential history from Plutarch than most men could from the whole British Museum. What is to be insisted upon is that the poet must develop or procure the consciousness of the past and that he should continue to develop this consciousness throughout his career.

What happens is a continual surrender of himself as he is at the moment to something which is more valuable. The progress of an artist is a continual self-sacrifice, a continual extinction of personality.

There remains to define this process of depersonalization and its relation to the sense of tradition. It is in this depersonalization that art may be said to approach the condition of science. I, therefore, invite you to consider, as a suggestive analogy, the action which takes place when a bit of finely filiated platinum is introduced into a chamber containing oxygen and sulphur dioxide.

I I

Honest criticism and sensitive appreciation are directed not upon the poet but upon the poetry. If we attend to the confused cries of the newspaper critics and the *susurrus* of popular repetition that follows, we shall hear the names of poets in great numbers; if we seek not Blue-book knowledge but the enjoyment of poetry, and ask for a poem, we shall seldom find it. I have tried to point out the importance of the relation of the poem to other poems by other authors, and suggested the conception of poetry as a living whole of all the poetry that has ever been written. The other aspect of this Impersonal theory of poetry is the relation of the poem to its author. And I hinted, by an analogy, that the mind of the mature poet differs from that of the immature one not precisely in any valuation of "personality," not being necessarily more interesting, or having "more to say," but rather by being a more finely perfected medium in which special, or very varied, feelings are at liberty to enter into new combinations.

The analogy was that of the catalyst. When the two gases previously mentioned are mixed in the presence of a filament of platinum, they form sulphurous acid. This combination takes place only if the platinum is present; nevertheless the newly formed acid contains no trace of platinum, and the platinum itself is apparently unaffected; has remained inert, neutral, and unchanged. The mind of the poet is the shred of platinum. It may partly or exclusively operate upon the experience of the man himself; but, the more perfect the artist, the more completely separate in him will be the man who suffers and the mind which creates; the more perfectly will the mind digest and transmute the passions which are its material.

The experience, you will notice, the elements which enter the presence of the transforming catalyst, are of two kinds: emotions and feelings. The effect of a work of art upon the person who enjoys it is an experience different in kind from any experience not of art. It may be formed out of one emotion, or may be a combination of several; and various feelings, inhering for the writer in particular words or phrases or images, may be added to compose the final result. Or great poetry may be made without the direct use of any emotion whatever: composed out of feelings solely. Canto XV of the *Inferno* (Brunetto Latini) is a working up of the emotion evident in the situation; but the effect, though single as that of any work of art, is obtained by considerable complexity of detail. The last quatrain gives an image, a feeling attaching to an image, which "came," which did not develop simply out of what precedes, but which was probably in suspension in the poet's mind until the proper combination arrived for it to add itself to. The poet's mind is in fact a receptacle for seizing and storing up numberless feelings, phrases, images, which remain there until all the particles which can unite to form a new compound are present together.

If you compare several representative passages of the greatest poetry you see how great is the variety of types of combination, and also how completely any semi-ethical criterion of "sublimity" misses the mark. For it is not the "greatness," the intensity, of the emotions, the components, but the intensity of the artistic process, the pressure, so to speak, under which the fusion takes place, that counts. The episode of Paolo and Francesca employs a definite emotion, but the intensity of the poetry is something quite different from whatever intensity in the supposed experience it may give the impression of. It is no more intense, furthermore, than Canto XXVI, the voyage of Ulysses, which has not the direct dependence upon an emotion. Great variety is possible in the process of transmutation of emotion: the murder of Agamemnon, or the agony of Othello, gives an artistic effect apparently closer to a possible original than the scenes from Dante.

In the *Agamemnon*, the artistic emotion approximates to the emotion of an actual spectator; in *Othello* to the emotion of the protagonist himself. But the difference between art and the event is always absolute; the combination which is the murder of Agamemnon is probably as complex as that which is the voyage of Ulysses. In either case there has been a fusion of elements. The ode of Keats contains a number of feelings which have nothing particular to do with the nightingale, but which the nightingale, partly, perhaps, because of its attractive name, and partly because of its reputation, served to bring together.

The point of view which I am struggling to attack is perhaps related to the metaphysical theory of the substantial unity of the soul: for my meaning is, that the poet has, not a "personality" to express, but a particular medium, which is only a medium and not a personality, in which impressions and experiences combine in peculiar and unexpected ways. Impressions and experiences which are important for the man may take no place in the poetry, and those which become important in the poetry may play quite a negligible part in the man, the personality.

I will quote a passage which is unfamiliar enough to be regarded with fresh attention in the light—or darkness—of these observations:

> *And now methinks I could e'en chide myself*
> *For doating on her beauty, though her death*
> *Shall be revenged after no common action.*
> *Does the silkworm expend her yellow labours*
> *For thee? For thee does she undo herself?*
> *Are lordships sold to maintain ladyships*
> *For the poor benefit of a bewildering minute?*
> *Why does yon fellow falsify highways,*
> *And put his life between the judge's lips,*
> *To refine such a thing—keeps horse and men*
> *To beat their valours for her? . . .*

In this passage (as is evident if it is taken in its context) there is a combination of positive and negative emotions: an intensely strong attraction toward beauty and an equally intense fascination by the ugliness which is contrasted with it and which destroys it. This balance of contrasted emotion is in the dramatic situation to which the speech is pertinent, but that situation alone is inadequate to it. This is, so to speak, the structural emotion, provided by the drama. But the whole effect, the dominant tone, is due to the fact that a number of floating feelings, having an affinity to this emotion by no means superficially evident, have combined with it to give us a new art emotion.

It is not in his personal emotions, the emotions provoked by particular events in his life, that the poet is in any way remarkable or interesting. His particular emotions may be simple, or crude, or flat. The emotion in his poetry will be a very complex thing, but not with the complexity of the emotions of people who have very complex or unusual emotions in life. One error, in fact, of eccentricity in poetry is to seek for new human emotions to express; and in this search for novelty in the wrong place it discovers the perverse. The business of the poet is not to find new emotions, but to use the ordinary ones and, in working them up into poetry, to express feelings which are not in actual emotions at all. And emotions which he has never experienced will serve his turn as well as those familiar to him. Consequently, we must believe that "emotion recollected in tranquillity" is an inexact formula. For it is neither emotion, nor recollection, nor, without distortion of meaning, tranquillity. It is a concentration, and a new thing resulting from the concentration, of a very great number of experiences which to the practical and active person would not seem to be experiences at all; it is a concentration which does not happen consciously or of deliberation. These experiences are not "recollected," and they finally unite in an atmosphere which is "tranquil" only in that it is a passive attending upon the event. Of course this is not quite the whole story. There is a great deal, in the writing of poetry, which must be conscious and deliberate. In fact, the bad poet is usually unconscious where he ought to be conscious, and conscious where he ought to be unconscious. Both errors tend to make him "personal." Poetry is not a turning loose of emotion, but an escape from emotion; it is not the expression of personality, but an escape from personality. But, of course, only those who have personality and emotions know what it means to want to escape from these things.

III

ὁ δὲ νοῦς ἴσως θειότερόν τι καὶ ἀπαθές ἐστιν.

This essay proposes to halt at the frontier of metaphysics or mysticism, and confine itself to such practical conclusions as can be applied by the responsible person interested in poetry. To divert interest from the poet to the poetry is a laudable aim: for it would conduce to a juster estimation of actual poetry, good and bad. There are many people who appreciate the expression of sincere emotion in verse, and there is a smaller number of people who can appreciate technical excellence. But very few know when there is an expression of *significant* emotion, emotion which has its life in the poem and not in the history of the poet. The emotion of art is impersonal. And the poet cannot reach this impersonality without surrendering himself wholly to the work to be done. And he is not likely to know what is to be done unless he lives in what is not merely the present, but the present moment of the past, unless he is conscious, not of what is dead, but of what is already living.

THE

FUNCTION OF CRITICISM

WRITING several years ago on the subject of the relation of the new to the old in art, I formulated a view to which I still adhere, in sentences which I take the liberty of quoting, because the present paper is an application of the principles they express:

"The existing monuments form an ideal order among themselves, which is modified by the introduction of the new (the really new) work of art among them. The existing order is complete before the new work arrives; for order to persist after the supervention of novelty, the *whole* existing order must be, if ever so slightly, altered; and so the relations, proportions, values of each work of art toward the whole are readjusted; and this is conformity between the old and the new. Whoever has approved this idea of order, of the form of European, of English literature, will not find it preposterous that the past should be altered by the present as much as the present is directed by the past."

I was dealing then with the artist, and the sense of tradition which, it seemed to me, the artist should have; but it was generally a problem of order; and the function of criticism seems to be essentially a problem of order too. I thought of literature then, as I think of it now, of the literature of the world, of the literature of Europe, of the literature of a single country, not as a collection of the writings of individuals, but as "organic wholes," as systems in relation to which, and only in relation to which, individual works of literary art, and the works of indi-

vidual artists, have their significance. There is accordingly something outside of the artist to which he owes allegiance, a devotion to which he must surrender and sacrifice himself in order
to earn and to obtain his unique position. A common inheritance
and a common cause unite artists consciously or unconsciously:
it must be admitted that the union is mostly unconscious. Between the true artists of any time there is, I believe, an unconscious community. And, as our instincts of tidiness imperatively
command us not to leave to the haphazard of unconsciousness
what we can attempt to do consciously, we are forced to conclude that what happens unconsciously we could bring about,
and form into a purpose, if we made a conscious attempt. The
second-rate artist, of course, cannot afford to surrender himself
to any common action; for his chief task is the assertion of all
the trifling differences which are his distinction: only the man
who has so much to give that he can forget himself in his work
can afford to collaborate, to exchange, to contribute.

If such views are held about art, it follows that *a fortiori*
whoever holds them must hold similar views about criticism.
When I say criticism, I mean of course in this place the com-
mentation and exposition of works of art by means of written
words; for of the general use of the word "criticism" to mean
such writings, as Matthew Arnold uses it in his essay, I shall
presently make several qualifications. No exponent of criticism
(in this limited sense) has, I presume, ever made the preposterous assumption that criticism is an autotelic activity. I do not
deny that art may be affirmed to serve ends beyond itself; but
art is not required to be aware of these ends, and indeed performs its function, whatever that may be, according to various
theories of value, much better by indifference to them. Criticism,
on the other hand, must always profess an end in view, which,
roughly speaking, appears to be the elucidation of works of art
and the correction of taste. The critic's task, therefore, appears to
be quite clearly cut out for him; and it ought to be comparatively easy to decide whether he performs it satisfactorily, and
in general, what kinds of criticism are useful and what are otiose.
But on giving the matter a little attention, we perceive that
criticism, far from being a simple and orderly field of beneficent

activity, from which impostors can be readily ejected, is no better than a Sunday park of contending and contentious orators,
who have not even arrived at the articulation of their differences.
Here, one would suppose, was a place for quiet co-operative
labour. The critic, one would suppose, if he is to justify his existence, should endeavour to discipline his personal prejudices
and cranks—tares to which we are all subject—and compose his
differences with as many of his fellows as possible, in the common pursuit of true judgment. When we find that quite the contrary prevails, we begin to suspect that the critic owes his liveli-
hood to the violence and extremity of his opposition to other
critics, or else to some trifling oddities of his own with which
he contrives to season the opinions which men already hold, and
which out of vanity or sloth they prefer to maintain. We are
tempted to expel the lot.

Immediately after such an eviction, or as soon as relief has
abated our rage, we are compelled to admit that there remain
certain books, certain essays, certain sentences, certain men, who
have been "useful" to us. And our next step is to attempt to
classify these, and find out whether we establish any principles
for deciding what kinds of book should be preserved, and what
aims and methods of criticism should be followed.

II

The view of the relation of the work of art to art, of the
work of literature to literature, of "criticism" to criticism, which
I have outlined above, seemed to me natural and self-evident.
I owe to Mr. Middleton Murry my perception of the contentious character of the problem; or rather, my perception that
there is a definite and final choice involved. To Mr. Murry I
feel an increasing debt of gratitude. Most of our critics are occupied in labour of obnubilation; in reconciling, in hushing up,
in patting down, in squeezing in, in glozing over, in concocting
pleasant sedatives, in pretending that the only difference between themselves and others is that they are nice men and the
others of very doubtful repute. Mr. Murry is not one of these.
He is aware that there are definite positions to be taken, and that

now and then one must actually reject something and select something else. He is not the anonymous writer who in a literary paper several years ago asserted that Romanticism and Classicism are much the same thing, and that the true Classical Age in France was the Age which produced the Gothic cathedrals and—Jeanne d'Arc. With Mr. Murry's formulation of Classicism and Romanticism I cannot agree; the difference seems to me rather the difference between the complete and the fragmentary, the adult and the immature, the orderly and the chaotic. But what Mr. Murry does show is that there are at least two attitudes toward literature and toward everything, and that you cannot hold both. And the attitude which he professes appears to imply that the other has no standing in England whatever. For it is made a national, a racial issue.

Mr. Murry makes his issue perfectly clear. "Catholicism," he says, "stands for the principle of unquestioned spiritual authority outside the individual; that is also the principle of Classicism in literature." Within the orbit within which Mr. Murry's discussion moves, this seems to me an unimpeachable definition, though it is of course not all that there is to be said about either Catholicism or Classicism. Those of us who find ourselves supporting what Mr. Murry calls Classicism believe that men cannot get on without giving allegiance to something outside themselves. I am aware that "outside" and "inside" are terms which provide unlimited opportunity for quibbling, and that no psychologist would tolerate a discussion which shuffled such base coinage; but I will presume that Mr. Murry and myself can agree that for our purpose these counters are adequate, and concur in disregarding the admonitions of our psychological friends. If you find that you have to imagine it as outside, then it is outside. If, then, a man's interest is political, he must, I presume, profess an allegiance to principles, or to a form of government, or to a monarch; and if he is interested in religion, and has one, to a Church; and if he happens to be interested in literature, he must acknowledge, it seems to me, just that sort of allegiance which I endeavoured to put forth in the preceding section. There is, nevertheless, an alternative, which Mr. Murry has expressed. "The English writer, the English divine, the English statesman, inherit no rules from their for-bears; they inherit only this: a sense that in the last resort they must depend upon the inner voice." This statement does, I ad-mit, appear to cover certain cases; it throws a flood of light upon Mr. Lloyd George. But why *"in the last resort"?* Do they, then, avoid the dictates of the inner voice up to the last ex-tremity? My belief is that those who possess this inner voice are ready enough to hearken to it, and will hear no other. The inner voice, in fact, sounds remarkably like an old principle which has been formulated by an elder critic in the now familiar phrase of "doing as one likes." The possessors of the inner voice ride ten in a compartment to a football match at Swansea, listen-ing to the inner voice, which breathes the eternal message of vanity, fear, and lust.

Mr. Murry will say, with some show of justice, that this is a wilful misrepresentation. He says: "If they (the English writer, divine, statesman) dig *deep enough* in their pursuit of self-knowledge—a piece of mining done not with the intellect alone, but with the whole man—they will come upon a self that is universal"—an exercise far beyond the strength of our football enthusiasts. It is an exercise, however, which I believe was of enough interest to Catholicism for several handbooks to be written on its practice. But the Catholic practitioners were, I believe, with the possible exception of certain heretics, not palpi-tating Narcissi; the Catholic did not believe that God and him-self were identical. "The man who truly interrogates himself will ultimately hear the voice of God," Mr. Murry says. In theory, this leads to a form of pantheism which I maintain is not European—just as Mr. Murry maintains that "Classicism" is not English. For its practical results, one may refer to the verses of *Hudibras*.

I did not realise that Mr. Murry was the spokesman for a considerable sect, until I read in the editorial columns of a dig-nified daily that "magnificent as the representatives of the clas sical genius have been in England, they are not the sole expres-sions of the English character, which remains at bottom obsti-nately 'humorous' and nonconformist." This writer is moderate in using the qualification *sole*, and brutally frank in attributing this "humorousness" to "the unreclaimed Teutonic element in us." But it strikes me that Mr. Murry, and this other voice, are either too obstinate or too tolerant. The question is, the first question, *not* what comes natural or what comes *easy* to us, but what is right? Either one attitude is better than the other, or else it is indifferent. But how can such a choice be indifferent? Surely the reference to racial origins, or the mere statement that the French are thus, and the English otherwise, is not expected to settle the question: which, of two antithetical views, is *right?* And I cannot understand why the opposition between Classicism and Romanticism should be profound enough in Latin countries (Mr. Murry says it is) and yet of no significance among ourselves. For if the French are *naturally* classical, why should there be any "opposition" in France, any more than there is here? And if Classicism is not natural to them, but something acquired, why not acquire it here? Were the French in the year 1600 classical, and the English in the same year romantic? A more important difference, to my mind, is that the French in the year 1600 *had already a more mature prose.*

I I I

This discussion may seem to have led us a long way from the subject of this paper. But it was worth my while to follow Mr. Murry's comparison of Outside Authority with the Inner Voice. For to those who obey the inner voice (perhaps "obey" is not the word) nothing that I can say about criticism will have the slightest value. For they will not be interested in the attempt to find any common principles for the pursuit of criticism. Why have principles, when one has the inner voice? If I like a thing, that is all I want; and if enough of us, shouting all together, like it, that should be all that *you* (who don't like it) ought to want. The law of art, said Mr. Clutton Brock, is all case law. And we can not only like whatever we like to like but we can like it for any reason we choose. We are not, in fact, concerned with literary *perfection* at all—the search for perfection is a sign of pettiness, for it shows that the writer has admitted the existence of an unquestioned spiritual authority outside himself, to which he has attempted to *conform*. We are not in fact interested in art. We will not worship Baal. "The principle of classical leadership is that obeisance is made to the office or to the tradition, never to the man." And we want, not principles, but men.

Thus speaks the Inner Voice. It is a voice to which, for convenience, we may give a name: and the name I suggest is Whiggery.

IV

Leaving, then, those whose calling and election are sure and returning to those who shamefully depend upon tradition and the accumulated wisdom of time, and restricting the discussion to those who sympathise with each other in this frailty, we may comment for a moment upon the use of the terms "critical" and "creative" by one whose place, on the whole, is with the weaker brethren. Matthew Arnold distinguishes far too bluntly, it seems to me, between the two activities: he overlooks the capital importance of criticism in the work of creation itself. Probably, indeed, the larger part of the labour of an author in composing his work is critical labour; the labour of sifting, combining, constructing, expunging, correcting, testing: this frightful toil is as much critical as creative. I maintain even that the criticism employed by a trained and skilled writer on his own work is the most vital, the highest kind of criticism; and (as I think I have said before) that some creative writers are superior to others solely because their critical faculty is superior. There is a tendency, and I think it is a whiggery tendency, to decry this critical toil of the artist; to propound the thesis that the great artist is an unconscious artist, unconsciously inscribing on his banner the words Muddle Through. Those of us who are Inner Deaf Mutes are, however, sometimes compensated by a humble conscience, which, though without oracular expertness, counsels us to do the best we can, reminds us that our compositions ought to be as free from defects as possible (to atone for their lack of inspiration), and, in short, makes us waste a good deal of time. We are aware, too, that the critical discrimination which comes so hardly to us has in more fortunate men flashed in the very heat of creation; and we do not assume that because works have been composed without apparent critical labour, no critical labour has been done. We do not know what previous labours have prepared, or what goes on, in the way of criticism, all the time in the minds of the creators.

But this affirmation recoils upon us. If so large a part of creation is really criticism, is not a large part of what is called "critical writing" really creative? If so, is there not creative criticism in the ordinary sense? The answer seems to be, that there is no equation. I have assumed as axiomatic that a creation, a work of art, is autotelic; and that criticism, by definition, is *about* something other than itself. Hence you cannot fuse creation with criticism as you can fuse criticism with creation. The critical activity finds its highest, its true fulfilment in a kind of union with creation in the labour of the artist.

But no writer is completely self-sufficient, and many creative writers have a critical activity which is not all discharged into their work. Some seem to require to keep their critical powers in condition for the real work by exercising them miscellaneously; others, on completing a work, need to continue the critical activity by commenting on it. There is no general rule. And as men can learn from each other, so some of these treatises have been useful to other writers. And some of them have been useful to those who were not writers.

At one time I was inclined to take the extreme position that the *only* critics worth reading were the critics who practised, and practised well, the art of which they wrote. But I had to stretch this frame to make some important inclusions; and I have since been in search of a formula which should cover everything I wished to include, even if it included more than I wanted. And the most important qualification which I have been able to find, which accounts for the peculiar importance of the criticism of practitioners, is that a critic must have a very highly developed sense of fact. This is by no means a trifling or frequent gift. And it is not one which easily wins popular commendations. The sense of fact is something very slow to develop, and its complete development means perhaps the very pinnacle of civilisation. For there are so many spheres of fact to be mastered, and our outermost sphere of fact, of knowledge, of control, will be ringed with narcotic fancies in the sphere beyond. To the member of the Browning Study Circle, the discussion of poets about poetry may seem arid, technical, and limited. It is merely that the practitioners have clarified and reduced to a state of fact all the feelings that the member can only enjoy in the most nebulous form; the dry technique implies, for those who have mastered it, all that the member thrills to; only that has been made into something precise, tractable, under control. That, at all events, is one reason for the value of the practitioner's criticism—he is dealing with his facts, and he can help us to do the same.

And at every level of criticism I find the same necessity regnant. There is a large part of critical writing which consists in "interpreting" an author, a work. This is not on the level of the Study Circle either; it occasionally happens that one person obtains an understanding of another, or a creative writer, which he can partially communicate, and which we feel to be true and illuminating. It is difficult to confirm the "interpretation" by external evidence. To any one who is skilled in fact on this level there will be evidence enough. But who is to prove his own skill? And for every success in this type of writing there are thousands of impostures. Instead of insight, you get a fiction. Your test is to apply it again and again to the original, with your view of the original to guide you. But there is no one to guarantee your competence, and once again we find ourselves in a dilemma.

We must ourselves decide what is useful to us and what is not; and it is quite likely that we are not competent to decide. But it is fairly certain that "interpretation" (I am not touching upon the acrostic element in literature) is only legitimate when it is not interpretation at all, but merely putting the reader in possession of facts which he would otherwise have missed. I have had some experience of Extension lecturing, and I have found only two ways of leading any pupils to like anything with the right liking: to present them with a selection of the simpler kind of facts about a work—its conditions, its setting, its genesis—or else to spring the work on them in such a way that they were not prepared to be prejudiced against it. There were many facts to help them with Elizabethan drama: the poems of T. E. Hulme only needed to be read aloud to have immediate effect.

Comparison and analysis, I have said before, and Remy de Gourmont has said before me (a real master of fact—sometimes, I am afraid, when he moved outside of literature, a master illusionist of fact), are the chief tools of the critic. It is obvious indeed that they *are* tools, to be handled with care, and not employed in an inquiry into the number of times giraffes are mentioned in the English novel. They are not used with conspicuous success by many contemporary writers. You must know what to compare and what to analyse. The late Professor Ker had skill in the use of these tools. Comparison and analysis need only the cadavers on the table; but interpretation is always producing parts of the body from its pockets, and fixing them in place. And any book, any essay, any note in *Notes and Queries*, which produces a fact even of the lowest order about a work of art is a better piece of work than nine-tenths of the most pretentious critical journalism, in journals or in books. We assume, of course, that we are masters and not servants of facts, and that we know that the discovery of Shakespeare's laundry bills would not be of much use to us; but we must always reserve final judgment as to the futility of the research which has discovered them, in the possibility that some genius will appear who will know of a use to which to put them. Scholarship, even in its humblest forms, has its rights; we assume that we know how to use it, and how to neglect it. Of course the multiplication of critical books and essays may create, and I have seen it create, a vicious taste for reading about works of art instead of reading the works themselves, it may supply opinion instead of educating taste. But *fact* cannot corrupt taste; it can at worst gratify one taste—a taste for history, let us say, or antiquities, or biography—under the illusion that it is assisting another. The real corrupters are those who supply opinion or fancy; and Goethe and Coleridge are not guiltless—for what is Coleridge's *Hamlet:* is it an honest inquiry as far as the data permit, or is it an attempt to present Coleridge in an attractive costume?

We have not succeeded in finding such a test as any one can apply; we have been forced to allow ingress to innumerable dull and tedious books; but we have, I think, found a test which, for those who are able to apply it, will dispose of the really vicious ones. And with this test we may return to the preliminary statement of the polity of literature and of criticism. For the kinds of critical work which we have admitted, there is the possibility of co-operative activity, with the further possibility of arriving at something outside of ourselves, which may provisionally be called truth. But if any one complains that I have not defined truth, or fact, or reality, I can only say apologetically that it was no part of my purpose to do so, but only to find a scheme into which, whatever they are, they will fit, if they exist.

II

"RHETORIC"

AND POETIC DRAMA

———

THE death of Rostand was the disappearance of
the poet whom, more than any other in France, we treated as
the exponent of "rhetoric," thinking of rhetoric as something
recently out of fashion. And as we find ourselves looking back
rather tenderly upon the author of *Cyrano* we wonder what this
vice or quality is that is associated as plainly with Rostand's
merits as with his defects. His rhetoric, at least, suited him at
times so well, and so much better than it suited a much greater
poet, Baudelaire, who is at times as rhetorical as Rostand.
And we begin to suspect that the word is merely a vague term
of abuse for any style that is bad, that is so evidently bad or
second-rate that we do not recognize the necessity for greater
precision in the phrases we apply to it.

Our own Elizabethan and Jacobean poetry—in so nice a problem it is much safer to stick to one's own language—is repeatedly
called "rhetorical." It had this and that notable quality, but,
when we wish to admit that it had defects, it is rhetorical. It
had serious defects, even gross faults, but we cannot be considered to have erased them from our language when we are so
unclear in our perception of what they are. The fact is that both
Elizabethan prose and Elizabethan poetry are written in a
variety of styles with a variety of vices. Is the style of Lyly, is
Euphuism, rhetorical? In contrast to the elder style of Ascham
and Elyot which it assaults, it is a clear, flowing, orderly and
relatively pure style, with a systematic if monotonous formula
of antitheses and similes. Is the style of Nashe? A tumid, flatu-

25

lent, vigorous style very different from Lyly's. Or it is perhaps the strained and the mixed figures of speech in which Shakespeare indulged himself. Or it is perhaps the careful declamation of Jonson. The word simply cannot be used as synonymous with bad writing. The meanings which it has been obliged to shoulder have been mostly opprobrious; but if a precise meaning can be found for it this meaning may occasionally represent a virtue. It is one of those words which it is the business of criticism to dissect and reassemble. Let us avoid the assumption that rhetoric is a vice of manner, and endeavour to find a rhetoric of substance also, which is right because it issues from what it has to express.

At the present time there is a manifest preference for the "conversational" in poetry—the style of "direct speech," opposed to the "oratorical" and the rhetorical; but if rhetoric is any convention of writing inappropriately applied, this conversational style can and does become a rhetoric—or what is supposed to be a conversational style, for it is often as remote from polite discourse as well could be. Much of the second and third rate in American *vers libre* is of this sort; and much of the second and third rate in English Wordsworthianism. There is in fact no conversational or other form which can be applied indiscriminately; if a writer wishes to give the effect of speech he must positively give the effect of himself talking in his own person or in one of his rôles; and if we are to express ourselves, our variety of thoughts and feelings, on a variety of subjects with inevitable rightness, we must adapt our manner to the moment with infinite variations. Examination of the development of Elizabethan drama shows this progress in adaptation, a development from monotony to variety, a progressive refinement in the perception of the variations of feeling, and a progressive elaboration of the means of expressing these variations. This drama is admitted to have grown away from the rhetorical expression, the bombast speeches, of Kyd and Marlowe to the subtle and dispersed utterance of Shakespeare and Webster. But this apparent abandonment or outgrowth of rhetoric is two things: it is partly an improvement in language and it is partly progressive variation in feeling. There is, of course, a long distance separating the furibund fluency of old Hieronimo and the broken words of Lear. There is also a difference between the famous

> *Oh eyes no eyes, but fountains full of tears!*
> *Oh life no life, but lively form of death!*

and the superb "additions to Hieronimo." [1]

We think of Shakespeare perhaps as the dramatist who concentrates everything into a sentence, "Pray you undo this button," or "Honest honest Iago"; we forget that there is a rhetoric proper to Shakespeare at his best period which is quite free from the genuine Shakespearean vices either of the early period or the late. These passages are comparable to the best bombast of Kyd or Marlowe, with a greater command of language and a greater control of the emotion. *The Spanish Tragedy* is bombastic when it descends to language which was only the trick of its age; *Tamburlaine* is bombastic because it is monotonous, inflexible to the alterations of emotion. The really fine rhetoric of Shakespeare occurs in situations where a character in the play *sees himself* in a dramatic light:

OTHELLO. *And say, besides,—that in Aleppo once* . . .

CORIOLANUS. *If you have writ your annals true, 'tis there,*
  That like an eagle in a dovecote, I
  Fluttered your Volscians in Corioli.
  Alone I did it. Boy!

TIMON. *Come not to me again; but say to Athens,*
  Timon hath made his everlasting mansion
  Upon the beachèd verge of the salt flood . . .

It occurs also once in *Antony and Cleopatra*, when Enobarbus is inspired to see Cleopatra in this dramatic light:

> *The barge she sat in* . . .

Shakespeare made fun of Marston, and Jonson made fun of Kyd. But in Marston's play the words were expressive of

---

[1] Of the authorship it can only be said that the lines are by some admirer of Marlowe. This might well be Jonson.

nothing; and Jonson was criticizing the feeble and conceited language, not the emotion, not the "oratory." Jonson is as oratorical himself, and the moments when his oratory succeeds are, I believe, the moments that conform to our formula. Notably the speech of Sylla's ghost in the induction to *Catiline*, and the speech of Envy at the beginning of *The Poetaster*. These two figures are contemplating their own dramatic importance, and quite properly. But in the Senate speeches in *Catiline*, how tedious, how dusty! Here we are spectators not of a play of characters, but of a play of forensic, exactly as if we had been forced to attend the sitting itself. A speech in a play should never appear to be intended to move us as it might conceivably move other characters in the play, for it is essential that we should preserve our position of spectators, and observe always from the outside though with complete understanding. The scene in *Julius Caesar* is right because the object of our attention is not the speech of Antony (*Bedeutung*) but the effect of his speech upon the mob, and Antony's intention, his preparation and consciousness of the effect. And in the rhetorical speeches from Shakespeare which have been cited, we have this necessary advantage of a new clue to the character, in noting the angle from which he views himself. But when a character *in* a play makes a direct appeal to us, we are either the victims of our own sentiment, or we are in the presence of a vicious rhetoric.

These references ought to supply some evidence of the propriety of Cyrano on Noses. Is not Cyrano exactly in this position of contemplating himself as a romantic, a dramatic figure? This dramatic sense on the part of the characters themselves is rare in modern drama. In sentimental drama it appears in a degraded form, when we are evidently intended to accept the character's sentimental interpretation of himself. In plays of realism we often find parts which are never allowed to be consciously dramatic, for fear, perhaps, of their appearing less real. But in actual life, in many of those situations in actual life which we enjoy consciously and keenly, we are at times aware of ourselves in this way, and these moments are of very great usefulness to dramatic verse. A very small part of acting is that which takes place on the stage! Rostand had—whether he had anything else or not—this dramatic sense, and it is what gives life to Cyrano. It is a sense which is almost a sense of humour (for when any one is conscious of himself as acting, something like a sense of humour is present). It gives Rostand's characters—Cyrano at least—a gusto which is uncommon on the modern stage. No doubt Rostand's people play up to this too steadily. We recognize that in the love scenes of Cyrano in the garden, for in *Romeo and Juliet* the profounder dramatist shows his lovers melting into unconsciousness of their isolated selves, shows the human soul in the process of forgetting itself. Rostand could not do that; but in the particular case of Cyrano on Noses, the character, the situation, the occasion were perfectly suited and combined. The tirade generated by this combination is not only genuinely and highly dramatic: it is possibly poetry also. If a writer is incapable of composing such a scene as this, so much the worse for his poetic drama.

Cyrano satisfies, as far as scenes like this can satisfy, the requirements of poetic drama. It must take genuine and substantial human emotions, such emotions as observation can confirm, typical emotions, and give them artistic form; the degree of abstraction is a question for the method of each author. In Shakespeare the form is determined in the unity of the whole, as well as single scenes; it is something to attain this unity, as Rostand does, in scenes if not the whole play. Not only as a dramatist, but as a poet, he is superior to Maeterlinck, whose drama, in failing to be dramatic, fails also to be poetic. Maeterlinck has a literary perception of the dramatic and a literary perception of the poetic, and he joins the two; the two are not, as sometimes they are in the work of Rostand, fused. His characters take no conscious delight in their rôle—they are sentimental. With Rostand the centre of gravity is in the expression of the emotion, not as with Maeterlinck in the emotion which cannot be expressed. Some writers appear to believe that emotions gain in intensity through being inarticulate. Perhaps the emotions are not significant enough to endure full daylight.

In any case, we may take our choice: we may apply the term "rhetoric" to the type of dramatic speech which I have instanced, and then we must admit that it covers good as well as bad. Or we may choose to except this type of speech from rhetoric. In that case we must say that rhetoric is any adornment or inflation of speech which is *not done for a particular effect* but for a general impressiveness. And in this case, too, we cannot allow the term to cover all bad writing.

A DIALOGUE

ON DRAMATIC POETRY

_E:_ YOU were saying, B., that it was all very well
for the older dramatic critics—you instanced Aristotle and Corneille and Dryden at random—to discuss the laws of drama as
they did; that the problem is altogether different and infinitely
more complicated for us. That fits in with a notion of my own,
which I will expound in a moment; but first I should like to
know what differences you find.

_B:_ I need not go into the matter very deeply to persuade you
of my contention. Take Aristotle first. He had only one type
of drama to consider; he could work entirely within the "categories" of that drama; he did not have to consider or criticise
the religious, ethical or artistic prejudices of his race. He did
not have to like so many things as we have to like, merely because he did not know so many things. And the less you know
and like, the easier to frame aesthetic laws. He did not have to
consider either what is universal or what is necessary for the
time. Hence he had a better chance of hitting on some of the
universals and of knowing what was right for the time. And as
for Dryden. I take Dryden because there is an obvious, a too
obvious, hiatus between the Tudor-Jacobean drama and that of
the Restoration. We know about the closing of the theatres, and
so on; and we are apt to magnify the differences and difficulties. But the differences between Dryden and Jonson are nothing to the differences between ourselves, who are sitting here to
discuss poetic drama, and Mr. Shaw and Mr. Galsworthy and
Sir Arthur Pinero and Mr. Jones and Mr. Arlen and Mr.

Coward: all of whom are almost contemporary with us. For the world of Dryden on the one hand and the world of Shakespeare and Jonson on the other were much the same world, with similar religious, ethical and artistic presuppositions. But what have we in common with the distinguished playwrights whom I have just mentioned?

And, to return to Aristotle for a moment, consider how much more we know (unfortunately) about Greek drama than he did. Aristotle did not have to worry about the relation of drama to religion, about the traditional morality of the Hellenes, about the relation of art to politics; he did not have to struggle with German or Italian aesthetics; he did not have to read the (extremely interesting) works of Miss Harrison or Mr. Cornford, or the translations of Professor Murray, or wrinkle his brow over the antics of the Todas and the Veddahs. Nor did he have to reckon with the theatre as a paying proposition.

Similarly, neither Dryden, nor Corneille, from whom he learned so much, was bothered by excessive knowledge about Greek civilisation. They had the Greek and Latin classics to read, and were not aware of *all* the differences between Greek and Roman civilisation and their own. As for us, we know too much, and are convinced of too little. Our literature is a substitute for religion, and so is our religion. We should do better if, instead of worrying about the place of drama in society, we simply decided what amused us. What is the purpose of the theatre except to amuse?

E: It is all very well to reduce the drama to "amusement." But it seems to me that that is just what has happened. I believe that the drama has something else to do except to divert us. What else does it do at the moment?

B: I have just given a list of dramatists. I admit that their intentions vary. Pinero, for instance, was concerned with setting, or, as is said in the barbarous jargon of our day, "posing" the problems of his generation. He was much more concerned with "posing" than with answering. Shaw, on the other hand, was much more concerned with answering than with "posing." Both of these accomplished writers had a strong ethical motive. This ethical motive is not apparent in Mr. Arlen or Mr. Coward.

Their drama is pure "amusement." The two excesses go together. The whole question is, whom does the drama amuse?
and what is the quality of the amusement?

C: I should not for my part admit that any of these people
are concerned to amuse. There is no such thing as mere amusement. They are concerned with flattering the prejudices of the
mob. And their own. I do not suppose for a moment that either
Shaw, or Pinero, or Mr. Coward has ever spent one hour in the
study of ethics. Their cleverness lies in finding out how much
their audiences would like to behave, and encouraging them to
do it by exhibiting personages behaving in that way.

D: But why should a dramatist be expected to spend even
five minutes in the study of ethics?

B: I consent. But they need to assume some moral attitude
in common with their audience. Aeschylus and Sophocles, the
Elizabethans, and the Restoration dramatists had this. But this
must be already given; it is not the job of the dramatist to impose it.

E: What is the moral attitude of Dryden's *Mr. Limberham?*

B: Impeccable. The morality of our Restoration drama cannot be impugned. It assumes orthodox Christian morality, and
laughs (in its comedy) at human nature for not living up to it.
It retains its respect for the divine by showing the failure of the
human. The attitude of Restoration drama towards morality is
like the attitude of the Blasphemer towards Religion. It is only
the irreligious who are shocked by blasphemy. Blasphemy is a
sign of Faith. Imagine Mr. Shaw blaspheming! He could not.
Our Restoration drama is all virtue. It depends upon virtue for
its existence. The author of *The Queen was in the Parlour* does
not depend upon virtue.

E: You are talking as if the drama was merely a matter of
established morals. Let me for a moment transfer the discussion
to the question of form. I speak as one who is satisfied neither
by Elizabethan drama nor by Pinero or Barrie. A few years
ago I—and you *B.* and you *C.* and *A.*—was delighted by the
Russian ballet. Here seemed to be everything that we wanted
in drama, except the poetry. It did not teach any "lesson," but
it had form. It seemed to revive the more formal element in

drama for which we craved. I concede that the more recent ballets have not given me the same pleasure. But for that I blame Mr. Diaghilev, not the ballet in principle. If there is a future for drama, and particularly for poetic drama, will it not be in the direction indicated by the ballet? Is it not a question of form rather than ethics? And is not the question of verse drama versus prose drama a question of degree of form?

A: There I am inclined to support you. People have tended to think of verse as a restriction upon drama. They think that the emotional range, and the realistic truth, of drama is limited and circumscribed by verse. People were once content with verse in drama, they say, because they were content with a restricted and artificial range of emotion. Only prose can give the full gamut of modern feeling, can correspond to actuality. But is not every dramatic representation artificial? And are we not merely deceiving ourselves when we aim at greater and greater realism? Are we not contenting ourselves with appearances, instead of insisting upon fundamentals? Has human feeling altered much from Aeschylus to ourselves? I maintain the contrary. I say that prose drama is merely a slight by-product of verse drama. The human soul, in intense emotion, strives to express itself in verse. It is not for me, but for the neurologists, to discover why this is so, and why and how feeling and rhythm are related. The tendency, at any rate, of prose drama is to emphasize the ephemeral and superficial; if we want to get at the permanent and universal we tend to express ourselves in verse.

D: But—to return to the point—can you hang all this on the ballet? How is the ballet concerned with the permanent and universal?

B: The ballet is valuable because it has, unconsciously, concerned itself with a permanent form; it is futile because it has concerned itself with the ephemeral in content. Apart from Stravinski, who is a real musician, and from Cocteau, who is a real playwright, what is the strength of the ballet? It is in a tradition, a training, an askesis, which, to be fair, is not of Russian but of Italian origin, and which ascends for several centuries. Sufficient to say that any efficient dancer has undergone a training which is like a moral training. Has any successful actor of our time undergone anything similar?

E: This seems to give me the opening for which I have been waiting. You all approve of the ballet because it is a system of physical training, of traditional, symbolical and highly skilled movements. It is a liturgy of very wide adaptability, and you seem to laud the liturgy rather than the variations. Very well. *B.* has spoken of our knowledge of Greek antecedents to Greek drama, and has implied that we know more about that than Dryden, or Aristotle, or the Greek dramatists themselves. I say that the consummation of the drama, the perfect and ideal drama, is to be found in the ceremony of the Mass. I say, with the support of the scholars whom *B.* mentions (and others), that drama springs from religious liturgy, and that it cannot afford to depart far from religious liturgy. I agree with *B.* that the problem of drama was simpler for Aristotle and for Dryden and for Corneille than for us. They had only to take things as they found them. But when drama has ranged as far as it has in our own day, is not the only solution to return to religious liturgy? And the only dramatic satisfaction that I find now is in a High Mass well performed. Have you not there everything necessary? And indeed, if you consider the ritual of the Church during the cycle of the year, you have the complete drama represented. The Mass is a small drama, having all the unities; but in the Church year you have represented the full drama of creation.

B: The question is not, whether the Mass is dramatic, but what is the relation of the drama to the Mass? We must take things as we find them. Are we to say that our cravings for drama are fulfilled by the Mass? I believe that a cursory examination is enough for us to reply, No. For I once knew a man who held the same views that you appear to hold, *E.* He went to High Mass every Sunday, and was particular to find a church where he considered the Mass efficiently performed. And as I sometimes accompanied him, I can testify that the Mass gave him extreme, I may even say immoderate, satisfaction. It was almost orgiastic. But when I came to consider his conduct, I realised that he was guilty of a *confusion des genres.*

His attention was not on the meaning of the Mass, for he was not a believer but a Bergsonian; it was on the Art of the Mass. His dramatic desires were satisfied by the Mass, precisely because he was not interested in the Mass, but in the drama of it. Now what I maintain is, that you have no business to care about the Mass unless you are a believer. And even if you are a believer you will have dramatic desires which crave fulfilment otherwise. For man lives in various degrees. We need (as I believe, but you need not believe this for the purpose of my argument) religious faith. And we also need amusement (the quality of the amusement will, of course, not be unrelated to the quality of our religious belief). Literature can be no substitute for religion, not merely because we need religion, but because we need literature as well as religion. And religion is no more a substitute for drama than drama is a substitute for religion. If we can do without religion, then let us have the theatre without pretending that it *is* religion; and if we can do without drama, then let us not pretend that religion is drama.

For there is a difference in attention. If we are religious, then we shall only be aware of the Mass as art, in so far as it is badly done and interferes with our devotion consequently. A devout person, in assisting at Mass, is not in the frame of mind of a person attending a drama, for he is *participating*—and that makes all the difference. In participating we are supremely conscious of certain realities, and unconscious of others. But we are human beings, and crave representations in which we are conscious, and critical, of these other realities. We cannot be aware solely of divine realities. We must be aware also of human realities. And we crave some liturgy less divine, something in respect of which we shall be more spectators and less participants. Hence we want the human drama, related to the divine drama, but not the same, as well as the Mass.

E: You have admitted all that I expected, and more. That is the essential relation of drama to religious liturgy.

D: I have a suggestion to put forward. It is this: can we not take it that the form of the drama must vary from age to age in accordance with religious assumptions of the age? That is, that drama represents a relation of the human needs and satisfactions to the religious needs and satisfactions which the age provides. When the age has a set religious practice and belief, then the drama can and should tend towards realism, I say *towards*, I do not say arrive at. The more definite the religious and ethical principles, the more freely the drama can move towards what is now called photography. The more fluid, the more chaotic the religious and ethical beliefs, the more the drama must tend in the direction of liturgy. Thus there would be some constant relation between drama and the religion of the time. The movement, in the time of Dryden and indeed of Corneille, and indeed of Aristotle, was towards freedom. Perhaps our movement should be towards what we called, in touching upon the ballet, form?

E: An interesting theory, with no historical backing whatever, but concluding in exactly what I said myself. But if you want form, you must go deeper than dramatic technique.

C: I should like to make an interruption. If I do not make it now I shall probably forget to make it at all. You are all talking of form and content, of freedom and restriction, as if everything was indefinitely variable. You are not, like myself, students of the popular drama of the *faubourgs*. And what I there remark is the fixity of morality. The suburban drama has today fundamentally the same morality as it had in the days of *Arden of Feversham* and *The Yorkshire Tragedy*. I agree with *B.* about Restoration comedy. It is a great tribute to Christian morality. Take the humour of our great English comedian, Ernie Lotinga. It is (if you like) bawdy. But such bawdiness is a tribute to, an acknowledgment of, conventional British morality. I am a member of the Labour Party. I believe in the King and the Islington Empire. I do not believe in the plutocratic St. Moritzers for whom our popular dramatists cater. But what I was saying is that our surburbian drama is morally sound, and out of such soundness poetry may come. Human nature does not change. Another port, please.

B: I suggest that I agree with the late William Archer about Elizabethan drama.

A, E, C and *D:* What!

B: Yes. William Archer was a very honest man. As a dramatic critic he had one fault: he knew nothing about poetry. Furthermore, he made the egregious error of supposing that the dramatic merit of a dramatic work could be estimated without reference to its poetic merit. Henrik Ibsen certainly had more dramatic ability than Cyril Tourneur. But as Archer did not realise that dramatic and poetic ability are less different than chalk and cheese, he made the mistake of supposing that Ibsen was a greater dramatist than Tourneur. Greater if you like, but he will not last as long. For the greatest drama is poetic drama, and dramatic defects *can* be compensated by poetic excellence. Let us ignore Tourneur. We can cite Shakespeare.

C: Do you mean that Shakespeare is a greater dramatist than Ibsen, not by being a greater dramatist, but by being a greater poet?

B: That is precisely what I mean. For, on the other hand, what great poetry is not dramatic? Even the minor writers of the Greek Anthology, even Martial, are dramatic. Who is more dramatic than Homer or Dante? We are human beings, and in what are we more interested than in human action and human attitudes? Even when he assaults, and with supreme mastery, the divine mystery, does not Dante engage us in the question of the human attitude towards this mystery—which is dramatic? Shakespeare was a great dramatist and a great poet. But if you isolate poetry from drama completely, have you the right to say that Shakespeare was a greater dramatist than Ibsen, or than Shaw? Shaw is right about Shakespeare, for Shaw is no poet. I am not quite right there neither, for Shaw *was* a poet—until he was born, and the poet in Shaw was stillborn. Shaw has a great deal of poetry, but all stillborn; Shaw is dramatically precocious, and poetically less than immature. The best you can say for Shaw is that he seems not to have read all the popular handbooks on science that Mr. Wells and Bishop Barnes have read.

E: Yes, Shakespeare fails us, and Mr. Archer is right. William Archer is only wrong in having attacked the minor figures of Elizabethan drama and not having understood that he was obliged to attack Shakespeare as well. He was wrong, as you said, in thinking that drama and poetry are two different things. If he had seen that they are the same thing he would have had to admit that Cyril Tourneur is a great dramatist, that Jonson is a great dramatist, that Marlowe is a very great dramatist, that Webster is a great dramatist, and that Shakespeare is so great a dramatist, so great a poet, that even Mr. Archer should have removed his shoes, instead of evading the question, rather than ask Shakespeare to abide it. Shakespeare would have abidden it if Mr. William Archer had chosen to ask it. But he did not choose.

D: I think both *B.* and *E.* are rather muddled about the relation of poetry and drama, but especially *B.* Just as Archer made a mechanical separation, so *B.* makes a mechanical re-union. Let us make it clearer by putting it about the other way, and taking up a point that *B.* let slip. If drama tends to poetic drama, not by adding an embellishment and still less by limiting its scale, we should expect a dramatic poet like Shakespeare to write his finest poetry in his most dramatic scenes. And this is just what we do find: what makes it most dramatic is what makes it most poetic. No one ever points to certain plays of Shakespeare as being the most poetic, and to *other* plays as being the most dramatic. The same plays are the most poetic and the most dramatic, and this not by a concurrence of two activities, but by the full expansion of one and the same activity. I agree that the dramatist who is not a poet is so much the less a dramatist.

C: The odd thing about William Archer's book is that he did, to some extent, recognise poetry when he saw it; but at any rate when he was dealing with an Elizabethan like Chapman, whenever he comes across a passage of poetry, he refuses to believe that it is dramatic. If this is poetry, he seems to say, that proves that it is not drama. I remember that when I read the book I noticed that Archer could certainly have picked out un-dramatic or defectively dramatic passages from Chapman's plays: instead he selects that splendidly dramatic speech of Clermont on seeing the ghosts—as an example of "mild surprise"!

B: Perhaps the ghosts put him off.

E: Yet nothing is more dramatic than a ghost.

C: To sum up: there is no "relation" between poetry and drama. All poetry tends towards drama, and all drama towards poetry.

F: A neat and dangerous generalisation. For you would admit that you enjoy a great deal of poetry in which hardly even your own practised eye could detect the "tendency" towards drama; and consequently you ought surely to be able to enjoy a great deal of drama which is unquestionably written in prose.

B: Of course he does. And some of the Elizabethan plays of which Mr. Archer disapproved are, in fact, bad plays. And a great many were also, as Mr. Shaw has observed, bad verse. Shaw points out that it is easier to write bad verse than good prose—which nobody ever denied; but it is easy for Shaw to write good prose and quite impossible for him to write good verse.

E: Running off on this wild-goose chase after William Archer, whom you might just as well have left alone, you have forgotten to tell us why Shakespeare fails us.

B: I mean that Archer's objections to Elizabethan drama were partly based upon a right instinct. He used some deplorable terms, such as "humanitarianism," in expressing his dislike. But had he observed that his fundamental objection applied as much to Shakespeare as to anybody, as much to the best as to the worst, he might have admitted an obligation to find another and profounder explanation for it.

A: Are we to infer that you criticise Shakespeare on the ground that his plays are not morally edifying?

B: In a sense, yes.

A: But a little while ago you were defending Restoration comedy against the charge of immorality and indecency.

B: Not against indecency, that was unnecessary. We all like its indecency when it is really witty, as it sometimes is. But the question of Wycherley and the question of Shakespeare are not on the same plane. Restoration comedy is a comedy of social manners. It presupposes the existence of a society, therefore of social and moral laws. (It owes much to Jonson, but little to Shakespeare—anyway, Shakespeare was too great to have much influence.) It laughs at the members of society who transgress its laws. The tragedy of Shakespeare goes much deeper and yet it tells us only that weakness of character leads to disaster. There is no background of social order such as you perceive behind Corneille and Sophocles.

C: Why should there be? You can't deduce from that that Shakespeare is inferior to Sophocles and Corneille.

B: No, I can't. All I know is that something is lacking, I am left dissatisfied and disturbed. I think there are other people who feel the same thing. So far as I can isolate Shakespeare, I prefer him to all other dramatists of every time. But I cannot do that altogether; and I find the age of Shakespeare moved in a steady current, with back-eddies certainly, towards anarchy and chaos.

C: But that has nothing to do with the question.

B: Possibly not.

E: Surely the dramatic poet, being when and where he is, has no business with his own background. He can't help that, and his business is with the audience. The Elizabethan drama, or at any rate Shakespeare, was good enough to justify artistically its own background. But it does seem to me that it is as much the lack of moral and social conventions as the lack of artistic conventions that stands in the way of poetic drama today. Shaw is our greatest stage moralist, and his conventions are only negative: they consist in all the things he doesn't believe. But there again, Shaw cannot help that.

A: This sort of moralising censorship would leave us nothing. Are you prepared to say that you are the worse for having read Shakespeare and seen him played?

B: No.

A: Are you prepared to maintain that you are none the better, none the wiser, and none the happier for it?

B: No.

A: Very well. I have also heard you railing at Wagner as "pernicious." But you would not willingly resign your experience of Wagner either. Which seems to show that a world in which there was no art that was not morally edifying would be a very poor world indeed.

B: So it would. I would not suppress anything that is good

measured by artistic standards. For there is always something
to be learned from it. I would not have Shakespeare any different from what he is. But it is like life in general. There are
heaps of things in the world which I should like to see changed;
but in a world without Evil life would not be worth living.

E: Well, you have taken a long time to leave us just where
we were before.

B: Not quite. You can never draw the line between aesthetic
criticism and moral and social criticism; you cannot draw a line
between criticism and metaphysics; you start with literary criticism, and however rigorous an aesthete you may be, you are
over the frontier into something else sooner or later. The best
you can do is to accept these conditions and know what you are
doing when you do it. And, on the other hand, you must know
how and when to retrace your steps. You must be very nimble.
I may begin by moral criticism of Shakespeare and pass over
into aesthetic criticism, or vice versa.

E: And all you do is to lead the discussion astray.

C: I cannot agree with that wild generalisation about the anarchy of Elizabethan drama. In fact it would only make the
present-day situation more puzzling. We seem to agree that
the modern world is chaotic, and we are inclined to agree that
its lack of social and moral conventions makes the task of the
dramatic poet more difficult, if not impossible. But if the Elizabethan and Jacobean period was also a period of chaos, and yet
produced great poetic drama, why cannot we?

B: I don't know.

C: You will have to qualify your statement about Elizabethan drama. You would have had to do that in any case, for
there are a great many more things to take account of than this
simple idea of decay. To begin with, there is no precedent for
a nation having *two* great periods of drama. And its great period
is always short, and is great because of a very small number of
great dramatists. And a very great period of any kind of poetry
is never repeated. Perhaps each great race has just strength
enough for one period of literary supremacy.

D: If *C.* is not side-tracked he will lead us presently into
politics.

A: All this is true and perfectly commonplace. But it does not help. When it comes to the present age, we are not going to be deterred by a fatalistic philosophy of history from wanting a poetic drama, and from believing that there must be some way of getting it. Besides, the craving for poetic drama is permanent in human nature. At this point I suspect that *F.* is waiting to let off on us what he calls the economic factors; and the state of the public, and the producers, and the cost of theatres; and the competition of cheap cinemas, et cetera. I believe that if you want a thing you can get it, and hang the economic factors.

F: And your way of getting it is to talk about it.

A: I like talking about things; it helps me to think.

C: I agree with *A.*, whether he has thought about it or not. All this talk about periods of art is interesting and sometimes useful when we are occupied with the past, but is quite futile when we come to consider the present in relation to the future. Let us begin by observing the several kinds of way in which contemporary drama fails. There are the plays written by poets who have no knowledge of the stage: this kind has been sufficiently abused. There are the plays written by men who know the stage and are not poets. Of these two extremes I will only remark that experience proves that neither is of any pertinence to our present subject.

A: But what is our present subject?

C: The possibility of poetic drama.

G: You seem to have covered nearly the whole field of discussion of contemporary drama, except for the topics of Gordon Craig, Reinhardt, Meierhold, Sir Barry Jackson, the Old Vic, Eugene O'Neill, Pirandello and Toller. And we are not here concerned with methods of production—which rules out the first four of these names—but with the production of something to produce. I have only one suggestion to offer, but it will be the only practical suggestion that has been made. We should hire a barn or studio, and produce plays of our own, or even disjected scenes of plays and produce them by ourselves and only for ourselves, no friends to be admitted. We might learn at least by practice first whether we have anything in common, and second what forms of versification are possible. We must find a new form of verse which shall be as satisfactory a vehicle for us as blank verse was for the Elizabethans.

F: And I know what will happen. We shall start selling tickets in order to pay the costs, we shall then have to import plays in order to supply the demand, and we shall end with a perfectly conventional cosmopolitan little-theatre or Sunday-society performance.

B: What is much more likely is that nothing will be done at all. We are all too busy; we have to earn our living in other ways. It is even doubtful whether we are sufficiently interested. We cannot make the plays unless we think there is a demand, and there will be no demand until we have made it. There is not one of us who has not a dozen things to do, within the next six months, which he knows to be more important for himself than to prance about in a stable-theatre.

C: One thing has struck me in this conversation. We started by speaking of Dryden, then passed to poetic drama in general; and we have not taken up one of the subjects that Dryden thought it worth while to discuss, and all of the subjects raised have been subjects that Dryden would never have thought of.

B: It is one thing to discuss the rules of an art when that art is alive, and quite another when it is dead. When there is a contemporary practice, the critic must start from that point, and all his criticism must return to it. Observe how confident Dryden is! Even the difference between the drama of his age and that of the Elizabethans, when the tumults and disorders of the Great Rebellion had hardly been subdued, seemed to him less important than they seem to us. He admits that his age is inferior, essentially in the respects in which we find it inferior, to the preceding; yet he thought of his generation—and at bottom he must have been thinking, with justifiable pride, of himself—as improving and polishing the earlier drama in many ways. He is quite right: the relation of his drama to that of the Elizabethans should be conceived as he conceived it; the chasm is not so vast as it is usually taken to be; and the French influence was far less than it is supposed to be. But the questions which he discussed are not out of date.

E: The Unities of Place and Time, for instance. Dryden gives what is the soundest and most commonsense view possible for his time and place. But the Unities have for me, at least, a perpetual fascination. I believe they will be found highly desirable for the drama of the future. For one thing, we want more concentration. All plays are now much too long. I never go to the theatre, because I hate to hurry over my dinner, and I dislike to dine early. A continuous hour and a half of *intense* interest is what we need. No intervals, no chocolate-sellers or ignoble trays. The Unities do make for intensity, as does verse rhythm.

A: You think that we need stronger stimulants, in a shorter space of time, to get the same exaltation out of the theatre that a sensitive contemporary may be supposed to have got out of a tragedy by Shakespeare or even out of one by Dryden.

E: And meanwhile let us drink another glass of port to the memory of John Dryden.

EURIPIDES

AND PROFESSOR MURRAY

———

THE appearance of Miss Sybil Thorndyke some
years ago as Medea at the Holborn Empire was an event which
had a bearing upon three subjects of considerable interest: the
drama, the present standing of Greek literature, and the importance of good contemporary translation. On the occasion on
which I was present the performance was certainly a success;
the audience was large, it was attentive, and its applause was
long. Whether the success was due to Euripides is uncertain;
whether it was due to Professor Murray is not proved; but
that it was in considerable measure due to Miss Thorndyke
there is no doubt. To have held the centre of the stage for
two hours in a rôle which requires both extreme violence and
restraint, a rôle which requires simple force and subtle variation; to have sustained so difficult a rôle almost without support; this was a legitimate success. The audience, or what could
be seen of it from one of the cheaper seats, was serious and re-
spectful and perhaps inclined to self-approval at having at-
tended the performance of a Greek play; but Miss Thorndyke's
acting might have held almost any audience. It employed all
the conventions, the theatricalities, of the modern stage; yet
her personality triumphed over not only Professor Murray's
verse but her own training.

The question remains whether the production was a "work
of art." The rest of the cast appeared slightly ill at ease; the
nurse was quite a tolerable nurse of the crone type; Jason was
negative; the messenger was uncomfortable at having to make

such a long speech; and the refined Dalcroze chorus had melli-
fluous voices which rendered their lyrics happily inaudible. All
this contributed toward the high-brow effect which is so depressing; and we imagine that the actors of Athens, who had
to speak clearly enough for 20,000 auditors to be able to criticise the versification, would have been pelted with figs and
olives had they mumbled so unintelligibly as most of this
troupe. But the Greek actor spoke in his own language, and
our actors were forced to speak in the language of Professor
Gilbert Murray.

I do not believe, however, that such performances will do
very much to rehabilitate Greek literature or our own, unless
they stimulate a desire for better translations. The serious auditors, many of whom I observed to be like myself provided
with Professor Murray's eighteenpenny translation, were probably not aware that Miss Thorndyke, in order to succeed as
well as she did, was really engaged in a struggle against the
translator's verse. She triumphed over it by attracting our attention to her expression and tone and making us neglect her
words; and this, of course, was not the dramatic method of
Greek acting at its best. The English and Greek languages remained where they were. But few persons realize that the Greek
language and the Latin language, and, *therefore*, we say, the
English language, are within our lifetime passing through a
critical period. The Classics have, during the latter part of the
nineteenth century and up to the present moment, lost their
place as a pillar of the social and political system—such as the
Established Church still is. If they are to survive, to justify
themselves as literature, as an element in the European mind, as
the foundation for the literature we hope to create, they are
very badly in need of persons capable of expounding them.
We need some one—not a member of the Church of Rome,
and perhaps preferably not a member of the Church of England—to explain how vital a matter it is, if Aristotle may be
said to have been a moral pilot of Europe, whether we shall or
shall not drop that pilot. And we need a number of educated
poets who shall at least have opinions about Greek drama, and
whether it is or is not of any use to us. And it must be said

that Professor Gilbert Murray is not the man for this. Greek poetry will never have the slightest vitalizing effect upon English poetry if it can only appear masquerading as a vulgar debasement of the eminently personal idiom of Swinburne. These are strong words to use against the most popular Hellenist of his time; but we must witness of Professor Murray ere we die that these things are not otherwise but thus.

This is really a point of capital importance. That the most conspicuous Greek propagandist of the day should almost habitually use two words where the Greek language requires one, and where the English language will provide him with one; that he should render σκιάν by "*grey* shadow"; and that he should stretch the Greek brevity to fit the loose frame of William Morris, and blur the Greek lyric to the fluid haze of Swinburne; these are not faults of infinitesimal insignificance. The first great speech of Medea Mr. Murray begins with:

> *Women of Corinth, I am come to show*
> *My face, lest ye despise me. . . .*

We find in the Greek ἐξῆλθον δόμον. "Show my face," therefore, is Mr. Murray's gift.

> *This thing undreamed of, sudden from on high,*
> *Hath sapped my soul: I dazzle where I stand,*
> *The cup of all life shattered in my hand. . . .*

Again, we find that the Greek is:

> ἐμοὶ δ' ἄελπτον πρᾶγμα προσπεσὸν τόδε
> ψυχὴν διέφθαρχ'· οἴχομαι δὲ καὶ βίου
> χάριν μεθεῖσα κατθανεῖν χρῄζω, φίλαι.

So, here are two striking phrases which we owe to Mr. Murray; it is he who has sapped our soul and shattered the cup of all life for Euripides. And these are only random examples.

> οὐκ ἔστιν ἄλλη φρὴν μιαιφονωτέρα

becomes "no bloodier spirit between heaven and hell"! Surely we know that Professor Murray is acquainted with "Sister

Helen"? Professor Murray has simply interposed between Euripides and ourselves a barrier more impenetrable than the Greek language. We do not reproach him for preferring, apparently, Euripides to Aeschylus. But if he does, he should at least appreciate Euripides. And it is inconceivable than any one with a genuine feeling for the sound of Greek verse should deliberately elect the William Morris couplet, the Swinburne lyric, as an equivalent.

As a poet, Mr. Murray is merely a very insignificant follower of the pre-Raphaelite movement. As a Hellenist, he is very much of the present day, and a very important figure in the day. This day began, in a sense, with Tylor and a few German anthropologists; since then we have acquired sociology and social psychology, we have watched the clinics of Ribot and Janet, we have read books from Vienna and heard a discourse of Bergson; a philosophy arose at Cambridge; social emancipation crawled abroad; our historical knowledge has of course increased; and we have a curious Freudian-social-mystical-rationalistic-higher-critical interpretation of the Classics and what used to be called the Scriptures. I do not deny the very great value of all work by scientists in their own departments, the great interest also of this work in detail and in its consequences. Few books are more fascinating than those of Miss Harrison, Mr. Cornford, or Mr. Cooke, when they burrow in the origins of Greek myths and rites; M. Durkheim, with his social consciousness, and M. Levy-Bruhl, with his Bororo Indians who convince themselves that they are parroquets, are delightful writers. A number of sciences have sprung up in an almost tropical exuberance which undoubtedly excites our admiration, and the garden, not unnaturally, has come to resemble a jungle. Such men as Tylor, and Robertson Smith, and Wilhelm Wundt, who early fertilized the soil, would hardly recognize the resulting vegetation; and indeed poor Wundt's *Völkerpsychologie* was a musty relic before it was translated.

All these events are useful and important in their phase, and they have sensibly affected our attitude towards the Classics; and it is this phase of classical study that Professor Murray— the friend and inspirer of Miss Jane Harrison—represents. The

Greek is no longer the awe-inspiring Belvedere of Winckel-mann, Goethe, and Schopenhauer, the figure of which Walter Pater and Oscar Wilde offered us a slightly debased re-edition. And we realize better how different—not how much more Olympian—were the conditions of the Greek civilization from ours; and at the same time Mr. Zimmern has shown us how the Greek dealt with analogous problems. Incidentally we do not believe that a good English prose style can be modelled upon Cicero, or Tacitus, or Thucydides. If Pindar bores us, we admit it; we are not certain that Sappho was *very* much greater than Catullus; we hold various opinions about Virgil; and we think more highly of Petronius than our grandfathers did.

It is to be hoped that we may be grateful to Professor Murray and his friends for what they have done, while we endeavour to neutralize Professor Murray's influence upon Greek litera-ture and English language in his translations by making better translations. The choruses from Euripides by H. D. are, allow-ing for errors and even occasional omissions of difficult passages, much nearer to both Greek and English than Mr. Murray's. But H. D. and the other poets of the "Poets' Translation Series" have so far done no more than pick up some of the more ro-mantic crumbs of Greek literature; none of them has yet shown himself competent to attack the *Agamemnon*. If we are to digest the heavy food of historical and scientific knowledge that we have eaten we must be prepared for much greater exertions. We need a digestion which can assimilate both Homer and Flaubert. We need a careful study of Renaissance Humanists and Translators, such as Mr. Pound has begun. We need an eye which can see the past in its place with its definite differences from the present, and yet so lively that it shall be as present to us as the present. This is the creative eye; and it is because Pro-fessor Murray has no creative instinct that he leaves Euripides quite dead.

SENECA IN
ELIZABETHAN TRANSLATION

═══

NO author exercised a wider or deeper influence
upon the Elizabethan mind or upon the Elizabethan form of
tragedy than did Seneca. To present the Elizabethan translations of the tragedies in their proper setting, it is necessary to
deal with three problems which at first may appear to be but
slightly connected: (1) the character, virtues and vices of the
Latin tragedies themselves; (2) the directions in which these
tragedies influenced our Elizabethan drama; (3) the history
of these translations, the part they played in extending the influence of Seneca, and their actual merit as translation and as
poetry. There are here several questions which, with the greater
number of important Tudor translations, do not arise. Most of
the better known translations are of authors whose intrinsic
merit is unquestioned, and the translations derive some of their
prestige from the merit and fame of the author translated; and
most of the better-known prose translations have an easy beauty
of style which arrests even the least prepared reader. But with
the Elizabethan translations of the *Tenne Tragedies* (for they
are by several hands) we are concerned first of all with a Latin
poet whose reputation would deter any reader but the most
curious; with translations of unequal merit, because by different scholars; and with translation into a metre—the "fourteener"—which is superficially a mere archaism, and which
repels readers who have not the patience to accustom their ears
and nerves to its beat. The translations have, as I hope to show,
considerable poetic charm and quite adequate accuracy, with

occasional flashes of real beauty; their literary value remains greater than that of any later translations of Seneca's tragedies that I have examined, either in English or French. But the appreciation of the literary value of these translations is inseparably engaged with the appreciation of the original and of its historical importance; so that although at first sight a consideration of the historical problems may appear irrelevant, it should in the end enhance our enjoyment of the translations as literature.

I

In the Renaissance, no Latin author was more highly esteemed than Seneca; in modern times, few Latin authors have been more consistently damned. The prose Seneca, the "Seneca morale" of Dante, still enjoys a measure of tepid praise, though he has no influence; but the poet and tragedian receives from the historians and critics of Latin literature the most universal reprobation. Latin literature provides poets for several tastes, but there is no taste for Seneca. Mackail, for instance, whose taste in Latin literature is almost catholic, dismisses Seneca with half a page of his *Short History of Latin Literature*, and a few of the usual adjectives such as rhetorical. Professor Mackail is inclined by his training to enjoy the purer and more classical authors, and is inclined by his temperament to enjoy the most romantic: like Shenstone or some other eighteenth-century poets, Seneca falls between. Nisard, in his *Poètes Latins de la décadence*, devotes many pages and much patience to the difference of conditions which produced great tragedy in Athens, and only rhetorical declamation in Rome. Butler, after a more detailed and more tolerant examination from a more literary point of view (*Post-Augustan Poetry*), commits himself to the damaging statement that "to Seneca more than to any other man is due the excessive predominance of declamatory rhetoric, which has characterised the drama throughout Western Europe from the Renaissance down to the latter half of the nineteenth century." The most recent critic, Mr. F. L. Lucas (*Seneca and Elizabethan Tragedy*), admits "the exasperatingly false rhetoric of the Senecan stage, with its far-fetched and frigid epigrams."

Yet this is a dramatist whom Scaliger preferred to Euripides, and whom the whole of Europe in the Renaissance delighted to honour. It is obviously a task of some difficulty to disentangle him from his reputation.

We must admit, first, that the tragedies of Seneca deserve the censure that has been directed upon them. On the other hand, it may be true—I think it is true—that the critics, especially the English critics, have been often biassed by Seneca's real and supposed bad influence upon the Renaissance, that they have included the demerits of his admirers in his own faults. But before we proceed to what redemption of his fame is possible, it is expedient to resume those universally admitted strictures and limitations which have become commonplaces of Senecan criticism. First, it is pretty generally agreed that the plays of Seneca were composed, not for stage performance, but for private declamation.[1] This theory attenuates the supposed "horrors" of the tragedies, many of which could hardly have been represented on a stage, even with the most ingenious machinery, without being merely ridiculous; the Renaissance assumption to the contrary gave licence to a taste which would probably have been indulged even without Seneca's authority. And if the plays were written to be declaimed, probably by a single speaker ("elocutionist" is really the word), we can account for other singularities. I say "account for," I do not say without qualification that this peculiar form was the "cause"; for the ultimate cause was probably the same Latin temper which made such an unacted drama possible. The cause lies in the Latin sensibility which is expressed by the Latin language. But if we imagine this unacted drama, we see at once that it is at one remove from reality, compared with the Greek. Behind the dialogue of Greek drama we are always conscious of a concrete visual actuality, and behind that of a specific emotional actuality. Behind the drama of words is the drama of action, the timbre of voice and voice, the uplifted hand or tense muscle, and the particular emotion. The spoken play, the words which we

[1] I must admit, however, that this view has recently been contested with great force by Léon Herrmann: *Le Théâtre de Sénèque* (Paris, 1924). See p. 19 of that book.

read, are symbols, a shorthand, and often, as in the best of
Shakespeare, a very abbreviated shorthand indeed, for the
acted and felt play, which is always the real thing. The phrase,
beautiful as it may be, stands for a greater beauty still. This is
merely a particular case of the amazing unity of Greek, the
unity of concrete and abstract in philosophy, the unity of thought
and feeling, action and speculation, in life. In the plays of
Seneca, the drama is all in the word, and the word has no further reality behind it. His characters all seem to speak with the
same voice, and at the top of it; they recite in turn.

I do not mean to suggest that the method of delivery of a
play of Seneca was essentially different from that of Greek
tragedy. It was probably nearer to the declamation of Greek
tragedy than was the delivery of Latin comedy. The latter
was acted by professional actors. I imagine that Seneca's plays
were declaimed by himself and other amateurs, and it is likely
that the Athenian tragedies were performed by amateurs. I
mean that the beauty of phrase in Greek tragedy is the shadow
of a greater beauty—the beauty of thought and emotion. In the
tragedies of Seneca the centre of value is shifted from what
the personage says to the way in which he says it. Very often
the value comes near to being mere smartness. Nevertheless, we
must remember that "verbal" beauty is still a kind of beauty.

The plays are admirably adapted for declamation before an
imperial highbrow audience of crude sensibility but considerable
sophistication in the ingenuities of language. They would have
been as unactable on the Greek stage as they are on the English. Superficially neat and trim, they are, for the stage, models
of formlessness. The Athenians were accustomed to long
speeches from Messengers, speeches which embarrass both the
modern actor and the modern audience; this was a convention
with practical advantages; their other long speeches usually
have some dramatic point, some place in the whole scheme of
the play. But the characters in a play of Seneca behave more
like members of a minstrel troupe sitting in a semicircle, rising
in turn each to do his "number," or varying their recitations by
a song or a little back-chat. I do not suppose that a Greek audience would have sat through the first three hundred lines of

the *Hercules Furens*. Only at the 523rd line does Amphitryon detect the sound of Hercules' tread, ascending from Hell, at which inopportune moment the chorus interrupt for two or three pages. When Hercules finally appears, he seems to be leading Cerberus, who presently evaporates, for he is not on the stage a few minutes later. After Amphitryon has in a rather round-about way, but more briefly than might have been expected, explained to Hercules the pressing danger to his family and country, Hercules makes off to kill Lycus. While Hercules is thus engaged in a duel on the result of which everybody's life depends, the family sit down calmly and listen to a long de-scription by Theseus of the Tartarean regions. This account is not a straight monologue, as Amphitryon from time to time puts leading questions about the fauna, and the administration and system of justice, of the world below. Meanwhile, Hercules has (contrary to the usual belief that Seneca murders all his victims in full view of the audience) despatched Lycus off-stage. At the end of the play, when Juno has stricken Hercules with madness, it is not at all clear whether he destroys his family on-stage or off. The slaughter is accompanied by a running commentary by Amphitryon, whose business it is to tell the audience what is going forward. If the children are slain in sight of the audience, this commentary is superfluous. Amphi-tryon also reports the collapse of Hercules; but presently Her-cules comes to, certainly on-stage, and spies his dead wife and children. The whole situation is inconceivable unless we assume the play to have been composed solely for recitation; like other of Seneca's plays, it is full of statements useful only to an au-dience which sees nothing. Seneca's plays might, in fact, be prac-tical models for the modern "broadcasted drama."

We need not look too closely into the conditions of the age which produced no genuine drama, but which allowed this curi-ous freak of non-theatrical drama. The theatre is a gift which has not been vouchsafed to every race, even of the highest cul-ture. It has been given to the Hindus, the Japanese, the Greeks; the English, the French, and the Spanish, at moments; in less measure to the Teutons and Scandinavians. It was not given to the Romans, or generously to their successors the Italians. The

Romans had some success in low comedy, itself an adaptation
of Greek models, but their instinct turned to shows and circuses,
as does that of the later race which created the Commedia del
l' Arte, which still provides the best puppet shows, and which
gives a home to Mr. Gordon Craig. No cause can be assigned,
for every cause demands a further cause. It is handy to speak
of "the genius of the language," and we shall continue to do
so, but why did the language adopt that particular genius? At
any rate, we should discourage any criticism which, in account-
ing for the defects and faults of the plays of Seneca, made much
of the "decadence" of the age of Nero. In the verse, yes, Seneca is unquestionably "silver age," or more exactly he is not a
poet of the *first* rank in Latin, he is far inferior to Virgil; but
for tragic drama, it would be a gross error to suppose that an
earlier and more heroic age of Rome could have produced anything better. Many of the faults of Seneca which appear "decadent" are, after all, merely Roman and (in the narrower
sense) Latin.

It is so with the characterisation. The characters of Seneca's
plays have no subtlety and no "private life." But it would be an
error to imagine that they are merely cruder and coarser versions of the Greek originals. They belong to a different race.
Their crudity is that which was of the Roman, as compared
with the Greek, in real life. The Roman was much the simpler
creature. At best, his training was that of devotion to the State,
his virtues were public virtues. The Greek knew well enough
the idea of the State, but he had also a strong traditional morality which constituted, so to speak, a direct relation between him
and the gods, without the mediation of the State, and he had
furthermore a sceptical and heterodox intelligence. Hence the
greater efficiency of the Roman, and the greater interest of the
Greek. Hence the difference between Greek Stoicism and Roman Stoicism—the latter being the form through which Stoicism
influenced later Europe. We must think of the characters of
Seneca as offspring of Rome, more than we think of them as
offspring of their age.

The drama of Antigone—which Seneca did not attempt—
could hardly have been transposed for Roman sentiment. In the

drama of Seneca there are no conflicts, except the conflict of passion, temper, or appetite with the external duties. The literary
consequence, therefore, is the tendency which persists in modern Italy; the tendency to "rhetoric"; and which, on such a
large scale, may be attributed to a development of language exceeding the development of sensibility of the people. If you
compare Catullus with Sappho, or Cicero with Demosthenes, or
Thucydides with a Latin historian, you find that the genius is
the genius of a different language, and what is lost is a gift of
sensibility. So with Seneca and the Greek dramatists. Hence we
should think of the long ranting speeches of Seneca, the beautiful but irrelevant descriptions, the smart stichomythia, rather
as peculiarities of Latin than as the bad taste of the dramatist.

The congeniality of Stoicism to the Roman mind is no part
of my duty to analyse; and it would be futile to attempt to decide what, in the dialogue and characterisation of Seneca's
plays, is due to Stoicism, what due to the Roman mind, and
what due to the peculiar form which Seneca elected. What is
certain is the existence of a large element of Stoicism in the
plays, enough to justify the belief that the plays and the prose
are by the hand of the same Seneca. In the plays, indeed, the
Stoicism is present in a form more quickly to catch the fancy of
the Renaissance than in the prose epistles and essays. Half of
the commonplaces of the Elizabethans—and the more commonplace half—are of Senecan origin. This ethic of sententious
maxims was, as we shall see, much more sympathetic to the
temper of the Renaissance than would have been the morals of
the elder Greek dramatists; the Renaissance itself was much
more Latin than Greek. In the Greek tragedy, as Nisard and
others have pointed out, the moralising is not the expression of
a conscious "system" of philosophy; the Greek dramatists mor-
alise only because morals are woven through and through the
texture of their tragic idea. Their morals are a matter of feeling trained for generations, they are hereditary and religious,
just as their dramatic forms themselves are the development
of their early liturgies. Their ethics of thought are one with
their ethics of behaviour. As the dramatic form of Seneca is
no growth, but a construction, so is his moral philosophy and

that of Roman Stoicism in general. Whether the Roman scepticism was, as Nisard suggests, the result of a too rapid and great
expansion and mixture of races cancelling each other's beliefs,
rather than the product of a lively inquiring intelligence, the
"beliefs" of Stoicism are a consequence of scepticism; and the
ethic of Seneca's plays is that of an age which supplied the lack
of moral habits by a system of moral attitudes and poses. To
this the natural public temper of Rome contributed. The ethic
of Seneca is a matter of postures. The posture which gives the
greatest opportunity for effect, hence for the Senecan morality,
is the posture of dying: death gives his characters the opportunity for their most sententious aphorisms—a hint which Elizabethan dramatists were only too ready to follow.

When all reserves have been made, there is still much to be
said for Seneca as a dramatist. And I am convinced that the
proper approach to his appreciation and enjoyment is not by
comparison and contrast—to which, in his case, criticism is violently tempted—but by isolation. I made a careful comparison
of the *Medea* and the *Hippolytus* of Seneca—perhaps his two
best plays—with the *Medea* of Euripides and the *Phèdre* of
Racine respectively; but I do not think that any advantage
would be gained by reporting the results of this inquiry, by
contrasting either the dramatic structure or the treatment of
the title figures. Such comparisons have already been made;
they magnify the defects and obscure the merits of the Senecan
tragedy. If Seneca is to be compared, he should rather be compared for versification, descriptive and narrative power, and
taste, with the earlier Roman poets. The comparison is fair,
though Seneca comes off rather ill. His prosody is monotonous;
in spite of a mastery of several metres, his choruses fall heavily
on the ear. Sometimes his chorus rhythms seem to hover between the more flexible measures of his predecessors and the
stiffer but more impressive beat of the mediaeval hymn.[2] But
within the limits of his declamatory purpose, Seneca obtains,
time after time, magnificent effects. In the verbal *coup de*

[2] E.g. *O mors amoris una sedamen mali,*
O mors pudoris maximum laesi decus.

(*Hippolytus,* 1188-89.)

théâtre no one has ever excelled him. The final cry of Jason to
Medea departing in her car is unique; I can think of no other
play which reserves such a shock for the last word:

> *Per alta vada spatia sublimi aethere;*
> *testare nullos esse, qua veheris, deos.*[3]

Again and again the epigrammatic observation on life or death
is put in the most telling way at the most telling moment. It is
not only in his brief ejaculations that Seneca triumphs. The sixteen lines addressed by the chorus to the dead sons of Hercules
(*Hercules Furens*, I. 1135 ff.), which are exquisitely rendered
by the Elizabethan translator, seem to me highly pathetic. The
descriptive passages are often of great charm, with phrases
which haunt us more than we should expect. The lines of
Hercules,

> *ubi sum? sub ortu solis, an sub cardine*
> *glacialis ursae?*

must have lain long in the memory of Chapman before they
came out in *Bussy d'Ambois* as

> *fly where men feel*
> *The cunning axle-tree, or those that suffer*
> *Under the chariot of the snowy Bear.*

Though Seneca is long-winded, he is not diffuse; he is capable
of great concision; there is even a monotony of forcefulness; but
many of his short phrases have for us as much oratorical impressiveness as they had for the Elizabethans. As (to take an
unworn example) the bitter words of Hecuba as the Greeks
depart:

> *concidit virgo ac puer;*
> *bellum peractum est.*

[3] Here the translator seems to me to have hit on the sense:

> *Bear witnesse, grace of God is none in place of thy repayre.*

A modern translator (Professor Miller, editing the Loeb Translation text)
gives "*bear witness, where thou ridest, that there are no gods.*" It seems to me
more effective if we take the meaning to be that there are no gods *where* (*ever*)
Medea is, instead of a mere outburst of atheism. But the old Farnaby edition
observes "*testimonium contra deorum justitiam, vel argumento nullos esse in
caelo deos.*"

Even the most sententious sayings of stoical commonplace preserve their solemnity in that Latin language which carries such thoughts more grandly than could any other:

> *Fatis agimur; cedite fatis.*
> *non sollicitae possunt curae*
> *mutare rati stamina fusi.*
> *quidquid patimur mortale genus,*
> *quidquid facimus venit ex alto,*
> *servatque suae decreta colus*
> *Lachesis nulla revoluta manu.*
> *omnia secto tramite vadunt*
> *primusque dies dedit extremum.*
>
> (*Oedipus,* 980 ff.)

But to quote Seneca is not criticism; it is merely to offer baits to a possible reader; it would indeed be bad criticism if we left the impression that these and such as these are moments in which Seneca excels himself, and which he could not sustain. An essential point to make about Seneca is the consistency of his writing, its maintenance on one level, below which he seldom falls and above which he never mounts. Seneca is not one of those poets who are to be remembered because they now and then rise to the tone and the vocabulary of greater poets. Seneca is wholly himself; what he attempted he executed, he created his own genre. And this leads us to a consideration which we must keep in mind in considering his later influence: whether we can treat him seriously as a *dramatist*. Critics are inclined to treat his drama as a bastard form. But this is an error which critics of the drama are in general apt to make; the forms of drama are so various that few critics are able to hold more than one or two in mind in pronouncing judgment of "dramatic" and "undramatic." What is "dramatic"? If one were saturated in the Japanese Noh, in Bhasa and Kalidasa, in Aeschylus, Sophocles and Euripides, Aristophanes and Menander, in the popular mediaeval plays of Europe, in Lope de Vega and Calderon, as well as the great English and French drama, and if one were (which is impossible) equally sensitive to them all, would one not hesitate to decide that one form is more dramatic

than another? And Seneca's is definitely a "form." It does not
fall within either of the categories of the defectively dramatic.
There are the "closet dramas" which are mostly simply inferior dramas: the plays of Tennyson, Browning, and Swinburne. (Whether a writer expected his play to be played or not
is irrelevant, the point is whether it is playable.) And there is
another, more interesting type, where the writer is trying to
do something more or something different from what the stage
can do, but yet with an implication of performance, where there
is a mixture of dramatic and extra-dramatic elements. This is
a modern and sophisticated form: it contains *The Dynasts*,
Goethe's *Faust*, and possibly (not having seen it played I cannot speak with confidence) *Peer Gynt*. Seneca's plays do not belong to either of these types. If, as I believe, they are intended
for *recitation*, they have a form of their own; and I believe
that they were intended for recitation because they are perfectly adapted for recitation—they are better recited than read.
And I have no doubt—though there is no external evidence—
that Seneca must have had considerable practice himself in reciting the plays. He would have been, therefore, a playwright
of as practical experience as Shakespeare or Molière. His form
is a practical form; it is even, I suggest, a form which might be
interesting to attempt in our own time, when the revival of the
theatre is obstructed by some of the difficulties which made the
stage an impossibility in the age of Seneca.

What lessons the Elizabethans learnt from Seneca, and
whether they were the same as those which we might learn
ourselves, is the next subject to consider. But whether they
profited by the study, or whether they admired him and pil-
laged him to their own detriment, we must remember that
we cannot justly estimate his influence unless we form our own
opinion of Senca first, without being influenced by his influence.

I I

The influence of Seneca upon Elizabethan drama has received
much more attention from scholars than from literary critics.
The historical treatment has been very thorough. The admir-

able edition of the works of Sir William Alexander, Earl of Stirling, by Kastner and Charlton (Manchester University Press, vol. i. 1921), has a full account of this influence both direct and through Italy and France; in this introduction also will be found the best bibliography of the subject. Dr. F. S. Boas, especially in his edition of Kyd's Plays, has treated the matter at length. Professor J. W. Cunliffe's *Influence of Seneca on Elizabethan Tragedy* (1893) remains, within its limits, the most useful of all books, and Mr. Cunliffe has handled the question in a more general way in his *Early English Classical Tragedies*. Indirect Senecan influences have also been studied in detail, as in Professor A. M. Witherspoon's *Influence of Robert Garnier on Elizabethan Drama*. And work which is now being done on the earlier drama (see Dr. A. W. Reed's recent *Early Tudor Drama*, 1926) will enable us to understand better the junction of the Senecan influence with the native tradition. It is not fitting that a literary critic should retrace all this labour of scholarship, where either his dissent or his approval would be an impertinence; but we may benefit by this scholarship to draw certain general conclusions.

The plays of Seneca exerted their influence in several ways and to several results. The results are of three main types: (1) the popular Elizabethan tragedy; (2) the "Senecal" drama, pseudo-classical, composed by and for a small and select body of persons not closely in touch or in sympathy with the popular drama of the day, and composed largely in protest against the defects and monstrosities of that drama; (3) the two Roman tragedies of Ben Jonson, which appear to belong between the two opposed classes, to constitute an attempt, by an active practising playwright, to improve the form of popular drama by the example of Seneca; not by slavish imitation but by adaptation, to make of popular drama a finished work of art. As for the ways in which Seneca influenced the Elizabethans, it must be remembered that these were never simple, and became more complicated. The Italian and the French drama of the day was already penetrated by Seneca. Seneca was a regular part of the school curriculum, while Greek drama was unknown to all but a few great scholars. Every schoolboy with a smattering of

Latin had a verse or two of Seneca in his memory; probably a
good part of the audiences could recognise the origin of the
occasional bits of Seneca which are quoted in Latin in some of
the popular plays (*e.g.* several times by Marston). And by the
time that *The Spanish Tragedy* and the old *Hamlet* had made
their success, the English playwright was under the influence of
Seneca by being under the influence of his own predecessors.
Here the influence of Kyd is of the greatest importance: if
Senecan Kyd had such a vogue, that was surely the path to
facile success for any hard-working and underpaid writer.

All that I wish to do is to consider certain misconceptions of
the Senecan influence, which I believe are still current in our
opinions of Elizabethan drama, although they do not appear in
works of scholarship. For such a purpose the contemporary
translations possess a particular value: whether they greatly affected the conception of Seneca, or greatly extended his influence, they give a reflection of the appearance of Seneca to the
Englishman of the time. I do not suggest that the influence of
Seneca has been exaggerated or diminished in modern criticism;
but I believe that too much importance has been attached to his
influence in some directions, and too little to his influence in
others. There is one point on which every one is agreed, and
hardly more than one: the five-act division of the modern European play is due to Seneca. What I chiefly wish to consider are,
first, his responsibility for what has been called since Symonds'
day the Tragedy of Blood—how far Seneca is the author of the
horrors which disfigure Elizabethan drama; second, his responsibility for *bombast* in Elizabethan diction; and third, his influence upon the *thought*, or what passes for thought, in the drama
of Shakespeare and his contemporaries. It is the first which I
think has been overestimated, the second misconstrued, the
third undervalued.

Certainly, among all national dramas, the Elizabethan tragedies are remarkable for the extent to which they employ the
horrible and revolting. It is true that but for this taste and
practice we should never have had *King Lear* or *The Duchess
of Malfy;* so impossible is it to isolate the vices from the virtues,

the failures from the masterpieces of Elizabethan tragedy. We cannot reprehend a custom but for which one great experiment of the human spirit must have been left unmade, even if we cannot like it; nor can we wholly deplore anything which brings with it some information about the soul. And even leaving Shakespeare apart, the genius of no other race could have manipulated the tragedy of horror into the magnificent farce of Marlowe, or the magnificent nightmare of Webster. We must therefore reserve two measures of comparison: one, that between the baser tragedy of the time and the best tragedy of the time, the other (which is perhaps a moral measure, the application of which would lead us too far for the present discussion) between the tragedy of the time as a whole and another tragedy of horror—we think of Dante's Ugolino and the Oedipus of Sophocles—in which, in the end, the mind seems to triumph. Here, the question of Seneca's influence is capital. If the taste for horror was a result of being trained on Seneca, then it has neither justification nor interest; if it was something inherent in the people and in the age, and Seneca merely the excuse and precedent, then it is a phenomenon of interest. Even to speak of Seneca as offering a precedent and excuse is probably to falsify; for it implies that the Elizabethans would otherwise have been a little uneasy in conscience at indulging such tastes— which is ridiculous to suppose. They merely assumed that Seneca's taste was like their own—which is not *wholly* untrue; and that Seneca represented the whole of classical antiquity—which is quite false. Where Seneca took part is in affecting the type of plot; he supported one tendency against another. But for Seneca, we might have had more plays in *The Yorkshire Tragedy* mould; that is to say, the equivalent of the *News of the World* murder report; Seneca, and particularly the Italianised Seneca, encouraged the taste for the foreign, remote, or exotic. No doubt *The Jew of Malta* or *Titus Andronicus* would have made the living Seneca shudder with genuine aesthetic horror; but his influence helped to recommend work with which he had little in common.

When we examine the plays of Seneca, the actual horrors are not so heinous or so many as are supposed. The most unpleasantly sanguinary is the *Thyestes*, a subject which, so far as I know, was not attempted by a Greek dramatist. Even here, if the view that the tragedies were intended only for recitation is true, the cultivated Roman audience were listening to a story which was part of their Hellenic culture, and which is in fact a common property of folklore. The story was sanctified by time. The plots of Elizabethan tragedy were, so far as the audience were concerned, novelties. This plot of *Thyestes* is not employed by any Elizabethan, but the play has undoubtedly more in common with the Tragedy of Blood, especially in its early form, than any other of Seneca's. It has a particularly tedious Ghost. It has, more emphatically than any other, the motive of Revenge, unregulated by any divine control or justice. Yet even in the *Thyestes* the performance of the horrors is managed with conventional tact; the only visible horror is the perhaps unavoidable presentation of the evidence—the children's heads in a dish.

The most significant popular play under Senecan influence is of course *The Spanish Tragedy*, and the further responsibility of Kyd for the translation of the pseudo-Senecan *Cornelia* of Garnier has marked him as the disciple of Seneca. But in *The Spanish Tragedy* there is another element, not always sufficiently distinguished from the Senecan, which (though it may have relations among the Italian Renaissance progeny of Seneca) allies it to something more indigenous. The Senecan apparatus, it is true, is impressive. The Ghost, and Revenge, who replace the Tantalus and the Fury of the *Thyestes*, use all the infernal allusions—Acheron, Charon, and the rest—so dear to Seneca. Temporary insanity is an expedient well known to Seneca. But in the type of plot there is nothing classical or pseudo-classical at all. "Plot" in the sense in which we find plot in *The Spanish Tragedy* does not exist for Seneca. He took a story perfectly well known to everybody, and interested his auditors entirely by his embellishments of description and narrative and by smartness and pungency of dialogue; suspense and surprise attached solely to verbal effects. *The Spanish Tragedy*, like the series of Hamlet plays, including Shakespeare's, has an affinity

to our contemporary detective drama.[4] The plot of Hieronymo
to compass his revenge by the play allies it with a small but interesting class of drama which certainly owes nothing essential
to Seneca: that which includes *Arden of Feversham* [5] and *The
Yorkshire Tragedy*. These two remarkable plays are both based
on contemporary or recent crimes committed in England. Unless it be the hint of divine retribution in the epilogue to *Arden*,
there is no token of foreign or classical influence in these two
plays. Yet they are bloody enough. The husband in *The Yorkshire Tragedy* kills his two young sons, throws the servant
downstairs and breaks her neck, and nearly succeeds in killing
his wife. In *Arden of Feversham* the wife and her conspirators
stab the husband to death upon the stage—the rest of the play
being occupied by a primitive but effective police inquiry. It is
only surprising that there are not more examples of this type
of play, since there is evidence of as lively a public interest in
police court horrors as there is today. One of the pieces of
evidence is associated with Kyd; it is a curious little account
of a poisoning case, *The Murder of John Brewen*. (A little
later, Dekker was to supply the deficiency of penny journalism
with his Plague Pamphlets.) In Kyd, whether *Arden* be by him
or by an imitator, we find the union of Senecan with native
elements, to the advantage of both. For the Senecan influence is
felt in the structure of the play—the structure of *The Spanish
Tragedy* is more dramatic than that of *Arden* or *The Yorkshire
Tragedy*; whilst the material of *The Spanish Tragedy*, like that
of the other two plays, is quite different from the Senecan material, and much more satisfying to an unlettered audience.

The worst that can be urged against Seneca, in the matter of
responsibility for what is disgusting in Elizabethan drama, is
that he may have provided the dramatist with a pretext or justification for horrors which were not Senecan at all, for which

[4] I suggest also that besides *Hamlet*, *Macbeth* and to some extent *Othello*
among Shakespeare's major tragedies have this "thriller" interest, whilst it is
not introduced into *King Lear*, *Antony and Cleopatra*, or *Coriolanus*. It is
present in *Oedipus Tyrannus*.
[5] I dissent from Dr. Boas, and agree with that body of opinion which attributes *Arden* to Kyd, *e.g.* Fleay, Robertson, Crawford, Dugdale Sykes, Oliphant.

there was certainly a taste, and the taste for which would certainly have been gratified at that time whether Seneca had ever written or not. Against my use of *The Yorkshire Tragedy*, it may be said that this play (the crime in question was committed only in 1603) and *Arden* also were written after the success of *The Spanish Tragedy*, and that the taste for horrors developed only after it had received Senecan licence. I cannot *prove* the contrary. But it must be admitted that the greater number of the horrors are such as Seneca himself would not have tolerated. In one of the worst offenders—indeed one of the stupidest and most uninspired plays ever written, a play in which it is incredible that Shakespeare had any hand at all, a play in which the best passages would be too highly honoured by the signature of Peele—in *Titus Andronicus* [6]—there is nothing really Senecan at all. There is a wantonness, an irrelevance, about the crimes of which Seneca would never have been guilty. Seneca's Oedipus has the traditional justification for blinding himself; and the blinding itself is far less offensive than that in *Lear*. In *Titus*, the hero cuts off his own hand in view of the audience, who can also testify to the mutilation of the hands and the tongue of Lavinia. In *The Spanish Tragedy*, Hieronymo bites off his own tongue. There is nothing like this in Seneca.

But if this is very unlike Seneca, it is very like the contemporary drama of Italy. Nothing could better illustrate the accidental character of literary "influence"—accidental, that is, with reference to the work exercising the influence—than the difference between Senecan drama in Italy and in France. The French drama is from the beginning restrained and decorous; to the French drama, especially to Garnier, the Senecan drama of Greville, Daniel and Alexander is allied. The Italian is bloodthirsty in the extreme. Kyd knew both; but it was to the Italian that he and Peele yielded themselves with sympathetic delight. We must remember, too, that Italy had developed stagecraft and stage machinery to the highest point—for the most sumptuous masques in England, Italian managers, engineers and artists were brought over; that the plastic arts were much more im-

[6] See J. M. Robertson: *An Introduction to the Study of the Shakespeare Canon.*

portant in Italy than elsewhere, and that consequently the spectacular and sensational elements of drama were insisted upon; that Italian civilisation had, in short, everything to dazzle the imagination of unsophisticated northerners emerging into a period of prosperity and luxury. I have no first-hand acquaintance with Italian plays of this epoch; it is a library which few readers would penetrate in pursuit of pleasure; but its character and influence in England are well attested. It is possible to say that Seneca hardly influenced this Italian drama at all; he was made use of by it and adopted into it; and for Kyd and Peele he was thoroughly Italianised.

The Tragedy of Blood is very little Senecan, in short, though it made much use of Senecan machinery; it is very largely Italian; and it added an ingenuity of plot which is native.

If we wished to find the reason for the sanguinary character of much Elizabethan drama—which persists to its end—we should have to allow ourselves some daring generalisations concerning the temper of the epoch. When we consider it, and reflect how much more refined, how much more *classical* in the profounder sense, is that earlier popular drama which reached its highest point in *Everyman*, I cannot but think that the change is due to some fundamental release of restraint. The tastes gratified are always latent: they were then gratified by the drama, as they are now gratified by crime reports in the daily press. It is no more reasonable to make Seneca responsible for this aspect of Elizabethan drama than it is to connect Aeschylus or Sophocles with *Jude the Obscure*. I am not sure that the latter association has not been made, though no one supposes that Hardy prepared himself by close application to the study of Greek drama.

It is pertinent to inquire, in this context, what was the influence of Seneca, in the way of horrors, upon the small body of "Senecal" dramatists who professedly imitated him. But this collation is relevant also to the question of Seneca's influence upon language; so that before making the comparison we may consider this latter question next. Here, the great influence of Seneca is unquestionable. Quotation after quotation, parallel after parallel, may be adduced; the most conspicuous are given in Cunliffe's *Influence of Seneca*, others in Lucas's *Seneca and Elizabethan Tragedy*. So great is this influence that we can say neither that it was good nor that it was bad; for we cannot imagine what Elizabethan dramatic verse would have been without it. The direct influence is restricted to the group of Marlowe and to Marston; Jonson and Chapman are, each in his own way, more sophisticated and independent; the later or Jacobean dramatists, Middleton, Webster, Tourneur, Ford, Beaumont and Fletcher, found their language upon their own predecessors, and chiefly upon Shakespeare. But none of these authors hesitated to draw upon Seneca when occasion served, and Chapman owes much, both good and bad, of his dramatic style to his admiration for Seneca. No better examples can be found, however, of plays which, while not Senecan in form, are yet deeply influenced by Seneca in language, than the *True Tragedy of Richard Duke of York*, and the Shakespearean *Richard II* and *Richard III*. These, with the work of Kyd and that of Marlowe and of Peele, and several of the plays included in the Shakespeare Apocrypha, have a great deal in common.

The precise pilferings and paraphrases have been thoroughly catalogued by the scholars I have mentioned, and others; hardly a dramatist, between Kyd and Massinger, is not many times indebted to Seneca. Instead of repeating this labour, I prefer to call attention to his universal influence. Not only the evolution of the dramatic structure, but the evolution of the blank verse cadence, took place under the shadow of Seneca; it is hardly too much to say that Shakespeare could not have formed the verse instrument which he left to his successors, Webster, Massinger, Tourneur, Ford, and Fletcher, unless he had received an instrument already highly developed by the genius of Marlowe and the influence of Seneca. Blank verse before 1600, or thereabouts, is a crude form of music compared to blank verse after that date; but its progress in fifteen years had been astonishing. In the first place, I believe that the establishment of blank verse as the vehicle of drama, instead of the old fourteener, or the heroic couplet, or (what might have happened) a particular form of prose rhythm, received considerable support from its being obviously the nearest equivalent to the solemnity and weight of the Senecan iambic. A comparison of the trotting metre of our translations with Surrey's translation of Virgil will show, I think, that while the former has undeniable poetic charms of its own, the latter would reveal more resources to the ear of the dramatist. The pre-Marlowe versification is competent, but extremely monotonous; it is literally a *monotone*, containing none of the musical counter-rhythms which Marlowe introduced, nor the rhythms of individual speech which were later added.

> *When this eternal substance of my soul*
> *Did live imprison'd in my wanton flesh,*
> *Each in their function serving other's need,*
> *I was a courtier in the Spanish court:*
> (Prologue, *Spanish Tragedy*, xxx.)

But to illustrate the early use of this metre under Senecan influence, a worse play serves our purpose better; the Senecan content justifies our quoting at some length from *Locrine*, an early play [1] of no merit whatever. Here is the Revival of Learning in the brain of a fourth-rate playwright:

HUMBER.

> *Where may I find some desert wilderness,*
> *Where I may breathe out curses as I would,*
> *And scare the earth with my condemning voice;*
> *Where every echo's repercussion*
> *May help me to bewail mine overthrow,*
> *And aid me in my sorrowful laments?*
> *Where may I find some hollow uncouth rock,*
> *Where I may damn, condemn, and ban my fill*
> *The heavens, the hell, the earth, the air, the fire,*
> *And utter curses to the concave sky,*
> *Which may infect the airy regions,*
> *And light upon the Brittain Locrine's head?*
> *You ugly sprites that in Cocytus mourn,*

---

[1] Usually attributed to Greene, and dated about 1585 (see Brooke, *Shakespeare Apocrypha*). Neither authorship nor date is important for my purpose: the play was obviously written by some one who had not yet experienced the influence of Marlowe.

And gnash your teeth with dolorous laments:
You fearful dogs that in black Lethe howl,
And scare the ghosts with your wide open throats:
You ugly ghosts that, flying from these dogs,
Do plunge yourselves in Puryflegiton:
Come, all of you, and with your shriking notes
Accompany the Brittain's conquering host.
Come, fierce Erynnys, horrible with snakes;
Come, ugly Furies, armed with your whips;
You threefold judges of black Tartarus,
And all the army of you hellish fiends,
With new-found torments rack proud Locrine's bones!
O gods, and stars! damned be the gods and stars
That did not drown me in fair Thetis' plains!
Curst be the sea, that with outrageous waves,
With surging billows did not rive my ships
Against the rocks of high Cerannia,
Or swallow me into her wat'ry gulf!
Would God we had arriv'd upon the shore
Where Polyphemus and the Cyclops dwell,
Or where the bloody Anthropophagi
With greedy jawes devours the wand'ring wights!

Enter the ghost of ALBANACT

But why comes Albanact's bloody ghost,
To bring a corsive to our miseries?
Is 't not enough to suffer shameful flight,
But we must be tormented now with ghosts,
With apparitions fearful to behold?

GHOST.
Revenge! revenge for blood!

HUMBER.
So nought will satisfy your wand'ring ghost
But dire revenge, nothing but Humber's fall,
Because he conquered you in Albany.
Now, by my soul, Humber would be condemned
To Tantal's hunger or Ixion's wheel.

Or to the vulture of Prometheus,
Rather than that this murther were undone.
When as I die I'll drag thy cursed ghost
Through all the rivers of foul Erebus,
Through burning sulphur of the Limbo-lake,
To allay the burning fury of that heat
That rageth in mine everlasting soul.

GHOST.

Vindicta, vindicta. [Exeunt.

This is the proper Ercles bombast, ridiculed by Shakespeare, Jonson, and Nashe. From this, even to *Tamburlaine*, is a long way; it is too absurdly distorted to serve even as a burlesque of Seneca; but the metre has something Senecan about it. From such verse there is a long distance to the melodies of

Now comes my lover tripping like a roe,
And brings my longings tangled in her hair.

or

Welcome, my son: who are the violets now
That strew the green lap of the new-come spring?

or

But look, the morn, in russet mantle clad,
Walks o'er the dew of yon high eastern hill:

that is to say, to the *lyrical* phase of blank verse, before Shakespeare had analysed it into true dramatic differentiation; it belongs to the first or *declamatory* phase. But this declamation is in its impulse, if not in its achievement, Senecan; and progress was made, not by rejection, but by dissociating this type of verse into products with special properties.

The next stage also was reached with the help of a hint from Seneca. Several scholars, Butler in particular, have called attention to a trick of Seneca of repeating one word of a phrase in the next phrase, especially in stichomythia, where the sentence of one speaker is caught up and twisted by the next. This was an effective stage trick, but it is something more; it is the crossing of one rhythm pattern with another.

—*Sceptrone nostro* famulus *est potior tibi?*
—*Quot iste* famulus *tradidit* reges *neci.*
—*Cur ergo* regi *servit et patitur iugum?*

                                        (*Hercules.*)

Seneca also gets a kind of double pattern by breaking up lines into minimum antiphonal units:

> *Rex est timendus.*
>   *Rex meus fuerat pater.*
> *Non metuis arma?*
>   *Sint licet terra edita.*
> *Moriere.*
>   *Cupio.*
>   *Profuge.*
>   *Paenituit fugae.*
> *Medea,*
>   *Fiam.*
>   *Mater es.*
>   *Cui sim vides.*
>   (*Medea,* 168 ff.)

A man like Marlowe, or even men with less scholarship and less genius for the use of words than he, could hardly have failed to learn something from this. At any rate, I believe that the study of Seneca had its part in the formation of verse like the following:

> —*Wrong not her birth, she is of royal blood.*
> —*To save her life, I'll say she is not so.*
> —*Her life is safest only in her birth.*
> —*And only in that safety died her brothers.*

It is only a step (and a few lines further) to the pun:

> *Cousins, indeed; and by their uncle cozen'd.*

Some of the effects in such plays as *Richard II* and *Richard III* are indeed of pre-Marlowe origin, as:

> *I had an Edward, till a Richard kill'd him;*
> *I had a Henry, till a Richard kill'd him;*

> *Thou hadst an Edward, till a Richard kill'd him;*
> *Thou hadst a Richard, till a Richard kill'd him.*

which is already in even *Locrine*, as:

> *The boisterous Boreas thundreth forth Revenge,*
> *The stony rocks cry out on sharp revenge,*
> *The thorny bush pronounceth dire revenge,*

but in the following lines from Clarence's Dream we see an immense advance over *Locrine* in the use of infernal machinery:

> *I pass'd, methought, the melancholy flood,*
> *With that grim ferryman which poets write of,*
> *Unto the kingdom of perpetual night.*
> *The first that there did greet my stranger soul,*
> *Was my great father-in-law, renowned Warwick;*
> *Who cried aloud, "What scourge for perjury*
> *Can this dark monarchy afford false Clarence?"* [8]

The "kingdom of perpetual night" and the last two lines are a real approximation in English to the magnificence of Senecan Latin at its best; they are far from being a mere burlesque. The best of Seneca has here been absorbed into English.

In *Richard II*, which is usually dated a little earlier than *Richard III*, I find such interesting variations of versification that I am convinced that it is a slightly later play,[9] or else that there is more of Shakespeare in it. There is the same play of words:

> *Give Richard leave to live till Richard die.*

> *A brittle glory shineth in his face;*
> *As brittle as the glory is the face.*

but there is less stichomythia, less mere repetition, and a dexterity in retaining and developing the same rhythm with greater

---

[8] I once expressed the opinion that these lines must be by Shakespeare. I am not so confident now. See J. M. Robertson: *The Shakespeare Canon*, Part II.

[9] I do not deny that some parts, or some lines, of *Richard III* are later than *Richard II* Both plays may have undergone revision from time to time, and in any case must be dated near together.

freedom and less obvious calculation. (See the long speeches of Richard in Act III, sc. ii. and sc. iii, and compare with the more carefully balanced verses of Queen Margaret's tirade in *Richard III*, Act IV, sc. iv.)

When blank verse has reached this point, and passed into the hands of its greatest master, there is no need to look for fresh infusions of Seneca. He has done his work, and the one influence on later dramatic blank verse is the influence of Shakespeare. Not that later dramatists do not make great use of Seneca's plays. Chapman uses him, and employs the old machinery; but Seneca's influence on Chapman was chiefly on Chapman's "thought." Jonson uses Seneca deliberately; the superb prologues of *Envy* and *Sylla's Ghost* are adaptations of the Senecan ghost-prologue form, not an inheritance from Kyd. Massinger, a most accomplished dramatist and versifier, sometimes falls back most lamentably upon ghosts and spectacles. But the verse is formed, and Seneca no further responsible for its vices or virtues.

Certainly, Elizabethan bombast can be traced to Seneca; Elizabethans themselves ridiculed the Senecan imitation. But if we reflect, not on the more grotesque exaggerations, but on the dramatic poetry of the first half of the period, as a whole, we see that Seneca had as much to do with its merits and its progress as with its faults and its delays. Certainly it is all "rhetorical," but if it had not been rhetorical, would it have been anything? Certainly it is a relief to turn back to the austere, close language of *Everyman*, the simplicity of the mysteries; but if new influences had not entered, old orders decayed, would the language not have left some of its greatest resources unexplored? Without bombast, we should not have had *King Lear*. The art of dramatic language, we must remember, is as near to oratory as to ordinary speech or to other poetry. If the Elizabethans distorted and travestied Seneca in some ways, if they learned from him tricks and devices which they applied with inexpert hands, they also learned from him the essentials of declaimed verse. Their subsequent progress is a process of splitting up the primitive rhetoric, developing out of it subtler poetry and subtler tones of conversation, eventually mingling, as no other school of dramatists has done, the oratorical, the conversational, the elaborate and the simple, the direct and the indirect; so that they were able to write plays which can still be viewed as plays, with any plays, and which can still be read as poetry, with any poetry.

It is improper to pass from the questions of Seneca's influence upon the Tragedy of Blood and upon the language of the Elizabethans without mentioning the group of "Senecal" plays, largely produced under the aegis of the Countess of Pembroke. The history of this type of play belongs rather to the history of scholarship and culture than to the history of the Drama: it begins in a sense with the household of Sir Thomas More, and therefore is doubly allied to the present subject by Jasper Heywood; it is continued in the conversations at Cambridge of Mr. Ascham, Mr. Watson, and Mr. (later Sir John) Cheke. The first to attack openly the common stage was Sir Philip Sidney, whose words are well known:

"Our Tragedies and Comedies (not without cause cried out against), observing rules neither of honest civility nor of skilful Poetry, excepting *Gorboduc* (againe, I say, of those that I have seen), which notwithstanding, as it is full of stately speeches and well sounding Phrases, climbing to the height of Seneca his style, and as full of notable morality, which it doth most delightfully teach, and so obtain the very end of Poesie, yet in troth it is very defectious in the circumstances, which grieveth me, because it might not remain as an exact model of all Tragedies. For it is faulty both in place and time, the two necessary companions of all corporal actions. . . . But if it be so in *Gorboduc,* how much more in all the rest, where you shall have Asia of the one side, and Afric of the other, and so many other under-kingdoms, that the Player, when he cometh in, must ever begin with telling where he is: or else the tale will not be conceived? Now ye shall have three Ladies walk to gather flowers, and then we must believe the stage to be a Garden. By and by, we hear news of shipwrack in the same place, and then we are to blame if we accept it not for a Rock."

It was after Sidney's death that his sister, the Countess of Pembroke, tried to assemble a body of wits to compose drama in the proper Senecan style, to make head against the popular melodrama of the time. Great poetry should be both an art and a diversion; in a large and cultivated public like the Athenian it can be both; the shy recluses of Lady Pembroke's circle were bound to fail. But we must not draw too sharp a line of separation between the careful workman who laboured to create a classical drama in England and the hurried purveyors of playhouse successes: the two worlds were not without communication, and the work of the earlier Senecals was not without fruit.

With the part played by the *Tenne Tragedies* in this Senecan tradition I shall deal in the next section of this essay. Here, I wish only to call attention to certain characteristics of Senecal Tragedy in its final form, in the work of Greville, Daniel and Alexander. I would only remind the reader that these final Senecal plays were written after any real hope of altering or reforming the English stage had disappeared. In the early Elizabethan years appeared a succession of tragedies, mostly performed by the Inns of Court, and therefore not popular productions, which might in favourable circumstances have led to a living Senecan drama. Notably, *Gorboduc* (mentioned by Sidney above), *Jocasta*, and *Gismond of Salerne* (three of the four plays contained in Cunliffe's *Early English Classical Tragedies*). When *The Spanish Tragedy* appeared (with, as I have suggested, its particularly non-classical element) these feeble lights were snuffed out. I pass on to the finished Senecal product, because I am only concerned to elicit the effect of Seneca upon his sedulous admirers and imitators who professed to be, and were, men of taste and culture.

The Monarchic Tragedies of Alexander, Earl of Stirling, are the last on our list, composed under the auspices of the scholarly King James I. They are poor stuff: I imagine that they are more important in the history of the Union than in the history of the Drama, since they represent the choice, by a Scotsman of accidental eminence, to write verse in English instead of in Scots. Their faults are the faults of the other plays of the group; but they have not the virtues of the others. The two plays of Fulke Greville, Lord Brooke, the friend and biographer of Sidney, have some magnificent passages, especially in the choruses; Greville had a true gift for sententious declamation. But they have much dullness also; and they do not imitate Seneca nearly so faithfully as either those of Alexander or those of Daniel. Greville not only cannot stick to one chorus, but will introduce, on one occasion, a chorus of "Bashas or Caddies," and after the next act, a chorus of "Mahometan Priests"; he introduces the still more doubtful practice of supernatural figures, a "dialogue of Good and Evil Spirits," or even a chorus of two allegorical figures, "Time and Eternity" (ending indeed with the fine line spoken by Eternity: *I am the measure of felicity*). The best, the best sustained, the most poetic and the most lyrical, are two tragedies of Samuel Daniel: *Cleopatra* and *Philotas*. They contain many lovely passages, they are readable all through, and they are well built.

Now, in comparison with the supposed influence of Seneca on the barbarity of Elizabethan tragedy, and his supposed bad influence upon the language, what do we find in the plays of those who took him as their model in their attack upon the popular stage, in that attack in which Daniel, in his dedication of *Cleopatra* to the Countess of Pembroke, declared himself the foe of "Gross Barbarism"? Deaths there are, of course, but there is none of these tragedies that is not far more restrained, far more discreet and sober, not only than the Tragedy of Blood, but than Seneca himself. Characters die so decently, so remote from the stage, and the report of their deaths is wrapped up in such long speeches by messengers stuffed with so many moral maxims, that we may read on unaware that any one concerned in the play has died at all. Where the popular playwrights travestied Seneca's melodrama and his fury, the Senecals travesty his reserve and his decorum. And as for the language, that, too, is a different interpretation of Seneca. How vague are our notions of bombast and rhetoric when they must include styles and vocabularies so different as those of Kyd and Daniel! It is by opposite excesses that Senecals and popular dramatists attract the same reproach. The language of Daniel is pure and restrained; the vocabulary choice, the expression clear; there is nothing far-fetched, conceited, or perverse.

CLEOPATRA.

> *What, hath my face yet power to win a Lover?*
>   *Can this torne remnant serve to grace me so,*
> *That it can Caesar's secret plots discover,*
>   *What he intends with me and mine to do?*
> *Why then, poor beauty, thou hast done thy last,*
>   *And best good service thou could'st do unto me;*
> *For now the time of death reveal'd thou hast,*
>   *Which in my life did'st serve but to undo me.*

The first two lines are admirable; the rest are good serviceable lines; almost any passage from *Cleopatra* is as good, and some are far better. The whole thing is in excellent taste. Yet we may ponder the fact that it would not have made the slightest difference, to the formation of our Augustan poetry, if Daniel and his friends had never written a line; that Dryden and Pope are nearer allied to—Cowley; and that they owe more to Marlowe than to the purest taste of the sixteenth century. Daniel and Greville are good poets, and there is something to be learned from them; but they, and Sir John Davies who somewhat resembles them, had no influence. The only one of Lady Pembroke's heroes who had influence is Edmund Spenser.

Within the limits of an essay it is impossible to do more than touch on the influence of Seneca upon the "thought" of the Elizabethans, or more exactly, upon their attitude toward life so far as it can be formulated in words. I would only say enough, at this point, to remind the reader that Seneca's influence upon dramatic form, upon versification and language, upon sensibility, and upon thought, must in the end be all estimated together; they cannot be divided. How the influence of Seneca is related, in the Elizabethan mind, with other influences, perhaps those of Montaigne and Machiavelli, I do not know; and I think it is a subject still to be investigated. But the frequency with which a quotation from Seneca, or a thought or figure ultimately derived from Seneca, is employed in Elizabethan plays whenever a moral reflection is required, is too remarkable to be ignored; and when an Elizabethan hero or villain dies, he usually dies in the odour of Seneca. These facts are known to scholars; but if known, they are usually ignored by literary critics. In a comparison of Shakespeare with Dante, for instance, it is assumed that Dante leant upon a system of philosophy which he accepted whole, whereas Shakespeare created his own: or that Shakespeare had acquired some extra- or ultra-intellectual knowledge superior to a philosophy. This occult kind of information is sometimes called "spiritual knowledge" or "insight." Shakespeare and Dante were both merely poets (and Shakespeare a dramatist as well); our estimate of the intellectual material they absorbed does not affect our estimate of their poetry, either absolutely or relatively to each other. But it must affect our vision of them and the use we make of them, the fact that Dante, for instance, had behind him an Aquinas, and Shakespeare behind him a Seneca. Perhaps it was Shakespeare's special rôle in history to have effected this peculiar union—perhaps it is a part of his special eminence to have expressed an inferior philosophy in the greatest poetry. It is certainly one cause of the terror and awe with which he inspires us.

> *Omnia certo tramite vadunt*
> *primusque dies dedit extremum.*
> *non illa deo vertisse licet*
> *quae nexa suis currunt causis.*
> *it cuique ratus prece non ulla*
> *mobilis ordo.*
> *multis ipsum timuisse nocet.*
> *multi ad fatum venere suum*
> *dum fata timent.*

Compare with *Edward III*, Act iv, sc. iv (see Cunliffe, *Influence of Seneca*, p. 87), and with *Measure for Measure*, Act iii, sc. i. And

Men must endure
Their going hence, even as their coming hither,
Ripeness is all.[10]

III

The *Tenne Tragedies* were translated and printed separately
over a space of about eight years, with the exception of the
Thebais, which was translated by Newton in 1581 to complete
the work for his edition of the whole. The order and dates
of the several translations are of interest. The first and best of
the translators was Jasper Heywood:[11] his *Troas* was printed
in 1559, his *Thyestes* in 1560, his *Hercules Furens* in 1561.
The *Oedipus* by Alexander Nevyle (translated 1560) was
printed in 1563. In 1566 appeared the *Octavia* of Nuce, the
Agamemnon, Medea, and *Hercules Oetaeus* of Studley in 1566,
and the *Hippolytus* of Studley probably in 1567. About four-
teen years then elapsed before Newton produced his complete
edition, and it may be presumed that he translated the *Thebais*
for that purpose.[12]

It has never been supposed, in spite of the acid taunt of
Nashe, that any of the Elizabethan dramatists owe any great

[10] Mr. F. L. Lucas, in his *Seneca and Elizabethan Tragedy*, says (p. 122):
"But it must be said once for all about the bulk of Shakespeare's supposed
borrowings from Seneca, that one grows more and more sceptical." What has
been said once for all is not for me to dispute, but I would point out that I
am not here concerned with Shakespeare's "borrowings" (where I am inclined
to agree) but with Shakespeare as the voice of his time, and this voice in
poetry is, in the most serious matters of life and death, most often the voice
of Seneca. I subscribe to the observation of Cunliffe (*op. cit.* p. 85): "We
have [in *King Lear*] Seneca's hopeless fatalism, not only in the catastrophe,
but repeatedly brought forward in the course of the play."

> *As flies to wanton boys are we to the gods;*
> *They kill us for their sport.*

[11] Sometime Fellow of All Souls College, and later an eminent Jesuit; but
chiefly remembered as the uncle of John Donne. Much information about
Heywood and his family is contained in A. W. Reed's *Early Tudor Drama*.
[12] These facts are given succinctly in Cunliffe's *Influence of Seneca*. The
slight textual differences between the early editions and that of 1581 are
given by E. M. Spearing: *The Elizabethan Translations of Seneca's Tragedies.*

debt to these translations.[13] Most of the playwrights, as I have
intimated before, may be supposed to have had a smattering
of Seneca at school; two of the popular dramatists who exercised a decisive influence at an important moment—Kyd and
Peele—were acquainted with several languages, and therefore
themselves subjected to several influences. But if we look at
the dates we cannot overlook the probability that these translations helped to direct the course of events. They (all but one)
appeared between 1559 and 1566. The first plays of Senecan form
which could be called popular were Sackville and Norton's
Gorboduc, which appeared in 1561, Gascoyne's *Jocasta* in 1566,
and *Gismond of Salerne* in 1567. We must also take account, of
course, of the fact that plays of Seneca, and plays in imitation
of Seneca, were being produced in Latin at the Universities.[14]
The *Troades* was performed in Latin at Trinity College, Cambridge, in 1551. Trinity resumed its enterprise in 1559—the
year of Heywood's *Troas*—and between 1559 and 1561 the College produced in Latin four plays of Seneca. And during the
'sixties the two Universities first, and the Inns of Court subsequently, composed and performed a number of Latin plays on
the Senecan model. This would have occurred, no doubt, even
had Heywood never translated Seneca at all. But there can be
little doubt that his translations indicate a nascent interest in a
new vernacular drama to vie with classical drama, and that they
in turn stimulated the beginning of this drama. At the same
busy moment took place another event of capital importance,
which combined with this Senecan work to produce English
tragedy. In 1557 came the publication of Surrey's translation of
Book II of the *Aeneid,* in the new "blank verse," the instrument without which the Elizabethan drama would have been
impossible. The first-fruits, *Gorboduc,* are inconsiderable; but
this play marks a new epoch; there is no clearer division in
the whole of English literature.

We have, in fact, within a period of about forty years, three
distinct phases in the development of English tragedy: the first,

[13] See E. M. Spearing: *op. cit.*

[14] For a convenient summary of the Senecan movement throughout Europe,
and particularly in England, see Kastner and Charlton's edition of Alexander,
above mentioned.

from 1559 to some time in the early 'eighties, is announced by
Heywood's translations; the second is the period in which
flourished Kyd and Peele, both of whom came to be influenced by the sudden and soon extinguished genius of Marlowe;
the third is the period of Shakespeare up to his culminating
tragedies. Then follows a period of Jacobean drama which belongs not so much to Shakespeare, although Shakespeare's last
plays fall within the first years of it, as to Beaumont and
Fletcher: it is the period, not typically of tragedy, but of tragi-
comic romance.

In the preceding section I insisted upon the difference between Seneca's influence upon popular drama and his influence
upon those fastidious spirits, the Senecals, who tried to observe
his dramatic laws. But this difference of tendency is hardly
apparent in the first period, or until the appearance of Kyd and
Peele. During this period the fashions set at the Universities
were followed at the Inns of Court. The plays produced by
the legal wits were sometimes acted at the Queen's Court, with
which, indeed, the Inns had a kind of formal connection. And in
turn the plays produced at the Royal Court affected the more
popular drama.[15] *Gorboduc* is followed by *Gismond of Salerne*,
and *Gismond* later by the popular and atrocious *Locrine* (in
which Peele almost certainly had a heavy hand); *The Misfor-
tunes of Arthur* was probably too tardy to play much part in
the transition. Another play of importance, which shows the
persistence of the influence from the Universities upon popular
drama, is Legge's *Richardus Tertius*, a Latin chronicle play
acted at St. John's College, Cambridge, in 1573, and apparently
repeated in 1579 and 1582. This play is the parent of *The True
Tragedy of Richard III*, and consequently of the entire brood
of chronicle plays.

Another point which I have already considered, but which
must be mentioned here in a different context, is the relation
of Seneca to *Italian* Seneca, and of both to the native tendencies
of the time. Italian Seneca is not conspicuous until the period of
Kyd and Peele; but even among the translations of Heywood
we can find evidence that he was to be by no means unwelcome.

[15] See J. M. Manly's introduction (p. v) to F. S. Miller's translation of
The Tragedies of Seneca (1907).

Besides other peculiarities of these translations which we must examine, there is an interesting addition made by Heywood to the *Troas*. In the play of Seneca Achilles' Ghost makes no appearance; it is merely mentioned as having been seen. The play was the first to be translated, and there is some reason for believing that the translation was intended to be played. The "divers and sundrye" additions which Heywood invents render this supposition all the more plausible; for they are such as a translator would be much more likely to make if he had a performance in view, than if his translation were intended only for reading; in the latter event he might be expected to stick pretty closely to the text. Between the second and third acts of the *Troas* Heywood allows himself the liberty of interpolating a new scene of his own invention, which is a long soliloquy in thirteen stanzas by the Ghost of Achilles. And this independent "Sprite" rants in a tone which hardly Peele could outdo:

> *From burning lakes the furies wrath I threate,*
> *And fire that nought but streames of bloud may slake*
> *The rage of wind and seas their shippes shall beate,*
> *And Ditis deepe on you shall vengeance take,*
> *The sprites crye out, the earth and seas do quake,*
> *The poole of Styx ungratefull Greekes it seath,*
> *With slaughtred bloud revenge Achilles' death.*

It is to be observed that Nevyle and Studley both joined Inns of Court; that Nevyle came there to know Gascoyne, the author of *Jocasta*; and that Heywood knew, or at least knew of, Sackville and Norton before they had written *Gorboduc*. The impulse toward the Tragedy of Blood is already present in these translators, and they do not hesitate to add or to alter; the distortion of Seneca begins in his translation.

It is not only as an embryonic form of Elizabethan tragedy that these translations have documentary interest. They represent the transformation of the older form of versification into the new—consequently the transformation of language and sensibility as well. Few things that can happen to a nation are more important than the invention of a new form of verse. And at no other time, and to no other country than England at that time, has such an achievement as that of Henry Howard, Earl of Surrey, had greater consequences. To the French or to the Italians it could not have mattered so much. Their sensibility had already learned to express itself in large part in prose: Boccaccio and Machiavelli in one country, and the chroniclers—Froissart, Joinville, Commines—in the other, had already done a great work in forming the local mind. But the Elizabethan mind, far more than the contemporary mind in any other country, grew and matured through its verse rather than through its prose. The development of prose between Elyot and Bacon is certainly remarkable; but a comparison of styles between, say, Latimer and Andrewes shows a slower rate of change than the same space of time in verse, or the same space of time in prose in the next century. On the other hand, a study of the styles, the syntax, and the cadences of blank verse from *Gorboduc* to Shakespeare, and even after Shakespeare in the work of Webster and Tourneur, brings to light a process which is wholly astonishing.

The *Tenne Tragedies* must have shown conclusively to the most sensitive contemporary ears that the fourteener had had its day; it was certain that the verse of Surrey's *Aeneid* was in every way the verse in which to render the dignity and pomposity of the Senecan rhythm. And the slower iambic pentameter brought with it an alteration in vocabulary. The fourteener had served very well in rough comedy; it runs jollily in *Roister Doister* and *Gammer Gurton*. It is no vehicle for solemn tragedy, and the miracle is that Heywood and Studley made as good a job with it as they did. The fourteener, and the kindred loose metres of the interlude, are not adapted to a highly Latinised vocabulary; they are adapted to a vocabulary containing a large proportion of short words and monosyllables of Germanic origin; a vocabulary which must have come to seem, as it seems to us, rather clownish, if fresh and vigorous. The language of early Tudor times is indeed in some ways a deterioration from the language of Chaucer. One reason for this is no doubt the change in pronunciation, the suppression of syllables; the melody of the older tongue had gone, and with this melody much of its dignity; new rhythms, and new infusions from abroad, were very much needed. At first, in fact, the innovations overpowered the language; the Elizabethan bombast was a verbal even more than an emotional debauch; it was not until the prose of Dryden and Hobbes that English settled down to something like sobriety.

In the *Iliad* of Chapman we see new wine bursting old bottles; the poem is a magnificent *tour de force* in which Chapman sometimes succeeds in fitting the new vocabulary to the old "stretched" metre. But it is, consequently, a poem of brilliant passages rather than sustained success. Heywood and Studley—particularly Studley—make no such attempt: their fourteener is early, not late Tudor; it is a different thing from Chapman's. Only in the pentameter rhymed choruses does their sensibility become more modern; the contrast between their dialogue and their chorus verse is interesting. Here is a random bit of Studley:

O wanny *jaws of Blacke Averne*, eake *Tartar dungeon* grim,
O *Lethes Lake of woful Soules the joy that therein swimme,*
And eake ye glummy *Gulphes destroy, destroy me wicked wight*
And still in pit of pangues *let me be plunged day and night.*
Now, now, come up ye Goblins grim from water creekes alow ..

The majority of the rhyme words are monosyllables. The most sonorous and canorous Latin names are truncated (it remained for Marlowe to discover, and Milton to perfect, the musical possibilities of classical names almost to the point of *incantation*). Alliteration, in as primitive a form as that of *Piers Plowman*, is constant. For instance, Heywood has

shal Sisyphus his stone
That slipper restles rollyng payse uppon my backe be borne,
Or shal my lymmes with swifter swinge of whirling whele be torne?
Or shal my paynes be Tytius panges th' encreasing liver still,
Whose growing guttes the gnawing gripes and fylthy foules do fyll?

To examine such lines under the microscope is not to do them justice; the vigorous vocabulary and swinging metre appear at their best when we read through a long descriptive or narrative passage: in the same play (the *Thyestes*) the messenger's account of the crime of Atreus (Act IV) is admirably rendered.

In their handling of the choruses the translators are less scrupulous. When they translate the dialogue they are literal to the best of their ability—occasional inaccuracies or mistranslations being admitted—but in the choruses they will sometimes lengthen or shorten, sometimes omit altogether, or substitute an invention of their own. On the whole, their alterations tend to make the play more dramatic; sometimes they may be suspected of adding a political innuendo to the Senecan moralising on the vanity of place and power. And it is especially in the choruses that we find, now and then, flashes of that felicity which is present in Tudor translation more perhaps than in the translations of any period into any language. For example, the whole of the chorus at the end of Act IV of Heywood's *Hercules Furens* is very fine, but the last six lines seem to me of singular beauty; and as the original, too, is a lovely passage, it is both fair and interesting to quote original and translation. The persons addressed are the dead children of Hercules, whom he has just slain in his madness.

> *ite ad Stygios, umbrae, portus*
> *ite, innocues, quas in primo*
> *limine vitae scelus oppressit*
> *patriusque furor;*
> *ite, iratos visite reges.*

And Heywood:

> *Goe hurtles soules, whom mischiefe hath opprest*
> *Even in first porch of life but lately had,*
> *And fathers fury goe unhappy kind*
> *O litle children, by the way ful sad*
>   *Of journey knowen.*
> *Goe see the angry kynges.*

Nothing can be said of such a translation except that it is perfect. It is a last echo of the earlier tongue, the language of Chaucer, with an overtone of that Christian piety and pity

which disappears with Elizabethan verse. The greater part of
the chorus work has not this purity: one feels a curious strain
on the old vocabulary to say new things; the fluctuation, the
shades of variation between the old world and the new deserve inquisitive study; the ambiguity probably contributes to
give these translations a unique mood, which is only to be extracted and enjoyed after patient perusals. They are not translations to be read in a hurry; they do not yield their charm
easily.

> *Such friendship finde wyth Gods yet no man myght,*
> *That he the morowe might be sure to lyve.*
> *The God our things all tost and turned quight*
> *Rolles with a whyrle wynde.*

III

FOUR ELIZABETHAN

DRAMATISTS

A PREFACE TO AN UNWRITTEN BOOK

———

T O attempt to supplement the criticism of Lamb, Coleridge, and Swinburne on these four Elizabethan dramatists —Webster, Tourneur, Middleton, and Chapman—is a task for which I now believe the time has gone by. What I wish to do is to define and illustrate a point of view toward the Elizabethan drama, which is different from that of the nineteenth century tradition. There are two accepted and apparently opposed critical attitudes toward Elizabethan drama, and what I shall endeavour to show is that these attitudes are identical, and that another attitude is possible. Furthermore, I believe that this alternative critical attitude is not merely a possible difference of personal bias, but that it is the inevitable attitude for our time. The statement and explication of a conviction about such an important body of dramatic literature, toward what is in fact the only distinct form of dramatic literature that England has produced, should be something more than an exercise in mental ingenuity or in refinement of taste: it should be something of revolutionary influence on the future of drama. Contemporary literature, like contemporary politics, is confused by the moment-to-moment struggle for existence; but the time arrives when an examination of principles is necessary. I believe that the theatre has reached a point at which a revolution in principles should take place.

The accepted attitude toward Elizabethan drama was estab-

lished on the publication of Charles Lamb's *Specimens*. By publishing these selections, Lamb set in motion the enthusiasm for
poetic drama which still persists, and at the same time encouraged the formation of a distinction which is, I believe, the ruin
of modern drama—the distinction between drama and literature. For the *Specimens* made it possible to read the plays as
poetry while neglecting their function on the stage. It is for
this reason that all modern opinion of the Elizabethans seems
to spring from Lamb, for all modern opinion rests upon the
admission that poetry and drama are two separate things, which
can only be *combined* by a writer of exceptional genius. The
difference between the people who prefer Elizabethan drama,
in spite of what they admit to be its dramatic defects, and the
people who prefer modern drama although acknowledging that
it is never good poetry, is comparatively unimportant. For in
either case, you are committed to the opinion that a play can
be good literature but a bad play and that it may be a good play
and bad literature—or else that it may be outside of literature
altogether.

On the one hand we have Swinburne, representative of the
opinion that plays exist as literature, and on the other hand
Mr. William Archer, who with great lucidity and consistency
maintains the view that a play need not be literature at all. No
two critics of Elizabethan drama could appear to be more
opposed than Swinburne and Mr. William Archer; yet their
assumptions are fundamentally the same, for the distinction
between poetry and drama, which Mr. Archer makes explicit,
is implicit in the view of Swinburne; and Swinburne as well
as Mr. Archer allows us to entertain the belief that the difference between modern drama and Elizabethan drama is represented by a gain of dramatic technique and the loss of poetry.

Mr. Archer in his brilliant and stimulating book [1] succeeded
in making quite clear all of the dramatic faults of Elizabethan
drama. What vitiates his analysis is his failure to see why these
faults are faults, and not simply different conventions. And he
gains his apparent victory over the Elizabethans for this reason,

---

[1] *The Old Drama and the New* (Heinemann, 1923).

that the Elizabethans themselves admit the same criteria of realism that Mr. Archer asserts. The great vice of English drama from Kyd to Galsworthy has been that its aim of realism was unlimited. In one play, *Everyman*, and perhaps in that one play only, we have a drama within the limitations of art; since Kyd, since *Arden of Feversham*, since *The Yorkshire Tragedy*, there has been no form to arrest, so to speak, the flow of spirit at any particular point before it expands and ends its course in the desert of exact likeness to the reality which is perceived by the most commonplace mind. Mr. Archer confuses faults with conventions; the Elizabethans committed faults and muddled their conventions. In their plays there are faults of inconsistency, faults of incoherency, faults of taste, there are nearly everywhere faults of carelessness. But their great weakness is the same weakness as that of modern drama, it is the lack of a convention. Mr. Archer facilitates his own task of destruction, and avoids offending popular opinion, by making an exception of Shakespeare: but Shakespeare, like all his contemporaries, was aiming in more than one direction. In a play of Aeschylus, we do not find that certain passages are literature and other passages drama; every style of utterance in the play bears a relation to the whole and because of this relation is dramatic in itself. The imitation of life is circumscribed, and the approaches to ordinary speech and withdrawals from ordinary speech are not without relation and effect upon each other. It is essential that a work of art should be self-consistent, that an artist should consciously or unconsciously draw a circle beyond which he does not trespass: on the one hand actual life is always the material, and on the other hand an abstraction from actual life is a necessary condition to the creation of the work of art.

Let us try to conceive how the Elizabethan drama would appear to us if we had in existence what has never existed in the English language: a drama formed within a conventional scheme—the convention of an individual dramatist, or of a number of dramatists working in the same form at the same time. And when I say convention, I do not necessarily mean any particular convention of subject matter, of treatment, of verse or of dramatic form, of general philosophy of life or any other

convention which has already been used. It may be some quite
new selection or structure or distortion in subject matter or
technique; any form or rhythm imposed upon the world of
action. We will take the point of view of persons accustomed
to this convention and finding the expression of their dramatic
impulses in it. From this point of view such performances as
were those of the Phoenix Society are most illuminating. For
the drama, the existence of which I suppose, will have its special
conventions of the stage and the actor as well as of the play
itself. An actor in an Elizabethan play is either too realistic or
too abstract in his treatment, whatever system of speech, of
expression and of movement he adopts. The play is for ever
betraying him. An Elizabethan play was in some ways as different from a modern play, its performance is almost as much
a lost art, as if it were a drama of Aeschylus or Sophocles. And
in some ways it is more difficult to reproduce. For it is easier
to present the effect of something in a firm convention, than the
effect of something which was aiming, blindly enough, at something else. The difficulty in presenting Elizabethan plays is that
they are liable to be made too modern, or falsely archaic. Why
are the asides ridiculous, which Mr. Archer reprehends in *A
Woman Killed with Kindness?* Because they are not a convention, but a subterfuge; it is not Heywood who assumes that
asides are inaudible, it is Mrs. Frankford who *pretends* not to
hear Wendoll. A convention is not ridiculous: a subterfuge
makes us extremely uncomfortable. The weakness of the Elizabethan drama is not its defect of realism, but its attempt at realism; not its conventions, but its lack of conventions.

In order to make an Elizabethan drama give a satisfactory
effect as a work of art, we should have to find a method of acting different from that of contemporary social drama, and at
the same time to attempt to express all the emotions of actual
life in the way in which they actually would be expressed: the
result would be something like a performance of *Agamemnon*
by the Guitrys. The effect upon actors who attempt to specialise
in Shakespearean or other seventeenth-century revivals is unfortunate. The actor is called upon for a great deal that is not
his business, and is left to his own devices for things in which

he should be trained. His stage personality has to be supplied from and confounded with his real personality. Any one who has observed one of the great dancers of the Russian school will have observed that the man or the woman whom we admire is a being who exists only during the performances, that it is a personality, a vital flame which appears from nowhere, disappears into nothing and is complete and sufficient in its appearance. It is a conventional being, a being which exists only in and for the work of art which is the ballet. A great actor on the ordinary stage is a person who also exists off it and who supplies the rôle which he performs with the person which he is. A ballet is apparently a thing which exists only as acted and would appear to be a creation much more of the dancer than of the choreographer. This is not quite true. It is a development of several centuries into a strict form. In the ballet only that is left to the actor which is properly the actor's part. The general movements are set for him. There are only limited movements that he can make, only a limited degree of emotion that he can express. He is not called upon for his personality. The differences between a great dancer and a merely competent dancer is in the vital flame, that impersonal, and, if you like, inhuman force which transpires between each of the great dancer's movements. So it would be in a strict form of drama; but in realistic drama, which is drama striving steadily to escape the conditions of art, the human being intrudes. Without the human being and without this intrusion, the drama cannot be performed, and this is as true of Shakespeare as it is of Henry Arthur Jones. A play of Shakespeare's and a play of Henry Arthur Jones's are essentially of the same type, the difference being that Shakespeare is very much greater and Mr. Jones very much more skilful. They are both dramatists to be read rather than seen, because it is precisely in that drama which depends upon the interpretation of an actor of genius, that we ought to be on our guard against the actor. The difference is, of course, that without the actor of genius the plays of Mr. Jones are nothing and the plays of Shakespeare are still to be read. But a true acting play is surely a play which does not depend upon the actor for anything but acting, in the sense in which a ballet depends upon the dancer for dancing. Lest any one should fall into a contrary misunderstanding, I will explain that I do not by any means intend the actor to be an automaton, nor would I admit that the human actor can be replaced by a marionette. A great dancer, whose attention is set upon carrying out an appointed task, provides the life of the ballet through his movements; in the same way the drama would depend upon a great trained actor. The advantages of convention for the actor are precisely similar to its advantages for the author. No artist produces great art by a deliberate attempt to express his personality. He expresses his personality indirectly through concentrating upon a task which is a task in the same sense as the making of an efficient engine or the turning of a jug or a table-leg.

The art of the Elizabethans is an impure art. If it be objected that this is a prejudice of the case, I can only reply that one must criticise from some point of view and that it is better to know what one's point of view is. I know that I rebel against most [2] performances of Shakespeare's plays because I want a direct relationship between the work of art and myself, and I want the performance to be such as will not interrupt or alter this relationship any more than it is an alteration or interruption for me to superpose a second inspection of a picture or building upon the first. I object, in other words, to the interpretation, and I would have a work of art such that it needs only to be completed and cannot be altered by each interpretation. Now it is obvious that in realistic drama you become more and more dependent upon the actor. And this is another reason why the drama which Mr. Archer desires, as the photographic and gramophonic record of its time, can never exist. The closer a play is built upon real life, the more the performance by one actor will differ from another, and the more the performances of one generation of actors will differ from those of the next. It is furthermore obvious that what we ask involves a considerable sacrifice of a certain kind of interest. A character in the conventional play can never be as real as is the character in a realistic play while the rôle is being enacted by a great actor who has made

[2] A really good performance of Shakespeare, such as the very best productions of the Old Vic and Sadlers' Wells, may add much to our understanding.

the part his own. I can only say that wherever you have a form you make some sacrifice against some gain.

If we examine the faults which Mr. Archer finds in Elizabethan drama, it is possible to come to the conclusion (already indicated) that these faults are due to its tendencies rather than what are ordinarily called its conventions. I mean that no single convention of Elizabethan drama, however ridiculous it may be made to appear, is essentially bad. Neither the soliloquy, nor the aside, nor the ghost, nor the blood-and-thunder, nor absurdity of place or time is in itself absurd. There are, of course, definite faults of bad writing, careless writing, and bad taste. A line-by-line examination of almost any Elizabethan play, including those of Shakespeare, would be a fruitful exercise. But these are not the faults which weaken the foundations. What is fundamentally objectionable is that in the Elizabethan drama there has been no firm principle of what is to be postulated as a convention and what is not. The fault is not with the ghost but with the presentation of a ghost on a plane on which he is inappropriate, and with the confusion between one kind of ghost and another. The three witches in *Macbeth* are a distinguished example of correct supernaturalism amongst a race of ghosts who are too frequently equivocations. It seems to me strictly an error, although an error which is condoned by the success of each passage in itself, that Shakespeare should have introduced into the same play ghosts belonging to such different categories as the three sisters and the ghost of Banquo.[3] The aim of the Elizabethans was to attain complete realism without surrendering any of the advantages which as artists they observed in unrealistic conventions.

We shall take up the work of four Elizabethan dramatists and attempt to subject them to an analysis from the point of view which I have indicated. We shall take the objections of Mr. Archer to each one of these dramatists and see if the difficulty does not reside in this confusion of convention and realism, and we must make some attempt also to illustrate the faults as distinguished from the conventions. There were, of course,

[3] This will appear to be an objection as pedantic as that of Thomas Rymer to *Othello*. But Rymer makes out a very good case.

tendencies toward form. There was a general philosophy of life, if it may be called such, based on Seneca and other influences which we find in Shakespeare as in the others. It is a philosophy which, as Mr. Santayana observed in an essay which passed almost unheeded, may be summarised in the statement that Duncan is in his grave. Even the philosophical basis, the general attitude toward life of the Elizabethans, is one of anarchism, of dissolution, of decay. It is in fact exactly parallel and indeed one and the same thing with their artistic greediness, their desire for every sort of effect together, their unwillingness to accept any limitation and abide by it. The Elizabethans are in fact a part of the movement of progress or deterioration which has culminated in Sir Arthur Pinero and in the present regimen of Europe.[4]

The case of John Webster, and in particular *The Duchess of Malfy*, will provide an interesting example of a very great literary and dramatic genius directed toward chaos. The case of Middleton is an interesting one, because we have from the same hand plays so different as *The Changeling*, *Women Beware Women*, *The Roaring Girle*, and *A Game at Chesse*.[5] In the one great play of Tourneur's, the discord is less apparent, but not less real. Chapman appears to have been potentially perhaps the greatest artist of all these men: his was the mind which was the most classical, his was the drama which is the most independent in its tendency toward a dramatic form—although it may seem the most formless and the most indifferent to dramatic necessities. If we can establish the same consequence independently by an examination of the Elizabethan philosophy, the Elizabethan dramatic form, and the variations in the rhythms of Elizabethan blank verse as employed by several of the greatest

[4] Mr. Archer calls it progress. He has certain predispositions. "Shakespeare," he says, "was not alive to the great idea which differentiates the present age from all that have gone before—the idea of progress." And he admits speaking of Elizabethan drama in general, that "here and there a certain glimmer of humanitarian feeling is perceptible."

[5] I agree with Mr. Dugdale Sykes, to whose acute observations I am under a great debt, that certain work attributed to Middleton is not Middleton's, but there appears to be no reason for questioning the authorship of the plays I have just mentioned.

dramatists, we may come to conclusions which will enable us to understand why Mr. Archer, who is the opponent of the Elizabethans, should also be unconsciously their last champion, and why he should be a believer in progress, in the growth of humanitarian feeling, and in the superiority and efficiency of the present age.

MARLOWE

SWINBURNE observes of Marlowe that "the father of English tragedy and the creator of English blank verse was therefore also the teacher and the guide of Shakespeare." In this sentence there are two misleading assumptions and two misleading conclusions. Kyd has as good a title to the first honour as Marlowe; Surrey has a better title to the second; and Shakespeare was not taught or guided by one of his predecessors or contemporaries alone. The less questionable judgment is, that Marlowe exercised a strong influence over later drama, though not himself as great a dramatist as Kyd; that he introduced several new tones into blank verse, and commenced the dissociative process which drew it farther and farther away from the rhythms of rhymed verse; and that when Shakespeare borrowed from him, which was pretty often at the beginning, Shakespeare either made something inferior or something different.

The comparative study of English versification at various periods is a large tract of unwritten history. To make a study of blank verse alone would be to elicit some curious conclusions. It would show, I believe, that blank verse within Shakespeare's lifetime was more highly developed, that it became the vehicle of more varied and more intense feeling than it has ever conveyed since; and that after the erection of the Chinese Wall of Milton, blank verse has suffered not only arrest but retrogression. That the blank verse of Tennyson, for example, a consummate master of this form in certain applications, is cruder (*not* "rougher" or less perfect in technique) than that of half a dozen contemporaries of Shakespeare; cruder, because less

100

capable of expressing complicated, subtle, and surprising emotions.

Every writer who has written any blank verse worth saving has produced particular tones which his verse and no other's is capable of rendering; and we should keep this in mind when we talk about "influences" and "indebtedness." Shakespeare is "universal" because he has more of these tones than any one else; but they are all out of the one man; one man cannot be more than one man; there might have been six Shakespeares at once without conflicting frontiers; and to say that Shakespeare expressed nearly all human emotions, implying that he left very little for any one else, is a radical misunderstanding of art and the artist—a misunderstanding which, even when explicitly rejected, may lead to our neglecting the effort of attention necessary to discover the specific properties of the verse of Shakespeare's contemporaries. The development of blank verse may be likened to the analysis of that astonishing industrial product coal-tar. Marlowe's verse is one of the earlier derivatives, but it possesses properties which are not repeated in any of the analytic or synthetic blank verses discovered somewhat later.

The "vices of style" of Marlowe's and Shakespeare's age is a convenient name for a number of vices, no one of which, perhaps, was shared by all of the writers. It is pertinent, at least, to remark that Marlowe's "rhetoric" is not, or not characteristically, Shakespeare's rhetoric; that Marlowe's rhetoric consists in a pretty simple huffe-snuffe bombast, while Shakespeare's is more exactly a vice of style, a tortured perverse ingenuity of images which dissipates instead of concentrating the imagination, and which may be due in part to influences by which Marlowe was untouched. Next, we find that Marlowe's vice is one which he was gradually attenuating, and even, what is more miraculous, turning into a virtue. And we find that this poet of torrential imagination recognized many of his best bits (and those of one or two others), saved them, and reproduced them more than once, almost invariably improving them in the process.

It is worth while noticing a few of these versions, because they indicate, somewhat contrary to usual opinion, that Marlowe was a deliberate and conscious workman. Mr. J. M. Robertson has spotted an interesting theft of Marlowe's from Spenser. Here is Spenser (*Faerie Queene*, I, vii. 32):

> *Like to an almond tree y-mounted high*
> *On top of green Selinis all alone,*
> *With blossoms brave bedeckèd daintily;*
> *Whose tender locks do tremble every one*
> *At every little breath that under heaven is blown.*

And here Marlowe (*Tamburlaine*, Part II, Act iv, sc. iv):

> *Like to an almond tree y-mounted high*
> *Upon the lofty and celestial mount*
> *Of evergreen Selinus, quaintly deck'd*
> *With blooms more white than Erycina's brows,*
> *Whose tender blossoms tremble every one*
> *At every little breath that thorough heaven is blown.*

This is interesting, not only as showing that Marlowe's talent, like that of most poets, was partly synthetic, but also because it seems to give a clue to some particularly "lyric" effects found in *Tamburlaine*, not in Marlowe's other plays, and not, I believe, anywhere else. For example, the praise of Zenocrate in Part II, Act ii, sc. iv:

> *Now walk the angels on the walls of heaven,*
> *As sentinels to warn th' immortal souls*
> *To entertain divine Zenocrate.*

This is not Spenser's movement, but the influence of Spenser must be present. There had been no great blank verse before Marlowe; but there was the powerful presence of this great master of melody immediately precedent; and the combination produced results which could not be repeated. I do not think that it can be claimed that Peele had any influence here.

The passage quoted from Spenser has a further interest. It will be noted that the fourth line:

> *With blooms more white than Erycina's brows,*

is Marlowe's contribution. Compare this with these other lines
of Marlowe:

> *So looks my love, shadowing in her brows*
> > *(Tamburlaine)*
>
> *Like to the shadows of Pyramides*
> > *(Tamburlaine)*

and the final and best version:

> *Shadowing more beauty in their airy brows*
> *Than have the white breasts of the queen of love*
> > *(Doctor Faustus)*

and compare the whole set with Spenser again (*F. Q.*):

> *Upon her eyelids many graces sate*
> *Under the shadow of her even brows,*

a passage which Mr. Robertson says Spenser himself used in
three other places.

This economy is frequent in Marlowe. Within *Tamburlaine*
it occurs in the form of monotony, especially in the facile use
of resonant names (*e.g.* the recurrence of "Caspia" or "Cas-
pian" with the same tone effect), a practice in which Marlowe
was followed by Milton, but which Marlowe himself outgrew.
Again,

> *Zenocrate, lovelier than the love of Jove,*
> *Brighter than is the silver Rhodope,*

is paralleled later by

> *Zenocrate, the loveliest maid alive,*
> *Fairer than rocks of pearl and precious stone.*

One line Marlowe remodels with triumphant success:

> *And set black streamers in the firmament*
> > *(Tamburlaine)*

becomes

> *See, see, where Christ's blood streams in the firmament!*
> > *(Doctor Faustus)*

The verse accomplishments of *Tamburlaine* are notably two: Marlowe gets into blank verse the melody of Spenser, and he gets a new driving power by reinforcing the sentence period against the line period. The rapid long sentence, running line into line, as in the famous soliloquies "Nature compounded of four elements" and "What is beauty, saith my sufferings, then?" marks the certain escape of blank verse from the rhymed couplet, and from the elegiac or rather pastoral note of Surrey, to which Tennyson returned. If you contrast these two soliloquies with the verse of Marlowe's greatest contemporary, Kyd—by no means a despicable versifier—you see the importance of the innovation:

> *The one took sanctuary, and, being sent for out,*
> *Was murdered in Southwark as he passed*
> *To Greenwich, where the Lord Protector lay.*
> *Black Will was burned in Flushing on a stage;*
> *Green was hanged at Osbridge in Kent . . .*

which is not really inferior to:

> *So these four abode*
> *Within one house together; and as years*
> *Went forward, Mary took another mate;*
> *But Dora lived unmarried till her death.*
>
> (TENNYSON, *Dora*)

In *Faustus* Marlowe went farther: he broke up the line, to a gain in intensity, in the last soliloquy; and he developed a new and important conversational tone in the dialogues of Faustus with the devil. *Edward II* has never lacked consideration: it is more desirable, in brief space, to remark upon two plays, one of which has been misunderstood and the other underrated. These are *The Jew of Malta* and *Dido Queen of Carthage*. Of the first of these, it has always been said that the end, even the last two acts, are unworthy of the first three. If one takes *The Jew of Malta* not as a tragedy, or as a "tragedy of blood," but as a farce, the concluding act becomes intelligible; and if we attend with a careful ear to the versification, we find that Marlowe develops a tone to suit this farce, and even perhaps that this

tone is his most powerful and mature tone. I say farce, but with
the enfeebled humour of our times the word is a misnomer; it
is the farce of the old English humour, the terribly serious,
even savage comic humour, the humour which spent its last
breath in the decadent genius of Dickens. It has nothing in common with J. M. Barrie, Captain Bairnsfather, or *Punch*. It is
the humour of that very serious (but very different) play,
Volpone.

> *First, be thou void of these affections,*
> *Compassion, love, vain hope, and heartless fear;*
> *Be moved at nothing, see thou pity none . . .*
> *As for myself, I walk abroad o' nights,*
> *And kill sick people groaning under walls,*
> *Sometimes I go about and poison wells . . .*

and the last words of Barabas complete this prodigious caricature:

> *But now begins th' extremity of heat*
> *To pinch me with intolerable pangs,*
> *Die, life! fly, soul! tongue, curse thy fill, and die!*

It is something which Shakespeare could not do, and which he
did not want to do.

Dido appears to be a hurried play, perhaps done to order with
the *Aeneid* in front of him. But even here there is progress. The
account of the sack of Troy is in this newer style of Marlowe's,
this style which secures its emphasis by always hesitating on the
edge of caricature at the right moment:

> *The Grecian soldiers, tir'd with ten years' war,*
> *Began to cry, "Let us unto our ships,*
> *Troy is invincible, why stay we here?" . . .*
>
> *By this, the camp was come unto the walls,*
> *And through the breach did march into the streets,*
> *Where, meeting with the rest, "Kill, kill!" they*
> *   cried. . . .*
>
> *And after him, his band of Myrmidons,*
> *With balls of wild-fire in their murdering paws . . .*

At last, the soldiers pull'd her by the heels,
And swung her howling in the empty air. . . .

We saw Cassandra sprawling in the streets . . .

This is not Virgil, or Shakespeare; it is pure Marlowe. By comparing the whole speech with Clarence's dream, in *Richard III*, one acquires a little insight into the difference between Marlowe and Shakespeare:

What scourge for perjury
Can this dark monarchy afford false Clarence?

There, on the other hand, is what Marlowe's style could not do; the phrase has a concision which is almost classical, certainly Dantesque. Again, as often with the Elizabethan dramatists, there are lines in Marlowe, besides the many lines that Shakespeare adapted, that might have been written by either:

If thou wilt stay,
Leap in mine arms; mine arms are open wide;
If not, turn from me, and I'll turn from thee;
For though thou hast the heart to say farewell,
I have not power to stay thee.

But the direction in which Marlowe's verse might have moved, had he not "dyed swearing," is quite un-Shakespearean, is toward this intense and serious and indubitably great poetry, which, like some great painting and sculpture, attains its effects by something not unlike caricature.

SHAKESPEARE AND

THE STOICISM OF SENECA

———

THE last few years have witnessed a number of recrudescences of Shakespeare. There is the fatigued Shakespeare, a retired Anglo-Indian, presented by Mr. Lytton Strachey; there is the messianic Shakespeare, bringing a new philosophy and a new system of yoga, presented by Mr. Middleton Murry; and there is the ferocious Shakespeare, a furious Samson, presented by Mr. Wyndham Lewis in his interesting book, *The Lion and the Fox*. On the whole, we may all agree that these manifestations are beneficial. In any case so important as that of Shakespeare, it is good that we should from time to time change our minds. The last conventional Shakespeare is banished from the scene, and a variety of unconventional Shakespeares take his place. About any one so great as Shakespeare, it is probable that we can never be right; and if we can never be right, it is better that we should from time to time change our way of being wrong. Whether Truth ultimately prevails is doubtful and has never been proved; but it is certain that nothing is more effective in driving out error than a new error. Whether Mr. Strachey, or Mr. Murry, or Mr. Lewis, is any nearer to the truth of Shakespeare than Rymer, or Morgann, or Webster, or Jonson, is uncertain; they were all certainly more sympathetic in the year 1927 than Coleridge, or Swinburne, or Dowden. If they do not give us real Shakespeare—if there is one—they at least give us several up-to-date Shakespeares. If the only way to prove that Shakespeare did not feel and think exactly as people felt and thought in 1815, or in 1860, or in

1880, is to show that he felt and thought as we felt and thought in 1927, then we must accept gratefully that alternative.

But these recent interpreters of Shakespeare suggest a number of reflections on literary criticism and its limits, on general aesthetics, and on the limitations of the human understanding.

There are, of course, a number of other current interpretations of Shakespeare: that is, of the *conscious opinions* of Shakespeare: interpretations of category, so to speak: which make him either a Tory journalist or a Liberal journalist, or a Socialist journalist (though Mr. Shaw has done something to warn off his co-religionists from claiming Shakespeare, or from finding anything uplifting in his work); we have also a Protestant Shakespeare, and a sceptical Shakespeare, and some case may be made out for an Anglo-Catholic, or even a Papist Shakespeare. My own frivolous opinion is that Shakespeare may have held in private life very different views from what we extract from his extremely varied published works; that there is no clue in his writings to the way in which he would have voted in the last or would vote in the next election; and that we are completely in the dark as to his attitude about prayer-book revision. I admit that my own experience, as a minor poet, may have jaundiced my outlook; that I am used to having cosmic significances, which I never suspected, extracted from my work (such as it is) by enthusiastic persons at a distance; and to being informed that something which I meant seriously is *vers de société;* and to having my personal biography reconstructed from passages which I got out of books, or which I invented out of nothing because they sounded well; and to having my biography invariably ignored in what I *did* write from personal experience; so that in consequence I am inclined to believe that people are mistaken about Shakespeare just in proportion to the relative superiority of Shakespeare to myself.

One more personal "note": I believe that I have as high an estimate of the greatness of Shakespeare as poet and dramatist as any one living; I certainly believe that there is nothing greater. And I would say that my only qualification for venturing to talk about him is, that I am *not* under the delusion that Shakespeare in the least resembles myself, either as I am or as I should like to imagine myself. It seems to me that one of the chief reasons for questioning Mr. Strachey's Shakespeare, and Mr. Murry's, and Mr. Lewis's, is the remarkable resemblance which they bear to Mr. Strachey, and Mr. Murry, and Mr. Lewis respectively. I have not a very clear idea of what Shakespeare was like. But I do not conceive him as very like either Mr. Strachey, or Mr. Murry, or Mr. Wyndham Lewis, or myself.

We have had Shakespeare explained by a variety of influences. He is explained by Montaigne, and by Machiavelli. I imagine that Mr. Strachey would explain Shakespeare by Montaigne, though this would also be Mr. Strachey's Montaigne (for all of Mr. Strachey's favourite figures have a strong Strachey physiognomy) and not Mr. Robertson's. I think that Mr. Lewis, in the intensely interesting book mentioned, has done a real service in calling attention to the importance of Machiavelli in Elizabethan England, though this Machiavelli be only the Machiavelli of the *Contre-Machiavel*, and not in the least the real Machiavelli, a person whom Elizabethan England was as incapable of understanding as Georgian England, or any England, is. I think, however, that Mr. Lewis has gone quite wrong if he thinks (I am not sure what he thinks) that Shakespeare, and Elizabethan England in general, was "influenced" by the thought of Machiavelli. I think that Shakespeare, and other dramatists, used the popular Machiavellian idea, for stage purposes; but this idea was no more like Machiavelli, who was an Italian and a Roman Christian, than Mr. Shaw's idea of Nietzsche—whatever that is—is like the real Nietzsche.

I propose a Shakespeare under the influence of the stoicism of Seneca. But I do not believe that Shakespeare was under the influence of Seneca. I propose it largely because I believe that after the Montaigne Shakespeare (not that Montaigne had any philosophy whatever) and after the Machiavelli Shakespeare, a stoical or Senecan Shakespeare is almost certain to be produced. I wish merely to disinfect the Senecan Shakespeare before he appears. My ambitions would be realized if I could prevent him, in so doing, from appearing at all.

I want to be quite definite in my notion of the possible in-

fluence of Seneca on Shakespeare. I think it is quite likely that
Shakespeare read some of Seneca's tragedies at school. I think
it quite unlikely that Shakespeare knew anything of that ex-
traordinarily dull and uninteresting body of Seneca's prose,
which was translated by Lodge and printed in 1612. So far as
Shakespeare was influenced by Seneca, it was by his memories
of school conning and through the influence of the Senecan
tragedy of the day, through Kyd and Peele, but chiefly Kyd.
That Shakespeare deliberately took a "view of life" from Seneca there seems to be no evidence whatever.

Nevertheless, there is, in some of the great tragedies of
Shakespeare, a new attitude. It is not the attitude of Seneca, but
is derived from Seneca; it is slightly different from anything
that can be found in French tragedy, in Corneille or in Racine;
it is modern, and it culminates, if there is ever any culmina-
tion, in the attitude of Nietzsche. I cannot say that it is Shakespeare's "philosophy." Yet many people have lived by it;
though it may only have been Shakespeare's instinctive recognition of something of theatrical utility. It is the attitude of self-
dramatization assumed by some of Shakespeare's heroes at moments of tragic intensity. It is not peculiar to Shakespeare; it
is conspicuous in Chapman; Bussy, Clermont and Biron, all die
in this way. Marston—one of the most interesting and least ex-
plored of all the Elizabethans—uses it; and Marston and Chapman were particularly Senecan. But Shakespeare, of course,
does it very much better than any of the others, and makes it
somehow more integral with the human nature of his characters. It is less verbal, more real. I have always felt that I have
never read a more terrible exposure of human weakness—of
universal human weakness—than the last great speech of
Othello. I am ignorant whether any one else has ever adopted
this view, and it may appear subjective and fantastic in the extreme. It is usually taken on its face value, as expressing the
greatness in defeat of a noble but erring nature.

> *Soft you; a word or two before you go.*
> *I have done the state some service, and they know't,—*
> *No more of that.—I pray you, in your letters,*

When you shall these unlucky deeds relate,
Speak of me as I am; nothing extenuate,
Nor set down aught in malice: then must you speak
Of one that loved not wisely but too well;
Of one not easily jealous, but, being wrought,
Perplex'd in the extreme; of one whose hand,
Like the base Indian, threw a pearl away
Richer than all his tribe; of one whose subdued eyes,
Albeit unused to the melting mood,
Drop tears as fast as the Arabian trees
Their medicinal gum. Set you down this;
And say, besides,—that in Aleppo once,
Where a malignant and a turban'd Turk
Beat a Venetian and traduced the state,
I took by the throat the circumcised dog,
And smote him—thus.

What Othello seems to me to be doing in making this speech is *cheering himself up.* He is endeavouring to escape reality, he has ceased to think about Desdemona, and is thinking about himself. Humility is the most difficult of all virtues to achieve; nothing dies harder than the desire to think well of oneself. Othello succeeds in turning himself into a pathetic figure, by adopting an *aesthetic* rather than a moral attitude, dramatising himself against his environment. He takes in the spectator, but the human motive is primarily to take in himself. I do not believe that any writer has ever exposed this *bovarysme,* the human will to see things as they are not, more clearly than Shakespeare.

If you compare the deaths of several of Shakespeare's heroes —I do not say *all,* for there are very few generalizations that can be applied to the whole of Shakespeare's work—but notably Othello, Coriolanus and Antony—with the deaths of heroes of dramatists such as Marston and Chapman, consciously under Senecan influence, you will find a strong similarity—except only that Shakespeare does it both more poetically and more lifelike.

You may say that Shakespeare is merely illustrating, consciously or unconsciously, human nature, not Seneca. But I am not so much concerned with the influence of Seneca on Shake-speare as with Shakespeare's illustration of Senecan and stoical principles. Much of Chapman's Senecanism has lately been shown by Professor Schoell to be directly borrowed from Eras-mus and other sources. I am concerned with the fact that Seneca is the *literary* representative of Roman stoicism, and that Ro-man stoicism is an important ingredient in Elizabethan drama. It was natural that in a time like that of Elizabeth stoicism should appear. The original stoicism, and especially the Roman stoicism, was of course a philosophy suited to slaves: hence its absorption into early Christianity.

> *A man to join himself with the Universe*
> *In his main sway, and make in all things fit—*

A man does not join himself with the Universe so long as he has anything else to join himself with; men who could take part in the life of a thriving Greek city-state had something better to join themselves to; and Christians have had something better. Stoicism is the refuge for the individual in an indifferent or hos-tile world too big for him; it is the permanent substratum of a number of versions of cheering oneself up. Nietzsche is the most conspicuous modern instance of cheering oneself up. The stoical attitude is the reverse of Christian humility.

In Elizabethan England we have conditions apparently utterly different from those of imperial Rome. But it was a period of dissolution and chaos; and in such a period any emo-tional attitude which seems to give a man something firm, even if it be only the attitude of "I am myself alone," is eagerly taken up. I hardly need—and it is beyond my present scope—to point out how readily, in a period like the Elizabethan, the Senecan attitude of Pride, the Montaigne attitude of Scepticism, and the Machiavelli attitude [1] of Cynicism, arrived at a kind of fusion in the Elizabethan individualism.

This individualism, this vice of Pride, was, of course, ex-ploited largely because of its dramatic possibilities. But other drama had before existed without depending on this human fail-

---

[1] I do not mean the attitude of Machiavelli, which is not cynical. I mean the attitude of Englishmen who had heard of Machiavelli.

ing. You do not find it in *Polyeucte*, or in *Phèdre* either. But
even Hamlet, who has made a pretty considerable mess of
things, and occasioned the death of at least three innocent people, and two more insignificant ones, dies fairly well pleased
with himself—

> *Horatio, I am dead;*
> *Thou liv'st; report me and my cause aright*
> *To the unsatisfied. . . .*
> *O good Horatio, what a wounded name,*
> *Things standing thus unknown, shall live behind me!*

Antony says, "I am Antony still," and the Duchess, "I am
Duchess of Malfy still"; would either of them have said that
unless Medea had said *Medea superest?*

I do not wish to appear to maintain that the Elizabethan hero
and the Senecan hero are identical. The influence of Seneca is
much more apparent in the Elizabethan drama than it is in the
plays of Seneca. The influence of any man is a different thing
from himself. The Elizabethan hero is much more stoical and
Senecan, in this way, than the Senecan hero. For Seneca was
following the Greek tradition, which was not stoical; he developed familiar themes and imitated great models; so that the
vast difference between his emotional attitude and that of the
Greeks is rather latent in his work, and more apparent in the
work of the Renaissance. And the Elizabethan hero, the hero of
Shakespeare, was not invariable even in Elizabethan England.
A notable exception is Faustus. Marlowe—not excepting Shakespeare or Chapman, the most *thoughtful* and philosophical
mind, though immature, among the Elizabethan dramatists—
could conceive the proud hero, as Tamburlaine, but also the
hero who has reached that point of horror at which even pride
is abandoned. In a recent book on Marlowe, Miss Ellis-Fermor
has put very well this peculiarity of Faustus, from another point
of view than mine, but in words from which I take support:

"Marlowe follows Faustus further across the borderline between consciousness and dissolution than do any of his contemporaries. With Shakespeare, with Webster, death is a
sudden severing of life; their men die, conscious to the last of

some part at least of their surroundings, influenced, even upheld, by that consciousness and preserving the personality and characteristics they have possessed through life. . . . In Marlowe's Faustus alone all this is set aside. He penetrates deeply into the experience of a mind isolated from the past, absorbed in the realization of its own destruction."

But Marlowe, the most thoughtful, the most blasphemous (and therefore, probably, the most Christian) of his contemporaries, is always an exception. Shakespeare is exceptional primarily by his immense superiority.

Of all of Shakespeare's plays, *King Lear* is often taken as the most Senecan in spirit. Cunliffe finds it to be imbued with a Senecan fatalism. Here, again, we must distinguish between a man and his influence. The differences between the fatalism of Greek tragedy, and the fatalism of Seneca's tragedies, and the fatalism of the Elizabethans, proceed by delicate shades; there is a continuity, and there is also a violent contrast, when we look at them from far off. In Seneca, the Greek ethics is visible underneath the Roman stoicism. In the Elizabethans, the Roman stoicism is visible beneath the Renaissance anarchism. In *King Lear* there are several significant phrases, such as those which caught the attention of Professor Cunliffe, and there is a tone of Senecan fatalism: *fatis agimur*. But there is much less and much more. And this is the point at which I must part company with Mr. Wyndham Lewis. Mr. Lewis proposes a Shakespeare who is a *positive* nihilist, an intellectual force *willing* destruction. I cannot see in Shakespeare either a deliberate scepticism, as of Montaigne, or a deliberate cynicism, as of Machiavelli, or a deliberate resignation, as of Seneca. I can see that he *used* all of these things, for dramatic ends: you get perhaps more Montaigne in *Hamlet*, and more Machiavelli in *Othello*, and more Seneca in *Lear*. But I cannot agree with the following paragraph:

"With the exception of Chapman, Shakespeare is the only thinker we meet with among the Elizabethan dramatists. By this is meant, of course, that his work contained, apart from poetry, phantasy, rhetoric or observation of manners, a body of matter representing explicit processes of the intellect which

would have furnished a moral philosopher like Montaigne with
the natural material for his essays. But the quality of this thinking—as it can be surprised springing naturally in the midst of
the consummate movements of his art—is, as must be the case
with such a man, of startling force sometimes. And if it is not
systematic, at least a recognisable physiognomy is there."

It is the general notion of "thinking" that I would challenge.
One has the difficulty of having to use the same words for different things. We say, in a vague way, that Shakespeare, or
Dante, or Lucretius, is a poet who thinks, and that Swinburne
is a poet who does not think, even that Tennyson is a poet who
does not think. But what we really mean is not a difference in
quality of thought, but a difference in quality of emotion. The
poet who "thinks" is merely the poet who can express the emotional equivalent of thought. But he is not necessarily interested
in the thought itself. We talk as if thought was precise and
emotion was vague. In reality there is precise emotion and
there is vague emotion. To express precise emotion requires as
great intellectual power as to express precise thought. But by
"thinking" I mean something very different from anything that
I find in Shakespeare. Mr. Lewis, and other champions of Shakespeare as a great philosopher, have a great deal to say about
Shakespeare's power of thought, but they fail to show that he
thought to any purpose; that he had any coherent view of life,
or that he recommended any procedure to follow. "We possess
a great deal of evidence," says Mr. Lewis, "as to what Shakespeare thought of military glory and martial events." Do we?
Or rather, did Shakespeare think anything at all? He was occupied with turning human actions into poetry.

I would suggest that none of the plays of Shakespeare has
a "meaning," although it would be equally false to say that a
play of Shakespeare is meaningless. All great poetry gives the
illusion of a view of life. When we enter into the world of
Homer, or Sophocles, or Virgil, or Dante, or Shakespeare, we
incline to believe that we are apprehending something that can
be expressed intellectually; for every precise emotion tends
towards intellectual formulation.

We are apt to be deluded by the example of Dante. Here, we think, is a poem which represents an exact intellectual system; Dante has a "philosophy," therefore every poet as great as Dante has a philosophy too. Dante had behind him the system of St. Thomas, to which his poem corresponds point to point. Therefore Shakespeare and behind him Seneca, or Montaigne, or Machiavelli; and if his work does not correspond point to point with any or a composition of these, then it must be that he did a little quiet thinking on his own, and was better than any of these people at their own job. I can see no reason for believing that either Dante or Shakespeare did any thinking on his own. The people who think that Shakespeare thought, are always people who are not engaged in writing poetry, but who are engaged in thinking, and we all like to think that great men were like ourselves. The difference between Shakespeare and Dante is that Dante had one coherent system of thought behind him; but that was just his luck, and from the point of view of poetry is an irrelevant accident. It happened that at Dante's time thought was orderly and strong and beautiful, and that it was concentrated in one man of the greatest genius; Dante's poetry receives a boost which in a sense it does not merit, from the fact that the thought behind it is the thought of a man as great and lovely as Dante himself: St. Thomas. The thought behind Shakespeare is of men far inferior to Shakespeare himself: hence the alternative errors, first, that as Shakespeare was as great a poet as Dante, he must have supplied, out of his own thinking, the difference in quality between a St. Thomas and a Montaigne or a Machiavelli or a Seneca, or second, that Shakespeare is inferior to Dante. In truth, neither Shakespeare nor Dante did any real thinking—that was not their job; and the relative value of the thought current at their time, the material enforced upon each to use as the vehicle of his feeling, is of no importance. It does not make Dante a greater poet, or mean that we can learn more from Dante than from Shakespeare. We can certainly learn more from Aquinas than from Seneca, but that is quite a different matter. When Dante says

la sua voluntade e nostra pace

it is great poetry, and there is a great philosophy behind it. When Shakespeare says

> As flies to wanton boys, are we to the gods;
> They kill us for their sport.

it is equally great poetry, though the philosophy behind it is not great. But the essential is, that each expresses in perfect language, some permanent human impulse. Emotionally, the latter is just as strong, just as true, and just as informative—just as useful and beneficial in the sense in which poetry is useful and beneficial, as the former.

What every poet starts from is his own emotions. And when we get down to these, there is not much to choose between Shakespeare and Dante. Dante's railings, his personal spleen—sometimes thinly disguised under Old Testamental prophetic denunciations—his nostalgia, his bitter regrets for past happiness —or for what seems happiness when it is past—and his brave attempts to fabricate something permanent and holy out of his personal animal feelings—as in the *Vita Nuova*—can all be matched out of Shakespeare. Shakespeare, too, was occupied with the struggle—which alone constitutes life for a poet—to transmute his personal and private agonies into something rich and strange, something universal and impersonal. The rage of Dante against Florence, or Pistoia, or what not, the deep surge of Shakespeare's general cynicism and disillusionment, are merely gigantic attempts to metamorphose private failures and disappointments. The great poet, in writing himself, writes his time.[2] Thus Dante, hardly knowing it, became the voice of the thirteenth century; Shakespeare, hardly knowing it, became the representative of the end of the sixteenth century, of a turning point in history. But you can hardly say that Dante believed, or did not believe, the Thomist philosophy; you can hardly say that Shakespeare believed, or did not believe, the mixed and muddled scepticism of the Renaissance. If Shakespeare had written according to a better philosophy, he would have written worse poetry; it was his business to express the greatest emotional intensity of his time, based on whatever his time hap-

---

[2] Remy de Gourmont said much the same thing, in speaking of Flaubert.

pened to think. Poetry is not a substitute for philosophy or theology or religion, as Mr. Lewis and Mr. Murry sometimes seem to think; it has its own function. But as this function is not intellectual but emotional, it cannot be defined adequately in intellectual terms. We can say that it provides "consolation": strange consolation, which is provided equally by writers so different as Dante and Shakespeare.

What I have said could be expressed more exactly, but at much greater length, in philosophical language: it would enter into the department of philosophy which might be called the Theory of Belief (which is not psychology but philosophy, or phenomenology proper)—the department in which Meinong and Husserl have made some pioneer investigation; the different meanings which belief has in different minds according to the activity for which they are oriented. I doubt whether belief proper enters into the activity of a great poet, *qua* poet. That is, Dante, *qua* poet, did not believe or disbelieve the Thomist cosmology or theory of the soul: he merely made use of it, or a fusion took place between his initial emotional impulses and a theory, for the purpose of making poetry. The poet makes poetry, the metaphysician makes metaphysics, the bee makes honey, the spider secretes a filament; you can hardly say that any of these agents believes: he merely does.

The problem of belief is very complicated and probably quite insoluble. We must make allowance for differences in the emotional quality of believing not only between persons of different occupation, such as the philosopher and the poet, but between different periods of time. The end of the sixteenth century is an epoch when it is particularly difficult to associate poetry with systems of thought or reasoned views of life. In making some quite commonplace investigations of the "thought" of Donne, I found it quite impossible to come to the conclusion that Donne believed anything. It seemed as if, at that time, the world was filled with broken fragments of systems, and that a man like Donne merely picked up, like a magpie, various shining fragments of ideas as they struck his eye, and stuck them about here and there in his verse. Miss Ramsay, in her learned and exhaustive study of Donne's sources, came to the conclusion that he was a "mediaeval thinker"; I could not find either any "mediaevalism" or any thinking, but only a vast jumble of incoherent erudition on which he drew for purely poetic effects. The recent work of Professor Schoell on the sources of Chapman seems to show Chapman engaged in the same task; and suggests that the "profundity" and "obscurity" of Chapman's dark thinking are largely due to his lifting long passages from the works of writers like Ficino and incorporating them in his poems completely out of their context.

I do not for a moment suggest that the method of Shakespeare was anything like this. Shakespeare was a much finer instrument for transformations than any of his contemporaries, finer perhaps even than Dante. He also needed less contact in order to be able to absorb all that he required. The element of Seneca is the most completely absorbed and transmogrified, because it was already the most diffused throughout Shakespeare's world. The element of Machiavelli is probably the most indirect, the element of Montaigne the most immediate. It has been said that Shakespeare lacks unity; it might, I think, be said equally well that it is Shakespeare chiefly that *is* the unity, that unifies so far as they could be unified all the tendencies of a time that certainly lacked unity. Unity, in Shakespeare, but not universality; no one can be universal: Shakespeare would not have found much in common with his contemporary St. Theresa. What influence the work of Seneca and Machiavelli and Montaigne seems to me to exert in common on that time, and most conspicuously through Shakespeare, is an influence toward a kind of self-consciousness that is new; the self-consciousness and self-dramatization of the Shakespearean hero, of whom Hamlet is only one. It seems to mark a stage, even if not a very agreeable one, in human history, or progress, or deterioration, or change. Roman stoicism was in its own time a development in self-consciousness; taken up into Christianity, it broke loose again in the dissolution of the Renaissance. Nietzsche, as I suggested, is a late variant: his attitude is a kind of stoicism upside-down: for there is not much difference between identifying oneself with the Universe and identifying the Universe with oneself. The influence of Seneca on Elizabethan drama has been exhaustively studied in its formal aspect, and in the borrowing and adaptation of phrases and situations; the penetration of Senecan sensibility would be much more difficult to trace.

HAMLET

_____

 Few critics have even admitted that _Hamlet_ the play is the primary problem, and Hamlet the character only secondary. And Hamlet the character has had an especial temptation for that most dangerous type of critic: the critic with a mind which is naturally of the creative order, but which through some weakness in creative power exercises itself in criticism instead. These minds often find in Hamlet a vicarious existence for their own artistic realization. Such a mind had Goethe, who made of Hamlet a Werther; and such had Coleridge, who made of Hamlet a Coleridge; and probably neither of these men in writing about Hamlet remembered that his first business was to study a work of art. The kind of criticism that Goethe and Coleridge produced, in writing of Hamlet, is the most misleading kind possible. For they both possessed unquestionable critical insight, and both make their critical aberrations the more plausible by the substitution—of their own Hamlet for Shakespeare's —which their creative gift effects. We should be thankful that Walter Pater did not fix his attention on this play.

 Two writers of our own time, Mr. J. M. Robertson and Professor Stoll of the University of Minnesota, have issued small books which can be praised for moving in the other direction. Mr. Stoll performs a service in recalling to our attention the labours of the critics of the seventeenth and eighteenth centuries,[1] observing that

"they knew less about psychology than more recent Hamlet critics, but they were nearer in spirit to Shakespeare's art; and

[1] I have never, by the way, seen a cogent refutation of Thomas Rymer's objections to _Othello_.

as they insisted on the importance of the effect of the whole rather than on the importance of the leading character, they were nearer, in their old-fashioned way, to the secret of dramatic art in general."

Qua work of art, the work of art cannot be interpreted; there is nothing to interpret; we can only criticise it according to standards, in comparison to other works of art; and for "interpretation" the chief task is the presentation of relevant historical facts which the reader is not assumed to know. Mr. Robertson points out, very pertinently, how critics have failed in their "interpretation" of *Hamlet* by ignoring what ought to be very obvious; that *Hamlet* is a stratification, that it represents the efforts of a series of men, each making what he could out of the work of his predecessors. The *Hamlet* of Shakespeare will appear to us very differently if, instead of treating the whole action of the play as due to Shakespeare's design, we perceive his *Hamlet* to be superposed upon much cruder material which persists even in the final form.

We know that there was an older play by Thomas Kyd, that extraordinary dramatic (if not poetic) genius who was in all probability the author of two plays so dissimilar as *The Spanish Tragedy* and *Arden of Feversham;* and what this play was like we can guess from three clues: from *The Spanish Tragedy* itself, from the tale of Belleforest upon which Kyd's *Hamlet* must have been based, and from a version acted in Germany in Shakespeare's lifetime which bears strong evidence of having been adapted from the earlier, not from the later, play. From these three sources it is clear that in the earlier play the motive was a revenge-motive simply; that the action or delay is caused, as in *The Spanish Tragedy*, solely by the difficulty of assassinating a monarch surrounded by guards; and that the "madness" of Hamlet was feigned in order to escape suspicion, and successfully. In the final play of Shakespeare, on the other hand, there is a motive which is more important than that of revenge, and which explicitly "blunts" the latter; the delay in revenge is unexplained on grounds of necessity or expediency; and the effect of the "madness" is not to lull but to arouse the king's suspicion. The alteration is not complete enough, however, to be convincing. Furthermore, there are verbal parallels so close to *The Spanish Tragedy* as to leave no doubt that in places Shakespeare was merely *revising* the text of Kyd. And finally there are unexplained scenes—the Polonius-Laertes and the Polonius-Reynaldo scenes—for which there is little excuse; these scenes are not in the verse style of Kyd, and not beyond doubt in the style of Shakespeare. These Mr. Robertson believes to be scenes in the original play of Kyd reworked by a third hand, perhaps Chapman, before Shakespeare touched the play. And he concludes, with very strong show of reason, that the original play of Kyd was, like certain other revenge plays, in two parts of five acts each. The upshot of Mr. Robertson's examination is, we believe, irrefragable: that Shakespeare's *Hamlet*, so far as it is Shakespeare's, is a play dealing with the effect of a mother's guilt upon her son, and that Shakespeare was unable to impose this motive successfully upon the "intractable" material of the old play.

Of the intractability there can be no doubt. So far from being Shakespeare's masterpiece, the play is most certainly an artistic failure. In several ways the play is puzzling, and disquieting as is none of the others. Of all the plays it is the longest and is possibly the one on which Shakespeare spent most pains; and yet he has left in it superfluous and inconsistent scenes which even hasty revision should have noticed. The versification is variable. Lines like

> *Look, the morn, in russet mantle clad,*
> *Walks o'er the dew of yon high eastern hill,*

are of the Shakespeare of *Romeo and Juliet*. The lines in Act v, sc. ii,

> *Sir, in my heart there was a kind of fighting*
> *That would not let me sleep . . .*
> *Up from my cabin,*
> *My sea-gown scarf'd about me, in the dark*
> *Grop'd I to find out them: had my desire;*
> *Finger'd their packet;*

are of his quite mature. Both workmanship and thought are in an unstable position. We are surely justified in attributing the play, with that other profoundly interesting play of "intractable" material and astonishing versification, *Measure for Measure,* to a period of crisis, after which follow the tragic successes which culminate in *Coriolanus. Coriolanus* may be not as "interesting" as *Hamlet,* but it is, with *Antony and Cleopatra,* Shakespeare's most assured artistic success. And probably more people have thought *Hamlet* a work of art because they found it interesting, than have found it interesting because it is a work of art. It is the "Mona Lisa" of literatui e.

The grounds of *Hamlet's* failure are not immediately obvious. Mr. Robertson is undoubtedly correct in concluding that the essential emotion of the play is the feeling of a son towards a guilty mother:

"[Hamlet's] tone is that of one who has suffered tortures on the score of his mother's degradation. . . . The guilt of a mother is an almost intolerable motive for drama, but it had to be maintained and emphasized to supply a psychological solution, or rather a hint of one."

This, however, is by no means the whole story. It is not merely the "guilt of a mother" that cannot be handled as Shakespeare handled the suspicion of Othello, the infatuation of Antony, or the pride of Coriolanus. The subject might conceivably have expanded into a tragedy like these, intelligible, self-complete, in the sunlight. *Hamlet,* like the sonnets, is full of some stuff that the writer could not drag to light, contemplate, or manipulate into art. And when we search for this feeling, we find it, as in the sonnets, very difficult to localize. You cannot point to it in the speeches; indeed, if you examine the two famous soliloquies you see the versification of Shakespeare, but a content which might be claimed by another, perhaps by the author of the *Revenge of Bussy d'Ambois,* Act v, sc. i. We find Shakespeare's Hamlet not in the action, not in any quotations that we might select, so much as in an unmistakable tone which is unmistakably not in the earlier play.

The only way of expressing emotion in the form of art is by finding an "objective correlative"; in other words, a set of objects, a situation, a chain of events which shall be the formula of that *particular* emotion; such that when the external facts, which must terminate in sensory experience, are given, the emotion is immediately evoked. If you examine any of Shakespeare's more successful tragedies, you will find this exact equivalence; you will find that the state of mind of Lady Macbeth walking in her sleep has been communicated to you by a skilful accumulation of imagined sensory impressions; the words of Macbeth on hearing of his wife's death strike us as if, given the sequence of events, these words were automatically released by the last event in the series. The artistic "inevitability" lies in this complete adequacy of the external to the emotion; and this is precisely what is deficient in *Hamlet*. Hamlet (the man) is dominated by an emotion which is inexpressible, because it is in *excess* of the facts as they appear. And the supposed identity of Hamlet with his author is genuine to this point: that Hamlet's bafflement at the absence of objective equivalent to his feelings is a prolongation of the bafflement of his creator in the face of his artistic problem. Hamlet is up against the difficulty that his disgust is occasioned by his mother, but that his mother is not an adequate equivalent for it; his disgust envelops and exceeds her. It is thus a feeling which he cannot understand; he cannot objectify it, and it therefore remains to poison life and obstruct action. None of the possible actions can satisfy it; and nothing that Shakespeare can do with the plot can express Hamlet for him. And it must be noticed that the very nature of the *données* of the problem precludes objective equivalence. To have heightened the criminality of Gertrude would have been to provide the formula for a totally different emotion in Hamlet; it is just *because* her character is so negative and insignificant that she arouses in Hamlet the feeling which she is incapable of representing.

The "madness" of Hamlet lay to Shakespeare's hand; in the earlier play a simple ruse, and to the end, we may presume, understood as a ruse by the audience. For Shakespeare it is less than madness and more than feigned. The levity of Hamlet, his repetition of phrase, his puns, are not part of a deliberate plan of dissimulation, but a form of emotional relief. In the character Hamlet it is the buffoonery of an emotion which can find no outlet in action; in the dramatist it is the buffoonery of an emotion which he cannot express in art. The intense feeling, ecstatic or terrible, without an object or exceeding its object, is something which every person of sensibility has known; it is doubtless a subject of study for pathologists. It often occurs in adolescence: the ordinary person puts these feelings to sleep, or trims down his feelings to fit the business world; the artist keeps them alive by his ability to intensify the world to his emotions. The Hamlet of Laforgue is an adolescent; the Hamlet of Shakespeare is not, he has not that explanation and excuse. We must simply admit that here Shakespeare tackled a problem which proved too much for him. Why he attempted it at all is an insoluble puzzle; under compulsion of what experience he attempted to express the inexpressibly horrible, we cannot ever know. We need a great many facts in his biography; and we should like to know whether, and when, and after or at the same time as what personal experience, he read Montaigne, II. xii, *Apologie de Raimond Sebond*. We should have, finally, to know something which is by hypothesis unknowable, for we assume it to be an experience which, in the manner indicated, exceeded the facts. We should have to understand things which Shakespeare did not understand himself.

BEN JONSON

THE reputation of Jonson has been of the most deadly kind that can be compelled upon the memory of a great poet. To be universally accepted; to be damned by the praise that quenches all desire to read the book; to be afflicted by the imputation of the virtues which excite the least pleasure; and to be read only by historians and antiquaries—this is the most perfect conspiracy of approval. For some generations the reputation of Jonson has been carried rather as a liability than as an asset in the balance-sheet of English literature. No critic has succeeded in making him appear pleasurable or even interesting. Swinburne's book on Jonson satisfies no curiosity and stimulates no thought. For the critical study in the "Men of Letters Series" by Mr. Gregory Smith there is a place; it satisfies curiosity, it supplies many just observations, it provides valuable matter on the neglected masques; it only fails to remodel the image of Jonson which is settled in our minds. Probably the fault lies with several generations of our poets. It is not that the value of poetry is only its value to living poets for their own work; but appreciation is akin to creation, and true enjoyment of poetry is related to the stirring of suggestion, the stimulus that a poet feels in his enjoyment of other poetry. Jonson has provided no creative stimulus for a very long time; consequently we must look back as far as Dryden—precisely, a poetic practitioner who learned from Jonson—before we find a living criticism of Jonson's work.

Yet there are possibilities for Jonson even now. We have no difficulty in seeing what brought him to this pass; how, in contrast, not with Shakespeare, but with Marlowe, Webster, Donne, Beaumont, and Fletcher, he has been paid out with reputation instead of enjoyment. He is no less a poet than these men, but his poetry is of the surface. Poetry of the surface cannot be understood without study; for to deal with the surface of life, as Jonson dealt with it, is to deal so deliberately that we too must be deliberate, in order to understand. Shakespeare, and smaller men also, are in the end more difficult, but they offer something at the start to encourage the student or to satisfy those who want nothing more; they are suggestive, evocative, a phrase, a voice; they offer poetry in detail as well as in design. So does Dante offer something, a phrase everywhere (*tu se' ombra ed ombra vedi*) even to readers who have no Italian; and Dante and Shakespeare have poetry of design as well as of detail. But the polished veneer of Jonson reflects only the lazy reader's fatuity; unconscious does not respond to unconscious; no swarms of inarticulate feelings are aroused. The immediate appeal of Jonson is to the mind; his emotional tone is not in the single verse, but in the design of the whole. But not many people are capable of discovering for themselves the beauty which is only found after labour; and Jonson's industrious readers have been those whose interest was historical and curious, and those who have thought that in discovering the historical and curious interest they had discovered the artistic value as well. When we say that Jonson requires study, we do not mean study of his classical scholarship or of seventeenth-century manners. We mean intelligent saturation in his work as a whole; we mean that in order to enjoy him at all, we must get to the centre of his work and his temperament, and that we must see him unbiased by time, as a contemporary. And to see him as a contemporary does not so much require the power of putting ourselves into seventeenth-century London as it requires the power of setting Jonson in our London.

It is generally conceded that Jonson failed as a tragic dramatist; and it is usually agreed that he failed because his genius was for satiric comedy and because of the weight of pedantic learning with which he burdened his two tragic failures. The second point marks an obvious error of detail; the first is too crude a statement to be accepted; to say that he failed because

his genius was unsuited to tragedy is to tell us nothing at all.
Jonson did not write a good tragedy, but we can see no reason
why he should not have written one. If two plays so different
as *The Tempest* and *The Silent Woman* are both comedies,
surely the category of tragedy could be made wide enough to
include something possible for Jonson to have done. But the
classification of tragedy and comedy, while it may be sufficient
to mark the distinction in a dramatic literature of more rigid
form and treatment—it may distinguish Aristophanes from
Euripides—is not adequate to a drama of such variations as the
Elizabethans. Tragedy is a crude classification for plays so different in their tone as *Macbeth*, *The Jew of Malta*, and *The
Witch of Edmonton;* and it does not help us much to say that
The Merchant of Venice and *The Alchemist* are comedies. Jonson had his own scale, his own instrument. The merit which
Catiline possesses is the same merit that is exhibited more tri-
umphantly in *Volpone; Catiline* fails, not because it is too laboured and conscious, but because it is not conscious enough;
because Jonson in this play was not alert to his own idiom, not
clear in his mind as to what his temperament wanted him to do.
In *Catiline* Jonson conforms, or attempts to conform, to conventions; not to the conventions of antiquity, which he had exquisitely under control, but to the conventions of tragico-his-
torical drama of his time. It is not the Latin erudition that sinks
Catiline, but the application of that erudition to a form which
was not the proper vehicle for the mind which had amassed
the erudition.

If you look at *Catiline*—that dreary Pyrrhic victory of
tragedy—you find two passages to be successful: Act ii, sc. i,
the dialogue of the political ladies, and the Prologue of Sylla's
ghost. These two passages are genial. The soliloquy of the
ghost is a characteristic Jonson success in content and in versification—

> *Dost thou not feel me, Rome? not yet! is night*
> *So heavy on thee, and my weight so light?*
> *Can Sylla's ghost arise within thy walls,*
> *Less threatening than an earthquake, the quick falls*

Of thee and thine? Shake not the frighted heads
Of thy steep towers, or shrink to their first beds?
Or as their ruin the large Tyber fills,
Make that swell up, and drown thy seven proud hills? . . .

This is the learned, but also the creative, Jonson. Without concerning himself with the character of Sulla, and in lines of invective, Jonson makes Sylla's ghost, while the words are spoken, a living and terrible force. The words fall with as determined beat as if they were the will of the morose Dictator himself. You may say: merely invective; but mere invective, even if as superior to the clumsy fisticuffs of Marston and Hall as Jonson's verse is superior to theirs, would not create a living figure as Jonson has done in this long tirade. And you may say: rhetoric; but if we are to call it "rhetoric" we must subject that term to a closer dissection than any to which it is accustomed. What Jonson has done here is not merely a fine speech. It is the careful, precise filling in of a strong and simple outline, and at no point does it overflow the outline; it is far more careful and precise in its obedience to this outline than are many of the speeches in *Tamburlaine*. The outline is not Sulla, for Sulla has nothing to do with it, but "Sylla's ghost." The words may not be suitable to an historical Sulla, or to anybody in history, but they are a perfect expression for "Sylla's ghost." You cannot say they are rhetorical "because people do not talk like that," you cannot call them "verbiage"; they do not exhibit prolixity or redundancy or the other vices in the rhetoric books; there is a definite artistic emotion which demands expression at that length. The words themselves are mostly simple words, the syntax is natural, the language austere rather than adorned. Turning then to the induction of *The Poetaster*, we find another success of the same kind—

Light, I salute thee, but with wounded nerves . . .

Men may not talk in that way, but the Spirit of Envy does, and in the words of Jonson envy is a real and living person. It is not human life that informs envy and Sylla's ghost, but it is energy of which human life is only another variety.

Returning to *Catiline*, we find that the best scene in the body of the play is one which cannot be squeezed into a tragic frame, and which appears to belong to satiric comedy. The scene between Fulvia and Galla and Sempronia is a living scene in a wilderness of oratory. And as it recalls other scenes—there is a suggestion of the college of ladies in *The Silent Woman*—it looks like a comedy scene. And it appears to be satire.

They shall all give and pay well, that come here,
If they will have it; and that, jewels, pearl,
Plate, or round sums to buy these. I'm not taken
With a cob-swan or a high-mounting bull,
As foolish Leda and Europa were;
But the bright gold, with Danaë. For such price
I would endure a rough, harsh Jupiter,
Or ten such thundering gamesters, and refrain
To laugh at 'em, till they are gone, with my much suffering.

This scene is no more comedy than it is tragedy, and the "satire" is merely a medium for the essential emotion. Jonson's drama is only incidentally satire, because it is only incidentally a criticism upon the actual world. It is not satire in the way in which the work of Swift or the work of Molière may be called satire: that is, it does not find its source in any precise emotional attitude or precise intellectual criticism of the actual world. It is satire perhaps as the work of Rabelais is satire; certainly not more so. The important thing is that if fiction can be divided into creative fiction and critical fiction, Jonson's is creative. That he was a great critic, our first great critic, does not affect this assertion. Every creator is also a critic; Jonson was a conscious critic, but he was also conscious in his creations. Certainly, one sense in which the term "critical" may be applied to fiction is a sense in which the term might be used of a method antithetical to Jonson's. It is the method of *Education Sentimentale*. The characters of Jonson, of Shakespeare, perhaps of all the greatest drama, are drawn in positive and simple outlines. They may be filled in, and by Shakespeare they are filled in, by much detail or many shifting aspects; but a clear and sharp and simple form remains through these—though it would be hard to say in what the clarity and sharpness and simplicity of Hamlet consists. But Frédéric Moreau is not made in that way. He is constructed partly by negative definition, built up by a great number of observations. We cannot isolate him from the environment in which we find him; it may be an environment which is or can be universalized; nevertheless it and the figure in it consist of very many observed particular facts, the actual world. Without this world the figure dissolves. The ruling faculty is a critical perception, a commentary upon experienced feeling and sensation. If this is true of Flaubert, it is true in a higher degree of Molière than of Jonson. The broad farcical lines of Molière may seem to be the same drawing as Jonson's. But Molière—say in Alceste or Monsieur Jourdain—is criticizing the actual; the reference to the actual world is more direct. And having a more tenuous reference, the work of Jonson is much less directly satirical.

This leads us to the question of Humours. Largely on the evidence of the two Humour plays, it is sometimes assumed that Jonson is occupied with types; typical exaggerations, or exaggerations of type. The Humour definition, the expressed intention of Jonson, may be satisfactory for these two plays. *Every Man in his Humour* is the first mature work of Jonson, and the student of Jonson must study it; but it is not the play in which Jonson found his genius: it is the last of his plays to read first. If one reads *Volpone*, and after that re-reads *The Jew of Malta*; then returns to Jonson and reads *Bartholomew Fair*, *The Alchemist*, *Epicoene* and *The Devil is an Ass*, and finally *Catiline*, it is possible to arrive at a fair opinion of the poet and the dramatist.

The Humour, even at the beginning, is not a type, as in Marston's satire, but a simplified and somewhat distorted individual with a typical mania. In the later work, the Humour definition quite fails to account for the total effect produced. The characters of Shakespeare are such as might exist in different circumstances than those in which Shakespeare sets them. The latter appear to be those which extract from the characters the most intense and interesting realization; but that realization has not exhausted their possibilities. Volpone's life, on the other hand, is bounded by the scene in which it is played; in fact, the life is the life of the scene and is derivatively the life of Volpone; the life of the character is inseparable from the life of the drama. This is not dependence upon a background, or upon a substratum of fact. The emotional effect is single and simple. Whereas in Shakespeare the effect is due to the way in which the characters *act upon* one another, in Jonson it is given by the way in which the characters *fit in* with each other. The artistic result of *Volpone* is not due to any effect that Volpone, Mosca, Corvino, Corbaccio, Voltore have upon each other, but simply to their combination into a whole. And these figures are not personifications of passions; separately, they have not even that reality, they are constituents. It is a similar indication of Jonson's method that you can hardly pick out a line of Jonson's and say confidently that it is great poetry; but there are many extended passages to which you cannot deny that honour.

> *I will have all my beds blown up, not stuft;*
> *Down is too hard; and then, mine oval room*
> *Fill'd with such pictures as Tiberius took*
> *From Elephantis, and dull Aretine*
> *But coldly imitated. Then, my glasses*
> *Cut in more subtle angles, to disperse*
> *And multiply the figures, as I walk. . . .*

Jonson is the legitimate heir of Marlowe. The man who wrote, in *Volpone:*

> *for thy love,*
> *In varying figures, I would have contended*
> *With the blue Proteus, or the hornèd flood. . . .*

and

> *See, a carbuncle*
> *May put out both the eyes of our Saint Mark;*
> *A diamond would have bought Lollia Paulina,*
> *When she came in like star-light, hid with jewels. . . .*

is related to Marlowe as a poet; and if Marlowe is a poet, Jonson is also. And, if Jonson's comedy is a comedy of humours, then Marlowe's tragedy, a large part of it, is a tragedy of humours. But Jonson has too exclusively been considered as the typical representative of a point of view toward comedy. He has suffered from his great reputation as a critic and theorist, from the effects of his intelligence. We have been taught to think of him as the man, the dictator (confusedly in our minds with his later namesake), as the literary politician impressing his views upon a generation; we are offended by the constant reminder of his scholarship. We forget the comedy in the humours, and the serious artist in the scholar. Jonson has suffered in public opinion, as any one must suffer who is forced to talk about his art.

If you examine the first hundred lines or more of *Volpone* the verse appears to be in the manner of Marlowe, more deliberate, more mature, but without Marlowe's inspiration. It looks like mere "rhetoric," certainly not "deeds and language such as men do use." It appears to us, in fact, forced and flagitious bombast. That it is not "rhetoric," or at least not vicious rhetoric, we do not know until we are able to review the whole play. For the consistent maintenance of this manner conveys in the end an effect not of verbosity, but of bold, even shocking and terrifying directness. We have difficulty in saying exactly what produces this simple and single effect. It is not in any ordinary way due to management of intrigue. Jonson employs immense dramatic constructive skill: it is not so much skill in plot as skill in doing without a plot. He never manipulates as complicated a plot as that of *The Merchant of Venice;* he has in his best plays nothing like the intrigue of Restoration comedy. In *Bartholomew Fair* it is hardly a plot at all; the marvel of the play is the bewildering rapid chaotic action of the fair; it is the fair itself, not anything that happens in the fair. In *Volpone,* or *The Alchemist,* or *The Silent Woman,* the plot is enough to keep the players in motion; it is rather an "action" than a plot. The plot does not hold the play together; what holds the play together is a unity of inspiration that radiates into plot and personages alike.

We have attempted to make more precise the sense in which it was said that Jonson's work is "of the surface"; carefully

avoiding the word "superficial." For there is work contemporary with Jonson's which is superficial in a pejorative sense in
which the word cannot be applied to Jonson—the work of Beaumont and Fletcher. If we look at the work of Jonson's great
contemporaries, Shakespeare, and also Donne and Webster and
Tourneur (and sometimes Middleton), they have a depth, a
third dimension, as Mr. Gregory Smith rightly calls it, which
Jonson's work has not. Their words have often a network of tentacular roots reaching down to the deepest terrors and desires.
Jonson's most certainly have not; but in Beaumont and Fletcher
we may think that at times we find it. Looking closer, we discover that the blossoms of Beaumont and Fletcher's imagination
draw no sustenance from the soil, but are cut and slightly withered flowers stuck into sand.

> *Wilt thou, hereafter, when they talk of me,*
> *As thou shalt hear nothing but infamy,*
> *Remember some of these things? . . .*
> *I pray thee, do; for thou shalt never see me so again.*
>
> *Hair woven in many a curious warp,*
> *Able in endless error to enfold*
> *The wandering soul; . . .*

Detached from its context, this looks like the verse of the
greater poets; just as lines of Jonson, detached from their
context, look like inflated or empty fustian. But the evocative
quality of the verse of Beaumont and Fletcher depends upon
a clever appeal to emotions and associations which they have
not themselves grasped; it is hollow. It is superficial with a
vacuum behind it; the superficies of Jonson is solid. It is what
it is; it does not pretend to be another thing. But it is so very
conscious and deliberate that we must look with eyes alert to
the whole before we apprehend the significance of any part. We
cannot call a man's work superficial when it is the creation of a
world; a man cannot be accused of dealing superficially with
the world which he himself has created; the superficies *is* the
world. Jonson's characters conform to the logic of the emotions
of their world. They are not fancy, because they have a logic

of their own; and this logic illuminates the actual world, because it gives us a new point of view from which to inspect it.

A writer of power and intelligence, Jonson endeavoured to promulgate, as a formula and programme of reform, what he chose to do himself; and he not unnaturally laid down in abstract theory what is in reality a personal point of view. And it is in the end of no value to discuss Jonson's theory and practice unless we recognize and seize this point of view, which escapes the formulae, and which is what makes his plays worth reading. Jonson behaved as the great creative mind that he was: he created his own world, a world from which his followers, as well as the dramatists who were trying to do something wholly different, are excluded. Remembering this, we turn to Mr. Gregory Smith's objection—that Jonson's characters lack the third dimension, have no life out of the theatrical existence in which they appear—and demand an inquest. The objection implies that the characters are purely the work of intellect, or the result of superficial observation of a world which is faded or mildewed. It implies that the characters are lifeless. But if we dig beneath the theory, beneath the observation, beneath the deliberate drawing and the theatrical and dramatic elaboration, there is discovered a kind of power, animating Volpone, Busy, Fitzdottrel, the literary ladies of *Epicoene*, even Bobadil, which comes from below the intellect, and for which no theory of humours will account. And it is the same kind of power which vivifies Trimalchio, and Panurge, and some but not all of the "comic" characters of Dickens. The fictive life of this kind is not to be circumscribed by a reference to "comedy" or to "farce"; it is not exactly the kind of life which informs the characters of Molière or that which informs those of Marivaux —two writers who were, besides, doing something quite different the one from the other. But it is something which distinguishes Barabas from Shylock, Epicure Mammon from Falstaff, Faustus from—if you will—Macbeth; Marlowe and Jonson from Shakespeare and the Shakespeareans, Webster, and Tourneur. It is not merely Humours: for neither Volpone nor Mosca is a humour. No theory of humours could account for Jonson's best plays or the best characters in them. We want to know at what point the comedy of humours passes into a work of art, and why Jonson is not Brome.

The creation of a work of art, we will say the creation of a character in a drama, consists in the process of transfusion of the personality, or, in a deeper sense, the life, of the author into the character. This is a very different matter from the orthodox creation in one's own image. The ways in which the passions and desires of the creator may be satisfied in the work of art are complex and devious. In a painter they may take the form of a predilection for certain colours, tones, or lightings; in a writer the original impulse may be even more strangely transmuted. Now, we may say with Mr. Gregory Smith that Falstaff or a score of Shakespeare's characters have a "third dimension" that Jonson's have not. This will mean, not that Shakespeare's spring from the feelings or imagination and Jonson's from the intellect or invention; they have equally an emotional source; but that Shakespeare's represent a more complex tissue of feelings and desires, as well as a more supple, a more susceptible temperament. Falstaff is not only the roast Manningtree ox with the pudding in his belly; he also "grows old," and, finally, his nose is as sharp as a pen. He was perhaps the *satisfaction* of more, and of more complicated feelings; and perhaps he was, as the great tragic characters must have been, the offspring of deeper, less apprehensible feelings: deeper, but not necessarily stronger or more intense, than those of Jonson. It is obvious that the spring of the difference is not the difference between feeling and thought, or superior insight, superior perception, on the part of Shakespeare, but his susceptibility to a greater range of emotion, and emotion deeper and more obscure. But his characters are no more "alive" than are the characters of Jonson.

The world they live in is a larger one. But small worlds—the worlds which artists create—do not differ only in magnitude; if they are complete worlds, drawn to scale in every part, they differ in kind also. And Jonson's world has this scale. His type of personality found its relief in something falling under the category of burlesque or farce—though when you are dealing with a *unique* world, like his, these terms fail to appease the desire for definition. It is not, at all events, the farce of Molière: the latter is more analytic, more an intellectual redistribution. It is not defined by the word "satire." Jonson poses as a satirist. But satire like Jonson's is great in the end not by hitting off its object, but by creating it; the satire is merely the means which leads to the aesthetic result, the impulse which projects a new world into a new orbit. In *Every Man in his Humour* there is a neat, a very neat, comedy of humours. In discovering and proclaiming in this play the new genre Jonson was simply recognizing, unconsciously, the route which opened out in the proper direction for his instincts. His characters are and remain, like Marlowe's, simplified characters; but the simplification does not consist in the dominance of a particular humour or monomania. That is a very superficial account of it. The simplification consists largely in reduction of detail, in the seizing of aspects relevant to the relief of an emotional impulse which remains the same for that character, in making the character conform to a particular setting. This stripping is essential to the art, to which is also essential a flat distortion in the drawing; it is an art of caricature, of great caricature, like Marlowe's. It is a great caricature, which is beautiful; and a great humour, which is serious. The "world" of Jonson is sufficiently large; it is a world of poetic imagination; it is sombre. He did not get the third dimension, but he was not trying to get it.

If we approach Jonson with less frozen awe of his learning, with a clearer understanding of his "rhetoric" and its applications, if we grasp the fact that the knowledge required of the reader is not archaeology but knowledge of Jonson, we can derive not only instruction in two-dimensional life—but enjoyment. We can even apply him, be aware of him as a part of our literary inheritance craving further expression. Of all the dramatists of his time, Jonson is probably the one whom the present age would find the most sympathetic, if it knew him. There is a brutality, a lack of sentiment, a polished surface, a handling of large bold designs in brilliant colours, which ought to attract about three thousand people in London and elsewhere. At least, if we had a contemporary Shakespeare and a contemporary Jonson, it might be the Jonson who would arouse the enthusiasm of the intelligentsia. Though he is saturated in literature, he never sacrifices the theatrical qualities—theatrical in the most favourable sense—to literature or to the study of character. His work is a titanic show. But Jonson's masques, an important part of his work, are neglected; our flaccid culture lets shows and literature fade, but prefers faded literature to faded shows. There are hundreds of people who have read *Comus* to ten who have read the *Masque of Blackness*. *Comus* contains fine poetry, and poetry exemplifying some merits to which Jonson's masque poetry cannot pretend. Nevertheless, *Comus* is the death of the masque; it is the transition of a form of art—even of a form which existed for but a short generation—into "literature," literature cast in a form which has lost its application. Even though *Comus* was a masque at Ludlow Castle, Jonson had, what Milton came perhaps too late to have, a sense for the living art; his art was applied. The masques can still be read, and with pleasure, by any one who will take the trouble—a trouble which in this part of Jonson is, indeed, a study of antiquities—to imagine them in action, displayed with the music, costumes, dances, and the scenery of Inigo Jones. They are additional evidence that Jonson had a fine sense of form, of the purpose for which a particular form is intended; evidence that he was a literary artist even more than he was a man of letters.

THOMAS MIDDLETON

═══

THOMAS MIDDLETON, the dramatic writer, was not very highly thought of in his own time; the date of his death is not known; we know only that he was buried on July 4, 1627. He was one of the most voluminous, and one of the best, dramatic writers of his time. But it is easy to understand why he is not better known or more popular. It is difficult to imagine his "personality." Several new personalities have recently been fitted to the name of Shakespeare; Jonson is a real figure—our imagination plays about him discoursing at the Mermaid, or laying down the law to Drummond of Hawthornden; Chapman has become a breezy British character as firm as Nelson or Wellington; Webster and Donne are real people for the more intellectual; even Tourneur (Churton Collins having said the last word about him) is a "personality." But Middleton, who collaborated shamelessly, who is hardly separated from Rowley, Middleton who wrote plays so diverse as *Women Beware Women* and *A Game at Chesse* and *The Roaring Girle*, Middleton remains merely a collective name for a number of plays—some of which, like *The Spanish Gipsie*, are patently by other people.[1]

If we write about Middleton's plays we must write about Middleton's plays, and not about Middleton's personality. Many of these plays are still in doubt. Of all the Elizabethan dramatists Middleton seems the most impersonal, the most indifferent to personal fame or perpetuity, the readiest, except Rowley, to accept collaboration. Also he is the most various. His greatest tragedies and his greatest comedies are as if writ-

[1] Mr. Dugdale Sykes has written authoritatively on this subject.

140

ten by two different men. Yet there seems no doubt that Middleton was both a great comic writer and a great tragic writer. There are a sufficient number of plays, both tragedies and comedies, in which his hand is so far unquestioned, to establish his greatness. His greatness is not that of a peculiar personality, but of a great artist or artisan of the Elizabethan epoch. We have among others *The Changeling, Women Beware Women,* and *A Game at Chesse;* and we have *The Roaring Girle* and *A Trick to Catch the Old One.* And that is enough. Between the tragedies and the comedies of Shakespeare, and certainly between the tragedies and the comedies of Jonson, we can establish a relation; we can see, for Shakespeare or Jonson, that each had in the end a personal point of view which can be called neither comic nor tragic. But with Middleton we can establish no such relation. He remains merely a name, a voice, the author of certain plays, which are all of them great plays. He has no point of view, is neither sentimental nor cynical; he is neither resigned, nor disillusioned, nor romantic, he has no message. He is merely the name which associates six or seven great plays.

For there is no doubt about *The Changeling.* Like all of the plays attributed to Middleton, it is long-winded and tiresome; the characters talk too much, and then suddenly stop talking and act; they are real and impelled irresistibly by the fundamental motions of humanity to good or evil. This mixture of tedious discourse and sudden reality is everywhere in the work of Middleton, in his comedy also. In *The Roaring Girle* we read with toil through a mass of cheap conventional intrigue, and suddenly realize that we are, and have been for some time without knowing it, observing a real and unique human being. In reading *The Changeling* we may think, till almost the end of the play, that we have been concerned merely with a fantastic Elizabethan morality, and then discover that we are looking on at a dispassionate exposure of fundamental passions of any time and any place. The usual opinion remains the just judgment: *The Changeling* is Middleton's greatest play. The morality of the convention seems to us absurd. To many intelligent readers this play has only an historical interest, and only serves to illustrate the moral taboos of the Elizabethans. The heroine is a young woman who, in order to dispose of a fiancé to whom she is indifferent, so that she may marry the man she loves, accepts the offer of an adventurer to murder the affianced, at the price (as she finds in due course) of becoming the murderer's mistress. Such a plot is, to a modern mind, absurd; and the consequent tragedy seems a fuss about nothing. But *The Changeling* is not merely contingent for its effect upon our acceptance of Elizabethan good form or convention; it is, in fact, no more dependent upon the convention of its epoch than a play like *A Doll's House*. Underneath the convention there is the stratum of truth permanent in human nature. The tragedy of *The Changeling* is an eternal tragedy, as permanent as *Oedipus* or *Antony and Cleopatra*; it is the tragedy of the not naturally bad but irresponsible and undeveloped nature, caught in the consequences of its own action. In every age and in every civilization there are instances of the same thing: the unmoral nature, suddenly trapped in the inexorable toils of morality—of morality not made by man but by Nature—and forced to take the consequences of an act which it had planned light-heartedly. Beatrice is not a moral creature; she becomes moral only by becoming damned. Our conventions are not the same as those which Middleton assumed for his play. But the possibility of that frightful discovery of morality remains permanent.

The words in which Middleton expresses his tragedy are as great as the tragedy. The process through which Beatrice, having decided that De Flores is the instrument for her purpose, passes from aversion to habituation, remains a permanent commentary on human nature. The directness and precision of De Flores are masterly, as is also the virtuousness of Beatrice on first realizing his motives—

> *Why, 'tis impossible thou canst be so wicked,*
> *Or shelter such a cunning cruelty,*
> *To make his death the murderer of my honour!*
> *Thy language is so bold and vicious,*
> *I cannot see which way I can forgive it*
> *With any modesty*

—a passage which ends with the really great lines of De Flores, lines of which Shakespeare or Sophocles might have been proud:

> *Can you weep Fate from its determined purpose?*
> *So soon may you weep me.*

But what constitutes the essence of the tragedy is something which has not been sufficiently remarked; it is the *habituation* of Beatrice to her sin; it becomes no longer sin but merely custom. Such is the essence of the tragedy of *Macbeth*—the habituation to crime. And in the end Beatrice, having been so long the enforced conspirator of De Flores, becomes (and this is permanently true to human nature) more *his* partner, *his* mate, than the mate and partner of the man for the love of whom she consented to the crime. Her lover disappears not only from the scene but from her own imagination. When she says of De Flores,

> *A wondrous necessary man, my lord,*

her praise is more than half sincere; and at the end she belongs far more to De Flores—towards whom, at the beginning, she felt strong physical repulsion—than to her lover Alsemero. It is De Flores, in the end, to whom she belongs as Francesca to Paolo:

> *Beneath the stars, upon yon meteor*
> *Ever hung my fate, 'mongst things corruptible;*
> *I ne'er could pluck it from him; my loathing*
> *Was prophet to the rest, but ne'er believed.*

And De Flores's cry is perfectly sincere and in character:

> *I loved this woman in spite of her heart;*
> *Her love I earned out of Piracquo's murder . . .*
> *Yes, and her honour's prize*
> *Was my reward; I thank life for nothing*
> *But that pleasure; it was so sweet to me,*
> *That I have drunk up all, left none behind*
> *For any man to pledge me.*

The tragedy of Beatrice is not that she has lost Alsemero, for whose possession she played; it is that she has won De Flores.

Such tragedies are not limited to Elizabethan times: they happen every day and perpetually. The greatest tragedies are occupied with great and permanent moral conflicts: the great tragedies of Aeschylus, of Sophocles, of Corneille, of Racine, of Shakespeare, have the same burden. In poetry, in dramatic technique, *The Changeling* is inferior to the best plays of Webster. But in the moral essence of tragedy it is safe to say that in this play Middleton is surpassed by one Elizabethan alone, and that is Shakespeare. In some respects in which Elizabethan tragedy can be compared to French or to Greek tragedy *The Changeling* stands above every tragic play of its time, except those of Shakespeare.

The genius which blazed in *The Changeling* was fitful but not accidental. The best tragedy after *The Changeling* is *Women Beware Women*. The thesis of the play, as the title indicates, is more arbitrary and less fundamental. The play itself, although less disfigured by ribaldry or clowning, is more tedious. Middleton sinks himself in conventional moralizing of the epoch; so that, if we are impatient, we decide that he gives merely a document of Elizabethan humbug—and then suddenly a personage will blaze out in genuine fire of vituperation. The wickedness of the personages in *Women Beware Women* is conventional wickedness of the stage of the time; yet slowly the exasperation of Bianca, the wife who married beneath her, beneath the ambitions to which she was entitled, emerges from the negative; slowly the real human passions emerge from the mesh of interest in which they begin. And here again Middleton, in writing what appears on the surface a conventional picture-palace Italian melodrama of the time, has caught permanent human feelings. And in this play Middleton shows his interest—more than any of his contemporaries—in innuendo and double meanings; and makes use of that game of chess, which he was to use more openly and directly for satire in that perfect piece of literary political art, *A Game at Chesse*. The irony could not improved upon:

> *Did I not say my duke would fetch you o'er, Widow?*
> *I think you spoke in earnest when you said it, madam.*

And my black king makes all the haste he can too.
Well, madam, we may meet with him in time yet.
I've given thee blind mate twice.

There is hardly anything truer in Elizabethan drama than
Bianca's gradual self-will and self-importance in consequence of
her courtship by the Duke:

Troth, you speak wondrous well for your old house here;
'Twill shortly fall down at your feet to thank you,
Or stoop, when you go to bed, like a good child,
To ask you blessing.

In spite of all the long-winded speeches, in spite of all the conventional Italianate horrors, Bianca remains, like Beatrice in
The Changeling, a real woman; as real, indeed, as any woman
of Elizabethan tragedy. Bianca is a type of the woman who is
purely moved by vanity.

But if Middleton understood women in tragedy better than
any of the Elizabethans—better than the creator of the Duchess
of Malfy, better than Marlowe, better than Tourneur, or Shirley, or Fletcher, better than any of them except Shakespeare
alone—he was also able, in his comedy, to present a finer woman
than any of them. *The Roaring Girle* has no apparent relation
to Middleton's tragedies, yet it is agreed to be primarily the
work of Middleton. It is typical of the comedies of Middleton,
and it is the best. In his tragedies Middleton employs all the
Italianate horrors of his time, and obviously for the purpose
of pleasing the taste of his time; yet underneath we feel always
a quiet and undisturbed vision of things as they are and not
"another thing." So in his comedies. The comedies are long-
winded; the fathers are heavy fathers, and rant as heavy fathers
should; the sons are wild and wanton sons, and perform all the
pranks to be expected of them; the machinery is the usual
Elizabethan machinery; Middleton is solicitous to please his
audience with what they expect; but there is underneath the
same steady impersonal passionless observation of human nature. *The Roaring Girle* is as artificial as any comedy of the
time; its plot creaks loudly; yet the Girl herself is always real.

She may rant, she may behave preposterously, but she remains a type of the sort of woman who has renounced all happiness for herself and who lives only for a principle. Nowhere more than in *The Roaring Girle* can the hand of Middleton be distinguished more clearly from the hand of Dekker. Dekker is all sentiment; and, indeed, in the so admired passages of *A Fair Quarrel,* exploited by Lamb, the mood if not the hand of Dekker seems to the unexpert critic to be more present than Middleton's. *A Fair Quarrel* seems as much, if not more, Dekker's than Middleton's. Similarly with *The Spanish Gipsie,* which can with difficulty be attributed to Middleton. But the feeling about Moll Cut-Purse of *The Roaring Girle* is Middleton's rather than anybody's. In Middleton's tragedy there is a strain of realism underneath, which is one with the poetry; and in his comedy we find the same thing.

In her recent book on *The Social Mode of Restoration Comedy,* Miss Kathleen Lynch calls attention to the gradual transition from Elizabethan-Jacobean to Restoration comedy. She observes, what is certainly true, that Middleton is the greatest "realist" in Jacobean comedy. Miss Lynch's extremely suggestive thesis is that the transition from Elizabethan-Jacobean to later Caroline comedy is primarily economic: that the interest changes from the citizen aping gentry to the citizen become gentry and accepting that code of manners. In the comedy of Middleton certainly there is as yet no code of manners; but the merchant of Cheapside is *aiming* at becoming a member of the country gentry. Miss Lynch remarks: "Middleton's keen concentration on the spectacle of the interplay of different social classes marks an important development in realistic comedy." She calls attention to this aspect of Middleton's comedy, that it marks, better than the romantic comedy of Shakespeare, or the comedy of Jonson, occupied with what Jonson thought to be permanent and not transient aspects of human nature, the transition between the aristocratic world which preceded the Tudors and the plutocratic modern world which the Tudors initiated and encouraged. By the time of the return of Charles II, as Miss Lynch points out, society had been reorganized and formed, and social conventions had been created. In the Tudor times birth still counted (though nearly all the great families were extinct); by the time of Charles II only breeding counted. The comedy of Middleton, and the comedy of Brome, and the comedy of Shirley, is intermediate, as Miss Lynch remarks. Middleton, she observes, marks the transitional stage in which the London tradesman was anxious to cease to be a tradesman and to become a country gentleman. The words of his City Magnate in *Michaelmas Terme* have not yet lost their point:

"A fine journey in the Whitsun holydays, i'faith, to ride with a number of cittizens and their wives, some upon pillions, some upon side-saddles, I and little Thomasine i' the middle, our son and heir, Sim Quomodo, in a peach-colour taffeta jacket, some horse length, or a long yard before us—there will be a fine show on's I can tell you."

But Middleton's comedy is not, like the comedy of Congreve, the comedy of a set social behaviour; it is still, like the later comedy of Dickens, the comedy of individuals, in spite of the continual motions of city merchants towards county gentility. In the comedy of the Restoration a figure such as that of Moll Cut-Purse would have been impossible. As a social document the comedy of Middleton illustrates the transition from government by a landed aristocracy to government by a city aristocracy gradually engrossing the land. As such it is of the greatest interest. But as literature, as a dispassionate picture of human nature, Middleton's comedy deserves to be remembered chiefly by its real—perpetually real—and human figure of Moll the Roaring Girl. That Middleton's comedy was "photographic," that it introduces us to the low life of the time far better than anything in the comedy of Shakespeare or the comedy of Jonson, better than anything except the pamphlets of Dekker and Greene and Nashe, there is little doubt. But it produced one great play—*The Roaring Girle*—a great play in spite of the tedious long speeches of some of the principal characters, in spite of the clumsy machinery of the plot: for the reason that Middleton was a great observer of human nature, without fear, without sentiment, without prejudice.

And Middleton in the end—after criticism has subtracted all

that Rowley, all that Dekker, all that others contributed—is a great example of great English drama. He has no message; he is merely a great recorder. Incidentally, in flashes and when the dramatic need comes, he is a great poet, a great master of versification:

> *I that am of your blood was taken from you*
> *For your better health; look no more upon 't,*
> *But cast it to the ground regardlessly,*
> *Let the common sewer take it from distinction:*
> *Beneath the stars, upon yon meteor*
> *Ever hung my fate, 'mongst things corruptible;*
> *I ne'er could pluck it from him; my loathing*
> *Was prophet to the rest, but ne'er believed.*

The man who wrote these lines remains inscrutable, solitary, unadmired; welcoming collaboration, indifferent to fame; dying no one knows when and no one knows how; attracting, in three hundred years, no personal admiration. Yet he wrote one tragedy which more than any play except those of Shakespeare has a profound and permanent moral value and horror; and one comedy which more than any Elizabethan comedy realizes a free and noble womanhood.

THOMAS HEYWOOD

—

THERE are a few of the Elizabethan dramatists, notably Marlowe and Ben Jonson, who always return to our minds with the reality of personal acquaintances. We know them unmistakably through their own writings—Jonson partly through his conversations with Drummond—and by a few anecdotes of the kind which, even when apocryphal, remain as evidence of the personal impression that such men must have made upon their contemporaries. There are others whom we can remember only by the association of their names with a play, or a group of plays. Of all these men Thomas Heywood is one of the dimmest figures; and it is interesting to remark how very dim he still remains even after Dr. Clark's exhaustive industry.[1] Dr. Clark appears to have discovered and assembled all the information that we can ever expect to have; and it is certainly not his fault that Heywood makes still but a faint impression; in fact, Dr. Clark's book can help us considerably to understand why this is so. The book is solidly documentary; it is not, like some biographical essays with scanty material, stuffed out with appreciation and conjecture. It is, in fact, an admirable account of the life of a typical literary jack-of-all-trades of the epoch; the summary of Heywood's activities as a pamphleteer, with his works of what may be termed popular theology in the Puritan cause, is full of interest for any one who cares about this lively and, in some respects, very remote age. And the book confirms the impression that Heywood—whom Dr. Clark shows convincingly to have been a Heywood of Mottram, in

[1] *Thomas Heywood: Playwright and Miscellanist*, by A. M. Clark. Oxford: Blackwell. 1931.

Cheshire, and not of the family of Heywood of Lincolnshire, the county of his birth—was a facile and sometimes felicitous purveyor of goods to the popular taste.

Heywood's reputation, which we owe primarily to Lamb and Hazlitt, is founded on *A Woman Killed with Kindness;* but *The English Traveller* and *The Wise-Woman of Hogsdon* are not far below it; and the first part of *The Fair Maid of the West,* when it has been performed—twice, we believe, in recent years—was revealed as a rollicking piece of popular patriotic sentiment. Before considering whether this output has enough coherence to be treated with the dignity of an *œuvre,* there are several interesting attributions of Dr. Clark's which demand attention. The first and most important is *Appius and Virginia.*

The date of this play, which has long been a difficulty to students of Webster—a play far below Webster's best work, and in some respects dissimilar to it—forms one of Dr. Clark's reasons for attributing the play primarily to Heywood. This was, of course, the guess of Rupert Brooke; but, given the initial doubt which strikes any admirer of Webster, the opinion, when it comes from a close student of Heywood, has much stronger authority. Dr. Clark, however, is not content to take issue only with Mr. Sykes (who gives the whole play to Webster), though that is a serious task in itself. He dismisses, with hardly more attention than a few footnotes, the moderate and so far, we believe, impregnable view of Mr. F. L. Lucas. He refers, certainly, to Mr. Lucas's "attempt to depreciate Heywood" as "uncritical"; because Mr. Lucas, in his introduction to the play in his complete edition of Webster, doubts whether Heywood

"could have produced unaided so well-planned and reasonable a play. For there is a peculiar oafish simplicity about him which made him unable ever to create a single piece, except perhaps *Edward IV,* which is not deformed by pages of utter drivel."

Mr. Lucas has perhaps written with a heat uncommon among Elizabethan scholars, though refreshing; yet his doubt whether

Heywood could have planned the play is one likely to strike any one who reads both Webster and Heywood without prejudices. To such a reader, the fact that Heywood is the author of *The Rape of Lucrece* strains credulity to the breaking point. But this, indeed, is the whole issue between Dr. Clark and Mr. Lucas. Neither doubts that both Heywood and Webster had a hand in the play; neither makes a claim for any third author. Dr. Clark concludes that Heywood wrote the play and that "at an unknown date Webster revised the play somewhat carelessly." Mr. Lucas can more easily believe that Webster wrote, or designed and partly wrote, the play, and that Heywood either revised or completed it. We are left with a narrow choice and a fine distinction; in fact, we are left to our personal impressions. The feeling of the present reviewer, at least, is that the structure of the play is more credibly assignable to Webster, as well as the good lines which nobody denies him.

Our inclination to this conclusion is confirmed, if anything, by Dr. Clark's theory of Heywood's hand in *The Jew of Malta*. It seems to us that here Dr. Clark's scholarly theory is really founded upon a critical presupposition. He holds a not uncommon view that "so far as [Marlowe's] conception of Barabas is concerned, the play might finish with the second act." But he adds, "so far as we know Marlowe invented the plot," which is a considerable concession; and also admits that there is a very little in Acts III, IV and V which Marlowe may have written. He says, "in the play we probably still have the main incidents as originally determined, but now crowded mostly into V to make room for certain ribaldry and gruesome farce." There is perhaps a little ribaldry which we should prefer not to attribute to Marlowe, and of a kind of which Heywood was certainly capable; but the most "gruesome farce" is found in Act IV, Scenes I and II; which the mere critic may maintain to be farce of a gruesomeness a cut above Heywood, and by no means unworthy of Marlowe. That the latter part of the play is garbled, few would doubt; that the writer who filled in the remains of Marlowe's play was Heywood, Dr. Clark makes out a good case; but mutilated and patched as the play probably is, we may

still see in it a conception of Barabaṣ which is by no means finished with the second act.

The third of Dr. Clark's interesting ascriptions concerns *A
Yorkshire Tragedy*. This abrupt little play has been somewhat
overrated, singularly so by Swinburne. Dr. Clark's association
of it with *The Miseries of Enforced Marriage*, and his explanation of its inconsistencies through this association, is an excellent piece of reasoning. So far as the verse is concerned, the most
of it is not too bad to be Heywood's, and the best line and a
half—

> *But you are playing in the angels' laps*
> *And will not look on me—*

strike us as a *trouvaille* which might have been possible to Heywood. The best of the play is the part of the "little son":

"What, ail you, father? are you not well? I cannot scourge
my top as long as you stand so: you take up all the room with
your wide legs. Puh, you cannot make me afeard with this;
I fear no vizards, nor bugbears"—

and as we cannot allege any other minor dramatist as more
competent to have written this touching dialogue than Heywood, we are hardly in a strong position to refuse it to him.
This then, we think, is the most valuable of Dr. Clark's ascriptions.

None of these attributions, interesting as is the last of them
in itself, can make very much difference to our estimate of Heywood as a dramatist and a poet; and it is upon the indisputable
plays that we found our opinion of him. These indisputable
plays exhibit what may be called the minimum degree of unity.
Similar subject-matter and treatment appear in several; the
same stage skill, the same versifying ability. The sensibility is
merely that of ordinary people in ordinary life—which is the
reason, perhaps, why Heywood is misleadingly called a "realist." Behind the motions of his personages, the shadows of the
human world, there is no reality of moral synthesis; to inform
the verse there is no vision, none of the artist's power to give
undefinable unity to the most various material. In the work of

nearly all of those of his contemporaries who are as well known
as he there is at least some inchoate pattern; there is, as it
would often be called, personality. Of those of Heywood's plays
which are worth reading, each is worth reading for itself, but
none throws any illumination upon any other.

Heywood's versification is never on a very high poetic level,
but at its best is often on a high dramatic level. This can be
illustrated by one of the best known of quotations from *A
Woman Killed with Kindness*:

> *O speak no more!*
> *For more than this I know, and have recorded*
> *Within the red-leaved table of my heart.*
> *Fair, and of all beloved, I was not fearful*
> *Bluntly to give my life into your hand,*
> *And at one hazard all my earthly means.*
> *Go, tell your husband; he will turn me off,*
> *And I am then undone. I care not, I;*
> *'Twas for your sake. Perchance in rage he'll kill me,*
> *I care not, 'twas for you. Say I incur*
> *The general name of villain through the world,*
> *Of traitor to my friend; I care not, I.*
> *Beggary, shame, death, scandal, and reproach,*
> *For you I'll hazard all: why, what care I?*
> *For you I'll live, and in your love I'll die.*

The image at the beginning of this passage does not, it is true,
deserve its fame. "Table of my heart" is a legitimate, though
hardly striking, metaphor; but to call it *red-leaved* is to press
the anatomical aspect into a ridiculous figure. It is not a conceit,
as when Crashaw deliberately telescopes one image into another, but merely the irreflective grasping after a fine trope.
But in the lines that follow the most skilful use is made of regular blank verse to emphasize the argument; and it is, even to
the judicious couplet at the end, a speech which any actor should
be happy to declaim. The speech is perfect for the situation; the
most persuasive that Wendoll could have made to Mrs. Frankford; and it persuades us into accepting her surrender. And this
instance of verse which is only moderately poetical but very

highly dramatic is by no means singular in Heywood's work.

And undeniably Heywood was not without skill in the construction of plays. It is unreasonable to complain of *A Woman Killed with Kindness* that it is improbable that a woman who has lived very happily with her husband and borne children should suddenly and easily be seduced by a man who had been living in the house the whole time; we consider that the seduction is made extremely plausible. What is perhaps clumsy is the beginning superfluously by a scene directly after the marriage of the Frankfords, instead of by a scene marking the happiness of the pair up to the moment of Wendoll's declaration. Sufficient verisimilitude is maintained to the end; we accept the Elizabethan convention of very quick death from heartbreak; and the last scene is really affecting. It is true that Mistress Frankford's words:

Out of my zeal to Heaven, whither now I'm bound,

seem to rely upon some curiously unorthodox theology; and even if death from broken heart secures the remission of sins, it hardly became Mrs. Frankford to be so certain of it. But such a moral sentiment is perhaps not unique in the ethics of Elizabethan drama; and other small touches in the play, such as the finding of the guitar, well deserve the praise they have received. It is in the underplot, as in some other plays, that Heywood is least skilful. This theme—a man ready to prostitute his sister as payment for a debt of honour—is too grotesque even to horrify us; but it is too obviously there merely because an underplot is required to fill out the play for us to feel anything but boredom when it recurs. Middleton's *The Changeling*, in every other respect a far finer play, must share with *A Woman Killed with Kindness* the discredit of having the weakest underplot of any important play in the whole Elizabethan repertory.

Indeed, Heywood suffers from one great handicap in attempting to write underplots at all—he was gifted with very little sense of humour, and therefore could not fall back upon the comic for the purpose. In attempting to be amusing he sometimes has recourse, as other men than harried playwrights have been known to do, to the lowest bawdiness, which leaves us less with a sense of repugnance for the man who could write it than with a sense of pity for the man who could think of nothing better. Here and there, in *The Wise-Woman of Hogsdon* for instance, he succeeds with something not too far below Jonson to be comparable to that master's work; the wise woman herself, and her scenes with her clientele, are capitally done, and earn for Heywood the title of "realist" if any part of his work can. The scene of the unmasking of Young Chartley must be excellent fun when played. The underplot of *The English Traveller*, on the other hand, is a clumsy failure to do that in which only Jonson could have succeeded. But Heywood has no imaginative humour; and as he has so often been spoken of in the same breath with Dekker, that is a comparison which may justly be made. Just as Bess, the Fair Maid of the West, is a purely melodramatic figure beside the heroine of *The Roaring Girle*, so Heywood could no more have created the character of Cuddie Banks, in *The Witch*, than he could have written the magnificent tirade (a tirade which, if anything can, goes to prove that Middleton wrote *The Revenger's Tragedy*) which Middleton puts into the mouth of the chief character in the same play. Cuddie Banks, loving the dog whom he knows to be a devil, but loving him as dog while reproving him as devil, is worthy to rank with clowns of Shakespeare; he is not "realistic," he is true.

It was in *The English Traveller* that Heywood found his best plot. Possibly the elder critics disapproved of the heroine's plighting herself to marry her admirer as soon as her elderly husband should die; but it is far less offensive to modern taste than many other situations in Elizabethan drama, and it is one which a modern novelist—not perhaps a quite modern novelist, but a Stendhal—might have made the most of. It is indeed a plot especially modern among Elizabethan plots; for the refinement of agony of the virtuous lover who has controlled his passion and then discovers that his lady has deceived both her husband, who is his friend, and himself, is really more poignant than the torment of the betrayed husband Frankford. The strange situation *à quatre*, Master Wincott and his wife, young Geraldine and his faithless companion Delavil—and old Geraldine neatly worked into the pattern as well—is not only well thought of but well thought out; and it is delicately phrased:

Y. GER.

Your husband's old, to whom my soul doth wish
A Nestor's age, so much he merits from me;
Yet if (as proof and Nature daily teach
Men cannot always live, especially
Such as are old and crazed) he be called hence,
Fairly, in full maturity of time,
And we two be reserved to after-life,
Will you confer your widowhood on me?

WIFE.

You ask the thing I was about to beg;
Your tongue hath spoke mine own thoughts. . . .

WIFE.

Till that day come, you shall reserve yourself
A single man; converse nor company
With any woman, contract nor combine
With maid or widow; which expected hour
As I do wish not haste, so when it happens
It shall not come unwelcome. You hear all;
Vow this.

Y. GER.

By all that you have said, I swear,
And by this kiss confirm.

WIFE.

You're now my brother;
But then, my second husband.

It could not have been done better. As in the passage from *A Woman Killed with Kindness* quoted above, the verse, which nowhere bursts into a flame of poetry, is yet economical and tidy, and formed to extract all the dramatic value possible from the situation. And it is by his refinement of sentiment, by his sympathetic delicacy in these two plays, that Heywood deserves, and well deserves, to be remembered; for here he has accomplished what none of his contemporaries succeeded in accomplishing.

Yet we must concede that the interest is always sentimental, and never ethical. One has seen plays in our time which are just the sort of thing that Heywood would have written had he been our contemporary. It is usual for inferior authors at any time to accept whatever morality is current, because they are interested not to analyse the ethics but to exploit the sentiment. Mrs. Frankford yields to her seducer with hardly a struggle, and her decline and death are a tribute to popular sentiment; not, certainly, a vindication of inexorable moral law. She is in the sentimental tradition which peopled a period of nineteenth-century fiction with Little Em'lys; and which, if it now produces a generation of rather robuster heroines, has yet made no moral advance, because it has no vital relation to morals at all. For a Corneille or a Racine, the centre of interest in the situation of Mrs. Frankford or Mrs. Wincott would have been the moral conflict leading up to the fall; and even the absence of conflict, as in the seduction of Mathilde (if seduction it can be called) in *Le Rouge et le Noir*, can be treated by a moralist. The capital distinction is that between representation of human actions which have moral reality and representation of such as have only sentimental reality; and beside this, any distinction between "healthy" and "morbid" sentiment is trivial. It is well enough to speak of Heywood, as does Dr. Clark, as "a man of tender charity . . . ever kindly to the fallen and with a gift of homely pathos and simple poetry"; though it does less than justice to Heywood to describe his pathos as "homely" (for the famous pathos of "Nan, Nan!" is no homelier than Lear's "Never, never, never, never, never," though far below it). What matters is not whether Heywood was inspired by tender charity, but whether his actual productions are any more edifying, any more moral, than what Dr. Clark would call "the slippery ethics" of Fletcher, Massinger and Ford.

The ethics of most of the greater Elizabethan dramatists is only intelligible as leading up to, or deriving from, that of Shakespeare: it has its significance, we mean, only in the light of Shakespeare's fuller revelation. There is another type of ethics, that of the satirist. In Shakespeare's work it is represented most nearly by *Timon* and *Troilus*, but in a mind with such prodigious capacity of development as Shakespeare's, the snarling vein could not endure. The kind of satire which is approached in *The Jew of Malta* reaches perhaps its highest point with *Volpone*; but it is a kind to which also approximates much of the work of Middleton and Tourneur, men who as writers must be counted morally higher than Fletcher, Ford or Heywood.

> *These by enchantments can whole lordships change*
> *To trunks of rich attire, turn ploughs and teams*
> *To Flanders mares and coaches, and huge trains*
> *Of servitors to a French butterfly.*
> *Have you not city-witches who can turn*
> *Their husbands' wares, whole standing shops of wares,*
> *To sumptuous tables, gardens of stolen sin;*
> *In one year wasting what scarce twenty win?*
> *Are not these witches?*

That dolorous aspect of human nature which in comedy is best portrayed by Molière, though Jonson and even Wycherley have the same burden, appears again and again in the tragic drama of Middleton and Tourneur. Without denying to Heywood what Dr. Clark attributes to him, a sense of "the pity of it," we can find a profounder sense of the "pity of it" in the lines quoted above which Middleton gives to the Witch of Edmonton. Heywood's sense of pity is genuine enough, but it is only the kind of pity that the ordinary playgoer, of any time, can appreciate. Heywood's is a drama of common life, not, in the highest sense, tragedy at all; there is no supernatural music from behind the wings. He would in any age have been a successful playwright; he is eminent in the pathetic, rather than the tragic. His nearest approach to those deeper emotions which shake the veil of Time is in that fine speech of Frankford which surely no man or woman past their youth can read without a twinge of personal feeling:

> *O God! O God! that it were possible*
> *To undo things done; to call back yesterday. . . .*

CYRIL TOURNEUR

━━━━

ALTHOUGH the tragedies which make immortal the name of Cyril Tourneur are accessible to every one in the Mermaid edition, it is still an event to have a new edition of the "work" of this strange poet. Fifty-two years have passed since the edition in two volumes by Churton Collins. And this sumptuous critical edition of Professor Nicoll's [1] reminds us that it is time to revalue the work of Tourneur.

None of the Elizabethan dramatists is more puzzling; none offers less foothold for the scholarly investigator; and none is more dangerous for the literary critic. We know almost nothing of his life; we trace his hand in no collaboration. He has left only two plays; and it has been doubted even whether the same man wrote both; and if he did, as most scholars agree, there is still some doubt as to which he wrote first. Yet in no plays by any minor Elizabethan is a more positive personality revealed than in *The Revenger's Tragedy*. No Elizabethan dramatist offers greater temptation: to the scholar, to hazard conjecture of fact; and to the critic, to hazard conjecture of significance. We may be sure that what Mr. Nicoll does not know is unknown to anybody; and it is no disrespect to his scholarship and diligence to remark how little, in the fifty-two years of Elizabethan research since Collins, has been added to our knowledge of the singular poet with the delightful name. Churton Collins, in his admirable introduction, really knows nothing at all about the man's life; and all that later students have been able to do is to piece together several probable shreds. That

[1] The works of Cyril Tourneur. Edited by Allardyce Nicoll, with decorations by Frederick Carter. London: The Fanfrolico Press.

there was a family of Tourneurs is certain; the precise place in
it of Cyril is, as Mr. Nicoll freely admits, a matter of speculation. And with all the plausible guesses possible, Mr. Nicoll tells
us that Tourneur's "whole early life is a complete blank." What
he does give us is good reason for believing that Tourneur, with
perhaps other members of the family, was a servant of the
Cecils; and he adds to our knowledge a prose piece, "The Character of Robert Earl of Salisbury." Besides the two tragedies,
he also gives "The Transformed Metamorphosis," the "Funeral
Poem upon the Death of Sir Francis Vere," and the Elegy on
the death of Prince Henry, already canonically attributed to
Tourneur; and "Laugh and Lie Down," a satirical pamphlet,
no better and no worse than dozens of others, which is probably Tourneur's—at least, it is attributed to him, and there is
no particular reason why he should not be the author.

The information of fifty years is meagre, and probably will
never be improved. It is astonishingly incongruous with what
we feel we know about Tourneur after reading the two plays:
two plays as different from all plays by known Elizabethans
as they are from each other. In Elizabethan drama, the critic is
rash who will assert boldly that any play is by a single hand.
But with each of these, *The Atheist's Tragedy* and *The Revenger's Tragedy*, the literary critic feels that, even were there
some collaboration, one mind guided the whole work; and
feels that the mind was not that of one of the other well-known
dramatic writers. Certainly, Tourneur has made a very deep
impression upon the minds of those critics who have admired
him. It is to be regretted, however, that Professor Nicoll, at
the beginning of his otherwise sober and just introduction, has
quoted the hysterical phrase of Marcel Schwob's *vie imaginaire*
of Tourneur. To say that Tourneur *naquit de l'union d'un dieu
inconnu avec une prostituée* is a pardonable excess of a romantic period, a pardonable excess on the part of a poet discovering
a foreign poet. But this is not criticism; and it is a misleading
introduction to the work of a man who was a great English
poet; and it produces an impression which is increased by the
excellent but too *macabre* decorations of Mr. Carter. What

matters first is the beauty of the verse and the unity of the dramatic pattern in the two plays.

The author of *The Atheist's Tragedy* and *The Revenger's Tragedy* belongs critically among the earlier of the followers of Shakespeare. If Ford and Shirley and Fletcher represent the decadence, and Webster the last ripeness, then Tourneur belongs a little earlier than Webster. He is nearer to Middleton, and has some affinity to that curious and still underestimated poet Marston. The difference between his mind and that of Webster is very great; if we assigned his plays to any other known dramatist, Webster would be the last choice. For Webster is a slow, deliberate, careful writer, very much the conscious artist. He was incapable of writing so badly or so ` telessly as Tourneur sometimes did, but he is never quite so surprising as Tourneur sometimes is. Moreover, Webster, in his greatest tragedies, has a kind of pity for *all* of his characters, an attitude towards good and bad alike which helps to unify the Webster pattern. Tourneur has no such feeling for any of his characters; and in this respect is nearer, as Professor Stoll has pointed out and Professor Nicoll has reminded us, to the author of *Antonio and Mellida*. Of all his other contemporaries, Middleton is the nearest. But Mr. Nicoll, we think quite rightly, rejects Mr. E. H. C. Oliphant's theory that Middleton is the author of *The Revenger's Tragedy,* and with Mr. Dugdale Sykes restores the play to Tourneur. And in spite of Mr. Oliphant's weight of probabilities, there is one quality of Middleton which we do not find in the two plays attributed to Tourneur. The finest of the tragic characters of Middleton live in a way which differs from Tourneur's, not in degree but kind; and they have flashes of a kind of satiric wit unknown to Tourneur, in whom wit is supplied by a fierce grotesquerie. In reading one play of Middleton, either *The Changeling* or *Women Beware Women,* for instance, we can recognize an author capable of considerable variety in his dramatic work; in reading either of Tourneur's plays we recognize a narrow mind, capable at most of the limited range of Marston.

Indeed, none of the characters of Tourneur, even the notable Vindice, the protagonist of *The Revenger's Tragedy,* is by himself invested with much humanity either for good or evil. But dramatic characters may live in more than one way; and a dramatist like Tourneur can compensate his defects by the intensity of his virtues. Characters should be real in relation to our own life, certainly, as even a very minor character of Shakespeare may be real; but they must also be real in relation to each other; and the closeness of emotional pattern in the latter way is an important part of dramatic merit. The personages of Tourneur have, like those of Marston, and perhaps in a higher degree, this togetherness. They may be distortions, grotesques, almost childish caricatures of humanity, but they are all distorted to scale. Hence the whole action, from their appearance to their ending, "no common action" indeed, has its own self-subsistent reality. For closeness of texture, in fact, there are no plays beyond Shakespeare's, and the best of Marlowe and Jonson, that can surpass *The Revenger's Tragedy*. Tourneur excels in three virtues of the dramatist: he knew how, in his own way, to construct a plot, he was cunning in his manipulation of stage effects, and he was a master of versification and choice of language. *The Revenger's Tragedy* starts off at top speed, as every critic has observed; and never slackens to the end. We are told everything we need to know before the first scene is half over; Tourneur employs his torrent of words with the greatest economy. The opening scene and the famous Scene V of Act III are remarkable feats of melodrama; and the suddenness of the end of the final scene of Act V matches the sudden explosiveness of the beginning.

Before considering the detail of the two plays, we must face two problems which have never been solved and probably never will be: whether the two plays are by the same hand and, if so, in which order they were written. For the first point, the consensus of scholarship, with the exception of Mr. Oliphant's brilliant ascription of *The Revenger's Tragedy* to Middleton—an ascription which leaves the other play more of a mystery than before—assigns the two plays to Tourneur. For the second point, the consensus of scholarship is counter to the first impressions of sensibility; for all existing evidence points to the priority of *The Revenger's Tragedy* in time. The records of Stationer's

Hall cannot be lightly disregarded; and Mr. Dugdale Sykes, who is perhaps our greatest authority on the texts of Tourneur and Middleton, finds stylistic evidence also. Professor Nicoll accepts the evidence, although pointing out clearly enough the anomaly. Certainly, any testimony drawn from the analogy of a modern poet's experience would urge that *The Atheist's Tragedy* was immature work, and that *The Revenger's Tragedy* represented a period of full mastery of blank verse. It is not merely that the latter play is in every way the better; but that it shows a highly original development of vocabulary and metric, unlike that of every other play and every other dramatist. The versification of *The Revenger's Tragedy* is of a very high order indeed. And yet, with the evidence before us, summed up briefly in Mr. Nicoll's preface, we cannot affirm that this is the later play. Among all the curiosities of that curious period, when dramatic poets worked and developed in ways alien to the modern mind, this is one of the most curious. But it is quite possible. We may conjecture either that *The Atheist's Tragedy* was composed, or partly composed, and laid by until after *The Revenger's Tragedy* was written and entered. Or that after exhausting his best inspiration on the latter play—which certainly bears every internal evidence of having been written straight off in one sudden heat—Tourneur, years after, in colder blood, with more attention to successful models—not only Shakespeare but also perhaps Chapman—produced *The Atheist's Tragedy*, with more regular verse, more conventional moralizing, more conventional scenes, but with here and there flashes of the old fire. Not that the scenes of *The Atheist's Tragedy* are altogether conventional; or, at least, he trespasses beyond the convention in a personal way. There was nothing remarkable in setting a graveyard scene at midnight; but we feel that to set it for the action of a low assignation and an attempted rape at the same time seems more to be expected of the author of *The Revenger's Tragdy* than of any one else; while the low comedy, more low than comic, does not seem of the taste of either Webster or Middleton. Webster's farcical prose is harmonious with his tragic verse; and in this respect Webster is a worthy follower of the tradition of the Porter in

Macbeth. Middleton again, in his tragedies, has a different feel of the relation of the tragic and the comic; whereas the transitions in the two tragedies of Tourneur—and especially in *The Atheist's Tragedy*—are exactly what one would expect from a follower of Marston; especially in *The Atheist's Tragedy* they have that offensive tastelessness which is so positive as to be itself a kind of taste, which we find in the work of Marston.

The Atheist's Tragedy is indeed a peculiar brew of styles. It has well-known passages like the following: [2]

> *Walking next day upon the fatal shore,*
> *Among the slaughtered bodies of their men,*
> *Which the full-stomached sea had cast upon*
> *The sands, it was my unhappy chance to light*
> *Upon a face, whose favour when it lived*
> *My astonished mind informed me I had seen.*
> *He lay in his armour, as if that had been*
> *His coffin; and the weeping sea (like one*
> *Whose milder temper doth lament the death*
> *Of him whom in his rage he slew) runs up*
> *The shore, embraces him, kisses his cheek;*
> *Goes back again, and forces up the sands*
> *To bury him, and every time it parts*
> *Sheds tears upon him, till, at last (as if*
> *It could no longer endure to see the man*
> *Whom it had slain, yet loth to leave him) with*
> *A kind of unresolved unwilling pace,*
> *Winding her waves one in another, (like*
> *A man that folds his arms, or wrings his hands*
> *For grief) ebbed from the body, and descends;*
> *As if it would sink down into the earth*
> *And hide itself for shame of such a deed.*

The present writer was once convinced that *The Atheist's Tragedy* was the earlier play. But lines like these, masterly but artificial, might well belong to a later period; the regularity of

[2] The text used in the following quotations is the critical text of Professor Nicoll; but for convenience and familiarity the modernized spelling and punctuation of the "Mermaid" text is used.

the versification, the elaboration of the long suspended sentences, with three similes expressed in brackets, remind us even of Massinger. It is true that Charles Lamb, commenting on this passage, refers this parenthetical style to Sir Philip Sidney, who "seems to have set the example to Shakespeare"; but these lines have closer syntactical parallels in Massinger than in Shakespeare. But lines like

To spend our substance on a minute's pleasure

remind one of *The Revenger's Tragedy*, and lines like

Your gravity becomes your perished soul
As hoary mouldiness does rotten fruit

of *The Revenger's Tragedy* where it is likest Middleton.

As a parallel for admitting the possibility of *The Atheist's Tragedy* being the later play, Professor Nicoll cites the fact that *Cymbeline* is later than *Hamlet*. This strikes us as about the most unsuitable parallel that could be found. Even though some critics may still consider *Cymbeline* as evidence of "declining powers," it has no less a mastery of words than *Hamlet*, and possibly more; and, like every one of Shakespeare's plays, it adds something or develops something not explicit in any previous play; it has its place in an orderly sequence. Now accepting the canonical order of Tourneur's two plays, *The Atheist's Tragedy* adds nothing at all to what the other play has given us; there is no development, no fresh inspiration; only the skilful but uninspired use of a greater metrical variety. Cases are not altogether wanting, among poets, of a precocious maturity exceeding the limits of the poet's experience—in contrast to the very slow and very long development of Shakespeare—a maturity to which the poet is never again able to catch up. Tourneur's genius, in any case, is in *The Revenger's Tragedy*; his talent only in *The Atheist's Tragedy*.

Indeed, *The Revenger's Tragedy* might well be a specimen of such isolated masterpieces. It does express—and this, chiefly, is what gives it its amazing unity—an intense and unique and horrible vision of life; but is such a vision as might come, as the

result of few or slender experiences, to a highly sensitive adolescent with a gift for words. We are apt to expect of youth only
a fragmentary view of life; we incline to see youth as exagger-
ating the importance of its narrow experience and imagining the
world as did Chicken Licken. But occasionally the intensity of
the vision of its own ecstasies or horrors, combined with a mastery of word and rhythm, may give to a juvenile work a universality which is beyond the author's knowledge of life to give,
and to which mature men and women can respond. Churton
Collins's introduction to the works is by far the most penetrating interpretation of Tourneur that has been written; and
this introduction, though Collins believed *The Revenger's
Tragedy* to be the later play, and although he thinks of Tourneur as a man of mature experience, does not invalidate this
theory. "Tourneur's great defect as a dramatic poet," says
Collins, "is undoubtedly the narrowness of his range of vision":
and this narrowness of range might be that of a young man.
The cynicism, the loathing and disgust of humanity, expressed
consummately in *The Revenger's Tragedy*, are immature in the
respect that they exceed the object. Their objective equivalents
are characters practising the grossest vices; characters which
seem merely to be spectres projected from the poet's inner
world of nightmare, some horror beyond words. So the play is a
document on humanity chiefly because it is a document on one
human being, Tourneur; its motive is truly the death-motive,
for it is the loathing and horror of life itself. To have realized
this motive so well is a triumph; for the hatred of life is an
important phase—even, if you like, a mystical experience—in
life itself.

The *Revenger's Tragedy*, then, is in this respect quite different from any play by any minor Elizabethan; it can, in this
respect, be compared only to *Hamlet*. Perhaps, however, its
quality would be better marked by contrasting it with a later
work of cynicism and loathing, *Gulliver's Travels*. No two compositions could be more dissimilar. Tourneur's "suffering, cynicism and despair," to use Collins's words, are static; they might
be prior to experience, or be the fruit of but little; Swift's is the

progressive cynicism of the mature and disappointed man of the world. As an objective comment on the world, Swift's is by far the more terrible. For Swift had himself enough pettiness, as well as enough sin of pride, and lust of dominion, to be able to expose and condemn mankind by its universal pettiness and pride and vanity and ambition; and his poetry, as well as his prose, attests that he hated the very smell of the human animal. We may think as we read Swift, "how loathesome human beings are"; in reading Tourneur we can only think, "how terrible to loathe human beings so much as that." For you cannot make humanity horrible merely by presenting human beings as consistent and monotonous maniacs of gluttony and lust.

Collins, we think, tended to read into the plays of Tourneur too much, or more than is necessary, of a lifetime's experience. Some of his phrases, however, are memorable and just. But what still remains to be praised, after Swinburne and Collins and Mr. Nicoll, is Tourneur's unique style in blank verse. His occasional verses are mediocre at best; he left no lyric verse at all; but it is hardly too much to say that, after Marlowe, Shakespeare and Webster, Tourneur is the most remarkable technical innovator—an innovator who found no imitators. The style of *The Revenger's Tragedy* is consistent throughout; there is little variation, but the rapidity escapes monotony.

> *Faith, if the truth were known, I was begot*
> *After some gluttonous dinner; some stirring dish*
> *Was my first father, when deep healths went round*
> *And ladies' cheeks were painted red with wine,*
> *Their tongues, as short and nimble as their heels,*
> *Uttering words sweet and thick; and when they rose,*
> *Were merrily disposed to fall again.*
> *In such a whispering and withdrawing hour . . .*
> *   . . . and, in the morning*
> *When they are up and drest, and their mask on,*
> *Who can perceive this, save that eternal eye*
> *That sees through flesh and all? Well, if anything be*
> *   damned,*
> *It will be twelve o'clock at night. . . .*

His verse hurries:

> *O think upon the pleasure of the palace!*
> *Secured ease and state! the stirring meats,*
> *Ready to move out of the dishes, that e'en now*
> *Quicken when they are eaten!*
> *Banquets abroad by torchlight! music! sports!*
> *Bareheaded vassals, that had ne'er the fortune*
> *To keep on their own hats, but let horns wear 'em!*
> *Nine coaches waiting—hurry, hurry, hurry—*

His phrases seem to contract the images in his effort to say everything in the least space, the shortest time:

> *Age and bare bone*
> *Are e'er allied in action . . .*

> *To suffer wet damnation to run through 'em . . .*

> *The poor benefit of a bewildering minute . . .*

(*Bewildering* is the reading of the "Mermaid" text; both Churton Collins and Mr. Nicoll give *bewitching* without mentioning any alternative reading: it is a pity if they be right, for *bewildering* is much the richer word here.)

> *forgetful feasts . . .*

> *falsify highways . . .*

And the peculiar abruptness, the frequent change of tempo, characteristic of *The Revenger's Tragedy*, is nowhere better shown than by the closing lines:

> *This murder might have slept in tongueless brass,*
> *But for ourselves, and the world died an ass.*
> *Now I remember too, here was Piato*
> *Brought forth a knavish sentence once;*
> *No doubt (said he), but time*
> *Will make the murderer bring forth himself.*
> *'Tis well he died; he was a witch.*
> *And now, my lord, since we are in forever,*

This work was ours, which else might have been slipped!
And if we list, we could have nobles clipped,
And go for less than beggars; but we hate
To bleed so cowardly, we have enough,
I' faith, we're well, our mother turned, our sister true,
We die after a nest of dukes. Adieu!

The versification, as indeed the whole style of *The Revenger's Tragedy*, is not that of the last period of the great drama. Although so peculiar, the metric of Tourneur is earlier in style than that of the later Shakespeare, or Fletcher, or Webster, to say nothing of Massinger, or Shirley, or Ford. It seems to derive, as much as from any one's, from that of Marston. What gives Tourneur his place as a great poet is this one play, in which a horror of life, singular in his own or any age, finds exactly the right words and the right rhythms.

JOHN FORD

AMONG other possible classifications, we might divide the Elizabethan and Jacobean dramatists into those who would have been great even had Shakespeare never lived, those who are positive enough to have brought some positive contribution after Shakespeare, and those whose merit consists merely in having exploited successfully a few Shakespearean devices or echoed here and there the Shakespearean verse. In the first class would fall Marlowe, Jonson and Chapman; in the second, Middleton, Webster and Tourneur; in the third, Beaumont and Fletcher and Shirley as tragedian. This kind of division could not support very close question, especially in its distinction between the second and the third class; but it is of some use at the beginning, in helping us to assign a provisional place to John Ford.

The standard set by Shakespeare is that of a continuous development from first to last, a development in which the choice both of theme and of dramatic and verse technique in each play seems to be determined increasingly by Shakespeare's state of feeling, by the particular stage of his emotional maturity at the time. What is "the whole man" is not simply his greatest or maturest achievement, but the whole pattern formed by the sequence of plays; so that we may say confidently that the full meaning of any one of his plays is not in itself alone, but in that play in the order in which it was written, in its relation to all of Shakespeare's other plays, earlier and later: we must know all of Shakespeare's work in order to know any of it. No other dramatist of the time approaches anywhere near to this perfection of pattern, of pattern superficial and profound; but

the measure in which dramatists and poets approximate to this
unity in a lifetime's work is one of the measures of major
poetry and drama. We feel a similar interest, in less degree,
in the work of Jonson and Chapman, and certainly in the unfinished work of Marlowe; in less degree still, the interest is
in the work of Webster, baffling as the chronological order of
Webster's plays makes it. Even without an *œuvre*, some dramatists can effect a satisfying unity and significance of pattern
in single plays, a unity springing from the depth and coherence
of a number of emotions and feelings, and not only from dramatic and poetic skill. The *Maid's Tragedy*, or *A King and No
King*, is better constructed, and has as many poetic lines, as *The
Changeling*, but is far inferior in the degree of inner necessity
in the feeling: something more profound and more complex
than what is ordinarily called "sincerity."

It is significant that the first of Ford's important plays to be
performed, so far as we have knowledge, is one which depends
very patently upon some of the devices, and still more upon
the feeling tone, of Shakespeare's last period. *The Lover's
Melancholy* was licensed for the stage in 1628; it could hardly
have been written but for *Cymbeline*, *The Winter's Tale*,
Pericles, and *The Tempest*. Except for the comic passages,
which are, as in all of Ford's plays, quite atrocious, it is a pleasant, dreamlike play without violence or exaggeration. As in
other of his plays, there are verbal echoes of Shakespeare
numerous enough; but what is more interesting is the use of
the Recognition Scene, so important in Shakespeare's later plays,
to the significance of which as a Shakespeare symbol Mr. Wilson Knight has drawn attention. In Shakespeare's plays, this
is primarily the recognition of a long-lost daughter, secondarily
of a wife; and we can hardly read the later plays attentively
without admitting that the father and daughter theme was
one of very deep symbolic value to him in his last productive
years: Perdita, Marina and Miranda share some beauty of which
his earlier heroines do not possess the secret. Now Ford is struck
by the dramatic and poetic effectiveness of the situation, and
uses it on a level hardly higher than that of the device of twins
in comedy; so in *The Lover's Melancholy* he introduces two

such scenes, one the recognition of Eroclea in the guise of
Parthenophil by her lover Palador, the second her recognition
(accompanied, as in *Pericles*, by soft music) by her aged father
Meleander. Both of these scenes are very well carried out, and
in the first we have a passage in that slow solemn rhythm which
is Ford's distinct contribution to the blank verse of the period.

> *Minutes are numbered by the fall of sands,*
> *As by an hourglass; the span of time*
> *Doth waste us to our graves, and we look on it:*
> *An age of pleasure, revelled out, comes home*
> *At last, and ends in sorrow; but the life,*
> *Weary of riot, numbers every sand,*
> *Wailing in sighs, until the last drop down;*
> *So to conclude calamity in rest.*

The tone and movement are so positive that when in a dull
masque by Ford and Dekker, called *The Sun's Darling*, we
come across such a passage as

> *Winter at last draws on the Night of Age;*
> *Yet still a humour of some novel fancy*
> *Untasted or untried, puts off the minute*
> *Of resolution, which should bid farewell*
> *To a vain world of weariness and sorrows. . . .*

we can hardly doubt the identity of the author. The scenes, as
said above, are well planned and well written, and are even
moving; but it is in such scenes as these that we are convinced
of the incommensurability of writers like Ford (and Beaumont
and Fletcher) with Shakespeare. It is not merely that they fail
where he succeeds; it is that they had no conception of what he
was trying to do; they speak another and cruder language. In
their poetry there is no symbolic value; theirs is good poetry
and good drama, but it is poetry and drama of the surface. And
in a play like *The Revenger's Tragedy*, or *Women Beware
Women*, or *The White Devil*, there is some of that inner significance which becomes the stronger and stronger undertone
of Shakespeare's plays to the end. You do not find that in Ford.

It is suggested, then, that a dramatic poet cannot create characters of the greatest intensity of life unless his personages, in their reciprocal actions and behaviour in their story, are somehow dramatizing, but in no obvious form, an action or struggle for harmony in the soul of the poet. In this sense Ford's most famous, though not necessarily best, play may be called "meaningless"; and in so far as we may be justified in disliking its horrors, we are justified by its lack of meaning. *'Tis Pity She's a Whore* is surely one of the most read of minor Jacobean plays, and the only one of Ford's which has been lately revived upon the stage. It is the best constructed, with the exception of *Perkin Warbeck,* and the latter play is somewhat lacking in action. To the use of incest between brother and sister for a tragic plot there should be no objection of principle: the test is, however, whether the dramatic poet is able to give universal significance to a perversion of nature which, unlike some other aberrations, is defended by no one. The fact that it is defended by no one might, indeed, lend some colour of inoffensiveness to its dramatic use. Certainly, it is to Ford's credit that, having chosen this subject—which was suggested by an Italian tale—he went in for it thoroughly. There is none of the prurient flirting with impropriety which makes Beaumont and Fletcher's *King and No King* meretricious, and which is most evident and nauseous in the worst play which Ford himself ever wrote, *The Fancies Chaste and Noble;* a kind of prurience from which the comedy of Wycherley is entirely free. Furthermore, Ford handles the theme with all the seriousness of which he is capable, and he can hardly be accused here of wanton sensationalism. It is not the sort of play which an age wholly corrupt would produce; and the signs of decay in Ford's age are more clearly visible in the plays of Beaumont and Fletcher than in his own. Ford does not make the unpleasant appear pleasant; and when, at the moment of avowed love, he makes Annabella say

> *Brother, even by our mother's dust, I charge you,*
> *Do not betray me to your mirth or hate . . .*

he is certainly double-stressing the horror, which from that moment he will never allow you to forget; but if he did not stress the horror he would be the more culpable. There is noth-

ing in the play to which could be applied the term appropriately
used in the advertisements of some films: the "peppy situation."

We must admit, too, th ... the versification and poetry, for
example the fine speech of Annabella in Act v, sc. v., are of a
very high order:

> *Brother, dear brother, know what I have been,*
> *And know that now there's but a dining-time*
> *'Twixt us and our confusion. . . .*
> *Be not deceived, my brother;*
> *This banquet is an harbinger of death*
> *To you and me; resolve yourself it is,*
> *And be prepared to welcome it.*

Finally, the low comedy, bad as it is, is more restrained in space,
and more relevant to the plot, than is usual with Ford; and the
death of Bergetto ("Is all this mine own blood?") is almost
pathetic. When all is said, however, there are serious shortcomings to render account of. The sub-plot of Hippolita is tedious,
and her death superfluous. More important, the passion of
Giovanni and Annabella is not shown as an affinity of temperament due to identity of blood; it hardly rises above the purely
carnal infatuation. In *Antony and Cleopatra* (which is no more
an apology for adultery than *'Tis Pity* is an apology for incest)
we are made to feel convinced of an overpowering attraction
towards each other of two persons, not only in defiance of conventional morality, but against self-interest: an attraction as
fatal as that indicated by the love-potion motif in *Tristran und
Isolde*. We see clearly why Antony and Cleopatra find each
other congenial, and we see their relation, during the course of
the play, become increasingly serious. But Giovanni is merely
selfish and self-willed, of a temperament to want a thing the
more because it is forbidden; Annabella is pliant, vacillating
and negative: the one almost a monster of egotism, the other
virtually a moral defective. Her rebellious taunting of her
violent husband has an effect of naturalness and arouses some
sympathy; but the fact that Soranzo is himself a bad lot does
not extenuate her willingness to ruin him. In short, the play
has not the general significance and emotional depth (for the

two go together) without which no such action can be justified; and this defect separates it completely from the best plays of Webster, Middleton and Tourneur.

There are two other plays, however, which are superior to *'Tis Pity She's a Whore*. The first is *The Broken Heart*, in which, with *'Tis Pity* and *The Lover's Melancholy*, we find some of the best "poetical" passages. Some of the best lines in *The Broken Heart* are given to the distraught Penthea; and being reminded of another fine passage given to a crazed woman in *Venice Preserved*, we might be tempted to generalize, and suggest that it is easier for an inferior dramatic poet to write poetry when he has a lunatic character to speak it, because in such passages he is less tied down to relevance and ordinary sense. The quite irrelevant and apparently meaningless lines

> *Remember,*
> *When we last gathered roses in the garden,*
> *I found my wits; but truly you lost yours.*

are perhaps the purest poetry to be found in the whole of Ford's writings; but the longer and better known passage preceding them is also on a very high level:

> *Sure, if we were all Sirens, we should sing pitifully,*
> *And 'twere a comely music, when in parts*
> *One sung another's knell: the turtle sighs*
> *When he hath lost his mate; and yet some say*
> *He must be dead first: 'tis a fine deceit*
> *To pass away in a dream; indeed, I've slept*
> *With mine eyes open a great while. No falsehood*
> *Equals a broken faith; there's not a hair*
> *Sticks on my head but, like a leaden plummet,*
> *It sinks me to the grave: I must creep thither;*
> *The journey is not long.*

Between the first and the second of these passages there is, however, a difference of kind rather than degree: the first is real poetry, the second is the echo of a mood which other dramatic poets had caught and realized with greater mastery. Yet it exhibits that which gives Ford his most certain claim to perpetuity: the distinct personal rhythm in blank verse which could be no one's but his alone.

As for the play itself, the plot is somewhat overloaded and distracted by the affairs of unfortunate personages, all of whom have an equal claim on our attention; Ford overstrains our pity and terror by calling upon us to sympathize now with Penthea, now with Calantha, now with Orgilus, now with Ithocles; and the recipe by which good and evil are mixed in the characters of Orgilus and Ithocles is one which renders them less sympathetic, rather than more human. The scene in which Calantha, during the revels, is told successively the news of the death of her father, of Penthea and of her betrothed, and the scene in the temple which follows, must have been very effective on the stage; and the style is elevated and well sustained. The end of the play almost deserves the extravagant commendation of Charles Lamb; but to a later critic it appears rather as a recrudescence of the Senecan mood:

> *They are the silent griefs which cut the heart-strings,*
> *Let me die smiling.*

than as a profound searching of the human heart. The best of the play, and it is Ford at his best, is the character and the action of Penthea, the lady who, after having been betrothed to the man she loves, is taken from him and given to a rival to gratify the ambitions of her brother. Even here, Ford misses an opportunity, and lapses in taste, by making the unloved husband, Bassanes, the vulgar jealous elderly husband of comedy: Penthea is a character which deserved, and indeed required, a more dignified and interesting foil. We are also diverted from her woes by the selfish revengefulness of her lost lover, who, having been robbed of happiness himself, is determined to contrive that no one else shall be happy. Penthea, on the other hand, commands all our sympathy when she pleads the cause of her brother Ithocles, the brother who has ruined her life, with the Princess Calantha whom he loves. She is throughout a dignified, consistent and admirable figure; Penthea, and the Lady Katherine Gordon in *Perkin Warbeck*, are the most memorable of all Ford's characters.

Perkin Warbeck is little read, and does not contain any lines and passages such as those which remain in the memory after reading the other plays; but it is unquestionably Ford's highest achievement, and is one of the very best historical plays outside of the works of Shakespeare in the whole of Elizabethan and Jacobean drama. To make this base-born pretender to the throne of England into a dignified and heroic figure was no light task, and is not one which we should, after reading the other plays, have thought Ford competent to perform; but here for once there is no lapse of taste or judgment. Warbeck is made to appear as quite convinced that he is the lawful heir to the throne of England. We ourselves are left almost believing that he was; in the right state of uncertainty, wondering whether his kingly and steadfast behaviour is due to his royal blood, or merely due to his passionate conviction that he is of royal blood. What is more remarkable still, is that Ford has succeeded, not merely, as with Penthea, in creating one real person among shadows, but in fixing the right fitness and the right contrast between characters. Even at the end, when the earlier pretender, Lambert Simnel, who contentedly serves the King (Henry VII) in the humble capacity of falconer, is brought forward to plead with Perkin to accept a similar destiny, the scene is not degrading, but simply serves to emphasize the nobility and constancy of the hero. But to make a man who went down to history as an impostor into a heroic figure was not Ford's only difficulty and success. The King of Scotland, in order to demonstrate his faith, and emphasize his support, of Perkin Warbeck's claim to the English throne, gives him to wife his own niece, the Lady Katherine Gordon, very much against her father's wishes. To make a lady so abruptly given away to a stranger and dedicated to such very doubtful fortunes into not only a loyal but a devoted wife, is not easy; but Ford succeeds. The introduction of her admirer, her countryman Lord Dalyell, does not disturb the effect, for Katherine is not shown as having already reciprocated his affection. Dalyell is merely present as a reminder of the kind of happy and suitable marriage which Katherine would have made in her own country but for the appearance of Warbeck and the caprice of the King;

and his touching devotion to her cause throughout the action only exhibits more beautifully her own devotion to her husband. Ford for once succeeded in a most difficult attempt; and the play of *Perkin Warbeck* is almost flawless.

Of Ford's other plays, *Love's Sacrifice* is reprinted in the "Mermaid" selection. It has a few fine scenes, but is disfigured by all the faults of which Ford was capable. In the complete editions—the Moxon edition with introduction (to Ford and Massinger) by Hartley Coleridge is obtainable, and there is also the edition of the Quarto texts published at the University of Louvain, the first volume edited by the late Professor Bang, and the second (1927) by Professor De Vocht—there are no other plays solely by Ford which retain any interest. It is difficult now to assent to Lamb's words, "Ford was of the first order of poets," or to Mr. Havelock Ellis's attempt (in his excellent introduction to the "Mermaid" volume) to present Ford as a modern man and a psychologist. Mr. Ellis makes the assertion that Ford is nearer to Stendhal and Flaubert than he is to Shakespeare. Ford, nevertheless, depended upon Shakespeare; but it would be truer to say that Shakespeare is nearer to Stendhal and Flaubert than he is to Ford. There is a very important distinction to be drawn at this point. Stendhal and Flaubert, and to them might be added Balzac, are analysts of the individual soul as it is found in a particular phase of society; and in their work is found as much sociology as individual psychology. Indeed, the two are aspects of one thing; and the greater French novelists, from Stendhal to Proust, chronicle the rise, the régime, and the decay of the upper bourgeoisie in France. In Elizabethan and Jacobean drama, and even in the comedy of Congreve and Wycherley, there is almost no analysis of the particular society of the times, except in so far as it records the rise of the City families, and their ambition to ally themselves with needy peerages and to acquire country estates. Even that rise of the City, in *Eastward Hoe* and *Michaelmas Terme*, is treated lightly as a foible of the age, and not as a symptom of social decay and change. It is indeed in the lack of this sense of a "changing world," of corruptions and abuses peculiar to their own time, that the Elizabethan and Jacobean dramatists are blessed. We feel that they believed in their own age, in a way in which no nineteenth- or twentieth-century writer of the greatest seriousness has been able to believe in his age. And accepting their age, they were in a position to concentrate their attention, to their respective abilities, upon the common characteristics of humanity in all ages, rather than upon the differences. We can partly criticize their age through our study of them, but they did not so criticize it themselves. In the work of Shakespeare as a whole, there is to be read the profoundest and indeed one of the most sombre studies of humanity that has ever been made in poetry; though it is in fact so comprehensive that we cannot qualify it as a whole as either glad or sorry. We recognize the same assumption of permanence in his minor fellows. Dante held it also, and the great Greek dramatists. In periods of unsettlement and change we do not observe this: it was a changing world which met the eyes of Lucian or of Petronius. But in the kind of analysis in which Shakespeare was supreme the other Elizabethan and Jacobean dramatists differed only in degree and in comprehensiveness.

Such observations are not made in order to cast doubt upon the ultimate value or the permanence of the greatest nineteenth-century fiction. But for the age in which Shakespeare lived and the age into which his influence extended after his death, it must be his work, and his work as a whole, that is our criterion. The whole of Shakespeare's work is *one* poem; and it is the poetry of it in this sense, not the poetry of isolated lines and passages or the poetry of the single figures which he created, that matters most. A man might, hypothetically, compose any number of fine passages or even of whole poems which would each give satisfaction, and yet not be a great poet, unless we felt them to be united by one significant, consistent, and developing personality. Shakespeare is the one, among all his contemporaries, who fulfils these conditions; and the nearest to him is Marlowe. Jonson and Chapman have the consistency, but a far lower degree of significant development; Middleton and Webster take a lower place than these; the author of *The Revenger's Tragedy*, whether we call him Tourneur or Middleton or another, accomplishes all that can be accomplished within the limits of a single play. But in all these dramatists there is the essential, as well as the superficies, of poetry; they give the pattern, or we may say the undertone, of the personal emotion, the personal drama and struggle, which no biography, however full and intimate, could give us; which nothing can give us but our experience of the plays themselves. Ford, as well as Fletcher, wrote enough plays for us to see the absence of essential poetry. Ford's poetry, as well as Beaumont and Fletcher's, is of the surface: that is to say, it is the result of the stock of expressions of feeling accumulated by the greater men. It is the absence of purpose—if we may use the word "purpose" for something more profound than any formulable purpose can be —in such dramatists as Ford, Beaumont, Fletcher, Shirley, and later Otway, and still later Shelley, which makes their drama tend towards mere sensationalism. Many reasons might be found, according to the particular historical aspect from which we consider the problem. But Ford, as dramatic poet, as writer of dramatic blank verse, has one quality which assures him of a higher place than even Beaumont and Fletcher; and that is a quality which any poet may envy him. The varieties of cadence and tone in blank verse are none too many, in the history of English verse; and Ford, though intermittently, was able to manipulate sequences of words in blank verse in a manner which is quite his own.

PHILIP MASSINGER

—————

MASSINGER has been more fortunately and more fairly judged than several of his greater contemporaries. Three critics have done their best by him: the notes of Coleridge exemplify Coleridge's fragmentary and fine perceptions; the essay of Leslie Stephen is a piece of formidable destructive analysis; and the essay of Swinburne is Swinburne's criticism at its best. None of these, probably, has put Massinger finally and irrefutably into a place.

English criticism is inclined to argue or persuade rather than to state; and, instead of forcing the subject to expose himself, these critics have left in their work an undissolved residuum of their own good taste, which, however impeccable, is something that requires our faith. The principles which animate this taste remain unexplained. Canon Cruickshank's book [1] is a work of scholarship; and the advantage of good scholarship is that it presents us with evidence which is an invitation to the critical faculty of the reader: it bestows a method, rather than a judgment.

It is difficult—it is perhaps the supreme difficulty of criticism —to make the facts generalize themselves; but Mr. Cruickshank at least presents us with facts which are capable of generalization. This is a service of value; and it is therefore wholly a compliment to the author to say that his appendices are as valuable as the essay itself.

The sort of labour to which Mr. Cruickshank has devoted himself is one that professed critics ought more willingly to undertake. It is an important part of criticism, more important

[1] *Philip Massinger.* By A. H. Cruickshank. Oxford: Blackwell. 1920.

than any mere expression of opinion. To understand Elizabethan drama it is necessary to study a dozen playwrights at
once, to dissect with all care the complex growth, to ponder
collaboration to the utmost line. Reading Shakespeare and several of his contemporaries is pleasure enough, perhaps all the
pleasure possible, for most. But if we wish to consummate and
refine this pleasure by understanding it, to distil the last drop
of it, to press and press the essence of each author, to apply
exact measurement to our own sensations, then we must compare; and we cannot compare without parcelling the threads of
authorship and influence. We must employ Mr. Cruickshank's
judgments; and perhaps the most important judgment to which
he has committed himself is this:

"Massinger, in his grasp of stagecraft, his flexible metre, his
desire in the sphere of ethics to exploit both vice and virtue, is
typical of an age which had much culture, but which, without
being exactly corrupt, lacked moral fibre."

Here, in fact, is our text: to elucidate this sentence would
be to account for Massinger. We begin vaguely with good taste,
by a recognition that Massinger is inferior: can we trace this
inferiority, dissolve it, and have left any element of merit?

We turn first to the parallel quotations from Massinger and
Shakespeare collocated by Mr. Cruickshank to make manifest
Massinger's indebtedness. One of the surest of tests is the way
in which a poet borrows. Immature poets imitate; mature poets
steal; bad poets deface what they take, and good poets make
it into something better, or at least something different. The
good poet welds his theft into a whole of feeling which is
unique, utterly different from that from which it was torn; the
bad poet throws it into something which has no cohesion. A
good poet will usually borrow from authors remote in time,
or alien in language, or diverse in interest. Chapman borrowed
from Seneca; Shakespeare and Webster from Montaigne. The
two great followers of Shakespeare, Webster and Tourneur,
in their mature work do not borrow from him; he is too close
to them to be of use to them in this way. Massinger, as Mr.
Cruickshank shows, borrows from Shakespeare a good deal.
Let us profit by some of the quotations with which he has provided us—

MASSINGER:

> *Can I call back yesterday, with all their aids*
> *That bow unto my sceptre? or restore*
> *My mind to that tranquillity and peace*
> *It then enjoyed?*

SHAKESPEARE:

> *Not poppy, nor mandragora,*
> *Nor all the drowsy syrops of the world*
> *Shall ever medicine thee to that sweet sleep*
> *Which thou owedst yesterday.*

Massinger's is a general rhetorical question, the language just and pure, but colourless. Shakespeare's has particular significance; and the adjective "drowsy" and the verb "medicine" infuse a precise vigour. This is, on Massinger's part, an echo, rather than an imitation or a plagiarism—the basest, because least conscious form of borrowing. "Drowsy syrop" is a condensation of meaning frequent in Shakespeare, but rare in Massinger.

MASSINGER:

> *Thou didst not borrow of Vice her indirect,*
> *Crooked, and abject means.*

SHAKESPEARE:

> *God knows, my son;*
> *By what by-paths and indirect crook'd ways*
> *I met this crown.*

Here, again, Massinger gives the general forensic statement, Shakespeare the particular image. "Indirect crook'd" is forceful in Shakespeare; a mere pleonasm in Massinger. "Crook'd ways" is a metaphor; Massinger's phrase only the ghost of a metaphor.

MASSINGER:

> *And now, in the evening,*
> *When thou should'st pass with honour to thy rest,*
> *Wilt thou fall like a meteor?*

SHAKESPEARE:

> *I shall fall*
> *Like a bright exhalation in the evening,*
> *And no man see me more.*

Here the lines of Massinger have their own beauty. Still, a
"bright exhalation" appears to the eye and makes us catch our
breath in the evening; "meteor" is a dim simile; the word is
worn.

MASSINGER:

> *What you deliver to me shall be lock'd up*
> *In a strong cabinet, of which you yourself*
> *Shall keep the key.*

SHAKESPEARE:

> *'Tis in my memory locked,*
> *And you yourself shall keep the key of it.*

In the preceding passage Massinger had squeezed his simile
to death, here he drags it round the city at his heels; and how
swift Shakespeare's figure is! We may add two more passages,
not given by our commentator; here the model is Webster.
They occur on the same page, an artless confession.

> *Here he comes,*
> *His nose held up; he hath something in the wind,*

is hardly comparable to

The Cardinal lifts up his nose like a foul porpoise before a storm,

and when we come upon

> *as tann'd galley-slaves*
> *Pay such as do redeem them from the oar*

it is unnecessary to turn up the great lines in the *Duchess of
Malfy*. Massinger fancied this galley-slave; for he comes with
his oar again in *The Bondman*—

> *Never did galley-slave shake off his chains,*
> *Or looked on his redemption from the oar. . . .*

Now these are mature plays; and *The Roman Actor* (from which we have drawn the two previous extracts) is said to have been the preferred play of its author.

We may conclude directly from these quotations that Massinger's feeling for language had outstripped his feeling for things; that his eye and his vocabulary were not in co-operation. One of the greatest distinctions of several of his elder contemporaries—we name Middleton, Webster, Tourneur—is a gift for combining, for fusing into a single phrase, two or more diverse impressions.

> *. . . in her strong toil of grace*

of Shakespeare is such a fusion; the metaphor identifies itself with what suggests it; the resultant is one and is unique—

> *Does the silk worm* expend *her* yellow labours? *. . .*
> *Why does yon fellow* falsify highways
> *And lays his life between the judge's lips*
> *To* refine *such a one? keeps horse and men*
> *To* beat their valours *for her?*
>
> *Let the common sewer take it from distinction. . . .*
> *Lust and forgetfulness have been amongst us. . . .*

These lines of Tourneur and of Middleton exhibit that perpetual slight alteration of language, words perpetually juxtaposed in new and sudden combinations, meanings perpetually *eingeschachtelt* into meanings, which evidences a very high development of the senses, a development of the English language which we have perhaps never equalled. And, indeed, with the end of Chapman, Middleton, Webster, Tourneur, Donne we end a period when the intellect was immediately at the tips of the senses. Sensation became word and word was sensation. The next period is the period of Milton (though still with a Marvell in it); and this period is initiated by Massinger.

It is not that the word becomes less exact. Massinger is, in a wholly eulogistic sense, choice and correct. And the decay of the senses is not inconsistent with a greater sophistication of language. But every vital development in language is a development of feeling as well. The verse of Shakespeare and the major

Shakespearean dramatists is an innovation of this kind, a true mutation of species. The verse practised by Massinger is a different verse from that of his predecessors; but it is not a development based on, or resulting from, a new way of feeling. On the contrary, it seems to lead us away from feeling altogether.

We mean that Massinger must be placed as much at the beginning of one period as at the end of another. A certain Boyle, quoted by Mr. Cruickshank, says that Milton's blank verse owes much to the study of Massinger's.

"In the indefinable touches which make up the music of a verse [says Boyle], in the artistic distribution of pauses, and in the unerring choice and grouping of just those words which strike the ear as the perfection of harmony, there are, if we leave Cyril Tourneur's *Atheist's Tragedy* out of the question, only two masters in the drama, Shakespeare in his latest period and Massinger."

This Boyle must have had a singular ear to have preferred Tourneur's secondary work to his *Revenger's Tragedy*, and one must think that he had never glanced at Ford. But though the appraisal be ludicrous, the praise is not undeserved. Mr. Cruickshank has given us an excellent example of Massinger's syntax—

> *What though my father*
> *Writ man before he was so, and confirm'd it,*
> *By numbering that day no part of his life*
> *In which he did not service to his country;*
> *Was he to be free therefore from the laws*
> *And ceremonious form in your decrees?*
> *Or else because he did as much as man*
> *In those three memorable overthrows,*
> *At Granson, Morat, Nancy, where his master,*
> *The warlike Charalois, with whose misfortunes*
> *I bear his name, lost treasure, men, and life,*
> *To be excused from payment of those sums*
> *Which (his own patrimony spent) his zeal*
> *To serve his country forced him to take up!*

It is impossible to deny the masterly construction of this passage; perhaps there is not one living poet who could do the like. It is impossible to deny the originality. The language is pure and correct, free from muddiness or turbidity. Massinger does not confuse metaphors, or heap them one upon another. He is lucid, though not easy. But if Massinger's age, "without being exactly corrupt, lacks moral fibre," Massinger's verse, without being exactly corrupt, suffers from cerebral anaemia. To say that an involved style is necessarily a bad style would be preposterous. But such a style should follow the involutions of a mode of perceiving, registering, and digesting impressions which is also involved. It is to be feared that the feeling of Massinger is simple and overlaid with received ideas. Had Massinger had a nervous system as refined as that of Middleton, Tourneur, Webster, or Ford, his style would be a triumph. But such a nature was not at hand, and Massinger precedes, not another Shakespeare, but Milton.

Massinger is, in fact, at a further remove from Shakespeare than that other precursor of Milton—John Fletcher. Fletcher was above all an opportunist, in his verse, in his momentary effects, never quite a pastiche; in his structure ready to sacrifice everything to the single scene. To Fletcher, because he was more intelligent, less will be forgiven. Fletcher had a cunning guess at feelings, and betrayed them; Massinger was unconscious and innocent. As an artisan of the theatre he is not inferior to Fletcher, and his best tragedies have an honester unity than *Bonduca*. But the unity is superficial. In *The Roman Actor* the development of parts is out of all proportion to the central theme; in *The Unnatural Combat*, in spite of the deft handling of suspense and the quick shift from climax to a new suspense, the first part of the play is the hatred of Malefort for his son and the second part is his passion for his daughter. It is theatrical skill, not an artistic conscience arranging emotions, that holds the two parts together. In *The Duke of Milan* the appearance of Sforza at the Court of his conqueror only delays the action, or rather breaks the emotional rhythm. And we have named three of Massinger's best.

A dramatist who so skilfully welds together parts which have no reason for being together, who fabricates plays so well knit and so remote from unity, we should expect to exhibit the same synthetic cunning in character. Mr. Cruickshank, Coleridge, and Leslie Stephen are pretty well agreed that Massinger is no master of characterization. You can, in fact, put together heterogeneous parts to form a lively play; but a character, to be living, must be conceived from some emotional unity. A character is not to be composed of scattered observations of human nature, but of parts which are felt together. Hence it is that although Massinger's failure to draw a moving character is no greater than his failure to make a whole play, and probably springs from the same defective sensitiveness, yet the failure in character is more conspicuous and more disastrous. A "living" character is not necessarily "true to life." It is a person whom we can see and hear, whether he be true or false to human nature as we know it. What the creator of character needs is not so much knowledge of motives as keen sensibility; the dramatist need not understand people; but he must be exceptionally aware of them. This awareness was not given to Massinger. He inherits the traditions of conduct, female chastity, hymeneal sanctity, the fashion of honour, without either criticizing or informing them from his own experience. In the earlier drama these conventions are merely a framework, or an alloy necessary for working the metal; the metal itself consisted of unique emotions resulting inevitably from the circumstances, resulting or inhering as inevitably as the properties of a chemical compound. Middleton's heroine, for instance, in *The Changeling,* exclaims in the well-known words—

> *Why, 'tis impossible thou canst be so wicked,*
> *To shelter such a cunning cruelty*
> *To make his death the murderer of my honour!*

The word "honour" in such a situation is out of date, but the emotion of Beatrice at that moment, given the conditions, is as permanent and substantial as anything in human nature. The emotion of Othello in Act V is the emotion of a man who discovers that the worst part of his own soul has been exploited by some one more clever than he; it is this emotion carried by the writer to a very high degree of intensity. Even in so late and so decayed a drama as that of Ford, the framework of emotions and morals of the time is only the vehicle for statements of feeling which are unique and imperishable: Ford's and Ford's only.

What may be considered corrupt or decadent in the morals of Massinger is not an alteration or diminution in morals; it is simply the disappearance of all the personal and real emotions which this morality supported and into which it introduced a kind of order. As soon as the emotions disappear the morality which ordered it appears hideous. Puritanism itself became repulsive only when it appeared as the survival of a restraint after the feelings which it restrained had gone. When Massinger's ladies resist temptation they do not appear to undergo any important emotion; they merely know what is expected of them; they manifest themselves to us as lubricous prudes. Any age has its conventions; and any age might appear absurd when its conventions get into the hands of a man like Massinger—a man, we mean, of so exceptionally superior a literary talent as Massinger's, and so paltry an imagination. The Elizabethan morality was an important convention; important because it was not consciously of one social class alone, because it provided a framework for emotions to which all classes could respond, and it hindered no feeling. It was not hypocritical, and it did not suppress; its dark corners are haunted by the ghost of Mary Fitton and perhaps greater. It is a subject which has not been sufficiently investigated. Fletcher and Massinger rendered it ridiculous; not by not believing it, but because they were men of great talents who could not vivify it; because they could not fit into it passionate, complete human characters.

The tragedy of Massinger is interesting chiefly according to the definition given before; the highest degree of verbal excellence compatible with the most rudimentary development of the senses. Massinger succeeds better in something which is not tragedy; in the romantic comedy. *A Very Woman* deserves all the praise that Swinburne, with his almost unerring gift of selection, has bestowed upon it. The probable collaboration of Fletcher had the happiest result; for certainly that admirable comic personage, the tipsy Borachia, is handled with more humour than we expect of Massinger. It is a play which would be enjoyable on the stage. The form, however, of romantic comedy is itself inferior and decadent. There is an inflexibility about the poetic drama which is by no means a matter of classical, or neoclassical, or pseudo-classical law. The poetic drama might develop forms highly different from those of Greece or England, India or Japan. Conceded the utmost freedom, the romantic drama would yet remain inferior. The poetic drama must have an emotional unity, let the emotion be whatever you like. It must have a dominant tone; and if this be strong enough, the most heterogeneous emotions may be made to reinforce it. The romantic comedy is a skilful concoction of inconsistent emotion, a *revue* of emotion. *A Very Woman* is surpassingly well plotted. The debility of romantic drama does not depend upon extravagant setting, or preposterous events, or inconceivable coincidences; all these might be found in a serious tragedy or comedy. It consists in an internal incoherence of feelings, a concatenation of emotions which signifies nothing.

From this type of play, so eloquent of emotional disorder, there was no swing back of the pendulum. Changes never come by a simple reinfusion into the form which the life has just left. The romantic drama was not a new form. Massinger dealt not with emotions so much as with the social abstractions of emotions, more generalized and therefore more quickly and easily interchangeable within the confines of a single action. He was not guided by direct communications through the nerves. Romantic drama tended, accordingly, toward what is sometimes called the "typical," but which is not the truly typical; for the *typical* figure in a drama is always particularized—an individual. The tendency of the romantic drama was toward a form which continued it in removing its more conspicuous vices, was toward a more severe external order. This form was the Heroic Drama. We look into Dryden's "Essay on Heroic Plays," and we find that "love and valour ought to be the subject of an heroic poem." Massinger, in his destruction of the old drama, had prepared the way for Dryden. The intellect had perhaps exhausted the old conventions. It was not able to supply the impoverishment of feeling.

Such are the reflections aroused by an examination of some of Massinger's plays in the light of Mr. Cruickshank's statement that Massinger's age "had much more culture, but, without being exactly corrupt, lacked moral fibre." The statement may be supported. In order to fit into our estimate of Massinger the two admirable comedies—*A New Way to Pay Old Debts* and *The City Madam*—a more extensive research would be required than is possible within our limits.

II

Massinger's tragedy may be summarized for the unprepared reader as being very dreary. It is dreary, unless one is prepared by a somewhat extensive knowledge of his livelier contemporaries to grasp without fatigue precisely the elements in it which are capable of giving pleasure; or unless one is incited by a curious interest in versification. In comedy, however, Massinger was one of the few masters in the language. He was a master in a comedy which is serious, even sombre; and in one aspect of it there are only two names to mention with his: those of Marlowe and Jonson. In comedy, as a matter of fact, a greater variety of methods were discovered and employed than in tragedy. The method of Kyd, as developed by Shakespeare, was the standard for English tragedy down to Otway and to Shelley. But both individual temperament, and varying epochs, made more play with comedy. The comedy of Lyly is one thing; that of Shakespeare, followed by Beaumont and Fletcher, is another; and that of Middleton is a third. And Massinger, while he has his own comedy, is nearer to Marlowe and Jonson than to any of these.

Massinger was, in fact, as a comic writer, fortunate in the moment at which he wrote. His comedy is transitional; but it happens to be one of those transitions which contain some merit not anticipated by predecessors or refined upon by later writers. The comedy of Jonson is nearer to caricature; that of Middleton a more photographic delineation of low life. Massinger is nearer to Restoration comedy, and more like his contemporary, Shirley, in assuming a certain social level, certain distinctions of class, as a postulate of his comedy. This resemblance to later comedy is also the important point of difference between Massinger and earlier comedy. But Massinger's comedy differs just as widely from the comedy of manners proper; he is closer to that in his romantic drama—in *A Very Woman*—than in *A New Way to Pay Old Debts*; in his comedy his interest is not in the follies of love-making or the absurdities of social pretence, but in the unmasking of villainy. Just as the Old Comedy of Molière differs in principle from the New Comedy of Marivaux, so the Old Comedy of Massinger differs from the New Comedy of his contemporary Shirley. And as in France, so in England, the more farcical comedy was the more serious. Massinger's great comic rogues, Sir Giles Overreach and Luke Frugal, are members of the large English family which includes Barabas and Sir Epicure Mammon, and from which Sir Tunbelly Clumsy claims descent.

What distinguishes Massinger from Marlowe and Jonson is in the main an inferiority. The greatest comic characters of these two dramatists are slight work in comparison with Shakespeare's best—Falstaff has a third dimension and Epicure Mammon has only two. But this slightness is part of the nature of the art which Jonson practised, a smaller art than Shakespeare's. The inferiority of Massinger to Jonson is an inferiority, not of one type of art to another, but within Jonson's type. It is a simple deficiency. Marlowe's and Jonson's comedies were a view of life; they were, as great literature is, the transformation of a personality into a personal work of art, their lifetime's work, long or short. Massinger is not simply a smaller personality: his personality hardly exists. He did not, out of his own personality, build a world of art, as Shakespeare and Marlowe and Jonson built.

In the fine pages which Remy de Gourmont devotes to Flaubert in his *Problème du Style*, the great critic declares:

"La vie est un dépouillement. Le but de l'activité propre de l'homme est de nettoyer sa personnalité, de la laver de toutes

les souillures qu'y déposa l'éducation, de la dégager de toutes
les empreintes qu'y laissèrent nos admirations adolescentes";

and again:

"Flaubert incorporait toute sa sensibilité à ses œuvres. . . .
Hors de ses livres, où il se transvasait goutte à gouette, jusqu'à
la lie, Flaubert est fort peu intéressant."

Of Shakespeare notably, of Jonson less, of Marlowe (and of
Keats to the term of life allowed him), one can say that they
se transvasaient goutte à gouette; and in England, which has
produced a prodigious number of men of genius and comparatively few works of art, there are not many writers of whom
one can say it. Certainly not of Massinger. A brilliant master of
technique, he was not, in this profound sense, an artist. And so
we come to inquire how, if this is so, he could have written two
great comedies. We shall probably be obliged to conclude that
a large part of their excellence is, in some way which should be
defined, fortuitous; and that therefore they are, however remarkable, not works of perfect art.

This objection raised by Leslie Stephen to Massinger's
method of revealing a villain has great cogency; but I am inclined to believe that the cogency is due to a somewhat different
reason from that which Leslie Stephen assigns. His statement
is too *apriorist* to be quite trustworthy. There is no reason why
a comedy or a tragedy villain should not declare himself, and
in as long a period as the author likes; but the sort of villain
who may run on in this way is a simple villain (simple not
simpliste). Barabas and Volpone can declare their character, because they have no inside; appearance and reality are coinci-
dent; they are forces in particular directions. Massinger's two
villains are not simple. Giles Overreach is essentially a great
force directed upon small objects; a great force; a small mind;
the terror of a dozen parishes instead of the conqueror of a
world. The force is misapplied, attenuated, thwarted, by the
man's vulgarity: he is a great man of the City, without fear,
but with the most abject awe of the aristocracy. He is accordingly not simple, but a product of a certain civilization, and he

is not wholly conscious. His monologues are meant to be, not what he thinks he is, but what he really is: and yet they are not the truth about him, and he himself certainly does not know the truth. To declare himself, therefore, is impossible.

> *Nay, when my ears are pierced with widows' cries,*
> *And undone orphans wash with tears my threshold,*
> *I only think what 'tis to have my daughter*
> *Right honourable; and 'tis a powerful charm*
> *Makes me insensible of remorse, or pity,*
> *Or the least sting of conscience.*

This is the wrong note. Elsewhere we have the right:

> *Thou art a fool;*
> *In being out of office, I am out of danger;*
> *Where, if I were a justice, besides the trouble,*
> *I might or out of wilfulness, or error,*
> *Run myself finely into a praemunire,*
> *And so become a prey to the informer,*
> *No, I'll have none of 't; 'tis enough I keep*
> *Greedy at my devotion: so he serve*
> *My purposes, let him hang, or damn, I care not . . .*

And how well tuned, well modulated, here, the diction! The man is audible and visible. But from passages like the first we may be permitted to infer that Massinger was unconscious of trying to develop a different kind of character from any that Marlowe or Jonson had invented.

Luke Frugal, in *The City Madam*, is not so great a character as Sir Giles Overreach. But Luke Frugal just misses being almost the greatest of all hypocrites. His humility in the first act of the play is more than half real. The error in his portraiture is not the extravagant hocus-pocus of supposed Indian necromancers by which he is so easily duped, but the premature disclosure of villainy in his temptation of the two apprentices of his brother. But for this, he would be a perfect chameleon of circumstance. Here, again, we feel that Massinger was conscious only of inventing a rascal of the old simpler farce type. But the play is not a farce, in the sense in which *The Jew of Malta, The*

Alchemist, Bartholomew Fair are farces. Massinger had not the personality to create great farce, and he was too serious to invent trivial farce. The ability to perform that slight distortion of *all* the elements in the world of a play or a story, so that this world is complete in itself, which was given to Marlowe and Jonson (and to Rabelais) and which is prerequisite to great farce, was denied to Massinger. On the other hand, his temperament was more closely related to theirs than to that of Shirley or the Restoration wits. His two comedies therefore occupy a place by themselves. His ways of thinking and feeling isolate him from both the Elizabethan and the later Caroline mind. He might almost have been a great realist; he is killed by conventions which were suitable for the preceding literary generation, but not for his. Had Massinger been a greater man, a man of more intellectual courage, the current of English literature immediately after him might have taken a different course. The defect is precisely a defect of personality. He is not, however, the only man of letters who, at the moment when a new view of life is wanted, has looked at life through the eyes of his predecessors, and only at manners through his own.

IV

DANTE

═══════

1. THE "INFERNO"

In my own experience of the appreciation of poetry I have always found that the less I knew about the poet and his work, before I began to read it, the better. A quotation, a critical remark, an enthusiastic essay, may well be the accident that sets one to reading a particular author; but an elaborate preparation of historical and biographical knowledge has always been to me a barrier. I am not defending poor scholarship; and I admit that such experience, solidified into a maxim, would be very difficult to apply in the study of Latin and Greek. But with authors of one's own speech, and even with some of those of other modern languages, the procedure is possible. At least, it is better to be spurred to acquire scholarship because you enjoy the poetry, than to suppose that you enjoy the poetry because you have acquired the scholarship. I was passionately fond of certain French poetry long before I could have translated two verses of it correctly. With Dante the discrepancy between enjoyment and understanding was still wider.

I do not counsel any one to postpone the study of Italian grammar until he has read Dante, but certainly there is an immense amount of knowledge which, until one has read some of his poetry with intense pleasure—that is, with as keen pleasure as one is capable of getting from any poetry—is positively undesirable. In saying this I am avoiding two possible extremes of criticism. One might say that understanding of the scheme, the philosophy, the concealed meanings, of Dante's verse was *essential* to appreciation; and on the other hand one might say that these things were quite irrelevant, that the poetry in his poems was one thing, which could be enjoyed by itself without studying a framework which had served the author in producing the poetry but could not serve the reader in enjoying it. The latter error is the more prevalent, and is probably the reason why many people's knowledge of the *Comedy* is limited to the *Inferno,* or even to certain passages in it. The enjoyment of the *Divine Comedy* is a continuous process. If you get nothing out of it at first, you probably never will; but if from your first deciphering of it there comes now and then some direct shock of poetic intensity, nothing but laziness can deaden the desire for fuller and fuller knowledge.

What is surprising about the poetry of Dante is that it is, in one sense, extremely easy to read. It is a test (a positive test, I do not assert that it is always valid negatively) that genuine poetry can communicate before it is understood. The impression can be verified on fuller knowledge; I have found with Dante and with several other poets in languages in which I was unskilled, that about such impressions there was nothing fanciful. They were not due, that is, to *mis*understanding the passage, or to reading into it something not there, or to accidental sentimental evocations out of my own past. The impression was new, and of, I believe, the objective "poetic emotion." There are more detailed reasons for this experience on the first reading of Dante, and for my saying that he is easy to read. I do not mean that he writes very simple Italian, for he does not; or that his content is simple or always simply expressed. It is often expressed with such a force of compression that the elucidation of three lines needs a paragraph, and their allusions a page of commentary. What I have in mind is that Dante is, in a sense to be defined (for the word means little by itself), the most *universal* of poets in the modern languages. That does not mean that he is "the greatest," or that he is the most comprehensive—there is greater variety and detail in Shakespeare. Dante's universality is not solely a personal matter. The Italian language, and especially the Italian language in Dante's age, gains much by being the product of universal Latin. There is something much more *local* about the languages in which Shakespeare and

Racine had to express themselves. This is not to say, either, that English and French are inferior, as vehicles of poetry, to Italian. But the Italian vernacular of the late Middle Ages was still very close to Latin, as literary expression, for the reason that the men, like Dante, who used it, were trained, in philosophy and all abstract subjects, in mediaeval Latin. Now mediaeval Latin is a very fine language; fine prose and fine verse were written in it; and it had the quality of a highly developed and literary Esperanto. When you read modern philosophy, in English, French, German, and Italian, you must be struck by national or racial differences of thought: modern languages *tend* to separate abstract thought (mathematics is now the only universal language); but mediaeval Latin tended to concentrate on what men of various races and lands could think together. Some of the character of this universal language seems to me to inhere in Dante's Florentine speech; and the localization ("Florentine" speech) seems if anything to emphasize the universality, because it cuts across the modern division of nationality. To enjoy any French or German poetry, I think one needs to have some sympathy with the French or German mind; Dante, none the less an Italian and a patriot, is first a European.

This difference, which is one of the reasons why Dante is "easy to read," may be discussed in more particular manifestations. The style of Dante has a peculiar lucidity—a *poetic* as distinguished from an *intellectual* lucidity. The thought may be obscure, but the word is lucid, or rather translucent. In English poetry words have a kind of opacity which is part of their beauty. I do not mean that the beauty of English poetry is what is called mere "verbal beauty." It is rather that words have associations, and the groups of words *in* association have associations, which is a kind of local self-consciousness, because they are the growth of a *particular* civilization; and the same thing is true of other modern languages. The Italian of Dante, though essentially the Italian of today, is not in this way a modern language. The culture of Dante was not of one European country but of Europe. I am aware, of course, of a directness of speech which Dante shares with other great poets of pre-Reformation and pre-Renaissance times, notably Chaucer and Villon.

Undoubtedly there is something in common between the three, so much that I should expect an admirer of any one of them to be an admirer of the others; and undoubtedly there is an opacity, or inspissation of poetic style throughout Europe after the Renaissance. But the lucidity and universality of Dante are far beyond those qualities in Villon and Chaucer, though they are akin.

Dante is "easier to read," for a foreigner who does not know Italian very well, for other reasons: but all related to this central reason, that in Dante's time Europe, with all its dissensions and dirtiness, was mentally more united than we can now conceive. It is not particularly the Treaty of Versailles that has separated nation from nation; nationalism was born long before; and the process of disintegration which for our generation culminates in that treaty began soon after Dante's time. One of the reasons for Dante's "easiness" is the following—but first I must make a digression.

I must explain why I have said that Dante is "easy to read," instead of talking about his "universality." The latter word would have been much easier to use. But I do not wish to be thought to claim a universality for Dante which I deny to Shakespeare or Molière or Sophocles. Dante is no more "universal" than Shakespeare: though I feel that we can come nearer to understanding Dante than a foreigner can come to understanding those others. Shakespeare, or even Sophocles, or even Racine and Molière, are dealing with what is as universally human as the material of Dante; but they had no choice but to deal with it in a more local way. As I have said, the Italian of Dante is very near in feeling to mediaeval Latin: and of the mediaeval philosophers whom Dante read, and who were read by learned men of his time, there were, for instance, St. Thomas who was an Italian, St. Thomas's predecessor Albertus, who was a German, Abelard who was French, and Hugh and Richard of St. Victor who were Scots. For the *medium* that Dante had to use compare the opening of the *Inferno*

> *Nel mezzo del cammin di nostra vita*
> *mi ritrovai per una selva oscura,*
> *che la diritta via era smarrita.*

In the middle of the journey of our life I found myself in a
dark wood, having lost the straight path.

with the lines with which Duncan is introduced to Macbeth's
castle:

> *This castle hath a pleasant seat; the air*
> *Nimbly and sweetly recommends itself*
> *Unto our gentle senses.*
> > *This guest of summer,*
> *The temple-haunting martlet, does approve*
> *By his loved masonry that the heaven's breath*
> *Smells wooingly here: no jutty, frieze,*
> *Buttress, nor coign of vantage, but this bird*
> *Hath made his pendant bed and procreant cradle:*
> *Where they most breed and haunt, I have observed*
> *The air is delicate.*

I do not at all pretend that we appreciate everything, even
in one single line of Dante, that a cultivated Italian can appreciate. But I do maintain that more is lost in translating Shakespeare into Italian than in translating Dante into English. How
can a foreigner find words to convey in his own language just
that combination of intelligibility and remoteness that we get
in many phrases of Shakespeare?

I am not considering whether the language of Dante or
Shakespeare is superior, for I cannot admit the question: I
merely affirm that the differences are such as make Dante easier
for a foreigner. Dante's advantages are not due to greater
genius, but to the fact that he wrote when Europe was still more
or less one. And even had Chaucer or Villon been exact contemporaries of Dante, they would still have been farther,
linguistically as well as geographically, from the centre of Europe than Dante.

But the simplicity of Dante has another detailed reason. He
not only thought in a way in which every man of his culture
in the whole of Europe then thought, but he employed a
method which was common and commonly understood throughout Europe. I do not intend, in this essay, to go into questions

of disputed interpretations of Dante's allegory. What is important for my purpose is the fact that the allegorical method was a definite method not confined to Italy; and the fact, apparently paradoxical, that the allegorical method makes for simplicity and intelligibility. We incline to think of allegory as a tiresome cross-word puzzle. We incline to associate it with dull poems (at best, *The Romance of the Rose*), and in a great poem to ignore it as irrelevant. What we ignore is, in a case like Dante's, its particular effect towards lucidity of style.

I do not recommend, in first reading the first canto of the *Inferno*, worrying about the identity of the Leopard, the Lion, or the She-Wolf. It is really better, at the start, not to know or care what they do mean. What we should consider is not so much the meaning of the images, but the reverse process, that which led a man having an idea to express it in images. We have to consider the type of mind which by nature and *practice* tended to express itself in allegory: and for a competent poet, allegory means *clear visual images*. And clear visual images are given much more intensity by having a meaning—we do not need to know what that meaning is, but in our awareness of the image we must be aware that the meaning is there too. Allegory is only one poetic method, but it is a method which has very great advantages.

Dante's is a *visual* imagination. It is a visual imagination in a different sense from that of a modern painter of still life: it is visual in the sense that he lived in an age in which men still saw visions. It was a psychological habit, the trick of which we have forgotten, but as good as any of our own. We have nothing but dreams, and we have forgotten that seeing visions—a practice now relegated to the aberrant and uneducated—was once a more significant, interesting, and disciplined kind of dreaming. We take it for granted that our dreams spring from below: possibly the quality of our dreams suffers in consequence.

All that I ask of the reader, at this point, is to clear his mind, if he can, of every prejudice against allegory, and to admit at least that it was not a device to enable the uninspired to write verses, but really a mental habit, which when raised to the point of genius can make a great poet as well as a great mystic or saint.

And it is the allegory which makes it possible for the reader who is not even a good Italian scholar to enjoy Dante. Speech varies, but our eyes are all the same. And allegory was not a local Italian custom, but a universal European method.

Dante's attempt is to make us see what he saw. He therefore employs very simple language, and very few metaphors, for allegory and metaphor do not get on well together. And there is a peculiarity about his *comparisons* which is worth noticing in passing.

There is a well-known comparison or simile in the great XVth canto of the *Inferno*, which Matthew Arnold singled out, rightly, for high praise; which is characteristic of the way in which Dante employs these figures. He is speaking of the crowd in Hell who peered at him and his guide under a dim light:

> *e si ver noi aguzzevan le ciglia,*
> *come vecchio sartor fa nella cruna.*

and sharpened their vision (knitted their brows) at us, like an old tailor peering at the eye of his needle.

The purpose of this type of simile is solely to make us see *more definitely* the scene which Dante has put before us in the preceding lines.

> *she looks like sleep,*
> *As she would catch another Antony*
> *In her strong toil of grace.*

The image of Shakespeare's is much more complicated than Dante's, and more complicated than it looks. It has the grammatical form of a kind of simile (the "as if" form), but of course "catch in her toil" is a metaphor. But whereas the simile of Dante is merely to make you see more clearly how the people looked, and is explanatory, the figure of Shakespeare is expansive rather than intensive; its purpose is to *add* to what you see (either on the stage or in your imagination) a reminder of that fascination of Cleopatra which shaped her history and that of the world, and of that fascination being so strong that it prevails even in death. It is more elusive, and it is less possible to convey without close knowledge of the English language.

Between men who could make such inventions as these there can be no question of greater or less. But as the whole poem of Dante is, if you like, one vast metaphor, there is hardly any place for metaphor in the detail of it.

There is all the more reason to acquaint oneself well with Dante's poem first part by part, even dwelling specially on the parts that one likes most at first, because we cannot extract the full significance of any part without knowing the whole. We cannot understand the inscription at Hell Gate:

> *Giustizia mosse il mio alto Fattore;*
> *fecemi la divina Potestate,*
> *la somma Sapienza e il primo Amore.*

Justice moved my high Maker; what made me were the divine Power, the supreme Wisdom, and the primal Love—

until we have ascended to the highest Heaven and returned. But we can understand the first Episode that strikes most readers, that of Paolo and Francesca, enough to be moved by it as much as by any poetry, on the first reading. It is introduced by two similes of the same explanatory nature as that which I have just quoted:

> *E come gli stornei ne portan l'ali,*
> *nel freddo tempo, a schiera larga e piena,*
> *cosi quel fiato gli spiriti mali;*

And as their wings bear along the starlings, at the cold season, in large full troop.

> *E come i gru van cantando lor lai*
> *facendo in aer di sè lunga riga;*
> *cosi vid' io venir, traendo guai,*
> *ombre portate dalla detta briga;*

And as the cranes go chanting their lays, making themselves a long streak in the air, so I saw the wailing shadows come, wailing, carried on the striving wind.

We can see and feel the situation of the two lost lovers, though we do not yet understand the meaning which Dante gives it.

Taking such an episode by itself, we can get as much out of it as we get from the reading of a whole single play of Shakespeare. We do not understand Shakespeare from a single reading, and certainly not from a single play. There is a relation between the various plays of Shakespeare, taken in order; and it is a work of years to venture even one individual interpretation of the pattern in Shakespeare's carpet. It is not certain that Shakespeare himself knew what it was. It is perhaps a larger pattern than Dante's, but the pattern is less distinct. We can read with full comprehension the lines:

> *Noi leggevamo un giorno per diletto*
> *di Lancillotto, come amor lo strinse;*
> *soli eravamo e senza alcun sospetto.*
> *Per più fiate gli occhi ci sospinse*
> *quella lettura, e scolorocci il viso;*
> *ma solo un punto fu quel che ci vinse.*
> *Quando leggemmo il disiato riso*
> *esser baciato da cotanto amante,*
> *questi, che mai da me non fia diviso,*
> *La bocca mi baciò tutto tremante:*

One day, for pastime, we read of Lancelot, how love constrained him; we were alone, and without all suspicion. Several times that reading urged our eyes to meet, and changed the colour of our faces; but one moment alone it was that overcame us. When we read how the fond smile was kissed by such a lover, he, who shall never be divided from me, kissed my mouth all trembling.

When we come to fit the episode into its place in the whole *Comedy*, and see how this punishment is related to all other punishments and to purgations and rewards, we can appreciate better the subtle psychology of the simple line of Francesca:

> *se fosse amico il re dell' universo*

if the King of the Universe were our friend. . . .

or of the line

> *Amor, che a nullo amato amar perdona*

Love, which to no loved one permits excuse for loving. . . .

or indeed of the line already quoted:

questi, che mai da me non fia diviso

he, who shall never be divided from me. . . .

Proceeding through the *Inferno* on a first reading, we get a succession of phantasmagoric but clear images, of images which are coherent, in that each reinforces the last; of glimpses of individuals made memorable by a perfect phrase, like that of the proud Farinata degli Uberti:

ed ei s' ergea col petto e colla fronte,
come avesse lo inferno in gran dispitto.

He rose upright with breast and countenance, as though he entertained great scorn of Hell.

and of particular longer episodes, which remain separately in the memory. I think that among those which impress themselves most at the first reading are the episode of Brunetto Latini (Canto XV), Ulysses (Canto XXVI), Bertrand de Born (Canto XXVIII), Adamo di Brescia (Canto XXX), and Ugolino (Canto XXXIII).

Although I think it would be a mistake to skip, and find it much better to await these episodes until we come to them in due course, they certainly remain in my memory as the parts of the *Inferno* which first convinced me, and especially the Brunetto and the Ulysses episodes, for which I was unprepared by quotation or allusion. And the two may well be put together: for the first is Dante's testimony of a loved master of arts, the second his reconstruction of a legendary figure of ancient epic; yet both have the quality of *surprise* which Poe declared to be essential to poetry. This *surprise*, at its highest, could by nothing be better illustrated than by the final lines with which Dante dismisses the damned master whom he loves and respects:

Poi si rivolse, e parve di coloro
che coronno a Verona il drappo verde

per la campagna; e parve di costoro
quegli che vince e non colui che perde.

*Then he turned, and seemed like one of those who run for the
green cloth at Verona through the open field; and of them he
seemed like him who wins, and not like him who loses.*

One does not need to know anything about the race for the
roll of green cloth, to be *hit* by these lines; and in making Brunetto, so fallen, *run like the winner*, a quality is given to the
punishment which belongs only to the greatest poetry. So
Ulysses, unseen in the hornèd wave of flame,

> *Lo maggior corno della fiamma antica*
> *cominciò a crollarsi mormorando,*
> *pur come quella cui vento affatica.*
> *Indi la cima qua e là menando,*
> *come fosse la lingua che parlasse,*
> *gittò voce di fuori e disse: "Quando*
> *mi diparti' da Circe, che sottrasse*
> *me più d'un anno la presso a Gaeta. . . ."*

*The greater horn of the ancient flame began to shake itself mur-
muring, like a flame struggling against the wind. Then moving
to and fro the peak, as though it were the tongue that spoke,
threw forth a voice and said: "When I left Circe, who kept me
more than a year there near Gaeta. . . ."*

is a creature of the pure poetic imagination, apprehensible apart
from place and time and the scheme of the poem. The Ulysses
episode may strike us first as a kind of excursion, an irrelevance, a self-indulgence on the part of Dante taking a holiday
from his Christian scheme. But when we know the whole poem,
we recognize how cunningly and convincingly Dante has made
to fit in real men, his contemporaries, friends, and enemies,
recent historical personages, legendary and Biblical figures, and
figures of ancient fiction. He has been reproved or smiled at for
satisfying personal grudges by putting in Hell men whom he
knew and hated; but these, as well as Ulysses, are transformed
in the whole; for the real and the unreal are all representative

of types of sin, suffering, fault, and merit, and all become of the same reality and contemporary. The Ulysses episode is particularly "readable," I think, because of its continuous straightforward narrative, and because to an English reader the comparison with Tennyson's poem—a perfect poem at that—is very instructive. It is worth while noticing the greatly superior degree of *simplification* of Dante's version. Tennyson, like most poets, like most even of those whom we can call great poets, has to get his effect with a certain amount of *forcing*. Thus the line about the sea which

> *moans round with many voices,*

a true specimen of Tennyson-Virgilianism, is too *poetical* in comparison with Dante, to be the highest poetry. (Only Shakespeare can be so "poetical" without giving any effect of overloading, or distracting us from the main issue:

> *Put up your bright swords or the dew will rust them.*)

Ulysses and his shipmates pass through the pillars of Hercules, that "narrow pass"

> *ov' Ercole segnò li suoi riguardi*
> *acciochè l'uom più oltre non si metta.*

where Hercules set his marks, so that man should pass no farther.

> *"O frati," dissi, "che per cento milia*
> *perigli siete giunti all' occidente,*
> *a questa tanto picciola vigilia*
> *de' vostri sensi, ch' è del rimanente,*
> *non vogliate negar l'esperienza*
> *di retro al sol, del mondo senza gente.*
> *Considerate la vostra semenza,*
> *fatti non foste a viver come bruti*
> *ma per seguir virtute e conoscenza."*

"O brothers!" I said, "who through a hundred thousand dangers have reached the West, deny not, to this so brief vigil of your senses that remains, experience of the world without men

*that lies behind the sun. Consider your nature, you were made
not to live like beasts, but to pursue virtue and knowledge."*

They fare forth until suddenly

*n'apparve una montagna bruna
per la distanza, e parvemi alta tanto
quanto veduta non n'aveva alcuna.
Noi ci allegrammo, e tosto tornò in pianto,
chè dalla nuova terra un turbo nacque,
e percosse del legno il primo canto.
Tre volte il fe' girar con tutte l'acque,
alla quarta levar la poppa in suso,
e la prora ire in giù, com' altrui piacque,
infin che il mar fu sopra noi richiuso.*

*there appeared a mountain brown in the distance; and it seemed
to me the highest that I had ever seen. We rejoiced, but soon
our joy was turned to lamentation: for a storm came up from
the new land, and caught the stem of our ship. Three times it
whirled her round with all the waters; the fourth time it heaved
up the stern and drove her down at the head, as pleased Another; until the sea closed over us.*

The story of Ulysses, as told by Dante, reads like a straightforward piece of romance, a well told seaman's yarn; Tennyson's Ulysses is primarily a very self-conscious poet. But Tennyson's poem is flat, it has only two dimensions; there is nothing
more in it than what the average Englishman, with a feeling
for verbal beauty, can see. We do not need, at first, to know
what mountain the mountain was, or what the words mean *as
pleased Another*, to feel that Dante's sense has further depths.

It is worth pointing out again how very right was Dante to
introduce among his historical characters at least one character who even to him could hardly have been more than a fiction.
For the *Inferno* is relieved from any question of pettiness or
arbitrariness in Dante's selection of damned. It reminds us that
Hell is not a place but a *state;* that man is damned or blessed
in the creatures of his imagination as well as in men who have
actually lived; and that Hell, though a state, is a state which

can only be thought of, and perhaps only experienced, by the projection of sensory images; and that the resurrection of the body has perhaps a deeper meaning than we understand. But these are such thoughts as come only after many readings; they are not necessary for the first poetic enjoyment.

The experience of a poem is the experience both of a moment and of a lifetime. It is very much like our intenser experiences of other human beings. There is a first, or an early moment which is unique, of shock and surprise, even of terror (*Ego dominus tuus*); a moment which can never be forgotten, but which is never repeated integrally; and yet which would become destitute of significance if it did not survive in a larger whole of experience; which survives inside a deeper and a calmer feeling. The majority of poems one outgrows and outlives, as one outgrows and outlives the majority of human passions: Dante's is one of those which one can only just hope to grow up to at the end of life.

The last canto (XXXIV) is probably the most difficult on first reading. The vision of Satan may seem grotesque, especially if we have fixed in our minds the curly-haired Byronic hero of Milton; it too like a Satan in a fresco in Siena. Certainly no more than the Divine Spirit can the Essence of Evil be confined in one form and place; and I confess that I tend to get from Dante the impression of a Devil suffering like the human damned souls; whereas I feel that the *kind* of suffering experienced by the Spirit of Evil should be represented as utterly different. I can only say that Dante made the best of a bad job. In putting Brutus, the noble Brutus, and Cassius with Judas Iscariot he will also disturb at first the English reader, for whom Brutus and Cassius must always be the Brutus and Cassius of Shakespeare: but if my justification of Ulysses is valid, then the presence of Brutus and Cassius is also. If any one is repelled by the last canto of the *Inferno*, I can only ask him to wait until he has read and lived for years with the last canto of the *Paradiso*, which is to my thinking the highest point that poetry has ever reached or ever can reach, and in which Dante amply repairs any failure of Canto XXXIV of the *Inferno;*

but perhaps it is better, on our first reading of the *Inferno,* to omit the last canto and return to the beginning:

Per me si va nella città dolente;
  per me si va nell' eterno dolore;
  per me si va tra la perduta gente.
Giustizia mosse il mio alto Fattore;
  fecemi la divina Potestate,
  la somma Sapienza e il primo Amore.

II. THE "PURGATORIO" AND THE "PARADISO"

For the science or art of writing verse, one has learned from the *Inferno* that the greatest poetry can be written with the greatest economy of words, and with the greatest austerity in the use of metaphor, simile, verbal beauty, and elegance. When I affirm that more can be learned about how to write poetry from Dante than from any English poet, I do not at all mean that Dante's way is the only right way, or that Dante is thereby *greater* than Shakespeare or, indeed, any other English poet. I put my meaning into other words by saying that Dante can do less *harm* to any one trying to learn to write verse than can Shakespeare. Most great English poets are *inimitable* in a way in which Dante was not. If you try to imitate Shakespeare you will certainly produce a series of stilted, forced, and violent distortions of language. The language of each great English poet is his own language; the language of Dante is the perfection of a common language. In a sense, it is more pedestrian than that of Dryden or Pope. If you follow Dante without talent, you will at worst be pedestrian and flat; if you follow Shakespeare or Pope without talent, you will make an utter fool of yourself.

But if one has learned this much from the *Inferno,* there are other things to be learnt from the two successive divisions of the poem. From the *Purgatorio* one learns that a straightforward philosophical statement can be great poetry; from the *Paradiso*, that more and more rarefied and remote *states of beatitude* can be the material for great poetry. And gradually we come to admit that Shakespeare understands a greater extent and variety of human life than Dante; but that Dante understands deeper degrees of degradation and higher degrees of exaltation. And a further wisdom is reached when we see clearly that this indicates the equality of the two men.

On the one hand, the *Purgatorio* and the *Paradiso* belong, in the way of understanding, together. It is apparently easier to accept damnation as poetic material than purgation or beatitude; less is involved that is strange to the modern mind. I insist that the full meaning of the *Inferno* can only be extracted after appreciation of the two later parts, yet it has sufficient meaning in and by itself for the first few readings. Indeed, the *Purgatorio* is, I think, the most difficult of the three parts. It cannot be enjoyed by itself like the *Inferno*, nor can it be enjoyed merely as a sequel to the *Inferno*; it requires appreciation of the *Paradiso* as well; which means that its first reading is arduous and apparently unremunerative. Only when we have read straight through to the end of the *Paradiso*, and re-read the *Inferno*, does the *Purgatorio* begin to yield its beauty. Damnation and even blessedness are more exciting than purgation.

By compensation, the *Purgatorio* has a few episodes which, so to speak, "let us up" (as the counterpart to letting down) more easily than the rest, from the *Inferno*. We must not stop to orient ourselves in the new astronomy of the Mount of Purgatory. We must linger first with the shades of Casella and Manfred slain, and especially Buonconte and La Pia, those whose souls were saved from Hell only at the last moment.

> "*Io fui di Montefeltro, io son Buonconte;*
>   *Giovanna o altri non ha di me cura;*
>   *perch' io vo tra costor con bassa fronte.*"
> *Ed io a lui:* "*Qual forza o qual ventura*
>   *ti traviò si fuor di Campaldino*
>   *che non si seppe mai tua sepoltura?*"

"Oh," rispos' egli, "a piè del Casentino
traversa un' acqua che ha nome l'Archiano,
che sopra l'Ermo nasce in Apennino.
Dove il vocabol suo diventa vano
arriva' io forato nella gola,
fuggendo a piede e sanguinando il piano.
Quivi perdei la vista, e la parola
nel nome di Maria finii: e quivi
caddi, e rimase la mia carne sola."

"I was of Montefeltro, I am Buonconte; neither Giovanna nor any other has care of me, wherefore I go with these, with lowered brow." I said to him: *"What force or chance led you so far away from Campaldino that your place of sepulture has always been unknown?"* *"Oh,"* said he, *"at the foot of Casentino a stream crosses, which is called Archiano, and rises in the Apennines above the Hermitage. There, where its name is lost, came I, jabbed in the throat, fleeing on foot, dripping blood over the plain. There my sight left me, and I ended speech with [crying on] the name of Mary. There I fell, and my flesh alone remained."*

When Buonconte ends his story, the third spirit speaks:

"Deh, quando tu sarai tornato al mondo,
e riposato della lunga via,"
seguito il terzo spirito al secondo,
"ricorditi di me, che son la Pia;
Siena mi fe', disfecemi Maremma:
salsi colui che innanellata, pria
disposando, m'avea con la sua gemma."

"O pray, when you return to the world, and are rested from your long journey," followed the third spirit after the second, *"remember me, who am La Pia. Siena made me, Maremma unmade me: this is known to him who after due engagement wedded me with his ring."*

The next episode that impresses the reader coming fresh

from the *Inferno* is the meeting with Sordello the poet (Canto VI), the soul who appeared

> *altera e disdegnosa*
> *e nel mover degli occhi onesta e tarda!*

proud and disdainful, superb and slow in the movement of his eyes!

> *E il dolce duca incominciava:*
> *"Mantova"* . . . *e l'ombra, tutta in sè romita,*
> *surse ver lui del loco ove pria stava,*
> *dicendo: "O Mantovano, io son Sordello*
> *della tua terra." E l'un l'altro abbracciava.*

The gentle guide (Virgil) began: "Mantua" . . . *and the shade, suddenly rapt, leapt towards him from the place where first it was, saying, "O Mantuan, I am Sordello of thy very soil." And the one embraced the other.*

The meeting with Sordello *a guisa di leon quando si posa,* like a couchant lion, is no more affecting than that with the poet Statius, in Canto XXI. Statius, when he recognizes his master Virgil, stoops to clasp his feet, but Virgil answers—the lost soul speaking to the saved:

> *"Frate,*
> *non far, chè tu se' ombra, ed ombra vedi."*
> *Ed ei surgendo: Or puoi la quantitate*
> *comprender dell' amor ch' a te mi scalda,*
> *quando dismento nostra vanitate,*
> *trattando l'ombre come cosa salda."*

"Brother! refrain, for you are but a shadow, and a shadow is but what you see." Then the other, rising: "Now can you understand the quantity of love that warms me towards you, so that I forget our vanity, and treat the shadows like the solid thing."

The last "episode" at all comparable to those of the *Inferno* is the meeting with Dante's predecessors, Guido Guinizelli and Arnaut Daniel (Canto XXVI). In this canto the Lustful are purged in flame, yet we see clearly how the flame of purgatory differs from that of hell. In hell, the torment issues from the

very nature of the damned themselves, expresses their essence;
they writhe in the torment of their own perpetually perverted
nature. In purgatory the torment of flame is deliberately and
consciously accepted by the penitent. When Dante approaches
with Virgil these souls in purgatory flame, they crowd towards
him:

> *Poi verso me, quanto potevan farsi,*
> *certi si feron, sempre con riguardo*
> *di non uscir dove non fossero arsi.*

*Then certain of them made towards me, so far as they could, but
ever watchful not to come so far that they should* not be in the
fire.

The souls in purgatory suffer because they *wish to suffer,* for
purgation. And observe that they suffer more actively and
keenly, being souls preparing for blessedness, than Virgil suffers
in eternal limbo. In their suffering is hope, in the anaesthesia of
Virgil is hopelessness; that is the difference. The canto ends
with the superb verses of Arnaut Daniel in his Provençal
tongue:

> *"Ieu sui Arnaut, que plor e vau cantan;*
> *consiros vei la passada folor,*
> *e vei jausen lo jorn, qu' esper, denan.*
> *Ara vos prec, per aquella valor*
> *que vos guida al som de l'escalina,*
> *sovegna vos a temps de ma dolor."*
> Poi s' ascose nel foco che gli affina.

*"I am Arnold, who weeps and goes singing. I see in thought all
the past folly. And I see with joy the day for which I hope, before me. And so I pray you, by that Virtue which leads you to
the topmost of the stair—be mindful in due time of my pain."
Then dived he back into that fire which refines them.*

These are the high episodes, to which the reader initiated by
the *Inferno* must first cling, until he reaches the shore of Lethe,
and Matilda, and the first sight of Beatrice. In the last cantos
(XXIX-XXXIII) of the *Purgatorio* we are already in the
world of the *Paradiso*.

But in between these episodes is the narrative of the ascent of the Mount, with meetings, visions, and philosophical expositions, all important, and all difficult for the uninstructed reader who finds it less exciting than the continuous phantasmagoria of the *Inferno*. The allegory in the *Inferno* was easy to swallow or ignore, because we could, so to speak, grasp the concrete end of it, its solidification into imagery; but as we ascend from Hell to Heaven we are more and more required to grasp the whole from idea to image.

Here I must make a diversion, before tackling a specifically philosophical passage of the *Purgatorio*, concerning the nature of Belief. I wish merely to indicate certain tentative conclusions of my own, which might affect one's reading of the *Purgatorio*.

Dante's debt to St. Thomas Aquinas, like his debt (a much smaller one) to Virgil, can be easily exaggerated; for it must not be forgotten that Dante read and made use of other great mediaeval philosophers as well. Nevertheless, the question of how much Dante took from Aquinas and how much from elsewhere is one which has been settled by others and is not relevant to my present essay. But the question of what Dante "believed" is always relevant. It would not matter, if the world were divided between those persons who are capable of taking poetry simply for what it is and those who cannot take it at all; if so, there would be no need to talk about this question to the former and no use in talking about it to the latter. But most of us are somewhat impure and apt to confuse issues: hence the justification of writing books about books, in the hope of straightening things out.

My point is that you cannot afford to *ignore* Dante's philosophical and theological beliefs, or to skip the passages which express them most clearly; but that on the other hand you are not called upon to believe them yourself. It is wrong to think that there are parts of the *Divine Comedy* which are of interest only to Catholics or to mediaevalists. For there is a difference (which here I hardly do more than assert) between philosophical *belief* and poetic *assent*. I am not sure that there is not as great a difference between philosophical belief and scientific belief; but that is a difference only now beginning to appear, and

certainly inapposite to the thirteenth century. In reading Dante
you must enter the world of thirteenth-century Catholicism:
which is not the world of modern Catholicism, as his world of
physics is not the world of modern physics. You are not called
upon to believe what Dante believed, for your belief will not
give you a groat's worth more of understanding and appreciation; but you are called upon more and more to understand it.
If you can read poetry as poetry, you will "believe" in Dante's
theology exactly as you believe in the physical reality of his
journey; that is, you suspend both belief and disbelief. I will
not deny that it may be in practice easier for a Catholic to grasp
the meaning, in many places, than for the ordinary agnostic; but
that is not because the Catholic believes, but because he has been
instructed. It is a matter of knowledge and ignorance, not of
belief or scepticism. The vital matter is that Dante's poem is a
whole; that you must in the end come to understand every part
in order to understand any part.

Furthermore, we can make a distinction between what Dante
believes as a poet and what he believed as a man. Practically, it
is hardly likely that even so great a poet as Dante could have
composed the *Comedy* merely with understanding and without
belief; but his private belief becomes a different thing in becoming poetry. It is interesting to hazard the suggestion that this is
truer of Dante than of any other philosophical poet. With
Goethe, for instance, I often feel too acutely "this is what
Goethe the man believed," instead of merely entering into a
world which Goethe has created; with Lucretius also; less with
the *Bhagavad-Gita*, which is the next greatest philosophical
poem to the *Divine Comedy* within my experience. That is the
advantage of a coherent traditional system of dogma and morals
like the Catholic: it stands apart, for understanding and assent
even without belief, from the single individual who propounds
it. Goethe always arouses in me a strong sentiment of disbelief
in what he believes: Dante does not. I believe that this is because
Dante is the purer poet, not because I have more sympathy
with Dante the man than Goethe the man.

We are not to take Dante for Aquinas or Aquinas for Dante.
It would be a grievous error in psychology. The *belief attitude*

of a man reading the *Summa* must be different from that of a man reading Dante, even when it is the same man, and that man a Catholic.

It is not necessary to have read the *Summa* (which usually means, in practice, reading some handbook) in order to understand Dante. But it is necessary to read the philosophical passages of Dante with the humility of a person visiting a new world, who admits that every part is essential to the whole. What is necessary to appreciate the poetry of the *Purgatorio* is not belief, but suspension of belief. Just as much effort is required of any modern person to accept Dante's allegorical method, as is required of the agnostic to accept his theology.

When I speak of understanding, I do not mean merely knowledge of books or words, any more than I mean belief: I mean a state of mind in which one sees certain beliefs, as the order of the deadly sins, in which treachery and pride are greater than lust, and despair the greatest, as *possible*, so that we suspend our judgment altogether.

In the XVIth Canto of the *Purgatorio* we meet Marco Lombardo, who discourses at some length on the Freedom of the Will, and on the Soul:

> *Esce di mano a lui, che la vagheggia*
> *prima che sia, a giusa di fanciulla*
> *che piangendo e ridendo pargoleggia,*
> *l'anima semplicetta, che sa nulla,*
> *salvo che, mossa da lieto fattore,*
> *volentier torna a ciò che la trastulla.*
> *Di picciol bene in pria sente sapore;*
> *quivi s'inganna, e retro ad esso corre,*
> *se guida o fren non torce suo amore.*
> *Onde convenne legge per fren porre;*
> *convenne regge aver, che discernesse*
> *della vera cittade almen la torre.*

From the hands of Him who loves her before she is, there issues like a little child that plays, with weeping and laughter, the simple soul, that knows nothing except that, come from the hands of a glad creator, she turns willingly to everything that delights her. First she tastes the flavour of a trifling good; then is beguiled, and pursues it, if neither guide nor check withhold her. Therefore laws were needed as a curb; a ruler was needed, who should at least see afar the tower of the true City.

Later (Canto XVII) it is Virgil himself who instructs Dante in the nature of Love:

> *"Nè creator nè creatura mai,"*
> *cominciò ei, "figiuol, fu senza amore,*
> *o naturale o d'animo; e tu il sai.*
> *Lo natural è sempre senza errore,*
> *ma l'altro puote errar per malo obbietto,*
> *o per poco o per troppo di vigore.*
> *Mentre ch' egli è ne' primi ben diretto,*
> *e ne' secondi sè stesso misura,*
> *esser non può cagion di mal diletto;*
> *ma, quando al mal si torce, o con più cura*
> *o con men che non dee corre nel bene,*
> *contra il fattore adopra sua fattura.*
> *Quinci comprender puoi ch' esser conviene*
> *amor sementa in voi d' ogni virtute,*
> *e d' ogni operazion che merta pene.*

He began: "neither Creator, nor creature, my son, was ever without love, either natural or rational: and you know it. The natural is always without error; but the other may err through mistaking the object, or through excess or deficiency of force. While it is directed towards the primal goods, and in the secondary moderates itself, it cannot be the cause of delight of sin; but when turned to evil, or hurries towards the good with more or less solicitude than is right, then the creature works against the Creator. Accordingly you may understand how Love must be the seed in you both of every virtue and of every act that merits punishment."

I have quoted these two passages at some length, because they are of the sort that a reader might be inclined to skip, thinking that they are only for scholars, not for readers of poetry, or thinking that it is necessary to have studied the philosophy un-

derlying them. It is not necessary to have traced the descent of
this theory of the soul from Aristotle's *De Anima* in order to
appreciate it as poetry. Indeed, if we worry too much about it
at first as philosophy we are likely to prevent ourselves from
receiving the poetic beauty. It is the philosophy of that world
of poetry which we have entered.

But with the XXVIIth canto we have left behind the stage
of punishment and the stage of dialectic, and approach the state
of Paradise. The last cantos have the quality of the *Paradiso*
and prepare us for it; they move straightforward, with no de-
tour or delay. The three poets, Virgil, Statius, and Dante, pass
through the wall of flame which separates Purgatory from the
Earthly Paradise. Virgil dismisses Dante, who henceforth shall
proceed with a higher guide, saying:

> *Non aspettar mio dir più, nè mio cenno.*
> *Libero, dritto e sano è tuo arbitrio,*
> *e fallo fora non fare a suo senno:*
> *per ch'io te sopra te corono e mitrio.*

*No more expect my word, or sign. Your Will is free, straight
and whole, and not to follow its direction would be sin: wherefore I crown and mitre you (king and bishop) over yourself.*

I.e. Dante has now arrived at a condition, for the purposes of
the rest of his journey, which is that of the blessed: for political and ecclesiastical organization are only required because of
the imperfections of the human will. In the Earthly Paradise
Dante encounters a lady named Matilda, whose identity need
not at first bother us,

> *una donna soletta, che si gia*
> *cantando ed iscegliendo fior da fiore,*
> *ond' era pinta tutta la sua via.*

*A lady alone, who went singing and plucking flower after flower,
wherewith her path was pied.*

After some conversation and explanation by Matilda of the reason and nature of the place, there follows a "Divine Pageant."
To those who dislike—not what are popularly called pageants—

but the serious pageants of royalty, of the church, of military funerals—the "pageantry" which we find here and in the *Paradiso* will be tedious; and still more to those, if there be any, who are unmoved by the splendour of the Revelations of St. John. It belongs to the world of what I call the *high dream*, and the modern world seems capable only of the *low dream*. I arrived at accepting it, myself, only with some difficulty. There were at least two prejudices, one against pre-Raphaelite imagery, which was natural to one of my generation, and perhaps affects generations younger than mine. The other prejudice—which affects this end of the *Purgatorio* and the whole of the *Paradiso*—is the prejudice that poetry not only must be found *through* suffering but can find its material only *in* suffering. Everything else was cheerfulness, optimism, and hopefulness; and these words stood for a great deal of what one hated in the nineteenth century. It took me many years to recognize that the states of improvement and beatitude which Dante describes are still further from what the modern world can conceive as cheerfulness, than are his states of damnation. And little things put one off: Rossetti's *Blessed Damozel*, first by my rapture and next by my revolt, held up my appreciation of Beatrice by many years.

We cannot understand fully Canto XXX of the *Purgatorio* until we know the *Vita Nuova*, which in my opinion should be read after the *Divine Comedy*. But at least we can begin to understand how skilfully Dante expresses the recrudescence of an ancient passion in a new emotion, in a new situation, which comprehends, enlarges, and gives a meaning to it.

> *sopra candido vel cinta d'oliva*
> > *donna m'apparve, sotto verde manto,*
> > *vestita di color di fiamma viva.*
> *E lo spirito mio, che già cotanto*
> > *tempo era stato che alla sua presenza*
> > *non era di stupor, tremando, affranto,*
> *senza degli occhi aver più conoscenza,*
> > *per occulta virtù che da lei mosse,*
> > *d'antico amor sentì la gran potenza.*

Tosto che nella vista mi percosse
l'alta virtù, che già m'avea trafitto
primo ch'io fuor di puerizia fosse,
volsemi alla sinistra col rispitto
col quale il fantolin corre alla mamma,
quando ha paura o quando egli è afflito,
per dicere a Virgilio: "Men che dramma
di sangue m' è rimaso, che non tremi;
conosco i segni dell' antica fiamma."

Olive-crowned over a white veil, a lady appeared to me, clad under a green mantle in colour of living flame. And my spirit, after so many years since trembling in her presence it had been broken with awe, without further knowledge by my eyes, felt, through hidden power which went out from her, the great strength of the old love. As soon as that lofty power struck my sense, which already had transfixed me before my adolescence, I turned leftwards with the trust of the little child who runs to his mama when he is frightened or distressed, to say to Virgil: "Hardly a drop of blood in my body does not shudder: I know the tokens of the ancient flame."

And in the dialogue that follows we see the passionate conflict of the old feelings with the new; the effort and triumph of a new renunciation, greater than renunciation at the grave, because a renunciation of feelings that persist beyond the grave. In a way, these cantos are those of the greatest *personal* intensity in the whole poem. In the *Paradiso* Dante himself, save for the Cacciaguida episode, becomes de- or super-personalized; and it is in these last cantos of the *Purgatorio*, rather than in the *Paradiso*, that Beatrice appears most clearly. But the Beatrice theme is essential to the understanding of the whole, *not* because we need to know Dante's biography—not, for instance, as the Wesendonck history is supposed to cast light upon *Tristan* —but because of Dante's *philosophy* of it. This, however, concerns more our examination of the *Vita Nuova*.

The *Purgatorio* is the most difficult because it is the *transitional* canto: the *Inferno* is one thing, comparatively easy; the *Paradiso* is another thing, more difficult as a whole than the

Purgatorio, because more a whole. Once we have got the hang of the kind of feeling in it no one part is difficult. The *Purgatorio,* here and there, might be called "dry": the *Paradiso* is never dry, it is either incomprehensible or intensely exciting. With the exception of the episode of Cacciaguida—a pardonable exhibition of family and personal pride, because it provides splendid poetry—it is not episodic. All the other characters have the best credentials. At first, they seem less distinct than the earlier unblessed people; they seem ingeniously varied but fundamentally monotonous variations of insipid blessedness. It is a matter of gradual adjustment of our vision. We have (whether we know it or not) a prejudice against beatitude as material for poetry. The eighteenth and nineteenth centuries knew nothing of it; even Shelley, who knew Dante well and who towards the end of his life was beginning to profit by it, the one English poet of the nineteenth century who could even have begun to follow those footsteps, was able to enounce the proposition that our sweetest songs are those which sing of saddest thought. The early work of Dante might confirm Shelley; the *Paradiso* provides the counterpart, though a different counterpart from the philosophy of Browning.

The *Paradiso* is not monotonous. It is as various as any poem. And take the *Comedy* as a whole, you can compare it to nothing but the *entire* dramatic work of Shakespeare. The comparison of the *Vita Nuova* with the *Sonnets* is another, and interesting, occupation. Dante and Shakespeare divide the modern world between them; there is no third.

We should begin by thinking of Dante fixing his gaze on Beatrice:

> *Nel suo aspetto tal dentro mi fei,*
>   *qual si fe' Glauco nel gustar dell' erba,*
>   *che il fe' consorto in mar degli altri dei.*
> *Trasumanar significar per verba*
>   *non si poria; pero l'esemplo basti*
>   *a cui esperienza grazia serba.*

Gazing on her, so I became within, as did Glaucus, on tasting of the grass which made him sea-fellow of the other gods. To transcend humanity may not be told in words, wherefore let the instance suffice for him for whom that experience is reserved by Grace.

And as Beatrice says to Dante: *"You make yourself dull with false fancy"*; warns him, that here there are divers sorts of blessedness, as settled by Providence.

If this is not enough, Dante is informed by Piccarda (Canto III) in words which even those who know no Dante know:

> *la sua voluntade è nostra pace.*

His will is our peace.

It is the mystery of the inequality, and of the indifference of that inequality, in blessedness, of the blessed. It is all the same, and yet each degree differs.

Shakespeare gives the greatest *width* of human passion; Dante the greatest altitude and greatest depth. They complement each other. It is futile to ask which undertook the more difficult job. But certainly the "difficult passages" in the *Paradiso* are Dante's difficulties rather than ours: his difficulty in making us apprehend sensuously the various states and stages of blessedness. Thus the long oration of Beatrice about the Will (Canto IV) is really directed at making us *feel* the reality of the condition of Piccarda; Dante has to educate our senses as he goes along. The insistence throughout is upon states of feeling; the reasoning takes only its proper place as a means of reaching these states. We get constantly verses like

> *Beatrice mi guardò con gli occhi pieni*
> *di faville d' amor cosi divini,*
> *che, vinta, mia virtù diedi le reni,*
> *e quasi mi perdei con gli occhi chini.*

Beatrice looked on me with eyes so divine filled with sparks of love, that my vanquished power turned away, and I became as lost, with downcast eyes.

The whole difficulty is in admitting that this is something that we are meant to feel, not merely decorative verbiage. Dante gives us every aid of images, as when

Come in peschiera, ch' è tranquilla e pura,
traggonsi i pesci a ciò che vien di fuori
per modo che lo stiman lor pastura;
sì vid' io ben più di mille splendori
trarsi ver noi, ed in ciascun s'udia:
Ecco che crescerà li nostri amori.

As in a fishpond still and clear, the fishes draw near to anything
that falls from without in such a way as to make them think it
something to eat, so I saw more than a thousand splendours
draw towards us, and in each was heard: Lo! here is one that
shall increase our loves.

About the persons whom Dante meets in the several spheres,
we need only to enquire enough to consider why Dante placed
them where he did.

When we have grasped the strict *utility* of the minor images,
such as the one given above, or even the simple comparison admired by Landor:

> *Quale alledetta che in aere si spazia*
> *primo cantando, e poi tace contenta*
> *dell' ultima dolcezza che la sazia,*

Like the lark which soars in the air, first singing, and then
ceases, content with the last sweetness that sates her,

we may study with respect the more elaborate imagery, such as
that of the figure of the Eagle composed by the spirits of the just,
which extends from Canto XVIII onwards for some space. Such
figures are not merely antiquated rhetorical devices, but serious
and practical means of making the spiritual visible. An understanding of the rightness of such imagery is a preparation for
apprehending the last and greatest canto, the most tenuous and
most intense. Nowhere in poetry has experience so remote from
ordinary experience been expressed so concretely, by a masterly
use of that imagery of *light* which is the form of certain types
of mystical experience.

> *Nel suo profondo vidi che s'interna,*
> *legato con amore in un volume,*
> *ciò che per l'universo si squaderna;*

sustanzia ed accidenti, e lor costume,
quasi conflati insieme per tal modo,
che ciò ch' io dico è un semplice lume.
La forma universal di questo nodo
credo ch' io vidi, perchè più di largo,
dicendo questo, mi sento ch' io godo.
Un punto solo m'è maggior letargo,
che venticinque secoli alla impresa,
che fe' Nettuno ammirar l'ombra d'Argo.

Within its depths I saw ingathered, bound by love in one mass,
the scattered leaves of the universe: substance and accidents and
their relations, as though together fused, so that what I speak of
is one simple flame. The universal form of this complex I think
I saw, because, as I say this, more largely I feel myself rejoice.
One single moment to me is more lethargy than twenty-five cen-
turies upon the enterprise which made Neptune wonder at the
shadow of the Argo (passing over him).

One can feel only awe at the power of the master who could
thus at every moment realize the inapprehensible in visual
images. And I do not know anywhere in poetry more authentic
sign of greatness than the power of association which could in
the last line, when the poet is speaking of the Divine vision,
yet introduce the Argo passing over the head of wondering
Neptune. Such association is utterly different from that of
Marino speaking in one breath of the beauty of the Magdalen
and the opulence of Cleopatra (so that you are not quite sure
what adjectives apply to which). It is the real right thing, the
power of establishing relations between beauty of the most
diverse sorts; it is the utmost power of the poet.

O quanto è corto il dire, e come fioco
al mio concetto!

How scant the speech, and how faint, for my conception!

In writing of the *Divine Comedy* I have tried to keep to a
few very simple points of which I am convinced. First that the
poetry of Dante is the one universal school of style for the

writing of poetry in any language. There is much, naturally, which can profit only those who write Dante's own Tuscan language; but there is no poet in any tongue—not even in Latin or Greek—who stands so firmly as a model for all poets. I tried to illustrate his universal mastery in the use of images. In the actual writing I went so far as to say that he is safer to follow, even for us, than any English poet, including Shakespeare. My second point is that Dante's "allegorical" method has great advantages for the writing of *poetry:* it simplifies the diction, and makes clear and precise the images. That in good allegory, like Dante's, it is not necessary to understand the meaning first to enjoy the poetry, but that our enjoyment of the poetry makes us want to understand the meaning. And the third point is that the *Divine Comedy* is a complete scale of the *depths* and *heights* of human emotion; that the *Purgatorio* and *Paradiso* are to be read as extensions of the ordinarily very limited human range. Every degree of the feeling of humanity, from lowest to highest, has, moreover, an intimate relation to the next above and below, and all fit together according to the logic of sensibility.

I have only now to make certain observations on the *Vita Nuova*, which may also amplify what I have suggested about the mediaeval mind expressed in allegory.

NOTE TO SECTION II

The theory of poetic belief and understanding here employed for a particular study is similar to that maintained by Mr. I. A. Richards (see his *Practical Criticism*, pp. 179 ff. and pp. 271 ff.). I say "similar," because my own *general* theory is still embryonic, and Mr. Richards's also is capable of much further development. I cannot therefore tell how far the similarity extends; but for those who are interested in the subject, I should point out one respect in which my view differs from that of Mr. Richards; and then proceed to qualify my own tentative conclusions.

I am in agreement with Mr. Richards's statement on p. 271 (*op. cit.*). I agree for the reason that if you hold any contradictory theory you deny, I believe, the existence of "literature" as well as of "literary criticism." We may raise the question whether "literature" exists; but for certain purposes, such as the purpose of this essay on Dante, we must assume that there is literature and literary appreciation; we must assume that the reader can obtain the full "literary" or (if you will) "aesthetic" enjoyment without sharing the beliefs of the author. *If* there is "literature," *if* there is "poetry," then it must be possible to have full literary or poetic appreciation without sharing the beliefs of the poet. That is as far as my thesis goes in the present essay. It may be argued whether there is literature, whether there is poetry, and whether there is any meaning in the term "full appreciation." But I have assumed for this essay that these things exist and that these terms are understood.

I deny, in short, that the reader must share the beliefs of the poet in order to enjoy the poetry fully. I have also asserted that we can distinguish between Dante's beliefs as a man and his beliefs as a poet. But we are forced to believe that there is a particular relation between the two, and that the poet "means what he says." If we learned, for instance, that *De Rerum Natura* was a Latin exercise which Dante had composed for relaxation after completing the *Divine Comedy*, and published under the name of one Lucretius, I am sure that our capacity for enjoying either poem would be mutilated. Mr. Richards's statement (*Science and Poetry*, p. 76 footnote) that a certain writer has effected "a complete severance between his poetry and *all* beliefs" is to me incomprehensible.

If you deny the theory that full poetic appreciation is possible without belief in what the poet believed, you deny the existence of "poetry" as well as "criticism"; and if you push this denial to its conclusion, you will be forced to admit that there is very little poetry that you can appreciate, and that your appreciation of it will be a function of your philosophy or theology or something else. If, on the other hand, I push *my* theory to the extreme, I find myself in as great a difficulty. I am quite aware of the ambiguity of the word "understand." In one sense, it means to understand without believing, for unless you can understand a view of life (let us say) without believing in it, the word "understand" loses all meaning, and the act of choice between one view and another is reduced to caprice. But if you yourself are convinced of a certain view of life, then you irresistibly and inevitably believe that if any one else comes to "understand" it fully, his understanding *must* terminate in belief. It is possible, and sometimes necessary, to argue that full understanding must identify itself with full belief. A good deal, it thus turns out, hangs on the meaning, if any, of this short word *full*.

In short, both the view I have taken in this essay, and the view which contradicts it, are, if pushed to the end, what I call heresies (not, of course, in the theological, but in a more general sense). Each is true only within a limited field of discourse, but unless you limit fields of discourse, you can have no discourse at all. Orthodoxy can only be found in such contradictions, though it must be remembered that a pair of contradictions may *both* be false, and that not all pairs of contradictions make up a truth.

And I confess to considerable difficulty, in analysing my own feelings, a difficulty which makes me hesitate to accept Mr. Richards's theory of "pseudo-statements." On reading the line which he uses,

Beauty is truth, truth beauty . . .

I am at first inclined to agree with him, because this statement of equivalence means nothing to me. But on re-reading the whole Ode, this line strikes me as a serious blemish on a beautiful poem; and the reason must be either that I fail to understand it, or that it is a statement which is untrue. And I suppose that Keats meant something by it, however remote his truth and his beauty may have been from these words in ordinary use. And I am sure that he would have repudiated any explanation of the line which called it a pseudo-statement. On the other hand the line I have often quoted of Shakespeare,

Ripeness is all,

or the line I have quoted of Dante,

la sua voluntade è nostra pace,

strikes very differently on my ear. I observe that the propositions in these words are very different in kind, not only from that of Keats, but from each other. The statement of Keats seems to me meaningless: or perhaps, the fact that it is grammatically meaningless conceals another meaning from me. The statement of Shakespeare seems to me to have profound emotional meaning, with, at least, no literal fallacy. And the statement of Dante seems to me *literally true*. And I confess that it has more beauty for me now, when my own experience has deepened its meaning, than it did when I first read it. So I can only conclude that I cannot, in practice, wholly separate my poetic appreciation from my personal beliefs. Also that the distinction between a statement and a pseudo-statement is not always, in particular instances, possible to establish. The theory of Mr. Richards is, I believe, incomplete until he defines the species of religious, philosophical, scientific, and other beliefs, as well as that of "everyday" belief.

I have tried to make clear some of the difficulties inhering in my own theory. Actually, one probably has more pleasure in the poetry when one shares the beliefs of the poet. On the other hand there is a distinct pleasure in enjoying poetry as poetry when one does *not* share the beliefs, analogous to the pleasure of "mastering" other men's philosophical systems. It would appear that "literary appreciation" is an abstraction, and pure poetry a phantom; and that both in creation and enjoyment much always enters which is, from the point of view of "Art," irrelevant.

III. THE "VITA NUOVA"

All of Dante's "minor works" are important, because they are works of Dante; but the *Vita Nuova* has a special importance, because it does more than any of the others help us to a fuller understanding of the *Divine Comedy*. I do not suggest that the others may be neglected; the *Convivio* is important, and also the *De Volgari Eloquio:* and every part of Dante's writings can give us some light on other parts. But the *Vita Nuova* is a youthful work, in which some of the method and design, and explicitly the intention, of the *Divine Comedy* are shown. Because it is an immature work, it requires some knowledge of the masterpiece to understand; and at the same time helps particularly towards understanding of the *Comedy*.

A great deal of scholarship has been directed upon examination of the early life of Dante, in connexion with the *Vita Nuova*. Critics may be roughly divided into those who regard it as primarily biographical, and those who regard it as primarily allegorical. It is much easier for the second group to make a good case than for the first. If this curious medley of verse and prose is biographical, then the biography has unquestionably been manipulated almost out of recognition to fit into conventional forms of allegory. The imagery of much of it is certainly in a very ancient tradition of vision literature: just as the scheme of the *Divine Comedy* has been shown to be closely similar to similar supernatural peregrination stories in Arabic and in old Persian literature—to say nothing of the descents of Ulysses and Aeneas—so there are parallels to the visions of the *Vita Nuova* such as the *Shepherd of Hermas* in Greek. And as the book is obviously not a literal statement, whether of vision or delusion, it is easy to make out a case for its being an entire allegory: for asserting, that is, that Beatrice is merely a personification of an abstract virtue, intellectual or moral.

I wish to make clear that my own opinions are opinions founded only upon reading the text. I do not think that they are such as can either be verified or refuted by scholars; I mean to restrict my comments to the unprovable and the irrefutable.

It appears likely, to any one who reads the *Vita Nuova* without prejudice, that it is a mixture of biography and allegory; but a mixture according to a recipe not available to the modern mind. When I say the "modern mind," I mean the minds of those who have read or could have read such a document as

Rousseau's *Confessions*. The modern mind can understand the
"confession," that is, the literal account of oneself, varying only
in degree of sincerity and self-understanding, and it can understand "allegory" in the abstract. Nowadays "confessions,"
of an insignificant sort, pour from the press; every one *met son
cœur à nu,* or pretends to; "personalities" succeed one another
in interest. It is difficult to conceive of an age (of many ages)
when human beings cared somewhat about the salvation of the
"soul," but not about each other as "personalities." Now Dante,
I believe, had experiences which seemed to him of some importance; not of importance because they had happened to
him and because he, Dante Alighieri, was an important person
who kept press-cutting bureaux busy; but important in themselves; and therefore they seemed to him to have some philosophical and impersonal value. I find in it an account of a particular kind of experience: that is, of something which had actual experience (the experience of the "confession" in the modern sense) *and* intellectual and imaginative experience (the experience of thought and the experience of dream) as its materials; and which became a third kind. It seems to me of importance to grasp the simple fact that the *Vita Nuova* is neither
a "confession" nor an "indiscretion" in the modern sense, nor
is it a piece of Pre-Raphaelite tapestry. If you have that sense
of intellectual and spiritual realities that Dante had, then a
form of expression like the *Vita Nuova* cannot be classed either
as "truth" or "fiction."

In the first place, the type of sexual experience which Dante
describes as occurring to him at the age of nine years is by no
means impossible or unique. My only doubt (in which I found
myself confirmed by a distinguished psychologist) is whether
it could have taken place so *late* in life as the age of nine years.
The psychologist agreed with me that it is more likely to
occur at about five or six years of age. It is possible that Dante
developed rather late, and it is also possible that he altered the
dates to employ some other significance of the number nine. But
to me it appears obvious that the *Vita Nuova* could only have
been written around a personal experience. If so, the details do
not matter: whether the lady was the Portinari or not, I do not

care; it is quite as likely that she is a blind for some one else, even for a person whose name Dante may have forgotten or never known. But I cannot find it incredible that what has happened to others should have happened to Dante with much greater intensity.

The same experience, described in Freudian terms, would be instantly accepted as fact by the modern public. It is merely that Dante, quite reasonably, drew other conclusions and used another mode of expression, which arouses incredulity. And we are inclined to think—as Remy de Gourmont, for once misled by his prejudices into the pedantic attitude, thought—that if an author like Dante follows closely a form of vision that has a long history, it proves that the story is mere allegory (in the modern sense) or fake. I find a much greater difference in sensibility between the *Vita Nuova* and the *Shepherd of Hermas* than Gourmont did. It is not at all the simple difference between the genuine and the fraud; it is a difference in mind between the humble author of early Christian times and the poet of the thirteenth century, perhaps as great as that between the latter and ourselves. The similarities might prove that a certain *habit* in dream-imagery can persist throughout many changes of civilization. Gourmont would say that Dante borrowed; but that is imputing our own mind to the thirteenth century. I merely suggest that possibly Dante, in his place and time, was following something more essential than merely a "literary" tradition.

The attitude of Dante to the fundamental experience of the *Vita Nuova* can only be understood by accustoming ourselves to find meaning in *final causes* rather than in origins. It is not, I believe, meant as a description of what he *consciously* felt on his meeting with Beatrice, but rather as a description of what that meant on mature reflection upon it. The final cause is the attraction towards God. A great deal of sentiment has been spilt, especially in the eighteenth and nineteenth centuries, upon idealizing the reciprocal feelings of man and woman towards each other, which various realists have been irritated to denounce: this sentiment ignoring the fact that the love of man and woman (or for that matter of man and man) is only explained and made reasonable by the higher love, or else is simply the coupling of animals.

Let us entertain the theory that Dante, meditating on the astonishment of an experience at such an age, which no subsequent experience abolished or exceeded, found meanings in it which we should not be likely to find ourselves. His account is then just as reasonable as our own; and he is simply prolonging the experience in a different direction from that which we, with different mental habits and prejudices, are likely to take.

We cannot, as a matter of fact, understand the *Vita Nuova* without some saturation in the poetry of Dante's Italian contemporaries, or even in the poetry of his Provençal predecessors. Literary parallels are most important, but we must be on guard not to take them in a purely literary and literal way. Dante wrote more or less, at first, like other poets, not simply because he had read their works, but because his modes of feeling and thought were much like theirs. As for the Provençal poets, I have not the knowledge to read them at first hand. That mysterious people had a religion of their own which was thoroughly and painfully extinguished by the Inquisition; so that we hardly know more about them than about the Sumerians. I suspect that the difference between this unknown, and possibly maligned, Albigensianism and Catholicism has some correspondence with the difference between the poetry of the Provençal school and the Tuscan. The system of Dante's organization of sensibility—the contrast between higher and lower carnal love, the transition from Beatrice living to Beatrice dead, rising to the Cult of the Virgin, seems to me to be his own.

At any rate, the *Vita Nuova*, besides being a sequence of beautiful poems connected by a curious vision-literature prose, is, I believe, a very sound psychological treatise on something related to what is now called "sublimation." There is also a practical sense of realities behind it, which is antiromantic: not to expect more from *life* than it can give or more from *human* beings than they can give; to look to *death* for what life cannot give. The *Vita Nuova* belongs to "vision literature"; but its philosophy is the Catholic philosophy of disillusion.

Understanding of the book is greatly advanced by acquaint-

ance with Guido Guinicelli, Cavalcanti, Cino, and others.
One ought, indeed, to study the development of the art of love
from the Provençal poets onwards, paying just attention to
both resemblances and differences in spirit; as well as the development of verse form and stanza form and vocabulary. But
such study is vain unless we have first made the conscious
attempt, as difficult and hard as rebirth, to pass through the
looking-glass into a world which is just as reasonable as our own.
When we have done that, we begin to wonder whether the
world of Dante is not both larger and more solid than our own.
When we repeat

Tutti li miei penser parlan d'Amore

we must stop to think what *amore* means—something different
from its Latin original, its French equivalent, or its definition in
a modern Italian dictionary.

It is, I repeat, for several reasons necessary to read the
Divine Comedy first. The first reading of the *Vita Nuova* gives
nothing but Pre-Raphaelite quaintness. The *Comedy* initiates
us into the world of mediaeval imagery, in the *Inferno* most
apprehensible, in the *Paradiso* most rarefied. It initiates us also
into the world of mediaeval thought and dogma: far easier for
those who have had the college discipline of Plato and Aristotle, but possible even without that. The *Vita Nuova* plunges
us direct into mediaeval sensibility. It is not, for Dante, a masterpiece, so that it is safer for us to read it, the first time, for the
light it can throw on the *Comedy* than for itself.

Read in this way, it can be more useful than a dozen com-
mentaries. The effect of many books about Dante is to give the
impression that it is more necessary to read about him than to
read what he has written. But the next step after reading Dante
again and again should be to read some of the books that he
read, rather than modern books about his work and life and
times, however good. We may easily be distracted by following
up the histories of Emperors and Popes. With a poet like Shakespeare, we are less likely to ignore the text for the commentary. With Dante there is just as much need for concentrating
on the text, and all the more because Dante's mind is more re-

mote from the ways of thinking and feeling in which we have been brought up. What we need is not information but knowledge: the first step to knowledge is to recognize the differences between his form of thought and feeling and ours. Even to attach great importance to Thomism, or to Catholicism, may lead us astray, in attracting us too much to such differences as are entirely capable of intellectual formulation. The English reader needs to remember that even had Dante not been a good Catholic, even had he treated Aristotle or Thomas with sceptical indifference, his mind would still be no easier to understand; the forms of imagination, phantasmagoria, and sensibility would be just as strange to us. We have to learn to accept these forms: and this *acceptance* is more important than anything that can be called belief. There is almost a definite moment of acceptance at which the New Life begins.

What I have written is, as I promised, not an "introduction" to the study but a brief account of my own introduction to it. In extenuation, it may be observed that to write in this way of men like Dante or Shakespeare is really less presumptuous than to write of smaller men. The very vastness of the subject leaves a possibility that one may have something to say worth saying; whereas with smaller men, only minute and special study is likely to justify writing about them at all.

V

THE METAPHYSICAL POETS

B<small>Y</small> collecting these poems [1] from the work of a generation more often named than read, and more often read than profitably studied, Professor Grierson has rendered a service of some importance. Certainly the reader will meet with many poems already preserved in other anthologies, at the same time that he discovers poems such as those of Aurelian Townshend or Lord Herbert of Cherbury here included. But the function of such an anthology as this is neither that of Professor Saintsbury's admirable edition of Caroline poets nor that of the *Oxford Book of English Verse*. Mr. Grierson's book is in itself a piece of criticism and a provocation of criticism; and we think that he was right in including so many poems of Donne, elsewhere (though not in many editions) accessible, as documents in the case of "metaphysical poetry." The phrase has long done duty as a term of abuse or as the label of a quaint and pleasant taste. The question is to what extent the so-called metaphysicals formed a school (in our own time we should say a "movement"), and how far this so-called school or movement is a digression from the main current.

Not only is it extremely difficult to define metaphysical poetry, but difficult to decide what poets practise it and in which of their verses. The poetry of Donne (to whom Marvell and Bishop King are sometimes nearer than any of the other authors) is late Elizabethan, its feeling often very close to that of Chapman. The "courtly" poetry is derivative from Jonson, who borrowed liberally from the Latin; it expires in the next

[1] *Metaphysical Lyrics and Poems of the Seventeenth Century:* Donne to Butler. Selected and edited, with an Essay, by Herbert J. C. Grierson (Oxford: Clarendon Press. London: Milford).

century with the sentiment and witticism of Prior. There is finally the devotional verse of Herbert, Vaughan, and Crashaw (echoed long after by Christina Rossetti and Francis Thompson); Crashaw, sometimes more profound and less sectarian than the others, has a quality which returns through the Elizabethan period to the early Italians. It is difficult to find any precise use of metaphor, simile, or other conceit, which is common to all the poets and at the same time important enough as an element of style to isolate these poets as a group. Donne, and often Cowley, employ a device which is sometimes considered characteristically "metaphysical"; the elaboration (contrasted with the condensation) of a figure of speech to the farthest stage to which ingenuity can carry it. Thus Cowley develops the commonplace comparison of the world to a chess-board through long stanzas (*To Destiny*), and Donne, with more grace, in *A Valediction*, the comparison of two lovers to a pair of compasses. But elsewhere we find, instead of the mere explication of the content of a comparison, a development by rapid association of thought which requires considerable agility on the part of the reader.

> On a round ball
> A workman that hath copies by, can lay
> An Europe, Afrique, and an Asia,
> And quickly make that, which was nothing, All,
> So doth each teare,
> Which thee doth weare,
> A globe, yea, world by that impression grow,
> Till thy tears mixt with mine doe overflow
> This world, by waters sent from thee, my heaven dissolved so.

Here we find at least two connexions which are not implicit in the first figure, but are forced upon it by the poet: from the geographer's globe to the tear, and the tear to the deluge. On the other hand, some of Donne's most successful and characteristic effects are secured by brief words and sudden contrasts:

> A bracelet of bright hair about the bone,

where the most powerful effect is produced by the sudden contrast of associations of "bright hair" and of "bone." This tele-
scoping of images and multiplied associations is characteristic
of the phrase of some of the dramatists of the period which
Donne knew: not to mention Shakespeare, it is frequent in Middleton, Webster, and Tourneur, and is one of the sources of the
vitality of their language.

Johnson, who employed the term "metaphysical poets," apparently having Donne, Cleveland, and Cowley chiefly in mind,
remarks of them that "the most heterogeneous ideas are yoked
by violence together." The force of this impeachment lies in the
failure of the conjunction, the fact that often the ideas are yoked
but not united; and if we are to judge of styles of poetry by
their abuse, enough examples may be found in Cleveland to
justify Johnson's condemnation. But a degree of heterogeneity
of material compelled into unity by the operation of the poet's
mind is omnipresent in poetry. We need not select for illustration such a line as:

Notre âme est un trois-mâts cherchant son Icarie;

we may find it in some of the best lines of Johnson himself
(*The Vanity of Human Wishes*):

> *His fate was destined to a barren strand,*
> *A petty fortress, and a dubious hand;*
> *He left a name at which the world grew pale,*
> *To point a moral, or adorn a tale.*

where the effect is due to a contrast of ideas, different in degree
but the same in principle, as that which Johnson mildly repre-
hended. And in one of the finest poems of the age (a poem
which could not have been written in any other age), the
Exequy of Bishop King, the extended comparison is used with
perfect success: the idea and the simile become one, in the passage in which the Bishop illustrates his impatience to see his
dead wife, under the figure of a journey:

> *Stay for me there; I will not faile*
> *To meet thee in that hollow Vale.*

And think not much of my delay;
I am already on the way,
And follow thee with all the speed
Desire can make, or sorrows breed.
Each minute is a short degree,
And ev'ry houre a step towards thee.
At night when I betake to rest,
Next morn I rise nearer my West
Of life, almost by eight houres sail,
Than when sleep breath'd his drowsy gale. . . .
But heark! My Pulse, like a soft Drum
Beats my approach, tells Thee *I come;*
And slow howere my marches be,
I shall at last sit down by Thee.

(In the last few lines there is that effect of terror which is several times attained by one of Bishop King's admirers, Edgar Poe.) Again, we may justly take these quatrains from Lord Herbert's Ode, stanzas which would, we think, be immediately pronounced to be of the metaphysical school:

So when from hence we shall be gone,
And be no more, nor you, nor I,
As one another's mystery,
Each shall be both, yet both but one.

This said, in her up-lifted face,
Her eyes, which did that beauty crown,
Were like two starrs, that having faln down,
Look up again to find their place:

While such a moveless silent peace
Did seize on their becalmed sense,
One would have thought some influence
Their ravished spirits did possess.

There is nothing in these lines (with the possible exception of the stars, a simile not at once grasped, but lovely and justified) which fits Johnson's general observations on the metaphysical poets in his essay on Cowley. A good deal resides in the richness of association which is at the same time borrowed from and given to the word "becalmed"; but the meaning is clear, the language simple and elegant. It is to be observed that the language of these poets is as a rule simple and pure; in the verse of George Herbert this simplicity is carried as far as it can go— a simplicity emulated without success by numerous modern poets. The *structure* of the sentences, on the other hand, is sometimes far from simple, but this is not a vice; it is a fidelity to thought and feeling. The effect, at its best, is far less artificial than that of an ode by Gray. And as this fidelity induces variety of thought and feeling, so it induces variety of music. We doubt whether, in the eighteenth century, could be found two poems in nominally the same metre, so dissimilar as Marvell's *Coy Mistress* and Crashaw's *Saint Teresa;* the one producing an effect of great speed by the use of short syllables, and the other an ecclesiastical solemnity by the use of long ones:

> *Love, thou art absolute sole lord*
> *Of life and death.*

If so shrewd and sensitive (though so limited) a critic as Johnson failed to define metaphysical poetry by its faults, it is worth while to inquire whether we may not have more success by adopting the opposite method: by assuming that the poets of the seventeenth century (up to the Revolution) were the direct and normal development of the precedent age; and, without prejudicing their case by the adjective "metaphysical," consider whether their virtue was not something permanently valuable, which subsequently disappeared, but ought not to have disappeared. Johnson has hit, perhaps by accident, on one of their peculiarities, when he observes that "their attempts were always analytic"; he would not agree that, after the dissociation, they put the material together again in a new unity.

It is certain that the dramatic verse of the later Elizabethan and early Jacobean poets expresses a degree of development of sensibility which is not found in any of the prose, good as it often is. If we except Marlowe, a man of prodigious intelligence, these dramatists were directly or indirectly (it is at least a tenable theory) affected by Montaigne. Even if we except also

Jonson and Chapman, these two were notably erudite, and
were notably men who incorporated their erudition into their
sensibility: their mode of feeling was directly and freshly
altered by their reading and thought. In Chapman especially
there is a direct sensuous apprehension of thought, or a recrea-
tion of thought into feeling, which is exactly what we find in
Donne:

> *in this one thing, all the discipline*
> *Of manners and of manhood is contained;*
> *A man to join himself with th' Universe*
> *In his main sway, and make in all things fit*
> *One with that All, and go on, round as it;*
> *Not plucking from the whole his wretched part,*
> *And into straits, or into nought revert,*
> *Wishing the complete Universe might be*
> *Subject to such a rag of it as he;*
> *But to consider great Necessity.*

We compare this with some modern passage:

> *No, when the fight begins within himself,*
> *A man's worth something. God stoops o'er his head,*
> *Satan looks up between his feet—both tug—*
> *He's left, himself, i' the middle; the soul wakes*
> *And grows. Prolong that battle through his life!*

It is perhaps somewhat less fair, though very tempting (as both
poets are concerned with the perpetuation of love by offspring),
to compare with the stanzas already quoted from Lord Herbert's Ode the following from Tennyson:

> *One walked between his wife and child,*
> *With measured footfall firm and mild,*
> *And now and then he gravely smiled.*
> > *The prudent partner of his blood*
> > *Leaned on him, faithful, gentle, good,*
> > *Wearing the rose of womanhood.*
> *And in their double love secure,*
> *The little maiden walked demure,*
> *Pacing with downward eyelids pure.*

These three made unity so sweet,
My frozen heart began to beat,
Remembering its ancient heat.

The difference is not a simple difference of degree between poets. It is something which had happened to the mind of England between the time of Donne or Lord Herbert of Cherbury and the time of Tennyson and Browning; it is the difference between the intellectual poet and the reflective poet. Tennyson and Browning are poets, and they think; but they do not feel their thought as immediately as the odour of a rose. A thought to Donne was an experience; it modified his sensibility. When a poet's mind is perfectly equipped for its work, it is constantly amalgamating disparate experience; the ordinary man's experience is chaotic, irregular, fragmentary. The latter falls in love, or reads Spinoza, and these two experiences have nothing to do with each other, or with the noise of the typewriter or the smell of cooking; in the mind of the poet these experiences are always forming new wholes.

We may express the difference by the following theory: The poets of the seventeenth century, the successors of the dramatists of the sixteenth, possessed a mechanism of sensibility which could devour any kind of experience. They are simple, artificial, difficult, or fantastic, as their predecessors were; no less nor more than Dante, Guido Cavalcanti, Guinizelli, or Cino. In the seventeenth century a dissociation of sensibility set in, from which we have never recovered; and this dissociation, as is natural, was aggravated by the influence of the two most powerful poets of the century, Milton and Dryden. Each of these men performed certain poetic functions so magnificently well that the magnitude of the effect concealed the absence of others. The language went on and in some respects improved; the best verse of Collins, Gray, Johnson, and even Goldsmith satisfies some of our fastidious demands better than that of Donne or Marvell or King. But while the language became more refined, the feeling became more crude. The feeling, the sensibility, expressed in the *Country Churchyard* (to say nothing of Tennyson and Browning) is cruder than that in the *Coy Mistress*.

The second effect of the influence of Milton and Dryden

followed from the first, and was therefore slow in manifestation. The sentimental age began early in the eighteenth century, and continued. The poets revolted against the ratiocinative, the descriptive; they thought and felt by fits, unbalanced; they reflected. In one or two passages of Shelley's *Triumph of Life*, in the second *Hyperion*, there are traces of a struggle toward unification of sensibility. But Keats and Shelley died, and Tennyson and Browning ruminated.

After this brief exposition of a theory—too brief, perhaps, to carry conviction—we may ask, what would have been the fate of the "metaphysical" had the current of poetry descended in a direct line from them, as it descended in a direct line to them? They would not, certainly, be classified as metaphysical. The possible interests of a poet are unlimited; the more intelligent he is the better; the more intelligent he is the more likely that he will have interests: our only condition is that he turn them into poetry, and not merely meditate on them poetically. A philosophical theory which has entered into poetry is established, for its truth or falsity in one sense ceases to matter, and its truth in another sense is proved. The poets in question have, like other poets, various faults. But they were, at best, engaged in the task of trying to find the verbal equivalent for states of mind and feeling. And this means both that they are more mature, and that they wear better, than later poets of certainly not less literary ability.

It is not a permanent necessity that poets should be interested in philosophy, or in any other subject. We can only say that it appears likely that poets in our civilization, as it exists at present, must be *difficult*. Our civilization comprehends great variety and complexity, and this variety and complexity, playing upon a refined sensibility, must produce various and complex results. The poet must become more and more comprehensive, more allusive, more indirect, in order to force, to dislocate if necessary, language into his meaning. (A brilliant and extreme statement of this view, with which it is not requisite to associate oneself, is that of M. Jean Epstein, *La Poésie d' aujourd-hui*.) Hence we get something which looks very much like the conceit—we get, in fact, a method curiously similar to that of the "metaphysical poets," similar also in its use of obscure words and of simple phrasing.

> O géraniums diaphanes, guerroyeurs sortilèges,
> Sacrilèges monomanes!
> Emballages, dévergondages, douches! O pressoirs
> Des vendanges des grands soirs!
> Layettes aux abois,
> Thyrses au fond des bois!
> Transfusions, représailles,
> Relevailles, compresses et l'éternal potion,
> Angélus! n'en pouvoir plus
> De débâcles nuptiales! de débâcles nuptiales!

The same poet could write also simply:

> Elle est bien loin, elle pleure,
> Le grand vent se lamente aussi . . .

Jules Laforgue, and Tristan Corbière in many of his poems, are nearer to the "school of Donne" than any modern English poet. But poets more classical than they have the same essential quality of transmuting ideas into sensations, of transforming an observation into a state of mind.

> Pour l'enfant, amoureux de cartes et d'estampes,
> L'univers est égal à son vaste appétit.
> Ah, que le monde est grand à la clarté des lampes!
> Aux yeux du souvenir que le monde est petit!

In French literature the great master of the seventeenth century—Racine—and the great master of the nineteenth—Baudelaire—are in some ways more like each other than they are like any one else. The greatest two masters of diction are also the greatest two psychologists, the most curious explorers of the soul. It is interesting to speculate whether it is not a misfortune that two of the greatest masters of diction in our language, Milton and Dryden, triumph with a dazzling disregard of the soul. If we continued to produce Miltons and Drydens it might not so much matter, but as things are it is a pity that English poetry has remained so incomplete. Those who object to the "artificiality" of Milton or Dryden sometimes tell us to "look into our hearts and write." But that is not looking deep enough; Racine or Donne looked into a good deal more than the heart. One must look into the cerebral cortex, the nervous system, and the digestive tracts.

May we not conclude, then, that Donne, Crashaw, Vaughan, Herbert and Lord Herbert, Marvell, King, Cowley at his best, are in the direct current of English poetry, and that their faults should be reprimanded by this standard rather than coddled by antiquarian affection? They have been enough praised in terms which are implicit limitations because they are "metaphysical" or "witty," "quaint" or "obscure," though at their best they have not these attributes more than other serious poets. On the other hand, we must not reject the criticism of Johnson (a dangerous person to disagree with) without having mastered it, without having assimilated the Johnsonian canons of taste. In reading the celebrated passage in his essay on Cowley we must remember that by wit he clearly means something more serious than we usually mean today; in his criticism of their versification we must remember in what a narrow discipline he was trained, but also how well trained; we must remember that Johnson tortures chiefly the chief offenders, Cowley and Cleveland. It would be a fruitful work, and one requiring a substantial book, to break up the classification of Johnson (for there has been none since) and exhibit these poets in all their difference of kind and of degree, from the massive music of Donne to the faint, pleasing tinkle of Aurelian Townshend—whose *Dialogue between a Pilgrim and Time* is one of the few regrettable omissions from the excellent anthology of Professor Grierson.

ANDREW MARVELL

———

THE tercentenary of the former member for Hull deserves not only the celebration proposed by that favoured borough, but a little serious reflection upon his writing. That is an act of piety, which is very different from the resurrection of a deceased reputation. Marvell has stood high for some years; his best poems are not very many, and not only must be well known, from the *Golden Treasury* and the *Oxford Book of English Verse*, but must also have been enjoyed by numerous readers. His grave needs neither rose nor rue nor laurel; there is no imaginary justice to be done; we may think about him, if there be need for thinking, for our own benefit, not his. To bring the poet back to life—the great, the perennial, task of criticism—is in this case to squeeze the drops of the essence of two or three poems; even confining ourselves to these, we may find some precious liquor unknown to the present age. Not to determine rank, but to isolate this quality, is the critical labour. The fact that of all Marvell's verse, which is itself not a great quantity, the really valuable part consists of a very few poems indicates that the unknown quality of which we speak is probably a literary rather than a personal quality; or, more truly, that it is a quality of a civilization, of a traditional habit of life. A poet like Donne, or like Baudelaire or Laforgue, may almost be considered the inventor of an attitude, a system of feeling or of morals. Donne is difficult to analyse: what appears at one time a curious personal point of view may at another time appear rather the precise concentration of a kind of feeling diffused in the air about him. Donne and his shroud, the shroud and his motive for wearing it, are inseparable, but they are not the same thing. The seventeenth century sometimes seems for more than a moment to gather up and to digest into its art all the experience of the human mind which (from the same point of view) the later centuries seem to have been partly engaged in repudiating. But Donne would have been an individual at any time and place; Marvell's best verse is the product of European, that is to say Latin, culture.

Out of that high style developed from Marlowe through Jonson (for Shakespeare does not lend himself to these genealogies) the seventeenth century separated two qualities: wit and magniloquence. Neither is as simple or as apprehensible as its name seems to imply, and the two are not in practice antithetical; both are conscious and cultivated, and the mind which cultivates one may cultivate the other. The actual poetry, of Marvell, of Cowley, of Milton, and of others, is a blend in varying proportions. And we must be on guard not to employ the terms with too wide a comprehension; for like the other fluid terms with which literary criticism deals, the meaning alters with the age, and for precision we must rely to some degree upon the literacy and good taste of the reader. The wit of the Caroline poets is not the wit of Shakespeare, and it is not the wit of Dryden, the great master of contempt, or of Pope, the great master of hatred, or of Swift, the great master of disgust. What is meant is some quality which is common to the songs in *Comus* and Cowley's Anacreontics and Marvell's Horatian Ode. It is more than a technical accomplishment, or the vocabulary and syntax of an epoch; it is, what we have designated tentatively as wit, a tough reasonableness beneath the slight lyric grace. You cannot find it in Shelley or Keats or Wordsworth; you cannot find more than an echo of it in Landor; still less in Tennyson or Browning; and among contemporaries Mr. Yeats is an Irishman and Mr. Hardy is a modern Englishman—that is to say, Mr. Hardy is without it and Mr. Yeats is outside of the tradition altogether. On the other hand, as it certainly exists in Lafontaine, there is a large part of it in Gautier. And of the magniloquence, the deliberate exploitation of the possibilities of magnificence in language which Milton used and abused, there is also use and even abuse in the poetry of Baudelaire.

Wit is not a quality that we are accustomed to associate with "Puritan" literature, with Milton or with Marvell. But if so, we are at fault partly in our conception of wit and partly in our generalizations about the Puritans. And if the wit of Dryden or of Pope is not the only kind of wit in the language, the rest is not merely a little merriment or a little levity or a little impropriety or a little epigram. And, on the other hand, the sense in which a man like Marvell is a "Puritan" is restricted. The persons who opposed Charles I and the persons who supported the Commonwealth were not all of the flock of Zeal-of-the-land Busy or the United Grand Junction Ebenezer Temperance Association. Many of them were gentlemen of the time who merely believed, with considerable show of rea·son, that government by a Parliament of gentlemen was better than government by a Stuart; though they were, to that extent, Liberal Practitioners, they could hardly foresee the tea-meeting and the Dissidence of Dissent. Being men of education and culture, even of travel, some of them were exposed to that spirit of the age which was coming to be the French spirit of the age. This spirit, curiously enough, was quite opposed to the tendencies latent or the forces active in Puritanism; the contest does great damage to the poetry of Milton; Marvell, an active servant of the public, but a lukewarm partisan, and a poet on a smaller scale, is far less injured by it. His line on the statue of Charles II, "It is such a King as no chisel can mend," may be set off against his criticism of the Great Rebellion: "Men . . . ought and might have trusted the King." Marvell, therefore, more a man of the century than a Puritan, speaks more clearly and unequivocally with the voice of his literary age than does Milton.

This voice speaks out uncommonly strong in the *Coy Mistress*. The theme is one of the great traditional commonplaces of European literature. It is the theme of *O mistress mine*, of *Gather ye rosebuds*, of *Go, lovely rose;* it is in the savage austerity of Lucretius and the intense levity of Catullus. Where

the wit of Marvell renews the theme is in the variety and order
of the images. In the first of the three paragraphs Marvell plays
with a fancy which begins by pleasing and leads to astonishment.

> *Had we but world enough and time,*
> *This coyness, lady, were no crime,*
> > *. . . I would*
> *Love you ten years before the Flood,*
> *And you should, if you please, refuse*
> *Till the conversion of the Jews;*
> *My vegetable love should grow*
> *Vaster than empires and more slow. . . .*

We notice the high speed, the succession of concentrated images,
each magnifying the original fancy. When this process has been
carried to the end and summed up, the poem turns suddenly
with that surprise which has been one of the most important
means of poetic effect since Homer:

> *But at my back I always hear*
> *Time's wingèd chariot hurrying near,*
> *And yonder all before us lie*
> *Deserts of vast eternity.*

A whole civilization resides in these lines:

> *Pallida Mors aequo pulsat pede pauperum tabernas,*
> *Regumque turris. . . .*

And not only Horace but Catullus himself:

> *Nobis, cum semel occidit brevis lux,*
> *Nox est perpetua una dormienda.*

The verse of Marvell has not the grand reverberation of
Catullus's Latin; but the image of Marvell is certainly more
comprehensive and penetrates greater depths than Horace's.
   A modern poet, had he reached the height, would very likely
have closed on this moral reflection. But the three strophes of
Marvell's poem have something like a syllogistic relation to
each other. After a close approach to the mood of Donne,

> *then worms shall try*
> *That long-preserved virginity . . .*
> *The grave's a fine and private place,*
> *But none, I think, do there embrace,*

the conclusion,

> *Let us roll all our strength and all*
> *Our sweetness up into one ball,*
> *And tear our pleasures with rough strife,*
> *Thorough the iron gates of life.*

It will hardly be denied that this poem contains wit; but it may not be evident that this wit forms the crescendo and diminuendo of a scale of great imaginative power. The wit is not only combined with, but fused into, the imagination. We can easily recognize a witty fancy in the successive images ("my *vegetable* love," "till the conversion of the Jews"), but this fancy is not indulged, as it sometimes is by Cowley or Cleveland, for its own sake. It is structural decoration of a serious idea. In this it is superior to the fancy of *L'Allegro, Il Penseroso,* or the lighter and less successful poems of Keats. In fact, this alliance of levity and seriousness (by which the seriousness is intensified) is a characteristic of the sort of wit we are trying to identify. It is found in

> *Le squelette était invisible*
> *Au temps heureux de l'art païen!*

of Gautier, and in the *dandysme* of Baudelaire and Laforgue. It is in the poem of Catullus which has been quoted, and in the variation by Ben Jonson:

> *Cannot we deceive the eyes*
> *Of a few poor household spies?*
> *'Tis no sin love's fruits to steal,*
> *But that sweet sin to reveal,*
> *To be taken, to be seen,*
> *These have sins accounted been.*

It is in Propertius and Ovid. It is a quality of a sophisticated literature; a quality which expands in English literature just at the moment before the English mind altered; it is not a quality which we should expect Puritanism to encourage. When we come to Gray and Collins, the sophistication remains only in the language, and has disappeared from the feeling. Gray and Collins were masters, but they had lost that hold on human values, that firm grasp of human experience, which is a formidable achievement of the Elizabethan and Jacobean poets. This wisdom, cynical perhaps but untired (in Shakespeare, a terrifying clairvoyance), leads toward, and is only completed by, the religious comprehension; it leads to the point of the *Ainsi tout leur a craqué dans la main* of Bouvard and Pécuchet.

The difference between imagination and fancy, in view of this poetry of wit, is a very narrow one. Obviously, an image which is immediately and unintentionally ridiculous is merely a fancy. In the poem *Upon Appleton House*, Marvell falls in with one of these undesirable images, describing the attitude of the house toward its master:

> *Yet thus the leaden house does sweat,*
> *And scarce endures the master great;*
> *But, where he comes, the swelling hall*
> *Stirs, and the square grows spherical;*

which, whatever its intention, is more absurd than it was intended to be. Marvell also falls into the even commoner error of images which are over-developed or distracting; which support nothing but their own misshapen bodies:

> *And now the salmon-fishers moist*
> *Their leathern boats begin to hoist;*
> *And, like Antipodes in shoes,*
> *Have shod their heads in their canoes.*

Of this sort of image a choice collection may be found in Johnson's *Life of Cowley*. But the images in the *Coy Mistress* are not only witty, but satisfy the elucidation of Imagination given by Coleridge:

"This power . . . reveals itself in the balance or reconcilement of opposite or discordant qualities: of sameness, with dif-

ference; of the general, with the concrete; the idea with the
image; the individual with the representative; the sense of
novelty and freshness with old and familiar objects; a more than
usual state of emotion with more than usual order; judgment
ever awake and steady self-possession with enthusiasm and feeling profound or vehement. . . ."

Coleridge's statement applies also to the following verses, which
are selected because of their similarity, and because they illustrate the marked caesura which Marvell often introduces in a
short line:

> *The tawny mowers enter next,*
> *Who seem like Israelites to be*
> *Walking on foot through a green sea . . .*

> *And now the meadows fresher dyed,*
> *Whose grass, with moister colour dashed,*
> *Seems as green silks but newly washed . . .*

> *He hangs in shades the orange bright,*
> *Like golden lamps in a green night . . .*

> *Annihilating all that's made*
> *To a green thought in a green shade . . .*

> *Had it lived long, it would have been*
> *Lilies without, roses within.*

The whole poem, from which the last of these quotations is
drawn (*The Nymph and the Fawn*), is built upon a very slight
foundation, and we can imagine what some of our modern practitioners of slight themes would have made of it. But we need
not descend to an invidious contemporaneity to point the difference. Here are six lines from *The Nymph and the Fawn*:

> *I have a garden of my own,*
> *But so with roses overgrown*
> *And lilies, that you would it guess*
> *To be a little wilderness;*
> *And all the spring-time of the year*
> *It only lovèd to be there.*

And here are five lines from *The Nymph's Song to Hylas* in the *Life and Death of Jason*, by William Morris:

> *I know a little garden close*
> *Set thick with lily and red rose.*
> *Where I would wander if I might*
> *From dewy dawn to dewy night,*
> *And have one with me wandering.*

So far the resemblance is more striking than the difference, although we might just notice the vagueness of allusion in the last line to some indefinite person, form, or phantom, compared with the more explicit reference of emotion to object which we should expect from Marvell. But in the latter part of the poem Morris divaricates widely:

> *Yet tottering as I am, and weak,*
> *Still have I left a little breath*
> *To seek within the jaws of death*
> *An entrance to that happy place;*
> *To seek the unforgotten face*
> *Once seen, once kissed, once reft from me*
> *Anigh the murmuring of the sea.*

Here the resemblance, if there is any, is to the latter part of *The Coy Mistress*. As for the difference, it could not be more pronounced. The effect of Morris's charming poem depends upon the mistiness of the feeling and the vagueness of its object; the effect of Marvell's upon its bright, hard precision. And this precision is not due to the fact that Marvell is concerned with cruder or simpler or more carnal emotions. The emotion of Morris is not more refined or more spiritual; it is merely more vague: if any one doubts whether the more refined or spiritual emotion can be precise, he should study the treatment of the varieties of discarnate emotion in the *Paradiso*. A curious result of the comparison of Morris's poem with Marvell's is that the former, though it appears to be more serious, is found to be the slighter; and Marvell's *Nymph and the Fawn*, appearing more slight, is the more serious.

So weeps the wounded balsam; so
The holy frankincense doth flow;
The brotherless Heliades
Melt in such amber tears as these.

These verses have the suggestiveness of true poetry; and the verses of Morris, which are nothing if not an attempt to suggest, really suggest nothing; and we are inclined to infer that the suggestiveness is the aura around a bright clear centre, that you cannot have the aura alone. The day-dreamy feeling of Morris is essentially a slight thing; Marvell takes a slight affair, the feeling of a girl for her pet, and gives it a connexion with that inexhaustible and terrible nebula of emotion which surrounds all our exact and practical passions and mingles with them. Again, Marvell does this in a poem which, because of its formal pastoral machinery, may appear a trifling object:

CLORINDA. *Near this, a fountain's liquid bell*
                Tinkles within the concave shell.

DAMON.   *Might a soul bathe there and be clean,*
                Or slake its drought?

where we find that a metaphor has suddenly rapt us to the image of spiritual purgation. There is here the element of *surprise*, as when Villon says:

Necessité faict gens mesprendre
Et faim saillir le loup des boys,

the surprise which Poe considered of the highest importance, and also the restraint and quietness of tone which make the surprise possible. And in the verses of Marvell which have been quoted there is the making the familiar strange, and the strange familiar, which Coleridge attributed to good poetry.

The effort to construct a dream-world, which alters English poetry so greatly in the nineteenth century, a dream-world utterly different from the visionary realties of the *Vita Nuova* or of the poetry of Dante's contemporaries, is a problem of which various explanations may no doubt be found; in any case, the result makes a poet of the nineteenth century, of the same size as Marvell, a more trivial and less serious figure. Marvell is no greater personality than William Morris, but he had something much more solid behind him: he had the vast and penetrating influence of Ben Jonson. Jonson never wrote anything purer than Marvell's *Horatian Ode;* this ode has that same quality of wit which was diffused over the whole Elizabethan product and concentrated in the work of Jonson. And, as was said before, this wit which pervades the poetry of Marvell is more Latin, more refined, than anything that succeeded it. The great danger, as well as the great interest and excitement, of English prose and verse, compared with French, is that it permits and justifies an exaggeration of particular qualities to the exclusion of others. Dryden was great in wit, as Milton in magniloquence; but the former, by isolating this quality and making it by itself into great poetry, and the latter, by coming to dispense with it altogether, may perhaps have injured the language. In Dryden wit becomes almost fun, and thereby loses some contact with reality; becomes pure fun, which French wit almost never is.

> *The midwife placed her hand on his thick skull,*
> *With this prophetic blessing: Be thou dull . . .*
>
> *A numerous host of dreaming saints succeed,*
> *Of the true old enthusiastic breed.*

This is audacious and splendid; it belongs to satire besides which Marvell's Satires are random babbling, but it is perhaps as exaggerated as:

> *Oft he seems to hide his face,*
> *But unexpectedly returns,*
> *And to his faithful champion hath in place*
> *Bore witness gloriously; whence Gaza mourns*
> *And all that band them to resist*
> *His uncontrollable intent.*

How oddly the sharp Dantesque phrase "whence Gaza mourns" springs out from the brilliant contortions of Milton's sentence!

Who from his private gardens, where
He lived reservèd and austere,
(As if his highest plot
To plant the bergamot)

Could by industrious valour climb
To ruin the great work of Time,
And cast the kingdoms old
Into another mold;

. . . . . .

The Pict no shelter now shall find
Within his parti-coloured mind,
But, from this valour sad,
Shrink underneath the plaid:

There is here an equipoise, a balance and proportion of tones, which, while it cannot raise Marvell to the level of Dryden or Milton, extorts an approval which these poets do not receive from us, and bestows a pleasure at least different in kind from any they can often give. It is what makes Marvell a classic; or classic in a sense in which Gray and Collins are not; for the latter, with all their accredited purity, are comparatively poor in shades of feeling to contrast and unite.

We are baffled in the attempt to translate the quality indicated by the dim and antiquated term wit into the equally unsatisfactory nomenclature of our own time. Even Cowley is only able to define it by negatives:

Comely in thousand shapes appears;
Yonder we saw it plain; and here 'tis now,
Like spirits in a place, we know not how.

It has passed out of our critical coinage altogether, and no new term has been struck to replace it; the quality seldom exists, and is never recognized.

In a true piece of Wit all things must be
Yet all things there agree;
As in the Ark, join'd without force or strife,
All creatures dwelt, all creatures that had life.

> *Or as the primitive forms of all*
> *(If we compare great things with small)*
> *Which, without discord or confusion, lie*
> *In that strange mirror of the Deity.*

So far Cowley has spoken well. But if we are to attempt even no more than Cowley, we, placed in a retrospective attitude, must risk much more than anxious generalizations. With our eye still on Marvell, we can say that wit is not erudition; it is sometimes stifled by erudition, as in much of Milton. It is not cynicism, though it has a kind of toughness which may be confused with cynicism by the tender-minded. It is confused with erudition because it belongs to an educated mind, rich in generations of experience; and it is confused with cynicism because it implies a constant inspection and criticism of experience. It involves, probably, a recognition, implicit in the expression of every experience, of other kinds of experience which are possible, which we find as clearly in the greatest as in poets like Marvell. Such a general statement may seem to take us a long way from *The Nymph and the Fawn,* or even from the *Horatian Ode;* but it is perhaps justified by the desire to account for that precise taste of Marvell's which finds for him the proper degree of seriousness for every subject which he treats. His errors of taste, when he trespasses, are not sins against this virtue; they are conceits, distended metaphors and similes, but they never consist in taking a subject too seriously or too lightly. This virtue of wit is not a peculiar quality of minor poets, or of the minor poets of one age or of one school; it is an intellectual quality which perhaps only becomes noticeable by itself, in the work of lesser poets. Furthermore, it is absent from the work of Wordsworth, Shelley, and Keats, on whose poetry nineteenth-century criticism has unconsciously been based. To the best of their poetry wit is irrelevant:

> *Art thou pale for weariness*
> *Of climbing heaven and gazing on the earth,*
> *Wandering companionless*
> *Among the stars that have a different birth,*

And ever changing, like a joyless eye,
That finds no object worth its constancy?

We should find it difficult to draw any useful comparison between these lines of Shelley and anything by Marvell. But later
poets, who would have been the better for Marvell's quality,
were without it; even Browning seems oddly immature, in some
way, beside Marvell. And nowadays we find occasionally good
irony, or satire, which lack wit's internal equilibrium, because
their voices are essentially protests against some outside senti-
mentality or stupidity; or we find serious poets who are afraid
of acquiring wit, lest they lose intensity. The quality which
Marvell had, this modest and certainly impersonal virtue—
whether we call it wit or reason, or even urbanity—we have
patently failed to define. By whatever name we call it, and
however we define that name, it is something precious and
needed and apparently extinct; it is what should preserve the
reputation of Marvell. *C'était une belle âme, comme on ne fait*
plus à Londres.

JOHN DRYDEN

IF the prospect of delight be wanting (which alone justifies the perusal of poetry) we may let the reputation of Dryden sleep in the manuals of literature. To those who are genuinely insensible of his genius (and these are probably the majority of living readers of poetry) we can only oppose illustrations of the following proposition: that their insensibility does not merely signify indifference to satire and wit, but lack of perception of qualities not confined to satire and wit and present in the work of other poets whom these persons feel that they understand. To those whose taste in poetry is formed entirely upon the English poetry of the nineteenth century— to the majority—it is difficult to explain or excuse Dryden: the twentieth century is still the nineteenth, although it may in time acquire its own character. The nineteenth century had, like every other, limited tastes and peculiar fashions; and, like every other, it was unaware of its own limitations. Its tastes and fashions had no place for Dryden; yet Dryden is one of the tests of a catholic appreciation of poetry.

He is a successor of Jonson, and therefore the descendant of Marlowe; he is the ancestor of nearly all that is best in the poetry of the eighteenth century. Once we have mastered Dryden—and by mastery is meant a full and essential enjoyment, not the enjoyment of a private whimiscal fashion—we can extract whatever enjoyment and edification there is in his contemporaries—Oldham, Denham, or the less remunerative Waller; and still more his successors—not only Pope, but Phillips, Churchill, Gray, Johnson, Cowper, Goldsmith. His inspiration is prolonged in Crabbe and Byron; it even extends, as Mr.

van Doren cleverly points out, to Poe. Even the poets responsible for the revolt were well acquainted with him: Wordsworth knew his work, and Keats invoked his aid. We cannot
fully enjoy or rightly estimate a hundred years of English
poetry unless we fully enjoy Dryden; and to enjoy Dryden
means to pass beyond the limitations of the nineteenth century
into a new freedom.

> *All, all of a piece throughout!*
> *Thy Chase had a Beast in View;*
> *Thy Wars brought nothing about;*
> *Thy Lovers were all untrue.*
> *'Tis well an Old Age is out,*
> *And time to begin a New.*
>
> . . . . . .
>
> *The world's great age begins anew,*
> *The golden years return,*
> *The earth doth like a snake renew*
> *Her winter weeds outworn:*
> *Heaven smiles, and faiths and empires gleam*
> *Like wrecks of a dissolving dream.*

The first of these passages is by Dryden, the second by Shelley;
the second is found in the *Oxford Book of English Verse*, the
first is not; yet we might defy any one to show that the second
is superior on intrinsically poetic merit. It is easy to see why
the second should appeal more readily to the nineteenth, and
what is left of the nineteenth under the name of the twentieth,
century. It is not so easy to see propriety in an image which
divests a snake of "winter weeds"; and this is a sort of blemish
which would have been noticed more quickly by a contemporary of Dryden than by a contemporary of Shelley.

These reflections are occasioned by an admirable book on
Dryden which has appeared at this very turn of time, when taste
is becoming perhaps more fluid and ready for a new mould.[1] It
is a book which every practitioner of English verse should

[1] *John Dryden*, by Mark van Doren (New York: Harcourt, Brace &
Howe).

study. The consideration is so thorough, the matter so compact, the appreciation so just, temperate, and enthusiastic, and supplied with such copious and well-chosen extracts from the poetry, the suggestion of astutely placed facts leads our thought so far, that there only remain to mention, as defects which do not detract from its value, two omissions: the prose is not dealt with, and the plays are somewhat slighted. What is especially impressive is the exhibition of the very wide range of Dryden's work, shown by the quotations of every species. Every one knows *MacFlecknoe*, and parts of *Absalom and Achitophel*; in consequence, Dryden has sunk by the persons he has elevated to distinction—Shadwell and Settle, Shaftesbury and Buckingham. Dryden was much more than a satirist; to dispose of him as a satirist is to place an obstacle in the way of our understanding. At all events, we must satisfy ourselves of our definition of the term satire; we must not allow our familiarity with the word to blind us to differences and refinements; we must not assume that satire is a fixed type, and fixed to the prosaic, suited only to prose; we must acknowledge that satire is not the same thing in the hands of two different writers of genius. The connotations of "satire" and of "wit," in short, may be only prejudices of nineteenth-century taste. Perhaps, we think, after reading Mr. van Doren's book, a juster view of Dryden may be given by beginning with some other portion of his work than his celebrated satires; but even here there is much more present, and much more that is poetry, than is usually supposed.

The piece of Dryden's which is the most fun, which is the most sustained display of surprise after surprise of wit from line to line, is *MacFlecknoe*. Dryden's method here is something very near to parody; he applies vocabulary, images, and ceremony which arouse epic associations of grandeur, to make an enemy helplessly ridiculous. But the effect, though disastrous for the enemy, is very different from that of the humour which merely belittles, such as the satire of Mark Twain. Dryden continually enhances: he makes his object great, in a way contrary to expectation; and the total effect is due to the transformation of the ridiculous into poetry. As an example may be taken a fine passage plagiarized from Cowley, from lines which Dryden must have marked well, for he quotes them directly in one of his prefaces. Here is Cowley:

> *Where their vast courts the mother-waters keep,*
> *And undisturbed by moons in silence sleep. . . .*
> *Beneath the dens where unfledged tempests lie,*
> *And infant winds their tender voices try.*

In *MacFlecknoe* this becomes:

> *Where their vast courts the mother-strumpets keep,*
> *And undisturbed by watch, in silence sleep.*
> *Near these, a nursery erects its head,*
> *Where queens are formed, and future heroes bred;*
> *Where unfledged actors learn to laugh and cry,*
> *Where infant punks their tender voices try,*
> *And little Maximins the gods defy.*

The passage from Cowley is by no means despicable verse. But it is a commonplace description of commonly poetic objects; it has not the element of surprise so essential to poetry, and this Dryden provides. A clever versifier might have written Cowley's lines; only a poet could have made what Dryden made of them. It is impossible to dismiss his verses as "prosaic"; turn them into prose and they are transmuted, the fragrance is gone. The reproach of the prosaic, levelled at Dryden, rests upon a confusion between the emotions considered to be poetic—which is a matter allowing considerable latitude of fashion—and the *result* of personal emotion in poetry; and also there is the emotion *depicted* by the poet in some kinds of poetry, of which the *Testaments* of Villon is an example. Again, there is the intellect, the originality and independence and clarity of what we vaguely call the poet's "point of view." Our valuation of poetry, in short, depends upon several considerations, upon the permanent and upon the mutable and transitory. When we try to isolate the essentially poetic, we bring our pursuit in the end to something insignificant; our standards vary with every poet whom we consider. All we can hope to do, in the attempt to introduce some order into our preferences, is to clarify our reasons for finding pleasure in the poetry that we like.

With regard to Dryden, therefore, we can say this much. Our taste in English poetry has been largely founded upon a partial perception of the value of Shakespeare and Milton, a perception which dwells upon sublimity of theme and action. Shakespeare had a great deal more; he had nearly everything to satisfy our various desires for poetry. The point is that the depreciation or neglect of Dryden is not due to the fact that his work is not poetry, but to a prejudice that the material, the feelings, out of which he built is not poetic. Thus Matthew Arnold observes, in mentioning Dryden and Pope together, that "their poetry is conceived and composed in their wits, genuine poetry is conceived in the soul." Arnold was, perhaps, not altogether the detached critic when he wrote this line; he may have been stirred to a defence of his own poetry, conceived and composed in the soul of a mid-century Oxford graduate. Pater remarks that Dryden:

"Loved to emphasize the distinction between poetry and prose, the protest against their confusion coming with somewhat diminished effect from one whose poetry was so prosaic."

But Dryden was right, and the sentence of Pater is cheap journalism. Hazlitt, who had perhaps the most uninteresting mind of all our distinguished critics, says:

"Dryden and Pope are the great masters of the artificial style of poetry in our language, as the poets of whom I have already treated—Chaucer, Spenser, Shakespeare, and Milton—were of the natural."

In one sentence Hazlitt has committed at least four crimes against taste. It is bad enough to lump Chaucer, Spenser, Shakespeare, and Milton together under the denomination of "natural"; it is bad to commit Shakespeare to one style only; it is bad to join Dryden and Pope together; but the last absurdity is the contrast of Milton, our greatest master of the *artificial* style, with Dryden, whose *style* (vocabulary, syntax, and order of thought) is in a high degree natural. And what all these objections come to, we repeat, is repugnance for the material out of which Dryden's poetry is built.

It would be truer to say, indeed, even in the form of the unpersuasive paradox, that Dryden is distinguished principally by his *poetic* ability. We prize him, as we do Mallarmé, for what he made of his material. Our estimate is only in part the appreciation of ingenuity: in the end the result *is* poetry. Much of Dryden's unique merit consists in his ability to make the small into the great, the prosaic into the poetic, the trivial into the magnificent. In this he differs not only from Milton, who required a canvas of the largest size, but from Pope, who required one of the smallest. If you compare any satiric "character" of Pope with one of Dryden, you will see that the method and intention are widely divergent. When Pope alters, he diminishes; he is a master of miniature. The singular skill of his portrait of Addison, for example, in the *Epistle to Arbuthnot*, depends upon the justice and reserve, the apparent determination not to exaggerate. The genius of Pope is not for caricature. But the effect of the portraits of Dryden is to transform the object into something greater, as were transformed the verses of Cowley quoted above.

> *A fiery soul, which working out its way,*
> *Fretted the pigmy body to decay:*
> *And o'er informed the tenement of clay.*

These lines are not merely a magnificent tribute. They create the object which they contemplate. Dryden is, in fact, much nearer to the master of comic creation than to Pope. As in Jonson, the effect is far from laughter; the comic is the material, the result is poetry. The Civic Guards of Rhodes:

> *The country rings around with loud alarms,*
> *And raw in fields the rude militia swarms;*
> *Mouths without hands; maintained at vast expense,*
> *In peace a charge, in war a weak defence;*
> *Stout once a month they march, a blust'ring band,*
> *And ever, but in times of need, at hand;*

> *This was the morn, when issuing on the guard,*
> *Drawn up in rank and file they stood prepared*
> *Of seeming arms to make a short essay,*
> *Then hasten to be drunk, the business of the day.*

Sometimes the wit appears as a delicate flavour to the magnifi-cence, as in *Alexander's Feast:*

> *Sooth'd with the sound the king grew vain;*
> *Fought all his battles o'er again;*
> *And thrice he routed all his foes, and thrice he slew the slain.*

The great advantage of Dryden over Milton is that while the former is always in control of his ascent, and can rise or fall at will (and how masterfully, like his own Timotheus, he directs the transitions!), the latter has elected a perch from which he cannot afford to fall, and from which he is in danger of slipping.

> *food alike those pure*
> *Intelligential substances require*
> *As doth your Rational; and both contain*
> *Within them every lower faculty*
> *Of sense, whereby they hear, see, smell, touch, taste,*
> *Tasting concoct, digest, assimilate,*
> *And corporeal to incorporeal turn.*

Dryden might have made poetry out of that; his translation from Lucretius is poetry. But we have an ingenious example on which to test our contrast of Dryden and Milton: it is Dry-den's "Opera," called *The State of Innocence and Fall of Man,* of which Nathaniel Lee neatly says in his preface:

> *Milton did the wealthy mine disclose,*
> *And rudely cast what you could well dispose:*
> *He roughly drew, on an old-fashioned ground,*
> *A chaos, for no perfect world were found,*
> *Till through the heap, your mighty genius shined.*

In the author's preface Dryden acknowledges his debt gener-ously enough:

"The original being undoubtedly, one of the greatest, most noble, and most sublime poems, which either this age or nation has produced."

The poem begins auspiciously:

LUCIFER.
> *Is this the seat our conqueror has given?*
> *And this the climate we must change for Heaven?*
> *These regions and this realm my wars have got;*
> *This mournful empire is the loser's lot:*
> *In liquid burnings, or on dry to dwell,*
> *Is all the sad variety of hell.*

It is an early work; it is on the whole a feeble work; it is not deserving of sustained comparison with *Paradise Lost*. But "all the sad variety of hell"! Dryden is already stirring; he has assimilated what he could from Milton; and he has shown himself capable of producing as splendid verse.

The capacity for assimilation, and the consequent extent of range, are conspicuous qualities of Dryden. He advanced and exhibited his variety by constant translation; and his translations of Horace, of Ovid, of Lucretius, are admirable. His gravest defects are supposed to be displayed in his dramas, but if these were more read they might be more praised. From the point of view of either the Elizabethan or the French drama they are obviously inferior; but the charge of inferiority loses part of its force if we admit that Dryden was not quite trying to compete with either, but was pursuing a direction of his own. He created no character; and although his arrangements of plot manifest exceptional ingenuity, it is the pure magnificence of diction, of poetic diction, that keep his plays alive:

> *How I loved*
> *Witness ye days and nights, and all ye hours,*
> *That danced away with down upon your feet,*
> *As all your business were to count my passion.*
> *One day passed by, and nothing saw but love;*
> *Another came, and still 'twas only love:*
> *The suns were wearied out with looking on,*

And I untired with loving.
I saw you every day and all the day;
And every day was still but as the first:
So eager was I still to see you more . . .

> *While within your arms I lay,*
> *The world fell mould'ring from my hands each hour.*

Such language is pure Dryden: it sounds, in Mr. van Doren's phrase, "like a gong." *All for Love,* from which the lines are taken, is Dryden's best play, and this is perhaps the highest reach. In general, he is best in his plays when dealing with situations which do not demand great emotional concentration; when his situation is more trivial, and he can practise his art of making the small great. The back-talk between the Emperor and his Empress Nourmahal, in *Aurungzebe,* is admirable purple comedy:

EMPEROR.
Such virtue is the plague of human life:
A virtuous woman, but a cursèd wife.
In vain of pompous chastity y' are proud:
Virtue's adultery of the tongue, when loud.
I, with less pain, a prostitute could bear,
Than the shrill sound of virtue, virtue hear.
In unchaste wives—
There's yet a kind of recompensing ease:
Vice keeps 'em humble, gives 'em care to please:
But against clamorous virtue, what defence?
It stops our mouths, and gives your noise pretence. . . .

What can be sweeter than our native home?
Thither for ease, and soft repose, we come;
Home is the sacred refuge of our life:
Secure from all approaches but a wife.
If thence we fly, the cause admits no doubt:
None but an inmate foe could force us out.
Clamours, our privacies uneasy make:
Birds leave their nests disturbed, and beasts their haunts
*   forsake.*

But drama is a mixed form; pure magnificence will not carry it through. The poet who attempts to achieve a play by the single force of the word provokes comparison, however strictly he confine himself to his capacity, with poets of other gifts. Corneille and Racine do not attain their triumphs by magnificence of this sort; they have concentration also, and, in the midst of their phrases, an undisturbed attention to the human soul as they knew it.

Nor is Dryden unchallenged in his supreme ability to make the ridiculous, or the trivial, great.

> *Avez-vous observé que maints cercueils de vieilles*
> *Sont presque aussi petits que celui d'un enfant?*

Those lines are the work of a man whose verse is as magnificent as Dryden's, and who could see profounder possibilities in wit, and in violently joined images, than ever were in Dryden's mind. For Dryden, with all his intellect, had a commonplace mind. His powers were, we believe, wider, but no greater, than Milton's; he was confined by boundaries as impassable, though less strait. He bears a curious antithetical resemblance to Swinburne. Swinburne was also a master of words, but Swinburne's words are all suggestions and no denotation; if they suggest nothing, it is because they suggest too much. Dryden's words, on the other hand, are precise, they state immensely, but their suggestiveness is often nothing.

> *That short dark passage to a future state;*
> *That melancholy riddle of a breath,*
> *That something, or that nothing, after death.*

is a riddle, but not melancholy enough, in Dryden's splendid verse. The question, which has certainly been waiting, may justly be asked: whether, without this which Dryden lacks, verse can be poetry? What is man to decide what poetry is? Dryden's use of language is not, like that of Swinburne, weakening and demoralizing. Let us take as a final test his elegy upon Oldham, which deserves not to be mutilated:

Farewell, too little and too lately known,
Whom I began to think and call my own;
For sure our souls were near allied, and thine
Cast in the same poetic mould with mine.
One common note on either lyre did strike,
And knaves and fools we both abhorred alike.
To the same goal did both our studies drive;
The last set out the soonest did arrive.
Thus Nisus fell upon the slippery place,
Whilst his young friend performed and won the race.
O early ripe! to thy abundant store
What could advancing age have added more?
It might (what nature never gives the young)
Have taught the numbers of thy native tongue.
But satire needs not those, and wit will shine
Through the harsh cadence of a rugged line.
A noble error, and but seldom made,
When poets are by too much force betrayed.
Thy generous fruits, though gathered ere their prime,
Still showed a quickness; and maturing time
But mellows what we write to the dull sweets of rhyme.
Once more, hail, and farewell; farewell, thou young,
But ah! too short, Marcellus of our tongue!
Thy brows with ivy and with laurels bound;
But fate and gloomy night encompass thee around.

From the perfection of such an elegy we cannot detract; the lack of suggestiveness is compensated by the satisfying completeness of the statement. Dryden lacked what his master Jonson possessed, a large and unique view of life; he lacked insight, he lacked profundity. But where Dryden fails to satisfy, the nineteenth century does not satisfy us either; and where that century has condemned him, it is itself condemned. In the next revolution of taste it is possible that poets may turn to the study of Dryden. He remains one of those who have set standards for English verse which it is desperate to ignore.

WILLIAM BLAKE

IF one follows Blake's mind through the several stages of his poetic development it is impossible to regard him as a naïf, a wild man, a wild pet for the supercultivated. The strangeness is evaporated, the peculiarity is seen to be the peculiarity of all great poetry: something which is found (not everywhere) in Homer and Aeschylus and Dante and Villon, and profound and concealed in the work of Shakespeare—and also in another form in Montaigne and in Spinoza. It is merely a peculiar honesty, which, in a world too frightened to be honest, is peculiarly terrifying. It is an honesty against which the whole world conspires because it is unpleasant. Blake's poetry has the unpleasantness of great poetry. Nothing that can be called morbid or abnormal or perverse, none of the things which exemplify the sickness of an epoch or a fashion, have this quality; only those things which, by some extraordinary labour of simplification, exhibit the essential sickness or strength of the human soul. And this honesty never exists without great technical accomplishment. The question about Blake the man is the question of the circumstances that concurred to permit this honesty in his work, and what circumstances define its limitations. The favouring conditions probably include these two: that, being early apprenticed to a manual occupation, he was not compelled to acquire any other education in literature than he wanted, or to acquire it for any other reason than that he wanted it; and that, being a humble engraver, he had no journalistic-social career open to him.

There was, that is to say, nothing to distract him from his interests or to corrupt these interests: neither the ambitions of

parents or wife, nor the standards of society, nor the tempta-
tions of success; nor was he exposed to imitation of himself or
of any one else. These circumstances—not his supposed inspired
and untaught spontaneity—are what make him innocent. His
early poems show what the poems of a boy of genius ought to
show, immense power of assimilation. Such early poems are not,
as usually supposed, crude attempts to do something beyond the
boy's capacity; they are, in the case of a boy of real promise,
more likely to be quite mature and successful attempts to do
something small. So with Blake, his early poems are technically
admirable, and their originality is in an occasional rhythm. The
verse of *Edward III* deserves study. But his affection for certain
Elizabethans is not so surprising as his affinity with the very best
work of his own century. He is very like Collins, he is very
eighteenth century. The poem *Whether on Ida's Shady Brow*
is eighteenth-century work; the movement, the weight of it,
the syntax, the choice of words:

> *The* languid *strings do scarcely move!*
> *The sound is* forc'd, *the notes are few!*

this is contemporary with Gray and Collins, it is the poetry of
a language which has undergone the discipline of prose. Blake
up to twenty is decidedly a traditional.

Blake's beginnings as a poet, then, are as normal as the
beginnings of Shakespeare. His method of composition, in his
mature work, is exactly like that of other poets. He has an idea
(a feeling, an image), he develops it by accretion or expansion,
alters his verse often, and hesitates often over the final choice.[1]
The idea, of course, simply comes, but upon arrival it is subjected to prolonged manipulation. In the first phase Blake is
concerned with verbal beauty; in the second he becomes the

---

[1] I do not know why M. Berger should say, without qualification, in his
William Blake: mysticisme et poésie, that "son respect pour l'esprit qui souf-
flait en lui et qui dictait ses paroles l'empêchait de les corriger jamais." Dr.
Sampson, in his Oxford edition of Blake, gives us to understand that Blake
believed much of his writing to be automatic, but observes that Blake's
"meticulous care in composition is everywhere apparent in the poems preserved in rough draft . . . alteration on alteration, rearrangement after rearrangement, deletions, additions, and inversions. . . ."

apparent naïf, really the mature intelligence. It is only when the ideas become more automatic, come more freely and are less manipulated, that we begin to suspect their origin, to suspect that they spring from a shallower source.

The Songs of Innocence and of Experience, and the poems from the Rossetti manuscript, are the poems of a man with a profound interest in human emotions, and a profound knowledge of them. The emotions are presented in an extremely simplified, abstract form. This form is one illustration of the eternal struggle of art against education, of the literary artist against the continuous deterioration of language.

It is important that the artist should be highly educated in his own art; but his education is one that is hindered rather than helped by the ordinary processes of society which constitute education for the ordinary man. For these processes consist largely in the acquisition of impersonal ideas which obscure what we really are and feel, what we really want, and what really excites our interest. It is of course not the actual information acquired, but the conformity which the accumulation of knowledge is apt to impose, that is harmful. Tennyson is a very fair example of a poet almost wholly encrusted with opinion, almost wholly merged into his environment. Blake, on the other hand, knew what interested him, and he therefore presents only the essential, only, in fact, what can be presented, and need not be explained. And because he was not distracted, or frightened, or occupied in anything but exact statements, he understood. He was naked, and saw man naked, and from the centre of his own crystal. To him there was no more reason why Swedenborg should be absurd than Locke. He accepted Swedenborg, and eventually rejected him, for reasons of his own. He approached everything with a mind unclouded by current opinions. There was nothing of the superior person about him. This makes him terrifying.

I I

But if there was nothing to distract him from sincerity there were, on the other hand, the dangers to which the naked man is exposed. His philosophy, like his visions, like his insight, like his technique, was his own. And accordingly he was inclined to attach more importance to it than an artist should; this is what makes him eccentric, and makes him inclined to formlessness.

> *But most through midnight streets I hear*
> *How the youthful harlot's curse*
> *Blasts the new-born infant's tear,*
> *And blights with plagues the marriage hearse,*

is the naked vision;

> *Love seeketh only self to please,*
> *To bind another to its delight,*
> *Joys in another's loss of ease,*
> *And builds a Hell in Heaven's despite,*

is the naked observation; and *The Marriage of Heaven and Hell* is naked philosophy, presented. But Blake's occasional marriages of poetry and philosophy are not so felicitous.

> *He who would do good to another must do it in Minute*
>   *Particulars.*
> *General Good is the plea of the scoundrel, hypocrite, and*
>   *flatterer;*
> *For Art and Science cannot exist but in minutely organized*
>   *particulars. . . .*

One feels that the form is not well chosen. The borrowed philosophy of Dante and Lucretius is perhaps not so interesting, but it injures their form less. Blake did not have that more Mediterranean gift of form which knows how to borrow as Dante borrowed his theory of the soul; he must needs create a philosophy as well as a poetry. A similar formlessness attacks his draughtsmanship. The fault is most evident, of course, in the longer poems—or rather, the poems in which structure is important. You cannot create a very large poem without introducing a more impersonal point of view, or splitting it up into various personalities. But the weakness of the long poems is certainly not that they are too visionary, too remote from the world. It is that Blake did not see enough, became too much occupied with ideas.

We have the same respect for Blake's philosophy (and perhaps for that of Samuel Butler) that we have for an ingenious piece of home-made furniture: we admire the man who has put it together out of the odds and ends about the house. England has produced a fair number of these resourceful Robinson Crusoes; but we are not really so remote from the Continent, or from our own past, as to be deprived of the advantages of culture if we wish them.

We may speculate, for amusement, whether it would not have been beneficial to the north of Europe generally, and to Britain in particular, to have had a more continuous religious history. The local divinities of Italy were not wholly exterminated by Christianity, and they were not reduced to the dwarfish fate which fell upon our trolls and pixies. The latter, with the major Saxon deities, were perhaps no great loss in themselves, but they left an empty place; and perhaps our mythology was further impoverished by the divorce from Rome. Milton's celestial and infernal regions are large but insufficiently furnished apartments filled by heavy conversation; and one remarks about the Puritan mythology its thinness. And about Blake's supernatural territories, as about the supposed ideas that dwell there, we cannot help commenting on a certain meanness of culture. They illustrate the crankiness, the eccentricity, which frequently affects writers outside of the Latin traditions, and which such a critic as Arnold should certainly have rebuked. And they are not essential to Blake's inspiration.

Blake was endowed with a capacity for considerable understanding of human nature, with a remarkable and original sense of language and the music of language, and a gift of hallucinated vision. Had these been controlled by a respect for impersonal reason, for common sense, for the objectivity of science, it would have been better for him. What his genius required, and what it sadly lacked, was a framework of accepted and traditional ideas which would have prevented him from indulging in a philosophy of his own, and concentrated his attention upon the problems of the poet. Confusion of thought, emotion, and vision is what we find in such a work as *Also Sprach Zarathustra;* it is eminently not a Latin virtue. The concentration resulting from a framework of mythology and theology and philosophy is one of the reasons why Dante is a classic, and Blake only a poet of genius. The fault is perhaps not with Blake himself, but with the environment which failed to provide what such a poet needed; perhaps the circumstances compelled him to fabricate, perhaps the poet required the philosopher and mythologist; although the conscious Blake may have been quite unconscious of the motives.

SWINBURNE AS POET

IT is a question of some nicety to decide how much must be read of any particular poet. And it is not a question merely of the size of the poet. There are some poets whose every line has unique value. There are others who can be taken by a few poems universally agreed upon. There are others who need be read only in selections, but what selections are read will not very much matter. Of Swinburne, we should like to have the *Atalanta* entire, and a volume of selections which should certainly contain *The Leper, Laus Veneris,* and *The Triumph of Time.* It ought to contain many more, but there is perhaps no other single poem which it would be an error to omit. A student of Swinburne will want to read one of the Stuart plays and dip into *Tristram of Lyonesse.* But almost no one, today, will wish to read the whole of Swinburne. It is not because Swinburne is voluminous; certain poets, equally voluminous, must be read entire. The necessity and the difficulty of a selection are due to the peculiar nature of Swinburne's contribution, which, it is hardly too much to say, is of a very different kind from that of any other poet of equal reputation.

We may take it as undisputed that Swinburne did make a contribution; that he did something that had not been done before, and that what he did will not turn out to be a fraud. And from that we may proceed to inquire what Swinburne's contribution was, and why, whatever critical solvents we employ to break down the structure of his verse, this contribution remains. The test is this: agreed that we do not (and I think that the present generation does not) greatly enjoy Swinburne, and agreed that (a more serious condemnation) at one period

of our lives we did enjoy him and now no longer enjoy him;
nevertheless, the words which we use to state our grounds of
dislike or indifference cannot be applied to Swinburne as they
can to bad poetry. The words of condemnation are words which
express his qualities. You may say "diffuse." But the diffuseness is essential; had Swinburne practised greater concentration
his verse would be, not better in the same kind, but a different
thing. His diffuseness is one of his glories. That so little material as appears to be employed in *The Triumph of Time*
should release such an amazing number of words, requires what
there is no reason to call anything but genius. You could not
condense *The Triumph of Time*. You could only leave out.
And this would destroy the poem; though no one stanza seems
essential. Similarly, a considerable quantity—a volume of selections—is necessary to give the quality of Swinburne although
there is perhaps no one poem essential in this selection.

If, then, we must be very careful in applying terms of censure, like "diffuse," we must be equally careful of praise. "The
beauty of Swinburne's verse is the sound," people say, explaining, "he had little visual imagination." I am inclined to think
that the word "beauty" is hardly to be used in connexion with
Swinburne's verse at all; but in any case the beauty or effect
of sound is neither that of music nor that of poetry which can
be set to music. There is no reason why verse intended to be
sung should not present a sharp visual image or convey an important intellectual meaning, for it supplements the music by
another means of affecting the feelings. What we get in Swinburne is an expression by sound, which could not possibly associate itself with music. For what he gives is not images and
ideas and music, it is one thing with a curious mixture of suggestions of all three.

> Shall I come, if I swim? wide are the waves, you see;
> Shall I come, if I fly, my dear Love, to thee?

This is Campion, and an example of the kind of music that is
not to be found in Swinburne. It is an arrangement and choice
of words which has a sound-value and at the same time a
coherent comprehensible meaning, and the two things—the mu-

sical value and meaning—are two things, not one. But in Swinburne there is no *pure* beauty—no pure beauty of sound, or of image, or of idea.

> *Music, when soft voices die,*
> *Vibrates in the memory;*
> *Odours, when sweet violets sicken,*
> *Live within the sense they quicken.*
>
> *Rose leaves, when the rose is dead,*
> *Are heaped for the beloved's bed;*
> *And so thy thoughts, when thou art gone,*
> *Love itself shall slumber on.*

I quote from Shelley, because Shelley is supposed to be the master of Swinburne; and because his song, like that of Campion, has what Swinburne has not—a beauty of music and a beauty of content; and because it is clearly and simply expressed, with only two adjectives. Now, in Swinburne the meaning and the sound are one thing. He is concerned with the meaning of the word in a peculiar way: he employs, or rather "works," the word's meaning. And this is connected with an interesting fact about his vocabulary: he uses the most general word, because his emotion is never particular, never in direct line of vision, never focused; it is emotion reinforced, not by intensification, but by expansion.

> *There lived a singer in France of old*
> *By the tideless dolorous midland sea.*
> *In a land of sand and ruin and gold*
> *There shone one woman, and none but she.*

You see that Provence is the merest point of diffusion here. Swinburne defines the place by the most general word, which has for him its own value. "Gold," "ruin," "dolorous": it is not merely the sound that he wants, but the vague associations of idea that the words give him. He has not his eye on a particular place, as:

> *Li ruscelletti che dei verdi colli*
> *Del Casentin discendon giuso in Arno . . .*

It is, in fact, the word that gives him the thrill, not the object. When you take to pieces any verse of Swinburne, you find always that the object was not there—only the word. Compare.

> *Snowdrops that plead for pardon*
> *And pine for fright*

with the daffodils that come before the swallow dares. The snowdrop of Swinburne disappears, the daffodil of Shakespeare remains. The swallow of Shakespeare remains in the verse in *Macbeth;* the bird of Wordsworth

> *Breaking the silence of the seas*

remains; the swallow of "Itylus" disappears. Compare, again, a chorus of *Atalanta* with a chorus from Athenian tragedy. The chorus of Swinburne is almost a parody of the Athenian: it is sententious, but it has not even the significance of commonplace.

> *At least we witness of thee ere we die*
> *That these things are not otherwise, but thus. . . .*

> *Before the beginning of years*
> *There came to the making of man*
> *Time with a gift of tears;*
> *Grief with a glass that ran. . . .*

This is not merely "music"; it is effective because it appears to be a tremendous statement, like statements made in our dreams; when we wake up we find that the "glass that ran" would do better for time than for grief, and that the gift of tears would be as appropriately bestowed by grief as by time.

It might seem to be intimated, by what has been said, that the work of Swinburne can be shown to be a sham, just as bad verse is a sham. It would only be so if you could produce or suggest something that it pretends to be and is not. The world of Swinburne does not depend upon some other world which it simulates; it has the necessary completeness and self-sufficiency for justification and permanence. It is impersonal, and no one else could have made it. The deductions are true to the postulates. It is indestructible. None of the obvious complaints that were or might have been brought to bear upon the first *Poems and Ballads* holds good. The poetry is not morbid, it is not erotic, it is not destructive. These are adjectives which can be applied to the material, the human feelings, which in Swinburne's case do not exist. The morbidity is not of human feeling but of language. Language in a healthy state presents the object, is so close to the object that the two are identified.

They are identified in the verse of Swinburne solely because the object has ceased to exist, because the meaning is merely the hallucination of meaning, because language, uprooted, has adapted itself to an independent life of atmospheric nourishment. In Swinburne, for example, we see the word "weary" flourishing in this way independent of the particular and actual weariness of flesh or spirit. The bad poet dwells partly in a world of objects and partly in a world of words, and he never can get them to fit. Only a man of genius could dwell so exclusively and consistently among words as Swinburne. His language is not, like the language of bad poetry, dead. It is very much alive, with this singular life of its own. But the language which is more important to us is that which is struggling to digest and express new objects, new groups of objects, new feelings, new aspects, as, for instance, the prose of Mr. James Joyce or the earlier Conrad.

IN MEMORIAM

⸻

TENNYSON is a great poet, for reasons that are perfectly clear. He has three qualities which are seldom found together except in the greatest poets: abundance, variety, and complete competence. We therefore cannot appreciate his work unless we read a good deal of it. We may not admire his aims: but whatever he sets out to do, he succeeds in doing, with a mastery which gives us the sense of confidence that is one of the major pleasures of poetry. His variety of metrical accomplishment is astonishing. Without making the mistake of trying to write Latin verse in English, he knew everything about Latin versification that an English poet could use; and he said of himself that he thought he knew the quantity of the sounds of every English word except perhaps *scissors*. He had the finest ear of any English poet since Milton. He was the master of Swinburne; and the versification of Swinburne, himself a classical scholar, is often crude and sometimes cheap in comparison with Tennyson's. Tennyson extended very widely the range of active metrical forms in English: in *Maud* alone the variety is prodigious. But innovation in metric is not to be measured solely by the width of the deviation from accepted practice. It is a matter of the historical situation: at some moments a more violent change may be necessary than at others. The problem differs at every period. At some times, a violent revolution may be neither possible nor desirable; at such times, a change which may appear very slight is the change which the important poet will make. The innovation of Pope, after Dryden, may not seem very great; but it is the mark of the master to be able to make small changes which will be highly significant, as at another time to make radical changes, through which poetry will curve back again to its norm.

There is an early poem, only published in the official biography, which already exhibits Tennyson as a master. According to a note, Tennyson later expressed regret that he had removed the poem from his *Juvenilia*; it is a fragmentary *Hesperides*, in which only the "Song of the Three Sisters" is complete. The poem illustrates Tennyson's classical learning and his mastery of metre. The first stanza of the "Song of the Three Sisters" is as follows:

The Golden Apple, the Golden Apple, the hallow'd fruit,
Guard it well, guard it warily,
Singing airily,
Standing about the charmèd root.
Round about all is mute,
As the snowfield on the mountain peaks,
As the sandfield at the mountain foot.
Crocodiles in briny creeks
Sleep and stir not; all is mute.
If ye sing not, if ye make false measure,
We shall lose eternal pleasure,
Worth eternal want of rest.
Laugh not loudly: watch the treasure
Of the wisdom of the West.
In a corner wisdom whispers. Five and three
(Let it not be preach'd abroad) make an awful mystery:
For the blossom unto threefold music bloweth;
Evermore it is born anew,
And the sap in threefold music floweth,
From the root,
Drawn in the dark,
Up to the fruit,
Creeping under the fragrant bark,
Liquid gold, honeysweet through and through.
Keen-eyed Sisters, singing airily,
Looking warily
Every way,

Guard the apple night and day,
Lest one from the East come and take it away.

A young man who can write like that has not much to learn about metric; and the young man who wrote these lines somewhere between 1828 and 1830 was doing something new. There is something not derived from any of his predecessors. In some of Tennyson's early verse the influence of Keats is visible—in songs and in blank verse; and less successfully, there is the influence of Wordsworth, as in *Dora*. But in the lines I have just quoted, and in the two Mariana poems, *The Sea-Fairies*, *The Lotos-Eaters*, *The Lady of Shalott* and elsewhere, there is something wholly new.

> *All day within the dreamy house,*
> *The doors upon their hinges creak'd;*
> *The blue fly sung in the pane; the mouse*
> *Behind the mouldering wainscoat shriek'd,*
> *Or from the crevice peer'd about.*

The blue fly sung in the pane (the line would be ruined if you substituted *sang* for *sung*) is enough to tell us that something important has happened.

The reading of long poems is not nowadays much practised: in the age of Tennyson it appears to have been easier. For a good many long poems were not only written but widely circulated; and the level was high: even the second-rate long poems of that time, like *The Light of Asia*, are better worth reading than most long modern novels. But Tennyson's long poems are not long poems in quite the same sense as those of his contemporaries. They are very different in kind from *Sordello* or *The Ring and the Book*, to name the greatest by the greatest of his contemporary poets. *Maud* and *In Memoriam* are each a series of poems, given form by the greatest lyrical resourcefulness that a poet has ever shown. The *Idylls of the King* have merits and defects similar to those of *The Princess*. An idyll is a "short poem descriptive of some picturesque scene or incident"; in choosing the name Tennyson perhaps showed an appreciation of his limitations. For his poems are always descriptive, and always picturesque; they are never really narrative. The *Idylls of the King* are no different in kind from some of his early poems; the *Morte d'Arthur* is in fact an early poem. *The Princess* is still an idyll, but an idyll that is too long. Tennyson's versification in this poem is as masterly as elsewhere: it is a poem which we must read, but which we excuse ourselves from reading twice. And it is worth while recognizing the reason why we return again and again, and are always stirred by the lyrics which intersperse it, and which are among the greatest of all poetry of their kind, and yet avoid the poem itself. It is not, as we may think while reading, the outmoded attitude towards the relations of the sexes, the exasperating views on the subjects of matrimony, celibacy and female education, that make us recoil from *The Princess*.[1] We can swallow the most antipathetic doctrines if we are given an exciting narrative. But for narrative Tennyson had no gift at all. For a static poem, and a moving poem, on the same subject, you have only to compare his *Ulysses* with the condensed and intensely exciting narrative of that hero in the XXVIth Canto of Dante's *Inferno*. Dante is telling a story. Tennyson is only stating an elegiac mood. The very greatest poets set before you real men talking, carry you on in real events moving. Tennyson could not tell a story at all. It is not that in *The Princess* he tries to tell a story and failed: it is rather that an idyll protracted to such length becomes unreadable. So *The Princess* is a dull poem; one of the poems of which we may say that they are beautiful but dull.

But in *Maud* and in *In Memoriam*, Tennyson is doing what every conscious artist does, turning his limitations to good purpose. *Maud* consists of a few very beautiful lyrics, such as *O let the solid ground, Birds in the high Hall-garden,* and *Go not, happy day,* around which the semblance of a dramatic situation has been constructed with the greatest metrical virtuosity. The whole situation is unreal; the ravings of the lover on the edge of insanity sound false, and fail, as do the bellicose bellowings,

[1] For a revelation of the Victorian mind on these matters, and of opinions to which Tennyson would probably have subscribed, see the Introduction by Sir Edward Strachey, Bt., to his emasculated edition of the *Morte D'Arthur* of Malory, still current. Sir Edward admired the *Idylls of the King*.

to make one's flesh creep with sincerity. It would be foolish to suggest that Tennyson ought to have gone through some experience similar to that described: for a poet with dramatic gifts, a situation quite remote from his personal experience may release the strongest emotion. And I do not believe for a moment that Tennyson was a man of mild feelings or weak passions. There is no evidence in his poetry that he knew the experience of violent passion for a woman; but there is plenty of evidence of emotional intensity and violence—but of emotion so deeply suppressed, even from himself, as to tend rather towards the blackest melancholia than towards dramatic action. And it is emotion which, so far as my reading of the poems can discover, attained no ultimate clear purgation. I should reproach Tennyson not for mildness, or tepidity, but rather for lack of serenity.

> *Of love that never found his earthly close,*
> *What sequel?*

The fury of *Maud* is shrill rather than deep, though one feels in every passage what exquisite adaptation of metre to the mood Tennyson is attempting to express. I think that the effect of feeble violence, which the poem as a whole produces, is the result of a fundamental error of form. A poet can express his feelings as fully through a dramatic, as through a lyrical form; but *Maud* is neither one thing nor the other: just as *The Princess* is more than an idyll, and less than a narrative. In *Maud*, Tennyson neither identifies himself with the lover, nor identifies the lover with himself: consequently, the real feelings of Tennyson, profound and tumultuous as they are, never arrive at expression.

It is, in my opinion, in *In Memoriam*, that Tennyson finds full expression. Its technical merit alone is enough to ensure its perpetuity. While Tennyson's technical competence is everywhere masterly and satisfying, *In Memoriam* is the most unapproachable of all his poems. Here are one hundred and thirty-two passages, each of several quatrains in the same form, and never monotony or repetition. And the poem has to be comprehended as a whole. We may not memorize a few passages, we cannot find a "fair sample"; we have to comprehend the whole of a poem which is essentially the length that it is. We may choose to remember:

> Dark house, by which once more I stand
> Here in the long unlovely street,
> Doors, where my heart was used to beat
> So quickly, waiting for a hand,
>
> A hand that can be clasp'd no more—
> Behold me, for I cannot sleep,
> And like a guilty thing I creep
> At earliest morning to the door.
>
> He is not here; but far away
> The noise of life begins again,
> And ghastly thro' the drizzling rain
> On the bald street breaks the blank day.

This is great poetry, economical of words, a universal emotion related to a particular place; and it gives me the shudder that I fail to get from anything in *Maud*. But such a passage, by itself, is not *In Memoriam*: *In Memoriam* is the whole poem. It is unique: it is a long poem made by putting together lyrics, which have only the unity and continuity of a diary, the concentrated diary of a man confessing himself. It is a diary of which we have to read every word.

Apparently Tennyson's contemporaries, once they had accepted *In Memoriam*, regarded it as a message of hope and reassurance to their rather fading Christian faith. It happens now and then that a poet by some strange accident expresses the mood of his generation, at the same time that he is expressing a mood of his own which is quite remote from that of his generation. This is not a question of insincerity: there is an amalgam of yielding and opposition below the level of consciousness. Tennyson himself, on the conscious level of the man who talks to reporters and poses for photographers, to judge from remarks made in conversation and recorded in his son's Memoir, consistently asserted a convinced, if somewhat sketchy, Christian belief. And he was a friend of Frederick Denison Maurice—nothing seems odder about that age than the respect which its eminent people felt for each other. Nevertheless, I get a very different impression from *In Memoriam* from that which Tennyson's contemporaries seem to have got. It is of a very much more interesting and tragic Tennyson. His biographers have not failed to remark that he had a good deal of the temperament of the mystic—certainly not at all the mind of the theologian. He was desperately anxious to hold the faith of the believer, without being very clear about what he wanted to believe: he was capable of illumination which he was incapable of understanding. The "Strong Son of God, immortal Love," with an invocation of whom the poem opens, has only a hazy connexion with the Logos, or the Incarnate God. Tennyson is distressed by the idea of a mechanical universe; he is naturally, in lamenting his friend, teased by the hope of immortality and reunion beyond death. Yet the renewal craved for seems at best but a continuance, or a substitute for the joys of friendship upon earth. His desire for immortality never is quite the desire for Eternal Life; his concern is for the loss of man rather than for the gain of God.

> shall he,
> Man, her last work, who seem'd so fair,
>   Such splendid purpose in his eyes,
>   Who roll'd the psalm to wintry skies,
> Who built him fanes of fruitless prayer,
>
> Who trusted God was love indeed,
>   And love Creation's final law—
>   Tho' Nature, red in tooth and claw
> With ravine, shriek'd against his creed—
>
> Who loved, who suffer'd countless ills,
>   Who battled for the True, the Just,
>   Be blown about the desert dust,
> Or seal'd within the iron hills?

That strange abstraction, "Nature," becomes a real god or goddess, perhaps more real, at moments, to Tennyson than God (*"Are God and Nature then at strife?"*). The hope of immortality is confused (typically of the period) with the hope of the gradual and steady improvement of this world. Much has been said of Tennyson's interest in contemporary science, and of the impression of Darwin. *In Memoriam,* in any case, antedates *The Origin of Species* by several years, and the belief in social progress by democracy antedates it by many more; and I suspect that the faith of Tennyson's age in human progress would have been quite as strong even had the discoveries of Darwin been postponed by fifty years. And after all, there is no logical connexion: the belief in progress being current already, the discoveries of Darwin were harnessed to it:

> *No longer half-akin to brute,*
>   *For all we thought, and loved and did*
>   *And hoped, and suffer'd, is but seed*
> *Of what in them is flower and fruit;*
>
> *Whereof the man, that with me trod*
>   *This planet, was a noble type*
>   *Appearing ere the times were ripe,*
> *That friend of mine who lives in God,*
>
> *That God, which ever lives and loves,*
>   *One God, one law, one element,*
>   *And one far-off divine event,*
> *To which the whole creation moves.*

These lines show an interesting compromise between the religious attitude and, what is quite a different thing, the belief in human perfectibility; but the contrast was not so apparent to Tennyson's contemporaries. They may have been taken in by it, but I don't think that Tennyson himself was, quite: his feelings were more honest than his mind. There is evidence elsewhere—even in an early poem, *Locksley Hall,* for example—that Tennyson by no means regarded with complacency all the changes that were going on about him in the progress of industrialism and the rise of the mercantile and manufacturing and banking classes; and he may have contemplated the future of England, as his years drew out, with increasing gloom. Temperamentally, he was opposed to the doctrine that he was moved to accept and to praise.

Tennyson's feelings, I have said, were honest; but they were usually a good way below the surface. *In Memoriam* can, I think, justly be called a religious poem, but for another reason than that which made it seem religious to his contemporaries. It is not religious because of the quality of its faith, but because of the quality of its doubt. Its faith is a poor thing, but its doubt is a very intense experience. *In Memoriam* is a poem of despair, but of despair of a religious kind. And to qualify its despair with the adjective "religious" is to elevate it above most of its derivatives. For *The City of Dreadful Night*, and *A Shropshire Lad*, and the poems of Thomas Hardy, are small work in comparison with *In Memoriam:* It is greater than they and comprehends them.[2]

In ending we must go back to the beginning and remember that *In Memoriam* would not be a great poem, or Tennyson a great poet, without the technical accomplishment. Tennyson is the great master of metric as well as of melancholia; I do not think any poet in English has ever had a finer ear for vowel sound, as well as a subtler feeling for some moods of anguish:

> *Dear as remember'd kisses after death,*
> *And sweet as those by hopeless fancy feign'd*
> *On lips that are for others; deep as love,*
> *Deep as first love, and wild with all regret.*

And this technical gift of Tennyson's is no slight thing. Tennyson lived in a time which was already acutely time-conscious: a great many things seemed to be happening, railways were being built, discoveries were being made, the face of the world was changing. That was a time busy in keeping up to date. It had, for the most part, no hold on permanent things, on permanent truths about man and God and life and death. The surface of Tennyson stirred about with his time; and he had nothing to which to hold fast except his unique and unerring feeling for

[2] There are other kinds of despair. Davidson's great poem, *Thirty Bob a Week*, is not derivative from Tennyson. On the other hand, there are other things derivative from Tennyson besides *Atalanta in Calydon*. Compare the poems of William Morris with *The Voyage of Maeldune*, and *Barrack Room Ballads* with several of Tennyson's later poems.

the sounds of words. But in this he had something that no one else had. Tennyson's surface, his technical accomplishment, is intimate with his depths: what we most quickly see about Tennyson is that which moves between the surface and the depths, that which is of slight importance. By looking innocently at the surface we are most likely to come to the depths, to the abyss of sorrow. Tennyson is not only a minor Virgil, he is also with Virgil as Dante saw him, a Virgil among the Shades, the saddest of all English poets, among the Great in Limbo, the most instinctive rebel against the society in which he was the most perfect conformist.

Tennyson seems to have reached the end of his spiritual development with *In Memoriam;* there followed no reconciliation, no resolution.

> *And now no sacred staff shall break in blossom,*
> *No choral salutation lure to light*
> *A spirit sick with perfume and sweet night,*

or rather with twilight, for Tennyson faced neither the darkness nor the light in his later years. The genius, the technical power, persisted to the end, but the spirit had surrendered. A gloomier end than that of Baudelaire: Tennyson had no *singulier avertissement.* And having turned aside from the journey through the dark night, to become the surface flatterer of his own time, he has been rewarded with the despite of an age that succeeds his own in shallowness.

VI

LANCELOT ANDREWES

T HE Right Reverend Father in God, Lancelot
Bishop of Winchester, died on September 25, 1626. During his
lifetime he enjoyed a distinguished reputation for the excellence
of his sermons, for the conduct of his diocese, for his ability in
controversy displayed against Cardinal Bellarmine, and for
the decorum and devotion of his private life. Some years after
Andrewes's death Lord Clarendon, in his *History of the Rebellion*, expressed regret that Andrewes had not been chosen
instead of Abbott to the Archbishopric of Canterbury, for thus
affairs in England might have taken a different course. By authorities on the history of the English Church Andrewes is still
accorded a high, perhaps the highest, place; among persons interested in devotion his *Private Prayers* are not unknown. But
among those persons who read sermons, if they read them at
all, as specimens of English prose, Andrewes is little known.
His sermons are too well built to be readily quotable; they stick
too closely to the point to be entertaining. Yet they rank with
the finest English prose of their time, of any time. Before attempting to remove the remains of his reputation to a last rest-
ing place in the dreary cemetery of literature, it is desirable
to remind the reader of Andrewes's position in history.

The Church of England is the creation not of the reign of
Henry VIII or of the reign of Edward VI, but of the reign of
Elizabeth. The *via media* which is the spirit of Anglicanism was
the spirit of Elizabeth in all things; the last of the humble
Welsh family of Tudor was the first and most complete incarnation of English policy. The taste or sensibility of Elizabeth,
developed by her intuitive knowledge of the right policy for the

hour and her ability to choose the right men to carry out that policy, determined the future of the English Church. In its persistence in finding a mean between Papacy and Presbytery the English Church under Elizabeth became something representative of the finest spirit of England of the time. It came to reflect not only the personality of Elizabeth herself, but the best community of her subjects of every rank. Other religious impulses, of varying degrees of spiritual value, were to assert themselves with greater vehemence during the next two reigns. But the Church at the end of the reign of Elizabeth, and as developed in certain directions under the next reign, was a masterpiece of ecclesiastical statesmanship. The same authority that made use of Gresham, and of Walsingham, and of Cecil, appointed Parker to the Archbishopric of Canterbury; the same authority was later to appoint Whitgift to the same office.

To the ordinary cultivated student of civilization the genesis of a Church is of little interest, and at all events we must not confound the history of a Church with its spiritual meaning. To the ordinary observer the English Church in history means Hooker and Jeremy Taylor—and should mean Andrewes also: it means George Herbert, and it means the churches of Christopher Wren. This is not an error: a Church is to be judged by its intellectual fruits, by its influence on the sensibility of the most sensitive and on the intellect of the most intelligent, and it must be made real to the eye by monuments of artistic merit. The English Church has no literary monument equal to that of Dante, no intellectual monument equal to that of St. Thomas, no devotional monument equal to that of St. John of the Cross, no building so beautiful as the Cathedral of Modena or the basilica of St. Zeno in Verona. But there are those for whom the City churches are as precious as any of the four hundred odd churches in Rome which are in no danger of demolition, and for whom St. Paul's, in comparison with St. Peter's, is not lacking in decency; and the English devotional verse of the seventeenth century—admitting the one difficult case of conversion, that of Crashaw—finer than that of any other country or religious communion at the time.

The intellectual achievement and the prose style of Hooker and Andrewes came to complete the structure of the English Church as the philosophy of the thirteenth century crowns the Catholic Church. To make this statement is not to compare the *Laws of Ecclesiastical Polity* with the *Summa*. The seventeenth century was not an age in which the Churches occupied themselves with metaphysics, and none of the writings of the fathers of the English Church belongs to the category of speculative philosophy. But the achievement of Hooker and Andrewes was to make the English Church more worthy of intellectual assent. No religion can survive the judgment of history unless the best minds of its time have collaborated in its construction; if the Church of Elizabeth is worthy of the age of Shakespeare and Jonson, that is because of the work of Hooker and Andrewes.

The writings of both Hooker and Andrewes illustrate that determination to stick to essentials, that awareness of the needs of the time, the desire for clarity and precision on matters of importance, and the indifference to matters indifferent, which was the general policy of Elizabeth. These characteristics are illustrated in the definition of the Church in the second book of the *Ecclesiastical Polity*. ("The Church of Christ which was from the beginning is and continueth until the end.") And in both Hooker and Andrewes—the latter the friend and intimate of Isaac Casaubon—we find also that breadth of culture, an ease with humanism and Renaissance learning, which helped to put them on terms of equality with their Continental antagonists and to elevate their Church above the position of a local heretical sect. They were fathers of a national Church and they were Europeans. Compare a sermon of Andrewes with a sermon by another earlier master, Latimer. It is not merely that Andrewes knew Greek, or that Latimer was addressing a far less cultivated public, or that the sermons of Andrewes are peppered with allusion and quotation. It is rather that Latimer, the preacher of Henry VIII and Edward VI, is merely a Protestant; but the voice of Andrewes is the voice of a man who has a formed visible Church behind him, who speaks with the

old authority and the new culture. It is the difference of negative and positive: Andrewes is the first great preacher of the
English Catholic Church.

The sermons of Andrewes are not easy reading. They are
only for the reader who can elevate himself to the subject. The
most conspicuous qualities of the style are three: ordonnance,
or arrangement and structure, precision in the use of words, and
relevant intensity. The last remains to be defined. All of them
are best elucidated by comparison with a prose which is much
more widely known, but to which I believe that we must assign
a lower place—that of Donne. Donne's sermons, or fragments
from Donne's sermons, are certainly known to hundreds who
have hardly heard of Andrewes; and they are known precisely
for the reasons because of which they are inferior to those of
Andrewes. In the introduction to an admirable selection of passages from Donne's sermons, which was published a few years
ago by the Oxford Press, Mr. Logan Pearsall Smith, after
"trying to explain Donne's sermons and account for them in a
satisfactory manner," observes:

> "And yet in these, as in his poems, there remains something
> baffling and enigmatic which still eludes our last analysis. Read-
> ing these old hortatory and dogmatic pages, the thought sug-
> gests itself that Donne is often saying something else, some-
> thing poignant and personal, and yet, in the end, incommuni-
> cable to us."

We may cavil at the word "incommunicable," and pause to ask
whether the incommunicable is not often the vague and un-
formed; but the statement is essentially right. About Donne
there hangs the shadow of the impure motive; and impure motives lend their aid to a facile success. He is a little of the religious spellbinder, the Reverend Billy Sunday of his time,
the flesh-creeper, the sorcerer of emotional orgy. We emphasize
this aspect to the point of the grotesque. Donne had a trained
mind; but without belittling the intensity or the profundity of
his experience, we can suggest that this experience was not
perfectly controlled, and that he lacked spiritual discipline.

But Bishop Andrewes is one of the community of the born spiritual, one

che in questo mondo,
contemplando, gustò di quella pace.

Intellect and sensibility were in harmony; and hence arise the particular qualities of his style. Those who would prove this harmony would do well to examine, before proceeding to the sermons, the volume of *Preces Privatae*. This book, composed by him for his private devotions, was printed only after his death; a few manuscript copies may have been given away during his lifetime—one bears the name of William Laud. It appears to have been written in Latin and translated by him into Greek; some of it is in Hebrew; it has been several times translated into English. The most recent edition is the translation of the late F. E. Brightman, with an interesting introduction (Methuen, 1903). They are almost wholly an arrangement of Biblical texts, and of texts from elsewhere in Andrewes's immense theological reading. Dr. Brightman has a paragraph of admirable criticism of these prayers which deserves to be quoted in full:

"But the structure is not merely an external scheme or framework: the internal structure is as close as the external. Andrewes develops an idea he has in his mind: every line tells and adds something. He does not expatiate, but moves forward: if he repeats, it is because the repetition has a real force of expression; if he accumulates, each new word or phrase represents a new development, a substantive addition to what he is saying. He assimilates his material and advances by means of it. His quotation is not decoration or irrelevance, but the matter in which he expresses what he wants to say. His single thoughts are no doubt often suggested by the words he borrows, but the thoughts are made his own, and the constructive force, the fire that fuses them, is his own. And this internal, progressive, often poetic structure is marked outwardly. The editions have not always reproduced this feature of the *Preces*, nor perhaps is it possible in any ordinary page to represent the structure adequately; but in the manuscript the intention is clear enough.

The prayers are arranged, not merely in paragraphs, but in lines advanced and recessed, so as in a measure to mark the inner structure and the steps and stages of the movement. Both in form and in matter Andrewes's prayers may often be described rather as hymns."

The first part of this excellent piece of criticism may be applied equally well to the prose of Andrewes's sermons. The prayers themselves, which, as Canon Brightman seems to hint, should take for Anglicans a place beside the Exercises of St. Ignatius and the works of St. François de Sales, illustrate the devotion to private prayer (Andrewes is said to have passed nearly five hours a day in prayer) and to public ritual which Andrewes bequeathed to William Laud; and his passion for order in religion is reflected in his passion for order in prose.

Readers who hesitate before the five large volumes of Andrewes's sermons in *The Library of Anglo-Catholic Theology* may find their introduction more easy through the *Seventeen Sermons on the Nativity*, which were published separately in a small volume by Griffith, Farran, Okeden and Welsh, in *The Ancient and Modern Library of Theological Literature*, and which can still be picked up here and there. It is an additional advantage that these sermons are all on the same subject, the Incarnation; they are the Christmas Day sermons preached before King James between 1605 and 1624. And in the sermons preached before King James, himself a theologian, Andrewes was not hampered as he sometimes was in addressing more popular audiences. His erudition had full play, and his erudition is essential to his originality.

Bishop Andrewes, as was hinted above, tried to confine himself in his sermons to the elucidation of what he considered essential in dogma; he said himself that in sixteen years he had never alluded to the question of predestination, to which the Puritans, following their Continental brethren, attached so much importance. The Incarnation was to him an essential dogma, and we are able to compare seventeen developments of the same idea. Reading Andrewes on such a theme is like listening to a great Hellenist expounding a text of the *Posterior Analy-*

tics: altering the punctuation, inserting or removing a comma or a semicolon to make an obscure passage suddenly luminous, dwelling on a single word, comparing its use in its nearer and in its most remote contexts, purifying a disturbed or cryptic lecture-note into lucid profundity. To persons whose minds are habituated to feed on the vague jargon of our time, when we have a vocabulary for everything and exact ideas about nothing—when a word half-understood, torn from its place in some alien or half-formed science, as of psychology, conceals from both writer and reader the meaninglessness of a statement, when all dogma is in doubt except the dogmas of sciences of which we have read in the newspapers, when the language of theology itself, under the influence of an undisciplined mysticism of popular philosophy, tends to become a language of tergiversation—Andrewes may seem pedantic and verbal. It is only when we have saturated ourselves in his prose, followed the movement of his thought, that we find his examination of words terminating in the ecstasy of assent. Andrewes takes a word and derives the world from it; squeezing and squeezing the word until it yields a full juice of meaning which we should never have supposed any word to possess. In this process the qualities which we have mentioned, of ordonnance and precision, are exercised.

Take, almost at random, a passage from Andrewes's exposition of the text, "For unto you is born this day in the city of David a Saviour, which is Christ the Lord" (Luke ii. 11). Any passage that we can choose must be torn violently from its context.

"Who is it? Three things are said of this Child by the Angel. (1) He is 'a Saviour.' (2) 'Which is Christ.' (3) 'Christ the Lord.' Three of his titles, well and orderly inferred one of another by good consequence. We cannot miss one of them; they be necessary all. Our method on earth is to begin with great; in heaven they begin with good first.

"First, then, 'a Saviour'; that is His name, Jesus, *Soter*; and in that Name His benefit, *Salus*, 'saving health or salvation.' Such a name as the great Orator himself saith of it, *Soter*, *hoc quantum est? Ita magnum est ut latino uno verbo exprimi non possit.* 'This name Saviour is so great as no one word can express the force of it.'

"But we are not so much to regard the *ecce* how great it is, as *gaudium* what joy is in it; that is the point we are to speak to. And for that, men may talk what they will, but sure there is no joy in the world to the joy of a man saved; no joy so great, no news so welcome, as to one ready to perish, in case of a lost man, to hear of one that will save him. In danger of perishing by sickness, to hear of one will make him well again; by sentence of the law, of one with a pardon to save his life; by enemies, of one that will rescue and set him in safety. Tell any of these, assure them but of a Saviour, it is the best news he ever heard in his life. There is joy in the name of a Saviour. And even this way, this Child is a Saviour too. *Potest hoc facere, sed hoc non est opus Ejus.* 'This He can do, but this is not His work'; a farther matter there is, a greater salvation He came for. And it may be we need not any of these; we are not presently sick, in no fear of the law, in no danger of enemies. And it may be, if we were, we fancy to ourselves to be relieved some other way. But that which He came for, that saving we need all; and none but He can help us to it. We have therefore all cause to be glad for the Birth of this Saviour."

And then, after this succession of short sentences—no one is more master of the short sentence than Andrewes—in which the effort is to find the exact meaning and make that meaning live, he slightly but sufficiently alters the rhythm in proceeding more at large:

"I know not how, but when we hear of saving or mention of a Saviour, presently our mind is carried to the saving of our skin, of our temporal state, of our bodily life, and farther saving we think not of. But there is another life not to be forgotten, and greater the dangers, and the destruction more to be feared than of this here, and it would be well sometimes we were remembered of it. Besides our skin and flesh a soul we have, and it is our better part by far, that also hath need of a Saviour; that hath her destruction out of which, that hath her destroyer from which she would be saved, and those would be thought on. Indeed our chief thought and care would be for that; how to escape the wrath, how to be saved from the destruction to come, whither our sins will certainly bring us. Sin it is will destroy us all."

In this extraordinary prose, which appears to repeat, to stand still, but is nevertheless proceeding in the most deliberate and orderly manner, there are often flashing phrases which never desert the memory. In an age of adventure and experiment in language, Andrewes is one of the most resourceful of authors in his devices for seizing the attention and impressing the memory. Phrases such as "Christ is no wild-cat. What talk ye of twelve days?" or "the word within a word, unable to speak a word," do not desert us; nor do the sentences in which, before extracting all the spiritual meaning of a text, Andrewes forces a concrete presence upon us.

Of the wise men come from the East:

"It was no summer progress. A cold coming they had of it at this time of the year, just the worst time of the year to take a journey, and specially a long journey in. The ways deep, the weather sharp, the days short, the sun farthest off, *in solstitio brumali*, 'the very dead of winter.' "

Of "the Word made flesh" again:

"I add yet farther; what flesh? The flesh of an infant. What, *Verbum infans*, the Word of an infant? The Word, and not be able to speak a word? How evil agreeth this! This He put up. How born, how entertained? In a stately palace, cradle of ivory, robes of estate? No; but a stable for His palace, a manger for His cradle, poor clouts for His array."

He will not hesitate to hammer, to inflect, even to play upon a word for the sake of driving home its meaning:

"Let us then make this so accepted a time in itself twice acceptable by our accepting, which He will acceptably take at our hands."

We can now better estimate what is this that we have called relevant intensity, for we have had enough of passages from Andrewes to recognize the extremity of his difference from Donne.

Every one knows a passage from a sermon of Donne's, which is given by Mr. Pearsall Smith under the title of "I am Not all Here."

"I am here speaking to you, and yet I consider by the way, in the same instant, what it is likely you will say to one another, when I have done, you are not all here neither; you are here now, hearing me, and yet you are thinking that you have heard a better sermon somewhere else of this text before; you are here, and yet you think you could have heard some other doctrine of downright *Predestination* and *Reprobation* roundly delivered somewhere else with more edification to you; you are here, and you remember yourselves that now yee think of it: This had been the fittest time, now, when everybody else is at church, to have made such and such a private visit; and because you would bee there, you are there,"

after which Mr. Pearsall Smith very happily places the paragraph on "Imperfect Prayers":

"A memory of yesterday's pleasures, a feare of tomorrow's dangers, a straw under my knee, a noise in mine eare, a light in mine eye, an anything, a nothing, a fancy, a Chimera in my braine, troubles me in my prayer. So certainly is there nothing, nothing in spirituall things, perfect in this world."

These are thoughts which would never have come to Andrewes. When Andrewes begins his sermon, from beginning to end you are sure that he is wholly in his subject, unaware of anything else, that his emotion grows as he penetrates more deeply into his subject, that he is finally "alone with the Alone," with the mystery which he is seeking to grasp more and more firmly. One is reminded of the words of Arnold about the preaching of Newman. Andrewes's emotion is purely contemplative; it is not personal, it is wholly evoked by the object of contemplation, to which it is adequate; his emotions wholly contained in and explained by its object. But with Donne there is always the something else, the "baffling" of which Mr. Pearsall Smith speaks in his introduction. Donne is a "personality" in a sense in which Andrewes is not: his sermons, one feels, are a "means of self-expression." He is constantly finding an object which shall be adequate to his feelings; Andrewes is wholly absorbed in the object and therefore responds with the adequate emotion. Andrewes has the *goût pour la vie spirituelle*, which is not native to Donne. On the other hand, it would be a great mistake to remember only that Donne was called to the priesthood by King James against his will, and that he accepted a benefice because he had no other way of making a living. Donne had a genuine taste both for theology and for religious emotion; but he belonged to that class of persons, of which there are always one or two examples in the modern world, who seek refuge in religion from the tumults of a strong emotional temperament which can find no complete satisfaction elsewhere. He is not wholly without kinship to Huysmans.

But Donne is not the less valuable, though he is the more dangerous for this reason. Of the two men, it may be said that Andrewes is the more mediaeval, because he is the more pure, and because his bond was with the Church, with tradition. His intellect was satisfied by theology and his sensibility by prayer and liturgy. Donne is the more modern—if we are careful to take this word exactly, without any implication of value, or any suggestion that we must have more sympathy with Donne than with Andrewes. Donne is much less the mystic; he is primarily interested in man. He is much less traditional. In his thought Donne has, on the one hand, much more in common with the Jesuits, and, on the other hand, much more in common with the Calvinists, than has Andrewes. Donne many times betrays the consequences of early Jesuit influence and of his later studies in Jesuit literature; in his cunning knowledge of the weaknesses of the human heart, his understanding of human sin, his skill in coaxing and persuading the attention of the variable human mind to Divine objects, and in a kind of smiling tolerance among his menaces of damnation. He is dangerous only for those who find in his sermons an indulgence of their sensibility, or for those who, fascinated by "personality" in the romantic sense of the word—for those who find in "personality" an ultimate value—forget that in the spiritual hierarchy there are places higher than that of Donne. Donne will certainly have always more readers than Andrewes, for the reason that his sermons can be read in detached passages and for the reason that they can be read by those who have no interest in the subject. He has many means of appeal, and appeals to many temperaments and minds, and, among others, to those capable of a certain wantonness of the spirit. Andrewes will never have many readers in any one generation, and his will never be the immortality of anthologies. Yet his prose is not inferior to that of any sermons in the language, unless it be some of Newman's. And even the larger public which does not read him may do well to remember his greatness in history—a place second to none in the history of the formation of the English Church.

JOHN BRAMHALL[1]

J OHN BRAMHALL, Bishop of Derry under
Charles I and Primate of Ireland under Charles II, is not at all
an easy subject for biography. He was a great man; but either
by defect of genius or by ill-luck he is not known as he should
be known, and his works are not read as they should be read.
Indeed, it is largely ill-luck. Not only were his immense energy
and ability divided among a number of important actions, so
that he has never become the symbolical representative of anything, but some of his most important activity was exerted
upon causes which are now forgotten. As Bishop of Derry, as
the lieutenant of Wentworth and Laud, he did much to reform and establish the Irish Church and to bring it into conformity with the English Church; he saw his work largely undone by Cromwell; as Primate of Ireland during the first years
of Charles II, and in his old age, he set to work to build it up
again. Had his labours been in England instead of Ireland he
might now be better remembered. His middle years were
spent in exile; and perhaps it is the work he performed during
these years, often in illness, danger, and vicissitudes, that should
earn him particular gratitude from his Church. This is a chapter
of Church history which is too little known; few people realize
how near in those times the English Church came to perishing
utterly, or realize that had the Commonwealth survived a few
years longer the Church would have fallen into a disorder from
which it might never have recovered. During the exile Bramhall was the stoutest inheritor of the tradition of Andrewes and
Laud.

[1] *Archbishop Bramhall*, by W. J. Sparrow-Simpson, D.D. (In the English
Theologians Series.) S.P.C.K.

Canon Sparrow-Simpson has treated the history of Bramhall's career in Ireland and his activities abroad during the
Commonwealth fully, but with a proper sense of proportion.
He leaves himself space to devote several chapters to Bramhall's
controversial writings; he is specially to be praised for the skill
with which he has digested these writings and condensed and
organized so much various information into two hundred and
fifty-one pages. With the purely historical matter I am not
competent to deal; Bramhall's life includes an important part
of the history of the Church and the history of England. But
there is still much interest to be found in Bramhall's writings,
and some of them are very much to the point at the present day.
One part of his work that is of particular importance is his controversy with Hobbes. It is sometimes cited by historians of
philosophy, but has never received the attention it deserves.
Bramhall, as Dr. Sparrow-Simpson points out, had by no means
the worst of the argument, and the whole debate, with the two
striking and opposed personalities engaged in it, throws light
upon the condition of philosophy and theology at that time. The
most important of the questions at issue are two: the freedom of
the will and the relation between Church and State.

Thomas Hobbes was one of those extraordinary little up-
starts whom the chaotic motions of the Renaissance tossed into
an eminence which they hardly deserved and have never lost.
When I say the Renaissance I mean for this purpose the period
between the decay of scholastic philosophy and the rise of
modern science. There was nothing particularly new about the
determinism of Hobbes; but he gave to his determinism and
theory of sense perception a new point and piquancy by applying
it, so to speak, almost to topical questions; and by his metaphor
of Leviathan he provided an ingenious framework on which
there was some peg or other to hang every question of philosophy, psychology, government, and economics.

Hobbes shows considerable ingenuity and determination in
his attempt to carry out his theory of the Will rigorously to
explain the whole and every aspect of human behaviour. It is
certain that in the end he lands himself in sophistries. But at the
time of Hobbes and Bramhall, and indeed ever since until re-

cently, it was unlikely that a controversy on this subject would keep to the point. For a philosopher like Hobbes has already a mixed attitude, partly philosophic and partly scientific; the philosophy being in decay and the science immature. Hobbes's philosophy is not so much a philosophy as it is an adumbration of the universe of material atoms regulated by laws of motion which formed the scientific view of the world from Newton to Einstein. Hence there is quite naturally no place in Hobbes's universe for the human will; what he failed to see is that there was no place in it for consciousness either, or for human beings. So his only philosophical theory is a theory of sense perception, and his psychology leaves no place in the world for his theory of government. His theory of government has no philosophic basis: it is merely a collection of discrete opinions, prejudices, and genuine reflections upon experience which are given a spurious unity by a shadowy metaphysic.

The attitude of Hobbes toward moral philosophy has by no means disappeared from human thought; nor has the confusion between moral philosophy and a mechanistic psychology. There is a modern theory, closely akin to that of Hobbes, which would make value reside entirely in the degree of organization of natural impulses. I cite the following passage from an important book by one of the most acute of younger psychologists:

"Anything is valuable which will satisfy an appetency without involving the frustration of some equal or more important appetency; in other words, the only reason which can be given for not satisfying a desire is that more important desires will thereby be thwarted. Thus morals become purely prudential, and ethical codes merely the expression of the most general schemes of expediency to which an individual or a race has attained." [2]

And Mr. Bertrand Russell, in his book, *What I Believe*, p. 43, sings the same tune:

"The practical need of morals arises from the conflict of desires, whether of different people or of the same person at different times or even at one time. A man desires to drink, and

[2] Richards, *Principles of Literary Criticism*, p. 48.

also to be fit for his work next morning. We think him immoral if he adopts the course which gives him the smaller total
satisfaction of desire."

The difficulty with such theories [3] is that they merely remove
the inherently valuable a further degree; just as Hobbes's Theory of Will removes freedom from the individual considered as
the object of psychology, but really implies the reality of free-
will in society. It will be remembered that Hobbes wished to
maintain the activity of human legislation in his deterministic
universe; so he considered that law acts as a deterrent force. He
did not consider that if human laws themselves are created by
the same necessity under which human beings act when encouraged or deterred by the laws, th   th whole system ceases to
have any meaning, and all valu ., including his own value of
good government, disappear.

It is not to be expected that the arguments advanced by
Bramhall against this position should appear very powerful
when opposed to the reasonings of modern disciples of Hobbes.
But in their own time and place they were excellent. I disregard that part of Bramhall's reasoning which consists in showing that Hobbes's system was incompatible with Christianity.
Hobbes was here in a very weak position of which the Bishop
with praiseworthy slyness took full advantage. Hobbes was undoubtedly an atheist and could hardly have been unconscious
of the fact; but he was no Spinoza, and would hardly have been
willing to sacrifice his worldly prospects for the sake of establishing consistency in his argument. Therefore he has always the
worst of the debate. But this is a minor point. Bramhall was
able to meet Hobbes also on his own ground. His method of
attack illustrates very clearly his type of mind. It was not a
subtle mind: it had not the refinement necessary to make a
scholastic metaphysician, nor was it the mind of a doctor of the
Church who could develop and explicate the meaning of a
dogma. It was essentially common sense and right instinct, a
mind not gifted to discover truth but tenacious to hold it. It

[3] A thoroughgoing "Behaviorism," as of Professor Watson, is a different
affair.

was typical of the best theological minds of that age. Hobbes suffers from not only a tactful but a real disadvantage in his confusion of the spheres of psychology and ethics. Bramhall is single-minded; he does not penetrate the real philosophical incoherence of Hobbes's position; but he touches the point of practical importance and implies the profounder objection to Hobbes when he says simply that Hobbes makes praise and blame meaningless. "If a man be born blind or with one eye, we do not blame him for it; but if a man have lost his sight by his intemperance, we blame him justly." This objection is finally unanswerable.

I have asserted that Hobbes's psychological analysis of the human mind has no rational connection with his theory of the State. But it has, of course, an emotional connection; one can say that both doctrines belong naturally to the same temperament. Materialistic determinism and absolutist government fit into the same scheme of life. And this theory of the State shows the same lack of balance which is a general characteristic of philosophers after the Renaissance. Hobbes merely exaggerates one aspect of the good State. In doing so he developed a particularly lamentable theory of the relation between Church and State.

There is no question to which a man like Hobbes can give a less satisfactory answer than that of Church and State. For Hobbes thought in extremes, and in this problem the extreme is always wrong. In the relation of Church and State, a doctrine when pushed to the extreme may even be transformed to the opposite of itself. Hobbes has something in common with Suarez.

Bramhall's position on this subject is characteristic of his sense of realities and his ability to grasp what was expedient. He had also what Hobbes lacked, the historical sense, which is a gift not only of the historian, but of the efficient lawyer, statesman, or theologian. His account of the relations of the English kings with the Papacy, from the earliest times, and his selection of parallels from the history of continental Europe, show both wide knowledge and great skill in argument. His thinking is a perfect example of the pursuit of the *via media*, and the *via media* is of all ways the most difficult to follow. It requires discipline and self-control, it requires both imagination and hold on reality. In a period of debility like our own, few men have the energy to follow the middle way in government; for lazy or tired minds there is only extremity or apathy: dictatorship or communism, with enthusiasm or with indifference. An able Conservative writer, Mr. Keith Feiling, in his *England under the Tudors and Stuarts*, refers to Hobbes as "the acutest thinker of the age." It would be equally true to say that he is the most eminent example in his age of a particularly lazy type of thinker. At any rate, the age owes a very great part of its distinction, both in England and in France, to thinkers of wholly the opposite type to Hobbes.

The French Church in the time of Louis XIV (*"il fut galli-cain, ce siècle, et janseniste"*) resembled the English Church un-der the Stuarts in several respects. In both countries a strong and autocratic civil Government controlled and worked with a strongly national Church. In each country there was a certain balance of power; in France between the throne and the Papacy; in England an internal balance of power between strong per-sonalities. There was much in common between Bramhall and Bossuet. But between Bramhall and Hobbes there is no sym-pathy whatever. Superficially their theories of the kingship bear some resemblance to each other. Both men were violently hostile to democracy in any form or degree. Both men believed that the monarch should have absolute power. Bramhall affirmed the divine right of kings: Hobbes rejected this noble faith, and asserted in effect the divine right of power, however come by. But Bramhall's view is not so absurdly romantic, or Hobbes's so soundly reasonable, as might seem. To Bramhall the king himself was a kind of symbol, and his assertion of divine right was a way of laying upon the king a double responsibility. It meant that the king had not merely a civil but a religious obli-gation toward his people. And the kingship of Bramhall is less absolute than the kingship of Hobbes. For Hobbes the Church was merely a department of the State, to be run exactly as the king thought best. Bramhall does not tell us clearly what would be the duties of a private citizen if the king should violate or overturn the Christian religion, but he obviously leaves a wide expedient margin for resistance or justified rebellion. It is curious that the system of Hobbes, as Dr. Sparrow-Simpson has observed, not only insists on autocracy but tolerates *unjustified* revolution. Hobbes's theory is in some ways very near to that of Machiavelli, with this important exception, that he has none of Machiavelli's profound observation and none of Machiavelli's limiting wisdom. The sole test and justification for Hobbes is in the end merely material success. For Hobbes all standards of good and evil are frankly relative.

It is extraordinary that a philosophy so essentially revolutionary as that of Hobbes, and so similar to that of contemporary Russia, should ever have been supposed to give any support to Toryism. But its ambiguity is largely responsible for its success. Hobbes was a revolutionary in thought and a timid conservative in action; and his theory of government is congenial to that type of person who is conservative from prudence but revolutionary in his dreams. This type of person is not altogether uncommon. In Hobbes there are symptoms of the same mentality as Nietzsche: his belief in violence is a confession of weakness. Hobbes's violence is of a type that often appeals to gentle people. His specious effect of unity between a very simple theory of sense perception and an equally simple theory of government is of a kind that will always be popular because it appears to be intellectual but is really emotional, and therefore very soothing to lazy minds.

Bramhall's abilities of thought and language are nowhere better displayed than in his *Just Vindication of the English Church*. As for the language of Bramhall, I think that Dr. Sparrow-Simpson does him less than justice. It is true that he employs in his vocabulary the most extraordinary confections of Latinity, but the catalogue of some of these expressions which Dr. Sparrow-Simpson gives would lead one to believe that they occur in every sentence. And although Bramhall is not an easy writer, his phrases are lucid and direct and occasionally have real beauty and rhythm. A theologian of his powers, at that period of English prose, a man trained on the theology and the style of Bishop Andrewes, could hardly fail to write prose of distinction.

"Every sudden passionate heat or misunderstanding or shaking of charity amongst Christians, though it were even between the principal pastors of the Church, is not presently schism. As that between Saint Paul and Barnabas in the Acts of the Apostles—who dare say that either of them were schismatic? or that between Saint Hierome and Ruffinus, who charged one another mutually with heresy; or that between Saint Chrysostom and Epiphanius, who refused to join in prayers; Saint Chrysostom wishing that Epiphanius might never return home alive, and Epiphanius wishing that Saint Chrysostom might not die a Bishop; both which things, by the just disposition of Almighty God, fell out according to the passionate and uncharitable desires of these holy persons; who had Christian charity still radicated in their hearts, though the violent torrent of sudden passion did for a time beat down all other respects before it."

This is rather heavy going, and the word "radicated" is one of those blemishes to which Dr. Sparrow-Simpson calls attention; but the style has distinction. In prose style, as well as in theology, Bramhall is a link between the generation of Andrewes and the generation of Jeremy Taylor. The prose of Bramhall is great prose only in the sense that it is good prose of a great epoch. I cannot believe that Bramhall was a great preacher. Andrewes and Donne and Taylor had a poetic sensibility; that is to say, they had the sensitiveness necessary to record and to bring to convergence on a theological point a multitude of fleeting but universal feelings. Their words linger and echo in the mind as Bramhall's never do; we forget Bramhall's phrases the moment we turn away from Bramhall's subject.

But for *ordonnance*, logical arrangement, for mastery of every fact relevant to a thesis, Bramhall is surpassed only by Hooker; and I am not sure that in the structure of the *Just Vindication of the English Church* he does not surpass even Hooker. And this book is no antiquity; it is a work which ought to be studied by any one to whom the relation of Church and State is an actual and importunate problem. There could hardly be a greater difference than that between the situation during the first half of the seventeenth century and the situation today. Yet the differences are such as to make the work of Bramhall the more pertinent to our problems. For they are differences in relation to a fundamental unity of thought between Bramhall, and what he represents, and ourselves.

THOUGHTS AFTER LAMBETH

T HE Church of England washes its dirty linen in
public. It is convenient and brief to begin with this metaphorical
statement. In contrast to some other institutions both civil and
ecclesiastical, the linen does get washed. To have linen to wash
is something; and to assert that one's linen never needed washing would be a suspicious boast. Without some understanding
of these habits of the Church, the reader of the Report of the
Lambeth Conference (1930) will find it a difficult and in some
directions a misleading document. The Report needs to be
read in the light of previous Reports; with some knowledge,
and with some sympathy for that oddest of institutions, the
Church of England.

The Conference is certainly more important than any report
of it can be. I mean that each Conference has its place in the
history of Lambeth Conferences, and that directions and tendencies are more significant than the precise formulation of the results obtained at any particular moment. To say that a significant direction can be traced, is not to applaud any aimless flux.
But I suspect that many readers of the Report, especially those
outside of the Anglican communion, are prepared to find (or
prepared to condemn because they know they will not find) the
clear hard and fast distinctions and decisions of a Papal Encyclical. Of such is Mr. George Malcolm Thomson, whose lively
pamphlet in this series [1] has given me food for thought. Between a Lambeth Conference Report and a Papal Encyclical
there is little similarity; there is a fundamental difference of

---

[1] *The Lambeth Conference*, by George Malcolm Thomson. Criterion Mis-
cellany.

intent. Perhaps the term "encyclical letter" for the archiepiscopal communication heading the Report is itself misleading, because it suggests to many minds the voice of final authority *de fide et moribus;* and to those who hope for the voice of absoluteness and the words of hard precision, the recommendations and pious hopes will be disappointing. Many, like Mr. Thomson, will exclaim that they find only platitudes, commonplaces, tergiversations and ambiguities. The Report of the Conference is not intended to be an absolute decree on questions of faith and morals; for the matter of that, the opinions expressed have no compulsion until ratified by Convocation. The Report, as a whole, is rather the expression of the ways in which the Church is moving, than an instruction to the faithful on belief and conduct.

Another consideration which we must keep in mind, before venturing to criticise the Report, is the manner of its composition. Some of the Report is to me, I admit at once, mere verbiage; some parts seem to me evasive; some parts seem to me to be badly expressed, at least if the ordinary uninstructed reader is acknowledged; one or two recommendations I deplore. But it ought not to be an occasion to us for mirth that three hundred bishops together assembled should, on pooling their views on most momentous matters, come out with a certain proportion of nonsense. I should not enjoy having to commit myself on any subject to any opinion which should also be that of any two hundred and ninety-nine of my acquaintance. Let us consider the quantity of nonsense that some of our most eminent scientists, professors and men of letters are able, each for himself, to turn out during every publishing season. Let us imagine (if we can imagine such persons agreeing to that extent) the fatuity of an encyclical letter produced by the joint efforts of Mr. H. G. Wells, Mr. Bernard Shaw and Mr. Russell; or Professors Whitehead, Eddington and Jeans; or Dr. Freud, Dr. Jung and Dr. Adler; or Mr. Murry, Mr. Fausset, the Huxley Brothers and the Reverend Dr. Potter of America.

With this comparison in mind, it is, I think, profitable to dispose first of those sections of the Report which are most insipid, and of that which has received most popular notice. I regret that what seem to me some of the best parts of the Report, such as the section on *The Christian Doctrine of God,* have been neglected in favour of those sections about which readers of the penny press are most ready to excite themselves. But if one is writing about the Report, one must be willing to offer one's own comment on these already over-commented sections. The report on "Youth and its Vocation" suggests that the bishops had been listening to ordinary popular drivel on the subject, or ordinary popular drivel about what the bishops themselves are supposed to believe. They begin with a protest which for any intelligent reader should be unnecessary. "We desire at the outset to protest emphatically against the contention that the Youth of today are, as a whole, less moral or less religious than youth of previous generations." It ought to be obvious that the Youth of today are not "as a whole" more or less anything than the youth of previous generations. The statement, not having much meaning, need not occupy much attention. "There are signs of a great intellectual stirring among the rising generation." One could wish that this journalistic hyperbole had been avoided. There can hardly be a great intellectual stirring among a whole generation, because the number of persons in any generation capable of being greatly stirred intellectually is always and everywhere very, very small. What the bishops might have said, I think, with justice, is this: that one does find here and there among educated young men a respect for the Church springing from a recognition of the intellectual ability which during two thousand years has gone to its formation. The number of persons interested in philosophy is always small; but whereas twenty years ago a young man attracted by metaphysical speculation was usually indifferent to theology, I believe that today a similar young man is more ready to believe that theology is a masculine discipline, than were those of my generation. If the capacity for faith be no greater, the prejudice against it is less; though one must remember to congratulate youth on finding themselves in this situation, before admiring them for taking advantage of it. I hope at this point that of the fifty bishops who committed themselves to the dismal trope that "youth of this generation . . . has admittedly struck its tents and is on the march," there was a large minority of dissentients. That is one of the troubles of the time: not only Youth but Middle Age is on the march; everybody, at least according to Fleet Street, is on the march; it does not matter what the destination is, the one thing contemptible is to sit still.

Youth, of course, is from one point of view merely a symptom of the results of what the middle-aged have been thinking and saying. I notice that the same fifty bishops refer guardedly to "the published works of certain authors whose recognized ability and position give undue weight to views on the relations of the sexes which are in direct conflict with Christian principles." I wish that they had mentioned names. For unfortunately, the only two authors of "recognized ability and position" officially disapproved in England are Mr. James Joyce and D. H. Lawrence; so that the fifty bishops have missed an opportunity of dissociating themselves from the condemnation of these two extremely serious and improving writers.[2] If, however, the fifty were thinking of Mr. Bertrand Russell or even of Mr. Aldous Huxley, then they are being apprehensive about what to me is a reason for cheerfulness; for if Youth has the spirit of a tomtit or the brain of a goose, it can hardly rally with enthusiasm to these two depressing life-forcers. (Not that Mr. Huxley, who has no philosophy that I can discover, and who succeeds to some extent in elucidating how sordid a world without any philosophy can be, has much in common with Mr. Russell.) I cannot regret that such views as Mr. Russell's, or what we may call the enervate *gospel of happiness*, are openly expounded and defended. They help to make clear, what the nineteenth century had been largely occupied in obscuring, that there is no such thing as just Morality; but that for any man who thinks clearly, as his Faith is so will his Morals be. Were my religion that of Mr. Russell, my views of conduct would very likely be his also; and I am sure in my own mind that I have not adopted my faith in order to defend my views of

[2] Some time ago, during the consulship of Lord Brentford, I suggested that if we were to have a Censorship at all, it ought to be at Lambeth Palace; but I suppose that the few persons who read my words thought that I was trying to be witty.

conduct, but have modified my views of conduct to conform with what seem to me the implications of my beliefs. The real conflict is not between one set of moral prejudices and another, but between the theistic and the atheistic faith; and it is all for the best that the division should be sharply drawn. Emancipation had some interest for venturous spirits when I was young, and must have been quite exciting to the previous generation; but the Youth to which the bishops' words apply is grey-haired now. Emancipation loses some of its charm in becoming respectable. Indeed, the gospel of happiness in the form preached by Mr. Russell in middle age is such as I cannot conceive as capable of making any appeal to Mr. Russell in youth, so mediocre and respectable is it. It has nothing to offer to those born into the world which Mr. Russell and others helped to create. The elders have had the satisfaction of throwing off prejudices; that is, of persuading themselves that the way they want to behave is the only moral way to behave; but there is not much in it for those who have no prejudices to reject. Christian morals gain immeasurably in richness and freedom by being seen as the consequence of Christian faith, and not as the imposition of tyrannical and irrational habit. What chiefly remains of the new freedom is its meagre impoverished emotional life; in the end it is the Christian who can have the more varied, refined and intense enjoyment of life; which time will demonstrate.

Before leaving the not very remunerative subject of Youth, I must mention another respect, not unrelated, in which Youth of today has some advantage over an earlier generation. (I dislike the word "generation," which has been a talisman for the last ten years; when I wrote a poem called *The Waste Land* some of the more approving critics said that I had expressed the "disillusionment of a generation," which is nonsense. I may have expressed for them their own illusion of being disillusioned, but that did not form part of my intention.) One of the most deadening influences upon the Church in the past, ever since the eighteenth century, was its acceptance, by the upper, upper middle and aspiring classes, as a political necessity and as a requirement of respectability. There are signs that the situation today is quite different. When, for instance, I brought out a small book of essays, several years ago, called *For Lancelot Andrewes*, the anonymous reviewer in the *Times Literary Supplement* made it the occasion for what I can only describe as a flattering obituary notice. In words of great seriousness and manifest sincerity, he pointed out that I had suddenly arrested my progress—whither he had supposed me to be moving I do not know—and that to his distress I was unmistakably making off in the wrong direction. Somehow I had failed, and had admitted my failure; if not a lost leader, at least a lost sheep; what is more, I was a kind of traitor; and those who were to find their way to the promised land beyond the waste, might drop a tear at my absence from the roll-call of the new saints. I suppose that the curiosity of this point of view will be apparent to only a few people. But its appearance in what is not only the best but the most respected and most respectable of our literary periodicals, came home to me as a hopeful sign of the times. For it meant that the orthodox faith of England is at last relieved from its burden of respectability. A new respectability has arisen to assume the burden; and those who would once have been considered intellectual vagrants are now pious pilgrims, cheerfully plodding the road from nowhere to nowhere, trolling their hymns, satisfied so long as they may be "on the march."

These changed conditions are so prevalent that any one who has been moving among intellectual circles and comes to the Church, may experience an odd and rather exhilarating feeling of isolation. The new orthodoxy, of course, has many forms, and the sectaries of one form sometimes speak hard words of others, but the outline of respectability is fairly clear. Mr. Middleton Murry, whose highly respectable new religion is continually heard to be "on the march" round the corner, though it has not reached us yet,[3] is able to say of his own version: "The words do not matter. If we can recreate the meaning—all the words of all the religions will be free to us, and we shall not want to use them." One is tempted to suggest that Mr. Murry has so many words in his employ already, including some of

[3] *I.e.*, in 1931.

his own creation, that he has no need to summon others. A writer still more respectable than Mr. Murry, because he is a Professor at an American University, is Mr. Norman Foerster, the fugleman of Humanism. Mr. Foerster, who has the honest simplicity to admit that he has very little acquaintance with Christianity beyond a narrow Protestantism which he repudiates, offers Humanism because it appeals to those "who can find in themselves no vocation for spiritual humility"! without perceiving at all that this is an exact parallel to saying that Companionate Marriage "appeals to those who can find in themselves no vocation for spiritual continence." It is true that to judge from his next paragraph he has at the back of his mind some foggy distinction between "spiritual humility" and "humility" plain, but the distinction, if present, is not developed. One can now be a distinguished professor, and a professional moralist to boot, without understanding the devotional sense of the word *vocation* or the theological sense of the virtue *humility;* a virtue, indeed, not conspicuous among modern men of letters. We have as many, as solemn, and as splendidly-robed prophets today as in any decade of the last century; and it is now the fashion to rebuke the Christian in the name of some higher "religion"—or more often, in the name of something higher called "religion" plain.

However low an opinion I held of Youth, I could not believe that it can long be deceived by that vacuous word "religion." The Press may continue for a time, for the Press is always behind the times, to organize battues of popular notables, with the religion of a this and of a that; and to excite such persons to talk nonsense about the revival or decay of "religion." Religion can hardly revive, because it cannot decay. To put the matter bluntly on the lowest level, it is not to anybody's interest that religion should disappear. If it did, many compositors would be thrown out of work; the audiences of our best-selling scientists would shrink to almost nothing; and the typewriters of the Huxley Brothers would cease from tapping. Without religion the whole human race would die, as according to W. H. R. Rivers, some Melanesian tribes have died, solely of boredom. Every one would be affected: the man who regularly has a run in his car and a round of golf on Sunday, quite as much as the punctilious churchgoer. Dr. Sigmund Freud, with characteristic delicacy of feeling, has reminded us that we should "leave Heaven to the angels and the sparrows"; following his hint, we may safely leave "religion" to Mr. Julian Huxley and Dr. Freud.

At this point I may make a transition from Youth to another point in the Report, at which I feel that the bishops also had their eyes on Youth. On page 19 we read:

"Perhaps most noteworthy of all, there is much in the scientific and philosophic thinking of our time which provides a climate more favourable to faith in God than has existed for generations."

I cannot help wishing that the bishops had consulted some of the able theologians and philosophers within the Church (such as Professor A. E. Taylor, who published an excellent article on the God of Whitehead, in *Theology*) before they had bestowed this benediction on our latest popular ramp of best-sellers. I do not disagree with the literal sense of the pronouncement which I have just quoted. Perhaps it is rather the tone of excessive amiability that I deprecate. I feel that the scientists should be received as penitents for the sins of an earlier scientific generation, rather than acclaimed as new friends and allies. And it may be an exceptional austerity or insensitiveness on my part, but I cannot consent to take climatic conditions so seriously as the phrase above seems to allow us to do. I do not wish to disparage the possible usefulness of the views set forth by Whitehead and Eddington and others. But it ought to be made quite clear that these writers cannot confirm any one in the faith; they can merely have the practical value of removing prejudices from the minds of those who have not the faith but who might possibly come to it: the distinction seems to me of capital importance.

One characteristic which increased my suspicion of the scientific paladins of religion is that they are all Englishmen, or at least all Anglo-Saxons. I have seen a few reported remarks on religion and philosophy from the lips of such men as Einstein,

Schroedinger and Planck; but they had the excuse of being interviewed by Mr. Sullivan; and the remarks were chiefly interesting, as I imagine Mr. Sullivan intended them to be, for the light they threw on the minds of these interesting scientists; none of these men has so far written a popular book of peeps into the fairyland of Reality. I suspect that there is some taint of Original H. G. Wells about most of us in English-speaking countries; and that we enjoy drawing general conclusions from particular disciplines, using our accomplishment in one field as the justification for theorizing about the world in general. It is also a weakness of Anglo-Saxons to like to hold personal and private religions and to promulgate them. And when a scientist gets loose into the field of religion, all that he can do is to give us the impression which his scientific knowledge and thought has produced upon his everyday, and usually commonplace, personal and private imagination.[4]

Even, however, in the section on Youth, we may find some wise and true sayings, if we have the patience to look for them. "The best of the younger generation in every section of the community," we are told, "and in every country of the world, are not seeking a religion that is watered down or robbed of the severity of its demands, but a religion that will not only give them a sure basis and an ultimate sanction for morals, but also a power to persevere in reaching out after the ideal which in their heart of hearts they recognize as the finest and best." I wish that this might have been said in fewer words, but the meaning is sound, and cannot be repeated too often. There is

[4] Under the heading *Nature of Space: Professor Einstein's Change of Mind*, I read in *The Times* of 6th February, 1931, the following news from New York:

"At the close of a 90-minute talk on his unified field theory to a group of physicists and astronomers in the Carnegie Institution at Pasadena yesterday, Professor Einstein startled his hearers by smilingly declaring, 'Space can never be anything similar to the old symmetrical spherical space theory.'

"That theory, he said, was not possible under the new equations. Thus he swept aside both his own former hypothesis that the universe and the space it occupied were both static and uniform, and the concept of his friend the Dutch astronomer, De Sitter, that though the universe was static it was non-uniform, which De Sitter had based upon the hypothesis that instead of

no good in making Christianity easy and pleasant; "Youth," or the better part of it, is more likely to come to a difficult religion than to an easy one. For some, the intellectual way of approach must be emphasized; there is need of a more intellectual laity. For them and for others, the way of discipline and asceticism must be emphasized; for even the humblest Christian layman can and must live what, in the modern world, is comparatively an ascetic life. Discipline of the emotions is even rarer, and in the modern world still more difficult, than discipline of the mind; some eminent lay preachers of "discipline" are men who know only the latter. Thought, study, mortification, sacrifice: it is such notions as these that should be impressed upon the young—who differ from the young of other times merely in having a different middle-aged generation behind them. You will never attract the young by making Christianity easy; but a good many can be attracted by finding it difficult: difficult both to the disorderly mind and to the unruly passions.

I refer with some reluctance, but with positive conviction, to the much-discussed Resolution 15 on marriage and birth control. On one part of the problem there is an admirable analytical study by the Master of Corpus in *Theology* for December, 1930. I can only add one suggestion to that statement, without attempting the problems of casuistry which the Master of Corpus discusses with great skill. I feel that the Conference was not only right and courageous to express a view on the subject of procreation radically different from that of Rome; but that the attitude adopted is more important than this particular ques-

matter determining space it was space that determined matter, and hence also the size of the universe.

"Astronomers who heard Professor Einstein make his declaration said it was an indication that he had accepted the work of two American scientists, Dr. Edwin P. Hubble, an astronomer in the Mount Wilson Observatory, and Dr. Richard C. Hace Tollman, a physicist of the California Institute of Technology, who hold that the universe is non-static, although uniformly distributed in space. In the belief of Dr. Hubble and Dr. Tollman the universe is constantly expanding and matter is constantly being converted into energy."

Our next revelation about the attitude of Science to Religion will issue, I trust, from Dr. Hubble and Dr. Tollman.

tion, important as it may be, and indicates a radical difference
between the Anglican and the Roman views on other matters. I
regret, however, that the bishops have placed so much reliance
upon the Individual Conscience; and by so doing jeopardized
the benefits of their independence. Certainly, any one who is
wholly sincere and pure in heart may seek for guidance from
the Holy Spirit; but who of us is always wholly sincere, especially where the most imperative of instincts may be strong
enough to simulate to perfection the voice of the Holy Spirit?

The Resolution shows pretty clearly both the strength and
the weakness of the Report, and the strength and weakness of
the Anglican Church. The recognition of contraception is, I feel
sure, something quite different from a concession to "modern"
opinion. It was a courageous facing of facts of life; and was
the only way of dealing with the question possible within the
Anglican organization. But before asserting the distinct character of the Anglican Church in this way, the bishops must have
taken a good deal of thought about it; all the more astonishing that they did not take a little more thought, and not proceed to a statement which seems to me almost suicidal. For to
allow that "each couple" should take counsel only *if perplexed
in mind* is almost to surrender the whole citadel of the Church.
It is ten to one, considering the extreme disingenuity of humanity, which ought to be patent to all after so many thousand years,
that only a very small minority will be "perplexed"; and in
view of the words of the bishops it is ten to one that the honest
minority which takes "competent advice" (and I observe that
the order of words is "*medical* and spiritual") will have to appeal to a clergy just as perplexed as itself, or else stung into an
obstinacy greater than that of any Roman clergy, by the futility
of this sentence.

In short, the whole resolution shows the admirable English
devotion to commonsense, but also the deplorable Anglican
habit of standing things on their heads in the name of commonsense. It is exactly this matter of "spiritual advice" which should
have been examined and analysed if necessary for years, before
making any pronouncement. But the principle is simple, though
the successful application might require time. I do not suggest

that the full Sacrament of Confession and Penance should be imposed upon every communicant of the Church; but the Church ought to be able to enjoin upon all its communicants that they should take spiritual advice upon specified problems of life; and both clergy and parishioners should recognize the full seriousness and responsibility of such consultation. I am not unaware that as opinions and theories vary at present, those seeking direction can always find the direction they seek, if they know where to apply; but that is inevitable. But here, if anywhere, is definitely a matter upon which the Individual Conscience is no reliable guide; spiritual guidance should be imperative; and it should be clearly placed above medical advice—where also, opinions and theories vary indefinitely. In short, a general principle of the greatest importance, exceeding the application to this particular issue alone, might have been laid down; and its enunciation was evaded.

To put it frankly, but I hope not offensively, the Roman view in general seems to me to be that a principle must be affirmed without exception; and that thereafter exceptions can be dealt with, without modifying the principle. The view natural to the English mind, I believe, is rather that a principle must be framed in such a way as to include all allowable exceptions. It follows inevitably that the Roman Church must profess to be fixed, while the Anglican Church must profess to take account of changed conditions. I hope that it is unnecessary to give the assurance that I do not consider the Roman way of thought dishonest, and that I would not endorse any cheap and facile gibes about the duplicity and dissimulation of that Church; it is another conception of human nature and of the means by which, on the whole, the greatest number of souls can be saved; but the difference goes deep. *Prudenti dissimulatione uti* [5] is not a precept which appeals to Anglo-Saxon theology; and here again, the Anglican Church can admit national (I do not mean nationalistic) differences in theory and practice

---

[5] See *Theology*, December, 1930, p. 307. It has been pointed out to me that here *dissimulatio* should perhaps be translated as "tactfulness" rather than "dissimulation"; but a tactfulness which consists primarily in not asking awkward questions seems to me to be pretty close to simulation and dissimulation.

which the more formal organization of Rome cannot recognize. What in England is the right balance between individual liberty and discipline?—between individual responsibility and obedience?—active co-operation and passive reception? And to what extremity are divergences of belief and practice permissible? These are questions which the English mind must always ask; and the answers can only be found, if with hesitation and difficulty, through the English Church. The admission of inconsistencies, sometimes ridiculed as indifference to logic and coherence, of which the English mind is often accused, may be largely the admission of inconsistencies inherent in life itself, and of the impossibility of overcoming them by the imposition of a uniformity greater than life will bear.

Even, however, if the Anglican Church affirmed, as I think it should affirm, the necessity for spiritual direction in admitting the exceptions, the Episcopate still has the responsibility of giving direction to the directors. I cannot but suspect that here the Roman doctrine, so far as I have seen it expounded, leaves us uncertain as does the Anglican. For example: according to the Roman doctrine, which is more commendable—prudent continence in marriage, or unlimited procreation up to the limit of the mother's strength? If the latter, the Church seems to me obliged to offer some solution to the economic questions raised by such a practice: for surely, if you lay down a moral law which leads, in practice, to unfortunate social consequences —such as over-population or destitution—you make yourself responsible for providing some resolution of these consequences. If the former, what motives are right motives? The latest Papal Encyclical appears to be completely decisive about the question of Resolution 15—at the cost of solving no individual's problems. And the Resolution is equally, though perhaps no more, unsatisfactory. The Roman statement leaves unanswered the questions: When is it right to limit the family? and: When is it wrong not to limit it? And the Anglican statement leaves unanswered the questions: When is it right to limit the family and right to limit it only by continence? and: When is it right to limit the family by contraception?

On the other hand, the fact that Resolution 15, as I take it, is wrong *primarily* in isolating and treating as independent a question which should be considered as a detail subsumed under the more general question which should have been treated first —that of Spiritual Direction and Authority; this fact does I think indicate one recurrent cause of weakness. When the episcopal mind sees that something is self-evidently desirable in itself, it seems inclined to turn first to consider the means for bringing it into being, rather than to find the theological grounds upon which it can be justified; and there are traces of this zeal here and there in the suggestions towards Reunion and fraternization. For instance (p. 117 of the Report), it is suggested that a bishop might authorize and encourage baptised communicant members of churches not in communion with our own, to communicate in his diocese with Anglicans "when the ministrations of their own Church are not available." It is true that this is to be done only under special and temporary local conditions; and it does not form part of my purpose to doubt that under the conditions which the bishops must have had in mind, such intercommunion is most desirable. But what does the suggestion imply? Surely, *if* dissenters should never communicate in Anglican churches, or *if* in certain circumstances they should be encouraged to do so, two very different theories of the Sacrament of the Altar are implied. For the innovation proposed, theological justification is required. What is required is some theory of degrees of reception of the Blessed Sacrament, as well as the validity of the ministration of a celebrant not episcopally ordained. My objection therefore is not to the admission of dissenters to the Altar—and I do not wish to attack what has not yet been defended—but to the propagation of this practice before theological justification has been expounded. Possibly theology is what Bradley said philosophy was: "the finding of bad reasons for what we believe upon instinct"; I think it may be the finding of good reasons for what we believe upon instinct; but if the Church of England cannot find these reasons, and make them intelligible to the more philosophically trained among the faithful, what can it do?

A similar danger seems to me to inhere in the statement about the Historic Episcopate. Mr. Malcolm Thomson, looking, as I suspect, for the Roman view, or for one of the tenable Roman views (as an outsider naturally would), and not finding it, extracts and exaggerates one possible perversion; on the other hand he does point to a danger of which we should be aware. He quotes the words of the Report:

"While we thus stand for the Historic Episcopate as a necessary element in any union in which the Anglican Church can take part . . . we do not require of others acceptance of those reasons, or of any particular theory or interpretation of the Episcopate as a condition of reunion."

What the bishops had in mind in committing themselves to this serious statement, I am sure, is the fact that the Church has never held one rigid theory of the nature of the Episcopate. Even in the Roman Church I understand that there are still at least two theories tenable. But such theological subtleties pass beyond the ordinary lay mind; and the greatest value of Mr. Thomson's interesting pamphlet, to me, is its exposure of the possibilities of misunderstanding in the wording of some of the Report. And I agree with him to this extent, that the words *we do not require of others acceptance of those reasons* might be taken to mean "we do not require of others acceptance of *any* reasons except expediency": in other words, we beg that Nonconformists should accept the Episcopate as a harmless formality, for the sake of a phantom unity.

I do not imagine for a moment that the "conversations" of the Church of England with the Free Churches will bear any fruit whatever in our time; and I rather hope they will not; for any fruit of this harvest would be unripe and bitter fruit, untimely nipped. But at the same time I cannot cat-call with those who accuse the Church of facing-both-ways, and making one profession to the innocent Levantines and Swedes, and another to the implacable Methodists. It would be very poor statesmanship indeed to envisage any reunion which should not fall ultimately within a scheme for complete reunion; and in spite of mirth, "reunion all round" is the only ideal tenable. To the Methodists, certainly, the Church of England owes a heavy responsibility, somewhat similar to that of the Church of Rome towards ourselves; and it would be almost effrontery for Anglican bishops to seek an alliance with Upsala and Constantinople without seeking some way of repatriating those descended from men who would (I am sure) never have left the Church of England had it been in the eighteenth century what it is now in the second quarter of the twentieth. In such difficult negotiations the Church is quite properly and conscientiously facing-both-ways: which only goes to show that the Church of England is at the present juncture the one church upon which the duty of working towards reunion most devolves. There are possible risks, which have been seized upon as actualities when they have been merely potentialities; the risk of feeling more orthodox when transacting with the Eastern and Baltic Churches, and more Evangelical when transacting with the Nonconformists. But I do not believe that the bishops have, according to the Report, conceded to the Nonconformists in England anything that the Eastern authorities could reasonably abhor. On the contrary, the attitude of eminent dissenters, in their objections still more than in their approval, seems to me to indicate that the bishops have stopped at the right point. The points of difference with the other orthodox churches are simple and direct, and in a near way of being settled. It is easier to agree with a man who differs from you in blood but less in faith, than to agree with one who is of your own blood but has different ideas: because the irrelevant differences between those of the same blood are less superable than the relevant differences between those of different blood. The problems of dissent between Anglicans and Free Churchmen are (we might just as well admit it) much more complicated than the problems between the Anglicans and the Swedish. Our doctrinal difficulties with Free Churchmen are complicated by divisions social, local and political; by traditions of prejudice on both sides; and it is likely that several generations must pass before the problems of theology and hierarchy can be fairly detached and faced. The Lambeth Conference of 1930 has accomplished in this direction this much: that it has determined the limits beyond which the Church cannot go in commending itself to Free Churchmen; further concession would be abandonment of the

Church itself, and mere incorporation, as possibly the most important member, in a loose federation of autonomous sects without stability and without significance.

The actuality of the approximation towards intercommunion with the Eastern Churches, however, has very much more than picturesque value. It brings with it the hope of a greater stability, instead of the old stability, real or apparent, which seemed to characterize an Establishment. On matters of doctrine, the summary of discussions between Anglican bishops and orthodox representatives (p. 138 ff.) is of great importance, especially paragraph 11:

"It was stated by the Anglican bishops that in the Sacrament of the Eucharist 'the Body and Blood of Christ are verily and indeed taken and received by the faithful in the Lord's Supper,' and that 'the Body of Christ is given, taken and eaten in the Supper only after an heavenly and spiritual manner,' and that after Communion the consecrated elements remaining are regarded sacramentally as the Body and Blood of Christ; further, that the Anglican Church teaches the doctrine of Eucharistic sacrifice as explained in the Answer of the Archbishops of Canterbury and York to Pope Leo XIII on Anglican Ordinations; and also that in the offering of the Eucharistic Sacrifice the Anglican Church prays that 'by the merits and death of Thy Son Jesus Christ, and through faith in His blood, we and all Thy whole Church may obtain remission of our sins, and all other benefits of His passion,' as including the whole company of faithful people, living and departed."

Reunion with the East is of the greatest significance for a Church the position of which in the national life is inevitably changing. We still think, and rightly, of the Church of England as the "National Church"; but the word *national* in this context can no longer mean what it once meant. I entirely sympathize with Mr. Malcolm Thomson, and with any other Scot, Irishman or Methodist, in his objection to the vapid phrase about St. Paul's, "the parish church of the British Empire." An "imperial" Church, perhaps under the patronage of the four evangelists of imperialism, Lords Rothermere, Beaverbrook, Riddell and Camrose, would be something more odious, because far more vulgar, than the Erastian Church of the eighteenth century. I prefer to think of the Church as what I believe it is more and more coming to be, not the "English Church," but national as "the Catholic Church in England."

For the last three hundred years the relation of Church to State has been constantly undergoing change. I do not propose in this essay to enter upon the difficult question of Disestablishment. I am not here concerned with the practical difficulties and anomalies which have made the problem of Church and State more acute in the last few years; I am not concerned with prognosticating their future relations, or with offering any facile solution for so complex a problem, or with discussing the future discipline within the Church itself. I wish to say nothing about Disestablishment, first because I have not made up my own mind, and second because it does not seem to me fitting at this time that one layman, with no special erudition in that subject, should publicly express his views. I am considering only the political and social changes within the last three hundred years. A National Church in the early Caroline sense depended upon the precarious harmony of the King, a strong Archbishop and a strong First Minister; and perhaps the Laudian Church came just too late to be more for us than the type of one form of order. The political-social Erastianism of the eighteenth century has gone its way too; there can be no more Hoadleys; there is not much financial or social advantage in holy orders; nowadays the smaller folk, who seek security, find their way if they can into the Civil Service, and the larger and more predatory seek success in the City. Less and less is there any reason for taking orders, but just vocation. I suspect that the rule by Prime Ministers is dwindling, too: no possible Prime Minister (except perhaps Lord Rothermere's sometime nominee, Lord Brentford, which God forfend) would now, I trust, venture to impose his own choice upon the Church in the way of episcopal preferment, or would do anything except consult the safest authorities. And the House of Commons, which has seemed to cling to the Church as the last reality in England over which it has any control, must eventually relinquish that tardy shadow of power too. The only powers left are those with which we must all reckon, the Chancellor of the Exchequer and the Bank of England.

Whether established or disestablished, the Church of England can never be reduced to the condition of a Sect, unless by some irrational act of suicide; even in the sense in which, with all due respect, the Roman Church is in England a sect. It is easier for the Church of England to become Catholic, than for the Church of Rome in England to become English; and if the Church of England was mutilated by separation from Rome, the Church of Rome was mutilated by separation from England. If England is ever to be in any appreciable degree converted to Christianity, it can only be through the Church of England.

To revert to the sense of the first paragraph of this essay, the Church of England may easily be made to appear in a better way, or in a worse way, than she is. The sudden heat of the Prayer Book controversy, the vivaciousness of Lord Brentford and Lord Cushendun, the "brawl" at St. Paul's, the unpleasantness in the diocese of Birmingham, the awareness of the Press that there is sometimes good copy in ecclesiastical affairs, the journalism of Dean Inge, and the large sales of popular theological literature; all these things together would seem to suggest that never was there such a lively interest in the Church as today. And the same dissensions, when interpreted to mean that opinion in the Church is divided to the point of disruption; the lack of ordinands and lack of funds, the anomalous and often humiliating relation of Church to State, the insurrection of what is popularly called the new morality, and the patent fact that the majority of Englishmen and women are wholly indifferent to the obligations of their faith, even when they have not quite repudiated it: such signs may seem to point towards collapse or superannuation.

I take such phenomena to be, for the most part, merely symptoms of the changing place, not only of the Anglican Church in the State, but of the Universal Church in the World. As I have said already, the Church of England can no longer be, and must no longer be, a National Church in the old nationalistic or in the old Erastian way. The high power it may seem to have lost was either a bad power, or an obsolete power, or the shadow of a power. The political pressure from without, a force of cohesion in the sixteenth and seventeenth centuries, no longer exists except as the spectral dread of Popery; the fear of the social consequences of disruption within no longer exists, for the disruption and secession have long since taken place, and the dread has been succeeded by the faint hope of reconstruction. The problem of the relation of Church and State—and I am not thinking here only of the Anglican Church, but of any body of believers in any country, and of the manifold and perplexing problems of the Holy See—is as acute as ever it was; but it takes ever new forms. I believe that in spite of the apparently insoluble problems with which it has to deal, the Church of England is strengthening its position as a branch of the Catholic Church, the Catholic Church in England. I am not thinking of the deliberate struggles of one party within the Church, but of an inevitable course of events which has not been directed by human hands.

At this point I must turn aside for a moment to protest against certain assumptions of Mr. Malcolm Thomson which are not peculiar to himself, but are probably shared by most of those who are only interested in church affairs as they read of them in the newspapers. When Mr. Thomson wrote his spirited pamphlet *Will the Scottish Church Survive?* [6] he was full of praise for the animation manifested in the English Church in the dissensions of Catholics, Evangelicals and Modernists. He may have slightly caricatured these differences for the sake of picturesqueness, if only as a stick to beat his Presbyterian victim. I think that his chief error in treating the Lambeth Conference is that he discusses the Report without reference to the history and development of the English Church, and treats it as if it were the creation of one individual intelligence, instead of considering what must be the composite production of three hundred minds. But on some matters he not only lacks perspective, but is definitely misleading. Mr. Thomson is a metaphor-addict.

[6] The Porpoise Press, Edinburgh.

and his mind is ridden by images of underground passages (very short ones), ferries, wherries, and other figures of easy transport from Canterbury to Rome. He remarks for instance:

"And the careers of several prominent Anglo-Catholics served to strengthen the general suspicion. For they had a habit of using the Church of England as a junction and not as a terminus."

I cannot see how *several* can form a habit; unless Mr. Thomson wishes to suggest that Father Knox and Father Vernon have formed the "habit" of leaving the English Church. I should like to know the names of the "few well-known authors" who have been converted: I doubt whether Mr. Thomson's list would contain many names that I do not know—one or two of his converts may even have started life as Presbyterians; and by the sum of the names which I know, I am not greatly impressed. And here again, I suspect that more capital is made of the transit of an Anglo-Catholic to Rome, than of that of a plain Low Churchman. For some souls, I admit, there is no satisfaction outside of Rome; and if Anglo-Catholicism has helped a few such to find their way to where they belong, I am very glad; but if Anglo-Catholicism has assisted a few persons to leave the Church of England who could never have rested in that uneasy bed anyway, on the other hand it has helped many more, I believe—one cannot quote statistics in the negative—to remain within the Anglican Church. Why, for instance, has Lord Halifax not saved himself a deal of trouble, of generous toil and disappointment, by becoming a convert out of hand? And why are not Lord Brentford and Lord Cushendun taken by the neck and dropped respectively into Methodism and Presbyterianism? The Anglican Church is supposed to be divided, by newspaper verdict, either into Catholics and Modernists, or into Catholics and Evangelicals, or sometimes into Catholics, Modernists *and* Evangelicals. If the divisions were so clear as all that, there might be something to be said for a voluntary liquidation. To those for whom the English Church means Lord Brentford, the Bishop of Birmingham and *The Church Times*, it may well seem that nothing keeps it together but inertia, and the unwillingness, for various motives, to scrap an extensive plant of machinery.

To detached observers like Mr. Malcolm Thomson, entering England from the comparative calm of Edinburgh, Lhassa or Rome, the disorder of the Church of England may seem fatal. When clergymen hasten to reply with severity if a Bishop writes a letter to *The Times* [7] and when even plain people like myself can make use of such eminences as Lord Brentford and the Bishop of Birmingham for comic relief,[8] there is at least the opportunity for misunderstanding. For such freedom of speech and such diversity of opinion there is, however, something to be said: within limits—which, I grant, have been transgressed; but what matters is not so much uniformity of liturgy as fixity of dogma. There are, of course, differences of opinion which are fundamental and permanent; but I am not at all sure that it is not a very good thing for the intellectual life of the Church that there should be. When they come to light in the public press, they usually appear to be the clear and irreconcilable views of two or more well-regimented and hostile forces. But in practice, each division is itself divided, and the lines of sectional division are far from clear. You cannot point to one group of "Modernists": there are Catholics who may be called modernist, and Evangelicals who may call themselves modernist, as well as a few persons in whom Modernism seems to signify merely confused thinking. I have known Evangelicals to whom the name of Dr. Barnes was more displeasing than that of Lord Halifax. There are persons who do not *always* agree with the Editor of *The Church Times;* and I sometimes am moved to admire an article in *The Modern Churchman.* To a large degree accordingly the differences within the Church are healthy differences within a living body, and to the same degree their existence qualifies the Church of England for assuming the initiative toward Reunion.

And the Conference of 1930 has marked an important stage in that direction. It has affirmed, beyond previous conferences,

[7] See a remarkable letter from the Bishop of Durham in *The Times* of 2nd December, 1930, and the poverty of the replies.

[8] When I say "comic," I am considering their *essence*, not their *operation.*

the Catholicity of the Church; and in spite of defects and dubious statements in detail, the Report will have strengthened the Church both within and without. It has made clearer the limits beyond which the Church cannot go towards meeting Nonconformity, and the extent to which it is prepared to go to meet the Eastern and Baltic Churches. This advance is of no small importance in a world which will obviously divide itself more and more sharply into Christians and non-Christians. The Universal Church is today, it seems to me, more definitely set against the World than at any time since pagan Rome. I do not mean that our times are particularly corrupt; all times are corrupt. I mean that Christianity, in spite of certain local appearances, is not, and cannot be within measurable time, "official." The World is trying the experiment of attempting to form a civilized but non-Christian mentality. The experiment will fail; but we must be very patient in awaiting its collapse; meanwhile redeeming the time: so that the Faith may be preserved alive through the dark ages before us; to renew and rebuild civilization, and save the World from suicide.

RELIGION AND LITERATURE

WHAT I have to say is largely in support of the
following propositions: Literary criticism should be completed
by criticism from a definite ethical and theological standpoint.
In so far as in any age there is common agreement on ethical
and theological matters, so far can literary criticism be substantive. In ages like our own, in which there is no such common
agreement, it is the more necessary for Christian readers to
scrutinize their reading, especially of works of imagination, with
explicit ethical and theological standards. The "greatness" of
literature cannot be determined solely by literary standards;
though we must remember that whether it is literature or not
can be determined only by literary standards.[1]

We have tacitly assumed, for some centuries past, that there
is *no* relation between literature and theology. This is not to
deny that literature—I mean, again, primarily works of imagination—has been, is, and probably always will be judged by
some moral standards. But moral judgements of literary works
are made only according to the moral code accepted by each
generation, whether it lives according to that code or not. In an
age which accepts some precise Christian theology, the common
code may be fairly orthodox: though even in such periods the
common code may exalt such concepts as "honour," "glory" or
"revenge" to a position quite intolerable to Christianity. The
dramatic ethics of the Elizabethan Age offers an interesting
study. But when the common code is detached from its theological background, and is consequently more and more merely a

---

[1] As an example of literary criticism given greater significance by theological
interests, I would call attention to Theodor Haecker: *Virgil* (Sheed and
Ward).

343

matter of habit, it is exposed both to prejudice and to change. At such times morals are open to being altered *by* literature; so that we find in practice that what is "objectionable" in literature is merely what the present generation is not used to. It is a commonplace that what shocks one generation is accepted quite calmly by the next. This adaptability to change of moral standards is sometimes greeted with satisfaction as an evidence of human perfectibility: whereas it is only evidence of what unsubstantial foundations people's moral judgements have.

I am not concerned here with religious literature but with the application of our religion to the criticism of any literature. It may be as well, however, to distinguish first what I consider to be the three senses in which we can speak of "religious literature." The first is that of which we say that it is "religious literature" in the same way that we speak of "historical literature" or of "scientific literature." I mean that we can treat the Authorized translation of the Bible, or the works of Jeremy Taylor, as literature, in the same way that we treat the historical writing of Clarendon or of Gibbon—our two great English historians—as literature; or Bradley's *Logic*, or Buffon's *Natural History*. All of these writers were men who, incidentally to their religious, or historical, or philosophic purpose, had a gift of language which makes them delightful to read to all those who can enjoy language well written, even if they are unconcerned with the objects which the writers had in view. And I would add that though a scientific, or historical, or theological, or philosophic work which is also "literature," may become superannuated as anything but literature, yet it is not likely to be "literature" unless it had its scientific or other value for its own time. While I acknowledge the legitimacy of this enjoyment, I am more acutely aware of its abuse. The persons who enjoy these writings *solely* because of their literary merit are essentially parasites; and we know that parasites, when they become too numerous, are pests. I could fulminate against the men of letters who have gone into ecstasies over "the Bible as literature," the Bible as "the noblest monument of English prose." Those who talk of the Bible as a "monument of English prose" are merely admiring it as a monument over the grave of Christianity. I must try to avoid the by-paths of my discourse: it is enough to suggest that just as the work of Clarendon, or Gibbon, or Buffon, or Bradley would be of inferior literary value if it were insignificant as history, science and philosophy respectively, so the Bible has had a *literary* influence upon English literature *not* because it has been considered as literature, but because it has been considered as the report of the Word of God. And the fact that men of letters now discuss it as "literature" probably indicates the *end* of its "literary" influence.

The second kind of relation of religion to literature is that which is found in what is called "religious" or "devotional" poetry. Now what is the usual attitude of the lover of poetry—and I mean the person who is a genuine and first-hand enjoyer and appreciator of poetry, not the person who follows the admirations of others—towards this department of poetry? I believe, all that may be implied in his calling it a *department*. He believes, not always explicitly, that when you qualify poetry as "religious" you are indicating very clear limitations. For the great majority of people who love poetry, "*religious* poetry" is a variety of *minor* poetry: the religious poet is not a poet who is treating the whole subject matter of poetry in a religious spirit, but a poet who is dealing with a confined part of this subject matter: who is leaving out what men consider their major passions, and thereby confessing his ignorance of them. I think that this is the real attitude of most poetry lovers towards such poets as Vaughan, or Southwell, or Crashaw, or George Herbert, or Gerard Hopkins.

But what is more, I am ready to admit that up to a point these critics are right. For there is a kind of poetry, such as most of the work of the authors I have mentioned, which is the product of a special religious awareness, which may exist without the general awareness which we expect of the major poet. In some poets, or in some of their works, this general awareness may have existed; but the preliminary steps which represent it may have been suppressed, and only the end-product presented. Between these, and those in which the religious or devotional genius represents the *special* and limited awareness, it may be very difficult to discriminate. I do not pretend to offer Vaughan,

or Southwell, or George Herbert, or Hopkins as major poets: [2]
I feel sure that the first three, at least, are poets of this limited
awareness. They are not great religious poets in the sense in
which Dante, or Corneille, or Racine, even in those of their
plays which do not touch upon Christian themes, are great Christian religious poets. Or even in the sense in which Villon and
Baudelaire, with all their imperfections and delinquencies, are
Christian poets. Since the time of Chaucer, Christian poetry (in
the sense in which I shall mean it) has been limited in England
almost exclusively to minor poetry.

I repeat that when I am considering Religion and Literature,
I speak of these things only to make clear that I am not concerned primarily with Religious Literature. I am concerned with
what should be the relation between Religion and all Literature.
Therefore the third type of "religious literature" may be more
quickly passed over. I mean the literary works of men who are
sincerely desirous of forwarding the cause of religion: that which
may come under the heading of Propaganda. I am thinking, of
course, of such delightful fiction as Mr. Chesterton's *Man Who
Was Thursday*, or his *Father Brown*. No one admires and enjoys these things more than I do; I would only remark that
when the same effect is aimed at by zealous persons of less talent
than Mr. Chesterton the effect is negative. But my point is that
such writings do not enter into any serious consideration of the
relation of Religion and Literature: because they are conscious
operations in a world in which it is assumed that Religion and
Literature are not related. It is a conscious and limited relating.
What I want is a literature which should be *un*consciously, rather
than deliberately and defiantly, Christian: because the work of
Mr. Chesterton has its point from appearing in a world which
is definitely not Christian.

I am convinced that we fail to realize how completely, and yet
how irrationally, we separate our literary from our religious
judgements. If there could be a complete separation, perhaps it

[2] I note that in an address delivered in Swansea some years later (subsequently published in *The Welsh Review* under the title of "What Is Minor
Poetry?") I stated with some emphasis my opinion that Herbert is a major,
not a minor poet. I agree with my later opinion. [1949]

might not matter: but the separation is not, and never can be, complete. If we exemplify literature by the novel—for the novel is the form in which literature affects the greatest number —we may remark this gradual secularization of literature during at least the last three hundred years. Bunyan, and to some extent Defoe, had moral purposes: the former is beyond suspicion, the latter may be suspect. But since Defoe the secularization of the novel has been continuous. There have been three chief phases. In the first, the novel took the Faith, in its contemporary version, for granted, and omitted it from its picture of life. Fielding, Dickens and Thackeray belong to this phase. In the second, it doubted, worried about, or contested the Faith. To this phase belong George Eliot, George Meredith and Thomas Hardy. To the third phase, in which we are living, belong nearly all contemporary novelists except Mr. James Joyce. It is the phase of those who have never heard the Christian Faith spoken of as anything but an anachronism.

Now, do people in general hold a definite opinion, that is to say religious or anti-religious; and do they read novels, or poetry for that matter, with a separate compartment of their minds? The common ground between religion and fiction is behaviour. Our religion imposes our ethics, our judgement and criticism of ourselves, and our behaviour toward our fellow men. The fiction that we read affects our behaviour towards our fellow men, affects our patterns of ourselves. When we read of human beings behaving in certain ways, with the approval of the author, who gives his benediction to this behaviour by his attitude toward the result of the behaviour arranged by himself, we can be influenced towards behaving in the same way.[3] When the contemporary novelist is an individual thinking for himself in isolation, he may have something important to offer to those who are able to receive it. He who is alone may speak to the individual. But the majority of novelists are persons drifting in the stream, only a little faster. They have some sensitiveness, but little intellect.

[3] Here and later I am indebted to Montgomery Belgion. *The Human Parrot* (chapter on The Irresponsible Propagandist).

We are expected to be broadminded about literature, to put aside prejudice or conviction, and to look at fiction as fiction and at drama as drama. With what is inaccurately called "censorship" in this country—with what is much more difficult to cope with than an official censorship, because it represents the opinions of individuals in an irresponsible democracy, I have very little sympathy; partly because it so often suppresses the wrong books, and partly because it is little more effective than Prohibition of Liquor; partly because it is one manifestation of the desire that state control should take the place of decent domestic influence; and wholly because it acts only from custom and habit, not from decided theological and moral principles. Incidentally, it gives people a false sense of security in leading them to believe that books which are *not* suppressed are harmless. Whether there *is* such a thing as a harmless book I am not sure: but there very likely are books so utterly unreadable as to be incapable of injuring anybody. But it is certain that a book is not harmless merely because no one is consciously offended by it. And if we, as readers, keep our religious and moral convictions in one compartment, and take our reading merely for entertainment, or on a higher plane, for aesthetic pleasure, I would point out that the author, whatever his conscious intentions in writing, in practice recognizes no such distinctions. The author of a work of imagination is trying to affect us wholly, as human beings, whether he knows it or not; and we are affected by it, as human beings, whether we intend to be or not. I suppose that everything we eat has some other effect upon us than merely the pleasure of taste and mastication; it affects us during the process of assimilation and digestion; and I believe that exactly the same is true of anything we read.

The fact that what we read does not concern merely something called our *literary taste,* but that it affects directly, though only amongst many other influences, the whole of what we are, is best elicited, I think, by a conscientious examination of the history of our individual literary education. Consider the adolescent reading of any person with some literary sensibility. Everyone, I believe, who is at all sensible to the seductions of poetry, can remember some moment in youth when he or she was completely carried away by the work of one poet. Very likely he was carried away by several poets, one after the other. The reason for this passing infatuation is not merely that our sensibility to poetry is keener in adolescence than in maturity. What happens is a kind of inundation, of invasion of the undeveloped personality by the stronger personality of the poet. The same thing may happen at a later age to persons who have not done much reading. One author takes complete possession of us for a time; then another; and finally they begin to affect each other in our mind. We weigh one against another; we see that each has qualities absent from others, and qualities incompatible with the qualities of others: we begin to be, in fact, critical; and it is our growing critical power which protects us from excessive possession by any one literary personality. The good critic—and we should all try to be critics, and not leave criticism to the fellows who write reviews in the papers—is the man who, to a keen and abiding sensibility, joins wide and increasingly discriminating reading. Wide reading is not valuable as a kind of hoarding, an accumulation of knowledge, or what sometimes is meant by the term "a well-stocked mind." It is valuable because in the process of being affected by one powerful personality after another, we cease to be dominated by any one, or by any small number. The very different views of life, cohabiting in our minds, affect each other, and our own personality asserts itself and gives each a place in some arrangement peculiar to ourself.

It is simply not true that works of fiction, prose or verse, that is to say works depicting the actions, thoughts and words and passions of imaginary human beings, *directly* extend our knowledge of life. Direct knowledge of life is knowledge directly in relation to ourselves, it is our knowledge of *how* people behave in general, of *what* they are like in general, in so far as that part of life in which we ourselves have participated gives us material for generalization. Knowledge of life obtained through fiction is only possible by another stage of self-consciousness. That is to say, it can only be a knowledge of other people's knowledge of life, not of life itself. So far as we are taken up with the happenings in any novel in the same way in which we are taken up with what happens under our eyes, we are acquiring at least as much falsehood as truth. But when we are developed enough to say: "This is the view of life of a person who was a good observer within his limits, Dickens, or Thackeray, or George Eliot, or Balzac; but he looked at it in a different way from me, because he was a different man; he even selected rather different things to look at, or the same things in a different order of importance, because he was a different man; so what I am looking at is the world as seen by a particular mind"—then we are in a position to gain something from reading fiction. We are learning *something* about life from these authors direct, just as we learn something from the reading of history direct; but these authors are only really helping us when we can see, and allow for, their differences from ourselves.

Now what we get, as we gradually grow up and read more and more, and read a greater diversity of authors, is a variety of views of life. But what people commonly assume, I suspect, is that we gain this experience of other men's views of life only by "improving reading." This, it is supposed, is a reward we get by applying ourselves to Shakespeare, and Dante, and Goethe, and Emerson, and Carlyle, and dozens of other respectable writers. The rest of our reading for amusement is merely killing time. But I incline to come to the alarming conclusion that it is just the literature that we read for "amusement," or "purely for pleasure" that may have the greatest and least suspected influence upon us. It is the literature which we read with the least effort that can have the easiest and most insidious influence upon us. Hence it is that the influence of popular novelists, and of popular plays of contemporary life, requires to be scrutinized most closely. And it is chiefly *contemporary* literature that the majority of people ever read in this attitude of "purely for pleasure," of pure passivity.

The relation to my subject of what I have been saying should now be a little more apparent. Though we may read literature merely for pleasure, of "entertainment" or of "aesthetic enjoyment," this reading never affects simply a sort of special sense: it affects us as entire human beings; it affects our moral and religious existence. And I say that while individual modern writers of eminence can be improving, contemporary literature as a whole tends to be degrading. And that even the effect of the better writers, in an age like ours, may be degrading to some readers; for we must remember that what a writer does to people is not necessarily what he intends to do. It may be only what people are capable of having done to them. People exercise an unconscious selection in being influenced. A writer like D. H. Lawrence may be in his effect either beneficial or pernicious. I am not sure that I have not had some pernicious influence myself.

At this point I anticipate a rejoinder from the liberal-minded, from all those who are convinced that if everybody says what he thinks, and does what he likes, things will somehow, by some automatic compensation and adjustment, come right in the end. "Let everything be tried," they say, "and if it is a mistake, then we shall learn by experience." This argument might have some value, if we were always the same generation upon earth; or if, as we know to be not the case, people ever learned much from the experience of their elders. These liberals are convinced that only by what is called unrestrained individualism will truth ever emerge. Ideas, views of life, they think, issue distinct from independent heads, and in consequence of their knocking violently against each other, the fittest survive, and truth rises triumphant. Anyone who dissents from this view must be either a mediaevalist, wishful only to set back the clock, or else a fascist, and probably both.

If the mass of contemporary authors were really individualists, every one of them inspired Blakes, each with his separate vision, and if the mass of the contemporary public were really a mass of *individuals* there might be something to be said for this attitude. But this is not, and never has been, and never will be. It is not only that the reading individual today (or at any day) is not enough an individual to be able to absorb all the "views of life" of all the authors pressed upon us by the publishers' advertisements and the reviewers, and to be able to arrive at wisdom by considering one against another. It is that the contemporary authors are not individuals enough either. It is not that the world of separate individuals of the liberal democrat is undesirable; it is simply that this world does not exist. For the reader of contemporary literature is not, like the reader of the established great literature of all time, exposing himself to the influence of divers and contradictory personalities; he is exposing himself to a mass movement of writers who, each of them, think that they have something individually to offer, but are really all working together in the same direction. And there never was a time, I believe, when the reading public was so large, or so helplessly exposed to the influences of its own time. There never was a time, I believe, when those who read at all, read so many more books by living authors than books by dead authors; there never was a time so completely parochial, so shut off from the past. There may be too many publishers; there are certainly too many books published; and the journals ever incite the reader to "keep up" with what is being published. Individualistic democracy has come to high tide: and it is more difficult today to be an individual than it ever was before.

Within itself, modern literature has perfectly valid distinctions of good and bad, better and worse: and I do not wish to suggest that I confound Mr. Bernard Shaw with Mr. Noel Coward, Mrs. Woolf with Miss Mannin. On the other hand, I should like it to be clear that I am not defending a "high"-brow against a "low"-brow literature. What I do wish to affirm is that the whole of modern literature is corrupted by what I call Secularism, that it is simply unaware of, simply cannot understand the meaning of, the primacy of the supernatural over the natural life: of something which I assume to be our primary concern.

I do not want to give the impression that I have delivered a mere fretful jeremiad against contemporary literature. Assuming a common attitude between my readers, or some of my readers, and myself, the question is not so much, what is to be done about it? as, how should we behave towards it?

I have suggested that the liberal attitude towards literature will not work. Even if the writers who make their attempt to impose their "view of life" upon us were really distinct individuals, even if we as readers were distinct individuals, what would be the result? It would be, surely, that each reader would be impressed, in his reading, merely by what he was previously prepared to be impressed by; he would follow the "line of least resistance," and there would be no assurance that he would be made a better man. For literary judgement we need to be acutely aware of two things at once: of "what we like," and of "what we *ought* to like." Few people are honest enough to know either. The first means knowing what we really feel: very few know that. The second involves understanding our shortcomings; for we do not really know what we ought to like unless we also know why we ought to like it, which involves knowing why we don't yet like it. It is not enough to understand what we ought to be, unless we know what we are; and we do not understand what we are, unless we know what we ought to be. The two forms of self-consciousness, knowing what we are and what we ought to be, must go together.

It is our business, as readers of literature, to know what we like. It is our business, as Christians, *as well as* readers of literature, to know what we ought to like. It is our business as honest men not to assume that whatever we like is what we ought to like; and it is our business as honest Christians not to assume that we do like what we ought to like. And the last thing I would wish for would be the existence of two literatures, one for Christian consumption and the other for the pagan world. What I believe to be incumbent upon all Christians is the duty of maintaining consciously certain standards and criteria of criticism over and above those applied by the rest of the world; and that by these criteria and standards everything that we read must be tested. We must remember that the greater part of our current reading matter is written for us by people who have no real belief in a supernatural order, though some of it may be written by people with individual notions of a supernatural order which are not ours. And the greater part of our reading matter is coming to be written by people who not only have no such belief, but are even ignorant of the fact that there are still people in the world so "backward" or so "eccentric" as to continue to believe. So long as we are conscious of the gulf fixed between ourselves and the greater part of contemporary literature, we are more or less protected from being harmed by it, and are in a position to extract from it what good it has to offer us.

There are a very large number of people in the world today who believe that all ills are fundamentally economic. Some believe that various specific economic changes alone would be enough to set the world right; others demand more or less drastic changes in the social as well, changes chiefly of two opposed types. These changes demanded, and in some places carried out, are alike in one respect, that they hold the assumptions of what I call Secularism: they concern themselves only with changes of a temporal, material, and external nature; they concern themselves with morals only of a collective nature. In an exposition of one such new faith I read the following words:

"In our morality the one single test of any moral question is whether it impedes or destroys in any way the power of the individual to serve the State. [The individual] must answer the questions: 'Does this action injure the nation? Does it injure other members of the nation? Does it injure my ability to serve the nation?' And if the answer is clear on all those questions, the individual has absolute liberty to do as he will."

Now I do not deny that this is a kind of morality, and that it is capable of great good within limits; but I think that we should all repudiate a morality which had no higher ideal to set before us than that. It represents, of course, one of the violent reactions we are witnessing, against the view that the community is solely for the benefit of the individual; but it is equally a gospel of this world, and of this world alone. My complaint against modern literature is of the same kind. It is not that modern literature is in the ordinary sense "immoral" or even "amoral"; and in any case to prefer that charge would not be enough. It is simply that it repudiates, or is wholly ignorant of, our most fundamental and important beliefs; and that in consequence its tendency is to encourage its readers to get what they can out of life while it lasts, to miss no "experience" that presents itself, and to sacrifice themselves, if they make any sacrifice at all, only for the sake of tangible benefits to others in this world either now or in the future. We shall certainly continue to read the best of its kind, of what our time provides; but we must tirelessly criticize it according to our own principles, and not merely according to the principles admitted by the writers and by the critics who discuss it in the public press.

THE *PENSÉES* OF PASCAL

═══════════

IT might seem that about Blaise Pascal, and about the two works on which his fame is founded, everything that there is to say had been said. The details of his life are as fully known as we can expect to know them; his mathematical and physical discoveries have been treated many times; his religious sentiment and his theological views have been discussed again and again; and his prose style has been analysed by French critics. But Pascal is one of those writers who will be and who must be studied afresh by men in every generation. It is not he who changes, but we who change. It is not our knowledge of him that increases, but our world that alters and our attitudes towards it. The history of human opinions of Pascal and of men of his stature is a part of the history of humanity. That indicates his permanent importance.

The few facts of Pascal's life which need to be recalled in examining the *Pensées,* are as follows. He was born at Clermont in Auvergne in 1623. His family were people of substance of the upper middle class. His father was a government official, who was able to leave, when he died, a sufficient patrimony to his one son and his two daughters. In 1631 the father moved to Paris, and a few years later took up another government post at Rouen. Wherever he lived, the elder Pascal seems to have mingled with some of the best society, and with men of eminence in science and the arts. Blaise was educated entirely by his father at home. He was exceedingly precocious, indeed excessively precocious, for his application to studies in childhood and adolescence impaired his health and is held responsible for his death at thirty-nine. Prodigious though not incredible stories are preserved, especially of his precocity in mathematics. His mind was active rather than accumulative; he showed from his earliest years that disposition to find things out for himself, which has characterized the infancy of Clerk Maxwell and other scientists. Of his later discoveries in physics there is no need for mention here; it must only be remembered that he counts as one of the greatest physicists and mathematicians of all time; and that his discoveries were made during the years when most scientists are still apprentices.

The elder Pascal, Etienne, was a sincere Christian. About 1646 he fell in with some representatives of the religious revival within the Church which has become known as Jansenism—after Jansenius, Bishop of Ypres, whose theological work is taken as the origin of the movement. This period is usually spoken of as the movement of Pascal's "first conversion." The word "conversion," however, is too forcible to be applied at this point to Blaise Pascal himself. The family had always been devout, and the younger Pascal, though absorbed in his scientific work, never seems to have been afflicted with infidelity. His attention was then directed, certainly, to religious and theological matters; but the term "conversion" can only be applied to his sisters—the elder, already Madame Périer, and particularly the younger, Jacqueline, who at that time conceived a vocation for the religious life. Pascal himself was by no means disposed to renounce the world. After the death of the father in 1650 Jacqueline, a young woman of remarkable strength and beauty of character, wished to take her vows as a sister of Port-Royal, and for some time her wish remained unfulfilled owing to the opposition of her brother. His objection was on the purely worldly ground that she wished to make over her patrimony to the Order; whereas while she lived with him, their combined resources made it possible for him to live more nearly on a scale of expense congenial to his tastes. He liked, in fact, not only to mix with the best society, but to keep a coach and horses—six horses is the number at one time attributed to his carriage. Though he had no legal power to prevent his sister from disposing of her property as she elected the amiable Jacqueline shrank from doing so without her brother's willing approval. The Mother Superior, Mère Angélique—herself an eminent personage in the history of this religious movement—finally persuaded the young novice to enter the order without the satisfaction of bringing her patrimony with her; but Jacqueline remained so distressed by this situation that her brother finally relented.

So far as is known, the worldly life enjoyed by Pascal during this period can hardly be qualified as "dissipation," and certainly not as "debauchery." Even gambling may have appealed to him chiefly as affording a study of mathematical probabilities. He appears to have led such a life as any cultivated intellectual man of good position and independent means might lead and consider himself a model of probity and virtue. Not even a love-affair is laid at his door, though he is said to have contemplated marriage. But Jansenism, as represented by the religious society of Port-Royal, was morally a Puritan movement within the Church, and its standards of conduct were at least as severe as those of any Puritanism in England or America. The period of fashionable society in Pascal's life is, however, of great importance in his development. It enlarged his knowledge of men and refined his tastes; he became a man of the world and never lost what he had learnt; and when he turned his thoughts wholly towards religion, his worldly knowledge was a part of his composition which is essential to the value of his work.

Pascal's interest in society did not distract him from scientific research; nor did this period occupy much space in what is a very short and crowded life. Partly his natural dissatisfaction with such a life, once he had learned all it had to teach him, partly the influence of his saintly sister Jacqueline, partly increasing suffering as his health declined, directed him more and more out of the world and to thoughts of eternity. And in 1654 occurs what is called his "second conversion," but which might be called his conversion simply.

He made a note of his mystical experience, which he kept always about him, and which was found, after his death, sewn into the coat which he was wearing. The experience occurred on 23rd November, 1654, and there is no reason to doubt its genuineness unless we choose to deny all mystical experience. Now, Pascal was not a mystic, and his works are not to be classified amongst mystical writings; but what can only be called mystical experience happens to many men who do not become mystics. The work which he undertook soon after, the *Lettres écrites à un provincial*, is a masterpiece of religious controversy at the opposite pole from mysticism. We know quite well that he was at the time when he received his illumination from God in extremely poor health; but it is a commonplace that some forms of illness are extremely favourable, not only to religious illumination, but to artistic and literary composition. A piece of writing meditated, apparently without progress, for months or years, may suddenly take shape and word; and in this state long passages may be produced which require little or no retouch. I have no good word to say for the cultivation of automatic writing as the model of literary composition; I doubt whether these moments *can* be cultivated by the writer; but he to whom this happens assuredly has the sensation of being a vehicle rather than a maker. No masterpiece can be produced whole by such means: but neither does even the higher form of religious inspiration suffice for the religious life; even the most exalted mystic must return to the world, and use his reason to employ the results of his experience in daily life. You may call it communion with the Divine, or you may call it a temporary crystallization of the mind. Until science can teach us to reproduce such phenomena at will, science cannot claim to have explained them; and they can be judged only by their fruits.

From that time until his death, Pascal was closely associated with the society of Port-Royal which his sister Jacqueline, who predeceased him, had joined as a *religieuse;* the society was then fighting for its life against the Jesuits. Five propositions, judged by a committee of cardinals and theologians at Rome to be heretical, were found to be put forward in the work of Jansenius; and the society of Port-Royal, the representative of Jansenism among communities, suffered a blow from which it never revived. It is not the place here to review the bitter controversy and conflict; the best account, from the point of view of a critic of genius who took no side, who was neither Jansenist nor Jesuit, Christian nor infidel, is that in the great book of Sainte-Beuve, *Port-Royal.* And in this book the parts devoted to Pascal himself are among the most brilliant pages of criticism that Sainte-Beuve ever wrote. It is sufficient to notice that the next occupation of Pascal, after his conversion, was to write these eighteen *Letters*, which as prose are of capital importance in the foundation of French classical style, and which as polemic are surpassed by none, not by Demosthenes, or Cicero, or Swift. They have the limitation of all polemic and forensic: they persuade, they seduce, they are unfair. But it is also unfair to assert that, in these *Letters to a Provincial*, Pascal was attacking the Society of Jesus in itself. He was attacking rather a particular school of casuistry which relaxed the requirements of the Confessional; a school which certainly flourished amongst the Society of Jesus, at that time, and of which the Spaniards Escobar and Molina are the most eminent authorities. He undoubtedly abused the art of quotation, as a polemical writer is likely to do; but there were abuses for him to abuse; and he did the job thoroughly. His *Letters* must not be called theology. Academic theology was not a department in which Pascal was versed; when necessary, the fathers of Port-Royal came to his aid. The *Letters* are the work of one of the finest mathematical minds of any time, and of a man of the world who addressed, not theologians, but the world in general—all of the cultivated and many of the less cultivated of the French laity; and with this public they made an astonishing success.

During this time Pascal never wholly abandoned his scientific interests. Though in his religious writings he composed slowly and painfully, and revised often, in matters of mathematics his mind seemed to move with consummate natural ease and grace. Discoveries and inventions sprang from his brain without effort; among the minor devices of this later period, the first omnibus service in Paris is said to owe its origin to his inventiveness. But rapidly failing health, and absorption in the great work he had in mind, left him little time and energy during the last two years of his life.

The plan of what we call the *Pensées* formed itself about 1660. The completed book was to have been a carefully constructed defence of Christianity, a true Apology and a kind of Grammar of Assent, setting forth the reasons which will convince the intellect. As I have indicated before, Pascal was not a theologian, and on dogmatic theology had recourse to his spiritual advisers. Nor was he indeed a systematic philosopher. He was a man with an immense genius for science, and at the same time a natural psychologist and moralist. As he was a great literary artist, his book would have been also his own spiritual autobiography; his style, free from all diminishing idiosyncrasies, was yet very personal. Above all, he was a man of strong passions; and his intellectual passion for truth was reinforced by his passionate dissatisfaction with human life unless a spiritual explanation could be found.

We must regard the *Pensées* as merely the first notes for a work which he left far from completion; we have, in Sainte-Beuve's words, a tower of which the stones have been laid on each other, but not cemented, and the structure unfinished. In early years his memory had been amazingly retentive of anything that he wished to remember; and had it not been impaired by increasing illness and pain, he probably would not have been obliged to set down these notes at all. But taking the book as it is left to us, we still find that it occupies a unique place in the history of French literature and in the history of religious meditation.

To understand the method which Pascal employs, the reader must be prepared to follow the process of the mind of the intelligent believer. The Christian thinker—and I mean the man who is trying consciously and conscientiously to explain to himself the sequence which culminates in faith, rather than the public apologist—proceeds by rejection and elimination. He finds the world to be so and so; he finds its character inexplicable by any non-religious theory: among religions he finds Christianity, and Catholic Christianity, to account most satisfactorily for the world and especially for the moral world within; and thus, by what Newman calls "powerful and concurrent" reasons, he finds himself inexorably committed to the dogma of the Incarnation. To the unbeliever, this method seems disingenuous and perverse: for the unbeliever is, as a rule, not so greatly troubled to explain the world to himself, nor so greatly distressed by its disorder; nor is he generally concerned (in modern terms) to "preserve values." He does not consider that if certain emotional states, certain developments of character, and what in the highest sense can be called "saintliness" are inherently and by inspection known to be good, then the satisfactory explanation of the world must be an explanation which will admit the "reality" of these values. Nor does he consider such reasoning admissible; he would, so to speak, trim his values according to his cloth, because to him such values are of no great value. The unbeliever starts from the other end, and as likely as not with the question: Is a case of human parthenogenesis credible? and this he would call going straight to the heart of the matter. Now Pascal's method is, on the whole, the method natural and right for the Christian; and the opposite method is that taken by Voltaire. It is worth while to remember that Voltaire, in his attempt to refute Pascal, has given once and for all the type of such refutation; and that later opponents of Pascal's Apology for the Christian Faith have contributed little beyond psychological irrelevancies. For Voltaire has presented, better than anyone since, what is the unbelieving point of view; and in the end we must all choose for ourselves between one point of view and another.

I have said above that Pascal's method is "on the whole" that of the typical Christian apologist; and this reservation was directed at Pascal's belief in miracles, which plays a larger part in his construction than it would in that, at least, of the modern Catholic. It would seem fantastic to accept Christianity because we first believe the Gospel miracles to be true, and it would seem impious to accept it primarily because we believe more recent miracles to be true; we accept the miracles, or some miracles, to be true because we believe the Gospel of Jesus Christ: we found our belief in the miracles on the Gospel, not our belief in the Gospel on the miracles. But it must be remembered that Pascal had been deeply impressed by a contemporary miracle, known as the miracle of the Holy Thorn: a thorn reputed to have been preserved from the Crown of Our Lord was pressed upon an ulcer which quickly healed. Sainte-Beuve, who as a medical man felt himself on solid ground, discusses fully the possible explanation of this apparent miracle. It is true that the miracle happened at Port-Royal, and that it arrived opportunely to revive the depressed spirits of the community in its political afflictions; and it is likely that Pascal was the more inclined to believe a miracle which was performed upon his beloved sister. In any case, it probably led him to assign a place to miracles, in his study of faith, which is not quite that which we should give to them ourselves.

Now the great adversary against whom Pascal set himself, from the time of his first conversations with M. de Saci at Port-Royal, was Montaigne. One cannot destroy Pascal, certainly; but of all authors Montaigne is one of the least destructible. You could as well dissipate a fog by flinging hand-grenades into it. For Montaigne is a fog, a gas, a fluid, insidious element. He does not reason, he insinuates, charms, and influences; or if he reasons, you must be prepared for his having some other design upon you than to convince you by his argument. It is hardly too much to say that Montaigne is the most essential author to know, if we would understand the course of French thought during the last three hundred years. In every way, the influence of Montaigne was repugnant to the men of Port-Royal. Pascal studied him with the intention of demolishing him. Yet, in the *Pensées*, at the very end of his life, we find passage after passage, and the slighter they are the more significant, almost "lifted" out of Montaigne, down to a figure of speech or a word. The parallels [1] are most often with the long essay of Montaigne called *Apologie de Raymond Sébond*—an astonishing piece of writing upon which Shakespeare also probably drew in *Hamlet*. Indeed, by the time a man knew Montaigne well enough to attack him, he would already be thoroughly infected by him.

It would, however, be grossly unfair to Pascal, to Montaigne, and indeed to French literature, to leave the matter at that. It is no diminution of Pascal, but only an aggrandizement of Montaigne. Had Montaigne been an ordinary life-sized sceptic, a small man like Anatole France, or even a greater man like

---

[1] Cf. the use of the simile of the *couvreur*. For comparing parallel passages, the edition of the *Pensées* by Henri Massis (*A la cité des livres*) is better than the two-volume edition of Jacques Chevalier (Gabalda). It seems just possible that in the latter edition, and also in his biographical study (*Pascal*; by Jacques Chevalier, English translation, published by Sheed and Ward), M. Chevalier is a little over-zealous to demonstrate the perfect orthodoxy of Pascal.

Renan, or even like the greatest sceptic of all, Voltaire, this "influence" would be to the discredit of Pascal; but if Montaigne had been no more than Voltaire, he could not have affected Pascal at all. The picture of Montaigne which offers itself first to our eyes, that of the original and independent solitary "personality," absorbed in amused analysis of himself, is deceptive. Montaigne's is no *limited* Pyrrhonism, like that of Voltaire, Renan, or France. He exists, so to speak, on a plan of numerous concentric circles, the most apparent of which is the small inmost circle, a personal puckish scepticism which can be easily aped if not imitated. But what makes Montaigne a very great figure is that he succeeded, God knows how—for Montaigne very likely did not know that he had done it—it is not the sort of thing that men *can* observe about themselves, for it is essentially bigger than the individual's consciousness—he succeeded in giving expression to the scepticism of *every* human being. For every man who thinks and lives by thought must have his own scepticism, that which stops at the question, that which ends in denial, or that which leads to faith and which is somehow integrated into the faith which transcends it. And Pascal, as the type of one kind of religious believer, which is highly passionate and ardent, but passionate only through a powerful and regulated intellect, is in the first sections of his unfinished Apology for Christianity facing unflinchingly the demon of doubt which is inseparable from the spirit of belief.

There is accordingly something quite different from an influence which would prove Pascal's weakness; there is a real affinity between his doubt and that of Montaigne; and through the common kinship with Montaigne Pascal is related to the noble and distinguished line of French moralists, from La Rochefoucauld down. In the honesty with which they face the *données* of the actual world this French tradition has a unique quality in European literature, and in the seventeenth century Hobbes is crude in comparison.

Pascal is a man of the world among ascetics, and an ascetic among men of the world; he had the knowledge of worldliness and the passion of asceticism, and in him the two are fused into an individual whole. The majority of mankind is lazy-minded, incurious, absorbed in vanities, and tepid in emotion, and is therefore incapable of either much doubt or much faith; and when the ordinary man calls himself a sceptic or an unbeliever, that is ordinarily a simple pose, cloaking a disinclination to think anything out to a conclusion. Pascal's disillusioned analysis of human bondage is sometimes interpreted to mean that Pascal was really and finally an unbeliever, who, in his despair, was incapable of enduring reality and enjoying the heroic satisfaction of the free man's worship of nothing. His despair, his disillusion, are, however, no illustration of personal weakness; they are perfectly objective, because they are essential moments in the progress of the intellectual soul; and for the type of Pascal they are the analogue of the drought, the dark night, which is an essential stage in the progress of the Christian mystic. A similar despair, when it is arrived at by a diseased character or an impure soul, may issue in the most disastrous consequences though with the most superb manifestations; and thus we get *Gulliver's Travels;* but in Pascal we find no such distortion; his despair is in itself more terrible than Swift's, because our heart tells us that it corresponds exactly to the facts and cannot be dismissed as mental disease; but it was also a despair which was a necessary prelude to, and element in, the joy of faith.

I do not wish to enter any further than necessary upon the question of the heterodoxy of Jansenism; and it is no concern of this essay whether the Five Propositions condemned at Rome were really maintained by Jansenius in his book *Augustinus,* or whether we should deplore or approve the consequent decay (indeed with some persecution) of Port-Royal. It is impossible to discuss the matter without becoming involved as a controversialist either for or against Rome. But in a man of the type of Pascal—and the type always exists—there is, I think, an ingredient of what may be called Jansenism of temperament, without identifying it with the Jansenism of Jansenius and of other devout and sincere but not immensely gifted doctors. [2] It is accordingly needful to state in brief what the dangerous doctrine

[2] The great man of Port-Royal was of course Saint-Cyran, but anyone who is interested will certainly consult, first of all, the book of Sainte-Beuve mentioned.

of Jansenius was, without advancing too far into theological refinements. It is recognized in Christian theology—and indeed on
a lower plane it is recognized by all men in affairs of daily life
—that free-will of the natural effort and ability of the individual
man and also supernatural *grace*, a gift accorded we know not
quite how, are both required, in co-operation, for salvation.
Though numerous theologians have set their wits at the problem, it ends in a mystery which we can perceive but not finally
decipher. At least, it is obvious that, like any doctrine a slight
excess or deviation to one side or the other will precipitate a
heresy. The Pelagians, who were refuted by St. Augustine, emphasized the efficacy of human effort and belittled the importance of supernatural grace. The Calvinists emphasized the degradation of man through Original Sin, and considered mankind
so corrupt that the will was of no avail; and thus fell into the
doctrine of predestination. It was upon the doctrine of grace according to St. Augustine that the Jansenists relied; and the
Augustinus of Jansenius was presented as a sound exposition of
the Augustinian views.

Heresies are never antiquated, because they forever assume
new forms. For instance, the insistence upon good works and
"service" which is preached from many quarters, or the simple
faith that anyone who lives a good and useful life need have no
"morbid" anxieties about salvation, is a form of Pelagianism.
On the other hand, one sometimes hears enounced the view that
it will make no real difference if all the traditional religious
sanctions for moral behaviour break down, because those who
are born and bred to be nice people will always prefer to behave
nicely, and those who are not will behave otherwise in any case:
and this is surely a form of predestination—for the hazard of
being born a nice person or not is as uncertain as the gift of grace.

It is likely that Pascal was attracted as much by the fruits of
Jansenism in the life of Port-Royal as by the doctrine itself.
This devout, ascetic, thoroughgoing society, striving heroically
in the midst of a relaxed and easy-going Christianity, was
formed to attract a nature so concentrated, so passionate, and so
thoroughgoing as Pascal's. But the insistence upon the degraded
and helpless state of man, in Jansenism, is something also to

which we must be grateful, for to it we owe the magnificent analysis of human motives and occupations which was to have constituted the early part of his book. And apart from the Jansenism which is the work of a not very eminent bishop who wrote a Latin treatise which is now unread, there is also, so to speak, a Jansenism of the individual biography. A moment of Jansenism may naturally take place, and take place rightly, in the individual; particularly in the life of a man of great and intense intellectual powers, who cannot avoid seeing through human beings and observing the vanity of their thoughts and of their avocations, their dishonesty and self-deception, the insincerity of their emotions, their cowardice, the pettiness of their real ambitions.[3] Actually, considering that much greater maturity is required for these qualities, than for any mathematical or scientific greatness, how easily his brooding on *the misery of man without God* might have encouraged in him the sin of spiritual pride, the *concupiscence de l'esprit:* and how fast a hold he has of humility!

And although Pascal brings to his work the same powers which he exerted in science, it is not as a scientist that he presents himself. He does not seem to say to the reader: I am one of the most distinguished scientists of the day: I understand many matters which will always be mysteries to you, and through science I have come to the Faith; you therefore who are not initiated into science ought to have faith if I have it. He is fully aware of the difference of subject-matter; and his famous distinction between the *esprit de géométrie* and the *esprit de finesse* is one to ponder over.

En l'un, les principes sont palpables, mais éloignés de l'usage commun; de sorte qu'on a peine à tourner la tête de ce côté-là, manque d'habitude: mais pour peu qu'on l'y tourne, on voit les principes à plein; et il faudrait avoir tout à fait l'esprit faux pour

---

[3] Cette négligence en une affaire ou il s'agit d'eux-mêmes, de leur éternité, de leur tout, m'irrite plus qu'elle ne m'attendrit; elle m'étonne et m'épouvante, c'est un monstre pour moi. Je ne dis pas ceci par le zèle pieux d'une dévotion spirituelle. J'entends au contraire qu'on doit avoir ce sentiment par un principe d'intérêt humain et par un intérêt d'amour-propre: il ne faut pour cela que voir ce que voient les personnes les moins éclairées. *Pensées:* ed. Massis, p. 29.

*mal raisonner sur des principes si gros qu'il est presque im-
possible qu'ils échappent.*

*Mais dans l'esprit de finesse, les principes sont dans l'usage
commun et devant les yeux de tout le monde. On n'a que faire
de tourner la tête, ni de se faire violence; il n'est question que
d'avoir bonne vue, mais il faut l'avoir bonne; car les principes
sont si déliés et en si grand nombre, qu'il est presque impossible
qu'il n'en échappe. Or, l'omission d'un principe mène à l'erreur;
ainsi, il faut avoir la vue bien nette pour tous les principes, et
ensuite l'esprit juste pour ne pas raisonner faussement sur des
principes connus.*

It is the just combination of the scientist, the *honnête homme*,
and the religious nature with a passionate craving for God that
makes Pascal unique. He succeeds where Descartes fails; for in
Descartes the element of *esprit de géométrie* is excessive.[4] And
in a few phrases about Descartes, in the present book, Pascal laid
his finger on the place of weakness.

*Je ne puis pardonner à Descartes; il aurait bien voulu, dans
toute sa philosophie, se pouvoir passer de Dieu; mais il n'a pu
s'empêcher de lui faire donner une chiquenaude, pour mettre le
monde en mouvement; après cela, il n'a plus que faire de Dieu.*

He who reads this book will observe at once its fragmentary
nature; but only after some study will perceive that the frag-
mentariness lies in the expression more than in the thought. The
"thoughts" cannot be detached from each other and quoted as
if each were complete in itself. *Le cœur a ses raisons que la raison
ne connaît point*, how often one has heard that quoted, and
quoted often to the wrong purpose![5] For this is by no means
an exaltation of the "heart" over the "head," a defence of
unreason. The heart, in Pascal's terminology, is itself truly
rational if it is truly the heart. For him, in theological matters which seemed to him much larger, more difficult, and more

[4] For a brilliant criticism of the errors of Descartes from a theological point
of view the reader is referred to *Three Reformers* by Jacques Maritain (translation published by Sheed and Ward).

[5] And those who have quoted *C'est là ma place au soleil* have often forgotten to add *Voilà le commencement et l'image de l'usurpation de toute la terre.*

important than scientific matters, the whole personality is involved.

We cannot quite understand any of the parts, fragmentary as they are, without some understanding of the whole. Capital, for instance, is his analysis of the *three orders:* the order of nature, the order of mind, and the order of charity. These three are *discontinuous;* the higher is not implicit in the lower as in an evolutionary doctrine it would be.[6] In this distinction Pascal offers much about which the modern world would do well to think. And indeed, because of his unique combination and balance of qualities, I know of no religious writer more pertinent to our time. The great mystics, like St. John of the Cross, are primarily for readers with a special determination of purpose; the devotional writers, such as St. François de Sales, are primarily for those who already feel consciously desirous of the love of God; the great theologians are for those interested in theology. But I can think of no Christian writer, not Newman even, more to be commended than Pascal to those who doubt, but who have the mind to conceive, and the sensibility to feel, the disorder, the futility, the meaninglessness, the mystery of life and suffering, and who can only find peace through a satisfaction of the whole being.

[6] An important modern theory of discontinuity, suggested partly by Pascal, is sketched in the collected fragments of *Speculations* by T. E. Hulme (Kegan Paul).

VII

BAUDELAIRE

ANYTHING like a just appreciation of Baude-
laire has been slow to arrive in England, and still is defective
or partial even in France. There are, I think, special reasons for
the difficulty in estimating his worth and finding his place. For
one thing, Baudelaire was in some ways far in advance of the
point of view of his own time, and yet was very much of it, very
largely partook of its limited merits, faults, and fashions. For
one thing, he had a great part in forming a generation of poets
after him; and in England he had what is in a way the misfortune to be first and extravagantly advertised by Swinburne, and
taken up by the followers of Swinburne. He was universal, and
at the same time confined by a fashion which he himself did
most to create. To dissociate the permanent from the temporary,
to distinguish the man from his influence, and finally to detach
him from the associations of those English poets who first admired him, is no small task. His comprehensiveness itself makes
difficulty, for it tempts the partisan critic, even now, to adopt
Baudelaire as the patron of his own beliefs.

It is the purpose of this essay to affirm the importance of
Baudelaire's prose works, a purpose justified by the translation
of one of those works which is indispensable for any student of
his poetry.[1] This is to see Baudelaire as something more than
the author of the *Fleurs du Mal*, and consequently to revise
somewhat our estimate of that book. Baudelaire came into vogue
at a time when "Art for Art's sake" was a dogma. The care
which he took over his poems, and the fact that contrary to the

---

[1] *Intimes*, translated by Christopher Sherwood, and published by the Blackamore Press.

371

fluency of his time, both in France and England he restricted, himself to this one volume, encouraged the opinion that Baudelaire was an artist exclusively for art's sake. The doctrine does not, of course, really apply to anybody; no one applied it less than Pater, who spent many years, not so much in illustrating it, as in expounding it as a *theory of life*, which is not the same thing at all. But it was a doctrine which did affect criticism and appreciation, and which did obstruct a proper judgment of Baudelaire. He is in fact a greater man than was imagined, though perhaps not such a perfect poet.

Baudelaire has, I believe, been called a fragmentary Dante, for what that description is worth. It is true that many people who enjoy Dante enjoy Baudelaire; but the differences are as important as the similarities. Baudelaire's inferno is very different in quality and significance from that of Dante. Truer, I think, would be the description of Baudelaire as a later and more limited Goethe. As we begin to see him now, he represents his own age in somewhat the same way as that in which Goethe represents an earlier age. As a critic of the present generation, Mr. Peter Quennell has recently said in his book, *Baudelaire and the Symbolists*:

"He had enjoyed a *sense of his own age*, had recognized its pattern while the pattern was yet incomplete, and—because it is only our misapprehension of the present which prevents our looking into the immediate future, our ignorance of today and of its real as apart from its spurious tendencies and requirements—had anticipated many problems, both on the aesthetic and on the moral plane, in which the fate of modern poetry is still concerned."

Now the man who has this sense of his age is hard to analyse. He is exposed to its follies as well as sensitive to its inventions; and in Baudelaire, as well as in Goethe, is some of the outmoded nonsense of his time. The parallel between the German poet who has always been the symbol of perfect "health" in every sense, as well as of universal curiosity, and the French poet who has been the symbol of morbidity in mind and concentrated interests in work, may seem paradoxical. But after

this lapse of time the difference between "health" and "morbidity" in the two men becomes more negligible; there is something artificial and even priggish about Goethe's healthiness,
as there is about Baudelaire's unhealthiness; we have passed beyond both fashions, of health or malady, and they are both
merely men with restless, critical, curious minds and the "sense
of the age"; both men who understood and foresaw a great
deal. Goethe, it is true, was interested in many subjects which
Baudelaire left alone; but by Baudelaire's time it was no longer
necessary for a man to embrace such varied interests in order to
have the sense of the age; and in retrospect some of Gothe's
studies seem to us (not altogether justly) to have been merely
dilettante hobbies. The most of Baudelaire's prose writings
(with the exception of the translations from Poe, which are of
less interest to an English reader) are as important as the most
of Goethe. They throw light on the *Fleurs du Mal* certainly,
but they also expand immensely our appreciation of their author.

It was once the mode to take Baudelaire's Satanism seriously,
as it is now the tendency to present Baudelaire as a serious and
Catholic Christian. Especially as a prelude to the *Journaux
Intimes* this diversity of opinion needs some discussion. I think
that the latter view—that Baudelaire is essentially Christian—is
nearer the truth than the former, but it needs considerable reservation. When Baudelaire's Satanism is dissociated from its
less creditable paraphernalia, it amounts to a dim intuition of a
part, but a very important part, of Christianity. Satanism itself, so far as not merely an affectation, was an attempt to get
into Christianity by the back door. Genuine blasphemy, genuine
in spirit and not purely verbal, is the product of partial belief,
and is as impossible to the complete atheist as to the perfect
Christian. It is a way of affirming belief. This state of partial
belief is manifest throughout the *Journaux Intimes*. What is
significant about Baudelaire is his theological innocence. He is
discovering Christianity for himself; he is not assuming it as a
fashion or weighing social or political reasons, or any other
accidents. He is beginning, in a way, at the beginning; and
being a discoverer, is not altogether certain what he is exploring
and to what it leads; he might almost be said to be making

again, as one man, the effort of scores of generations. His Christianity is rudimentary or embryonic; at best, he has the excesses of a Tertullian (and even Tertullian is not considered wholly orthodox and well balanced). His business was not to practise Christianity, but—what was much more important for his time—to assert its *necessity*.

Baudelaire's morbidity of temperament cannot, of course, be ignored: and no one who has looked at the work of Crépet or the recent small biographical study of François Porché can forget it. We should be misguided if we treated it as an unfortunate ailment which can be discounted or to attempt to detach the sound from the unsound in his work. Without the morbidity none of his work would be possible or significant; his weaknesses can be composed into a larger whole of strength, and this is implied in my assertion that neither the health of Goethe nor the malady of Baudelaire matters in itself: it is what both men made of their endowments that matters. To the eye of the world, and quite properly for all questions of private life, Baudelaire was thoroughly perverse and insufferable: a man with a talent for ingratitude and unsociability, intolerably irritable, and with a mulish determination to make the worst of everything; if he had money, to squander it; if he had friends, to alienate them; if he had any good fortune, to disdain it. He had the pride of the man who feels in himself great weakness and great strength. Having great genius, he had neither the patience nor the inclination, had he had the power, to overcome his weakness; on the contrary, he exploited it for theoretical purposes. The morality of such a course may be a matter for endless dispute; for Baudelaire, it was the way to liberate his mind and give us the legacy and lesson that he has left.

He was one of those who have great strength, but strength merely to *suffer*. He could not escape suffering and could not transcend it, so he *attracted* pain to himself. But what he could do, with that immense passive strength and sensibilities which no pain could impair, was to study his suffering. And in this limitation he is wholly unlike Dante, not even like any character in Dante's Hell. But, on the other hand, such suffering as Baudelaire's implies the possibility of a positive state of beatitude. Indeed, in his way of suffering is already a kind of presence of the supernatural and of the superhuman. He rejects always the purely natural and the purely human; in other words, he is neither "naturalist" nor "humanist." Either because he cannot adjust himself to the actual world he has to reject it in favour of Heaven and Hell, or because he has the perception of Heaven and Hell he rejects the present world: both ways of putting it are tenable. There is in his statements a good deal of romantic detritus; *ses ailes de géant l'empêchent de marcher*, he says of the Poet and of the Albatross, but not convincingly; but there is also truth about himself and about the world. His *ennui* may of course be explained, as everything can be explained in psychological or pathological terms; but it is also, from the opposite point of view, a true form of *acedia*, arising from the unsuccessful struggle towards the spiritual life.

II

From the poems alone, I venture to think, we are not likely to grasp what seems to me the true sense and significance of Baudelaire's mind. Their excellence of form, their perfection of phrasing, and their superficial coherence, may give them the appearance of presenting a definite and final state of mind. In reality, they seem to me to have the external but not the internal form of classic art. One might even hazard the conjecture that the care for perfection of form, among some of the romantic poets of the nineteenth century, was an effort to support, or to conceal from view, an inner disorder. Now the true claim of Baudelaire as an artist is not that he found a superficial form, but that he was searching for a form of life. In minor form he never indeed equalled Théophile Gautier, to whom he significantly dedicated his poems: in the best of the slight verse of Gautier there is a satisfaction, a balance of inwards and form, which we do not find in Baudelaire. He had a greater technical ability than Gautier, and yet the content of feeling is constantly bursting the receptacle. His apparatus, by which I do not mean his command of words and rhythms, but his stock of imagery (and every poet's stock of imagery is circumscribed somewhere), is not wholly perdurable or adequate. His prostitutes, mulattoes, Jewesses, serpents, cats, corpses, form a machinery which has not worn very well; his Poet, or his Don Juan, has a romantic ancestry which is too clearly traceable. Compare with the costumery of Baudelaire the stock of imagery of the *Vita Nuova*, or of Cavalcanti, and you find Baudelaire's does not everywhere wear as well as that of several centuries earlier; compare him with Dante or Shakespeare, for what such a comparison is worth, and he is found not only a much smaller poet, but one in whose work much more that is perishable has entered.

To say this is only to say that Baudelaire belongs to a definite place in time. Inevitably the offspring of romanticism, and by his nature the first counter-romantic in poetry, he could, like any one else, only work with the materials which were there. It must not be forgotten that a poet in a romantic age cannot be a "classical" poet except in tendency. If he is sincere, he must express with individual differences the general state of mind— not as a *duty*, but simply because he cannot help participating in it. For such poets, we may expect often to get much help from reading their prose works and even notes and diaries; help in deciphering the discrepancies between head and heart, means and end, material and ideals.

What preserves Baudelaire's poetry from the fate of most French poetry of the nineteenth century up to his time, and has made him, as M. Valéry has said in a recent introduction to the *Fleurs du Mal*, the one modern French poet to be widely read abroad, is not quite easy to conclude. It is partly that technical mastery which can hardly be overpraised, and which has made his verse an inexhaustible study for later poets, not only in his own language. When we read

> *Maint joyau dort enseveli*
> *Dans les ténèbres et l'oubli,*
> *Bien loin des pioches et des sondes;*
> *Mainte fleur épanche à regret*
> *Son parfum doux comme un secret*
> *Dans les solitudes profondes,*

we might for a moment think it a more lucid bit of Mallarmé; and so original is the arrangement of words that we might easily overlook its borrowing from Gray's *Elegy*. When we read

> *Valse mélancolique et langoureux vertige!*

we are already in the Paris of Laforgue. Baudelaire gave to French poets as generously as he borrowed from English and American poets. The renovation of the versification of Racine has been mentioned often enough; quite genuine, but might be overemphasized, as it sometimes comes near to being a trick. But even without this, Baudelaire's variety and resourcefulness would still be immense.

Furthermore, besides the stock of images which he used that seems already second-hand, he gave new possibilities to poetry in a new stock of imagery of contemporary life.

> *. . . Au cœur d'un vieux faubourg, labyrinthe fangeux*
> *Ou l'humanité grouille en ferments orageux,*
>
> *On voit un vieux chiffonnier qui vient, hochant le tête*
> *Buttant, et se cognant aux murs comme un poète.*

This introduces something new, and something universal in modern life. (The last line quoted, which in ironic terseness anticipates Corbière, might be contrasted with the whole poem *Bénédiction* which begins the volume.) It is not merely in the use of imagery of common life, not merely in the use of imagery of the sordid life of a great metropolis, but in the elevation of such imagery to the *first intensity*—presenting it as it is, and yet making it represent something much more than itself—that Baudelaire has created a mode of release and expression for other men.

This invention of language, at a moment when French poetry in particular was famishing for such invention, is enough to make of Baudelaire a great poet, a great landmark in poetry. Baudelaire is indeed the greatest exemplar in *modern* poetry in any language, for his verse and language is the nearest thing to a complete renovation that we have experienced. But his renovation of an attitude towards life is no less radical and no less important. In his verse, he is now less a model to be imitated or a source to be drained than a reminder of the duty, the consecrated task, of sincerity. From a fundamental sincerity he could not deviate. The superficies of sincerity (as I think has not always been remarked) is not always there. As I have suggested, many of his poems are insufficiently removed from their romantic origins, from Byronic paternity and Satanic fraternity. The "satanism" of the Black Mass was very much in the air; in exhibiting it Baudelaire is the voice of his time; but I would observe that in Baudelaire, as in no one else, it is redeemed by *meaning something else*. He uses the same paraphernalia, but cannot limit its symbolism even to all that of which he is conscious. Compare him with Huysmans in *A rebours, En route,* and *Là-bas*. Huysmans, who is a first-rate realist of his time, only succeeds in making his diabolism interesting when he treats it externally, when he is merely describing a manifestation of his period (if such it was). His own interest in such matters is, like his interest in Christianity, a petty affair. Huysmans merely provides a document. Baudelaire would not even provide that, if he had been really absorbed in that ridiculous hocus-pocus. But actually Baudelaire is concerned, not with demons, black masses, and romantic blasphemy, but with the real problem of good and evil. It is hardly more than an accident of time that he uses the current imagery and vocabulary of blasphemy. In the middle nineteenth century, the age which (at its best) Goethe had prefigured, an age of bustle, programmes, platforms, scientific progress, humanitarianism and revolutions which improved nothing, an age of progressive degradation, Baudelaire perceived that what really matters is Sin and Redemption. It is a proof of his honesty that he went as far as he could honestly go and no further. To a mind observant of the post-Voltaire France (*Voltaire . . . le prédicateur des concierges*), a mind which saw the world of *Napoléon le petit* more lucidly than did that of Victor Hugo, a mind which at the same time had no affinity for the *Saint-Sulpicerie* of the day, the recognition of the reality of Sin is a New Life; and the possibility of damnation is so immense a relief in a world of electoral reform, plebiscites, sex reform and dress reform, that damnation itself is an immediate form of salvation—of salvation from the ennui of modern life, because it at last gives some significance to living. It is this, I believe, that Baudelaire is trying to express; and it is this which separates him from the modernist Protestantism of Byron and Shelley. It is apparently Sin in the Swinburnian sense, but really Sin in the permanent Christian sense, that occupies the mind of Baudelaire.

Yet, as I said, the sense of Evil implies the sense of good. Here too, as Baudelaire apparently confuses, and perhaps did confuse, Evil with its theatrical representations, Baudelaire is not always certain in his notion of the Good. The romantic idea of Love is never quite exorcised, but never quite surrendered to. In *Le Balcon*, which M. Valéry considers, and I think rightly, one of Baudelaire's most beautiful poems, there is all the romantic idea, but something more: the reaching out towards something which cannot be had *in*, but which may be had partly *through*, personal relations. Indeed, in much romantic poetry the sadness is due to the exploitation of the fact that no human relations are adequate to human desires, but also to the disbelief in any further object for human desires than that which, being human, fails to satisfy them. One of the unhappy necessities of human existence is that we have to "find things out for ourselves." If it were not so, the statement of Dante would have, at least for poets, have done once for all. Baudelaire has all the romantic sorrow, but invents a new kind of romantic nostalgia, a derivative of his nostalgia being the *poésie des dé parts*, the *poésie des salles d'attente*. In a beautiful paragraph of the volume in question, *Mon cœur mis à nu*, he imagines the vessels lying in harbour as saying: *Quand partons-nous vers le bonheur?* and his minor successor Laforgue exclaims: *Comme ils sont beaux, les trains manqués*. The poetry of flight—which, in contemporary France, owes a great debt to the poems of the A. O. Barnabooth of Valery Larbaud—is, in its origin in this paragraph of Baudelaire, a dim recognition of the direction of beatitude.

But in the adjustment of the natural to the spiritual, of the bestial to the human and the human to the supernatural, Baudelaire is a bungler compared with Dante; the best that can be said, and that is a very great deal, is that what he knew he found out for himself. In his book, the *Journaux Intimes,* and especially in *Mon cœur mis à nu,* he has a great deal to say of the love of man and woman. One aphorism which has been especially noticed is the following: *la volupté unique et suprême de l'amour gît dans la certitude de faire le mal.* This means, I think, that Baudelaire has perceived that what distinguishes the relations of man and woman from the copulation of beasts is the knowledge of Good and Evil (of *moral* Good and Evil which are not natural Good and Bad or puritan Right and Wrong). Having an imperfect, vague romantic conception of Good, he was at least able to understand that the sexual act as evil is more dignified, less boring, than as the natural, "life-giving," cheery automatism of the modern world. For Baudelaire, sexual operation is at least something not analogous to Kruschen Salts.

So far as we are human, what we do must be either evil or good; [2] so far as we do evil or good, we are human; and it is better, in a paradoxical way, to do evil than to do nothing: at least, we exist. It is true to say that the glory of man is his capacity for salvation; it is also true to say that his glory is his capacity for damnation. The worst that can be said of most of our malefactors, from statesmen to thieves, is that they are not men enough to be damned. Baudelaire was man enough for damnation: whether he *is* damned is, of course, another question, and we are not prevented from praying for his repose. In all his humiliating traffic with other beings, he walked secure in this high vocation, that he was capable of a damnation denied to the politicians and the newspaper editors of Paris.

III

Baudelaire's notion of beatitude certainly tended to the wishy-washy; and even in one of the most beautiful of his poems, *L'Invitation au voyage,* he hardly exceeds the *poésie des*

[2] "Know ye not, that to whom ye yield yourselves servants to obey, his servants ye are to whom ye obey: whether of sin unto death, or of obedience unto righteousness?"—Romans vi, 16.

départs. And because his vision is here so restricted, there is for him a gap between human love and divine love. His human love is definite and positive, his divine love vague and uncertain: hence his insistence upon the evil of love, hence his constant vituperations of the female. In this there is no need to pry for psychopathological causes, which would be irrelevant at best; for his attitude towards women is consistent with the point of view which he had reached. Had he been a woman he would, no doubt, have held the same views about men. He has arrived at the perception that a woman must be to some extent a symbol; he did not arrive at the point of harmonising his experience with his ideal needs. The complement, and the correction to the *Journaux Intimes*, so far as they deal with the relations of man and woman, is the *Vita Nuova*, and the *Divine Comedy*. But—I cannot assert it too strongly—Baudelaire's view of life, such as it is, is objectively apprehensible, that is to say, his idiosyncrasies can partly explain his view of life, but they cannot explain it away. And this view of life is one which has grandeur and which exhibits heroism; it was an evangel to his time and to ours. *La vraie civilisation*, he wrote, *n'est pas dans le gaz, ni dans la vapeur, ni dans les tables tournantes. Elle est dans la diminution des traces du péché originel*. It is not quite clear exactly what *diminution* here implies, but the tendency of his thought is clear, and the message is still accepted by but few. More than half a century later T. E. Hulme left behind him a paragraph which Baudelaire would have approved:

"In the light of these absolute values, man himself is judged to be essentially limited and imperfect. He is endowed with Original Sin. While he can occasionally accomplish acts which partake of perfection, he can never himself *be* perfect. Certain secondary results in regard to ordinary human action in society follow from this. A man is essentially bad, he can only accomplish anything of value by discipline—ethical and political. Order is thus not merely negative, but creative and liberating. Institutions are necessary."

ARNOLD AND PATER

ALTHOUGH Pater is as appropriate to the 'seventies as to the 'eighties, because of the appearance of *Studies in the History of the Renaissance* in 1873, I have chosen to discuss him in this volume [1] because of the date 1885, the middle of the decade, which marks the publication of *Marius the Epicurean*. The first may certainly be counted the more "influential" book; but *Marius* illustrates another but related aspect of Pater's work. His writing of course extended well into the 'nineties; but I doubt whether any one would consider the later books and essays of anything like the importance, in social history or in literary history, of the two I have mentioned.

The purpose of the present paper is to indicate a direction from Arnold, through Pater, to the 'nineties, with, of course, the solitary figure of Newman in the background.

It is necessary first of all to estimate the aesthetic and religious views of Arnold: in each of which, to borrow his own phrase against him, there is an element of *literature* and an element of *dogma*. As Mr. J. M. Robertson has well pointed out in his *Modern Humanists Reconsidered*, Arnold had little gift for consistency or for definition. Nor had he the power of connected reasoning at any length: his flights are either short flights or circular flights. Nothing in his prose work, therefore, will stand very close analysis, and we may well feel that the positive content of many words is very small. Culture and Conduct are the first things, we are told; but what Culture and Conduct are, I feel that I know less well on every reading. Yet Arnold does still hold us, at least with *Culture and Anarchy* and *Friendship's*

---

[1] A volume entitled *The Eighteen-Eighties*. Edited by Walter de la Mare for the Royal Society of Literature. Cambridge.

Garland. To my generation, I am sure, he was a more sympathetic prose writer than Carlyle or Ruskin; yet he holds his position and achieves his effects exactly on the same plane, by the power of his rhetoric and by representing a point of view which is particular though it cannot be wholly defined.

But the revival of interest in Arnold in our time—and I believe he is admired and read not only more than Carlyle and Ruskin, but than Pater—is a very different thing from the influence he exerted in his own time. We go to him for refreshment and for the companionship of a kindred point of view to our own, but not as disciples. And therefore it is the two books I have mentioned that are most readable. Even the *Essays in Criticism* cannot be read very often; *Literature and Dogma, God and the Bible*, and *Last Essays on Church and Religion*, have served their turn and can hardly be read through. In these books he attempts something which must be austerely impersonal; in them reasoning power matters, and it fails him; furthermore, we have now our modern solvers of the same problem Arnold there set himself, and they, or some of them, are more accomplished and ingenious in this sort of rationalizing than Arnold was. Accordingly, and this is my first point, his Culture survives better than his Conduct, because it can better survive vagueness of definition. But both Culture and Conduct were important for his own time.

Culture has three aspects, according as we look at it in *Culture and Anarchy*, in *Essays in Criticism*, or in the abstract. It is in the first of these two books that Culture shows to best advantage. And the reason is clear: Culture there stands out against a background to which it is contrasted, a background of definite items of ignorance, vulgarity and prejudice. As an invective against the crudities of the industrialism of his time, the book is perfect of its kind. Compared with Carlyle, it looks like clear thinking, and is certainly clearer expression; and compared with Arnold, Ruskin often appears long-winded and peevish. Arnold taught English expository and critical prose a restraint and urbanity it needed. And hardly, in this book, do we question the meaning of Culture; for the good reason that we do not need to. Even when we read that Culture "is a study of perfection," we do not at that point raise an eyebrow to admire how much Culture appears to have arrogated from Religion. For we have shortly before been hearing something about "the will of God," or of a joint firm called "reason and the will of God"; and soon after we are presented with Mr. Bright and Mr. Frederic Harrison as foils to Culture; and appearing in this way between the will of God and Mr. Bright, Culture is here sufficiently outlined to be recognizable. *Culture and Anarchy* is on the same side as *Past and Present* or *Unto this Last*. Its ideas are really no clearer;—one reason why Arnold, Carlyle and Ruskin were so influential, for precision and completeness of thought do not always make for influence. (Arnold, it is true, gave something else: he produced a kind of illusion of precision and clarity; that is, maintained these qualities as ideals of style.)

Certainly, the prophets of the period just before that of which I am supposed to be writing excelled in denunciation (each in his own way) rather than in construction; and each in his own fashion lays himself open to the charge of tedious querulousness. And an idea, such as that of Culture, is apt to lead to consequences which its author cannot foresee and probably will not like. Already, in the *Essays*, Culture begins to seem a little more priggish—I do not say "begins" in a chronological sense—and a little more anaemic. Where Sir Charles Adderley and Mr. Roebuck appear, there is more life than in the more literary criticism. Arnold is in the end, I believe, at his best in satire and in apologetics for literature, in his defence and enunciation of a needed attitude.

To us, as I have said, Arnold is rather a friend than a leader. He was a champion of "ideas" most of whose ideas we no longer take seriously. His Culture is powerless to aid or to harm. But he is at least a forerunner of what is now called Humanism, of which I must here say something, if only to contrast it and compare it with the Aestheticism of Pater. How far Arnold is responsible for the birth of Humanism would be difficult to say; we can at least say that it issues very naturally from his doctrine, that Charles Eliot Norton is largely responsible for its American form, and that therefore Arnold is another likely ancestor. But the resemblances are too patent to be ignored. The difference is

that Arnold could father something apparently quite different—
the view of life of Walter Pater. The resemblance is that literature, or Culture, tended with Arnold to usurp the place of
Religion. From one point of view, Arnold's theory of Art and
his theory of Religion are quite harmonious, and Humanism is
merely the more coherent structure. Arnold's prose writings fall
into two parts; those on Culture and those on Religion; and the
books about Christianity seem only to say again and again—
merely that the Christian faith is of course impossible to the man
of culture. They are tediously negative. But they are negative
in a peculiar fashion: their aim is to affirm that the emotions of
Christianity can and must be preserved without the belief. From
this proposition two different types of man can extract two different types of conclusion: (1) that Religion is Morals, (2) that
Religion is Art. The effect of Arnold's religious campaign is to
divorce Religion from thought.

In Arnold himself there was a powerful element of Puritan
morality, as in most of his contemporaries, however diverse.
And the strength of his moral feeling—we might add its blind-
ness also—prevented him from seeing how very odd might look
the fragments of the fabric which he knocked about so reck-
lessly. "The power of Christianity has been in the immense
emotion which it has excited," he says; not realizing at all that
this is a counsel to get all the emotional kick out of Christianity
one can, without the bother of believing it; without reading the
future to foresee *Marius the Epicurean*, and finally *De Pro-
fundis*. Furthermore, in his books dealing with Christianity he
seems bent upon illustrating in himself the provincialisms which
he rebuked in others. "M. de Lavelaye," he says in the preface
to *God and the Bible*, with as deferential a manner as if he were
citing M. Renan himself, "is struck, as any judicious Catholic
may well be struck, with the superior freedom, order, stability,
and religious earnestness, of the Protestant Nations as compared
with the Catholic." He goes on complacently, "Their religion
has made them what they are." I am not here concerned with
the genuine differences between Catholic and Protestant; only
with the tone which Arnold adopts in this preface and through-

out this book; and which is in no wise more liberal than that of Sir Charles Adderley or Mr. Roebuck or "Mr. Tennyson's great broad-shouldered Englishman." He girds at (apparently) Herbert Spencer for substituting *Unknowable* for *God;* quite unaware that his own Eternal not ourselves comes to exactly the same thing as the Unknowable. And when we read Arnold's discourses on Religion, we return to scrutinize his Culture with some suspicion.

For Arnold's Culture, at first sight so enlightened, moderate and reasonable, walks so decorously in the company of the will of God, that we may overlook the fact that it tends to develop its own stringent rules and restrictions.

"Certainly, culture will never make us think it an essential of religion whether we have in our Church discipline 'a popular authority of elders,' as Hooker calls it, or whether we have Episcopal jurisdiction."

Certainly, "culture" in itself can never make us think so, any more than it can make us think that the quantum theory is an essential of physical science: but such people as are interested in this question at all, however cultured they be, hold one or the other opinion pretty strongly; and Arnold is really affirming that to Culture all theological and ecclesiastical differences are indifferent. But this is a rather positive dogma for Culture to hold. When we take *Culture and Anarchy* in one hand, and *Literature and Dogma* in the other, our minds are gradually darkened by the suspicion that Arnold's objection to Dissenters is partly that they do hold strongly to that which they believe, and partly that they are not Masters of Arts of Oxford. Arnold, as Master of Arts, should have had some scruple about the use of words. But in the very preface to the second edition of *Literature and Dogma* he says:

"The *Guardian* proclaims 'the miracle of the incarnation' to be the 'fundamental truth' for Christians. How strange that on me should devolve the office of instructing the *Guardian* that the fundamental thing for Christians is not the Incarnation but the imitation of Christ!"

While wondering whether Arnold's own "imitation" is even a good piece of mimicry, we notice that he employs *truth* and *thing* as interchangeable: and a very slight knowledge of the field in which he was skirmishing should have told him that a "fundamental truth" in theology and a "fundamental thing" in his own loose jargon have nothing comparable about them. The total effect of Arnold's philosophy is to set up Culture in the place of Religion, and to leave Religion to be laid waste by the anarchy of feeling. And Culture is a term which each man not only may interpret as he pleases, but must indeed interpret as he can. So the gospel of Pater follows naturally upon the prophecy of Arnold.

Even before the 'seventies began Pater seems to have written, though not published, the words:

"The theory, or idea, or system, which requires of us the sacrifice of any part of this experience, in consideration of some interest into which we cannot enter, or some abstract morality we have not identified with ourselves, or what is only conventional, has no real claim upon us." [2]

Although more outspoken in repudiating any measure than man for all things, Pater is not really uttering anything more subversive than the following words of Arnold:

"Culture, disinterestedly seeking in its aim at perfection to see things as they really are, shows us how worthy and divine a thing is the religious side in man, though it is not the whole of man. But while recognizing the grandeur of the religious side in man, culture yet makes us eschew an inadequate conception of man's totality."

Religion, accordingly, is merely a " 'side' in (*sic*) man"; a side which so to speak must be kept in its place. But when we go to Arnold to enquire what is "man's totality," that we may ourselves aim at so attractive a consummation, we learn nothing; any more than we learn about the "secret" of Jesus of which he has so much to say.

[2] In quoting from *The Renaissance* I use the first edition throughout.

The degradation of philosophy and religion, skilfully initiated by Arnold, is competently continued by Pater. "The service of philosophy, and of religion and culture as well, to the human spirit," he says in the 1873 conclusion to *The Renaissance*, "is to startle it into a sharp and eager observation." "We shall hardly have time," he says, "to make theories about the things we see and touch." Yet we have to be "curiously testing new opinions"; so it must be—if opinions have anything to do with theories, and unless wholly capricious and unreasoning they must have— that the opinions we test can only be those provided for our enjoyment by an inferior sort of drudges who are incapable of enjoying our own free life, because all their time is spent (and "*we* hardly have time") in making theories. And this again is only a development of the intellectual Epicureanism of Arnold.

Had Pater not had one gift denied to Arnold, his permutation of Arnold's view of life would have little interest. He had a taste for painting and the plastic arts, and particularly for Italian painting, a subject to which Ruskin had introduced the nation. He had a visual imagination; he had also come into contact with another generation of French writers than that which Arnold knew; the zealous Puritanism of Arnold was in him considerably mitigated, but the zeal for culture was equally virulent. So his peculiar appropriation of religion into culture was from another side: that of emotion, and indeed of sensation; but in making this appropriation, he was only doing what Arnold had given license to do.

Marius the Epicurean marks indeed one of the phases of the fluctuating relations between religion and culture in England since the Reformation; and for this reason the year 1885 is an important one. Newman, in leaving the Anglican Church, had turned his back upon Oxford. Ruskin, with a genuine sensibility for certain types of art and architecture, succeeded in satisfying his nature by translating everything immediately into terms of morals. The vague religious vapourings of Carlyle, and the sharper, more literate social fury of Ruskin yield before the persuasive sweetness of Arnold. Pater is a new variation.

We are liable to confusion if we call this new variation the "aesthete." Pater was, like the other writers I have just men-

tioned (except Newman), a moralist. If, as the *Oxford Dictionary* tells us, an aesthete is a "professed appreciator of the beautiful," then there are at least two varieties: those whose profession is most vocal, and those whose appreciation is most professional. If we wish to understand painting, we do not go to Oscar
Wilde for help. We have specialists, such as Mr. Berenson, or
Mr. Roger Fry. Even in that part of his work which can only
be called literary criticism, Pater is always primarily the moralist. In his essay on Wordsworth he says:

"To treat life in the spirit of art, is to make life a thing in
which means and ends are identified: to encourage such treatment, the true moral significance of art and poetry."

That was his notion: to find the "true moral significance of art
and poetry." Certainly, a writer may be none the less classified
as a moralist, if his moralising is suspect or perverse. We
have today a witness in the person of M. André Gide. As always
in his imaginary portraits, so frequently in his choice of other
writers as the subjects of critical studies, Pater is inclined to
emphasize whatever is morbid or associated with physical malady. His admirable study of Coleridge is charged with this attraction.

"More than Childe Harold (he says of Coleridge), more
than Werther, more than René himself, Coleridge, by what he
did, what he was, and what he failed to do, represents that inexhaustible discontent, languor, and homesickness, that endless
regret, the chords of which ring all through our modern literature."

Thus again in Pascal he emphasizes the malady, with its consequences upon the thought; but we feel that somehow what is
important about Pascal has been missed. But it is not that he
treats philosophers "in the spirit of art," exactly; for when we
read him on Leonardo or Giorgione, we feel that there is the
same preoccupation, coming between him and the object as it
really is. He is, in his own fashion, moralizing upon Leonardo
or Giorgione, on Greek art or on modern poetry. His famous
dictum: "Of this wisdom, the poetic passion, the desire of beauty,

the love of art for art's sake has most; for art comes to you pro-
fessing frankly to give nothing but the highest quality to your
moments as they pass, and simply for those moments' sake," is
itself a theory of ethics; it is concerned not with art but with life.
The second half of the sentence is of course demonstrably untrue, or else being true of everything else besides art is meaningless; but it is a serious statement of morals. And the disap-
proval which greeted this first version of the Conclusion to *The
Renaissance* is implicitly a just recognition of that fact. "Art for
art's sake" is the offspring of Arnold's Culture; and we can
hardly venture to say that it is even a perversion of Arnold's
doctrine, considering how very vague and ambiguous that doctrine is.

When religion is in a flourishing state, when the whole mind
of society is moderately healthy and in order, there is an easy
and natural association between religion and art. Only when religion has been partly retired and confined, when an Arnold can
sternly remind us that Culture is wider than Religion, do we
get "religious art" and in due course "aesthetic religion." Pater
undoubtedly had from childhood a religious bent, naturally to
all that was liturgical and ceremonious. Certainly this is a real
and important part of religion; and Pater cannot thereby be accused of insincerity and "aestheticism." His attitude must be
considered both in relation to his own mental powers and to his
moment of time. There were other men like him, but without
his gift of style, and such men were among his friends. In the
pages of Thomas Wright, Pater, more than most of his devout
friends, appears a little absurd. His High Churchmanship is undoubtedly very different from that of Newman, Pusey and the
Tractarians, who, passionate about dogmatic essentials, were singularly indifferent to the sensuous expressions of orthodoxy. It
was also dissimilar to that of the priest working in a slum parish.
He was "naturally Christian"—but within very narrow limitations: the rest of him was just the cultivated Oxford don and
disciple of Arnold, for whom religion was a matter of feeling,
and metaphysics not much more. Being incapable of sustained
reasoning, he could not take philosophy or theology seriously;

just as being primarily a moralist, he was incapable of seeing any work of art simply as it is.

Marius the Epicurean represents the point of English history at which the repudiation of revealed religion by men of culture and intellectual leadership coincides with a renewed interest in the visual arts. It is Pater's most arduous attempt at a work of literature; for *Plato and Platonism* can be almost dissolved into a series of essays. *Marius* itself is incoherent; its method is a number of fresh starts; its content is a hodge-podge of the learning of the classical don, the impressions of the sensitive holiday visitor to Italy, and a prolonged flirtation with the liturgy. Even A. C. Benson, who makes as much of the book as any one can, observes in a passage of excellent criticism:

"But the weakness of the case is, that instead of emphasizing the power of sympathy, the Christian conception of Love, which differentiates Christianity from all other religious systems, Marius is after all converted, or brought near to the threshold of the faith, more by its sensuous appeal, its liturgical solemnities; the element, that is to say, which Christianity has in common with all religions, and which is essentially human in character. And more than that, even the very peace which Marius discerns in Christianity is the old philosophical peace over again."

This is sound criticism. But—a point with which Dr. Benson was not there concerned—it is surely a merit, on the part of Pater, and one which deserves recognition, to have clarified the issues. Matthew Arnold's religion is the more confused, because he conceals, under the smoke of strong and irrational moral prejudice, just the same, or no better, Stoicism and Cyrenaicism of the amateur classical scholar. Arnold Hellenizes and Hebraicizes in turns; it is something to Pater's credit to have Hellenized purely.

Of the essence of the Christian faith, as Dr. Benson frankly admits, Pater knew almost nothing. One might say also that his intellect was not powerful enough to grasp—I mean, to grasp as firmly as many classical scholars whose names will never be so renowned as that of Pater—the essence of Platonism or Aristotelianism or Neo-Platonism. He therefore,

or his Marius, moves quite unconcerned with the intellectual
activity which was then amalgamating Greek metaphysics with
the tradition of Christ; just as he is equally unconcerned with
the realities of Roman life as we catch a glimpse of them in
Petronius, or even in such a book as Dill's on the reign of
Marcus Aurelius. Marius merely *drifts* towards the Christian
Church, if he can be said to have any motion at all; nor does
he or his author seem to have any realization of the chasm to
be leapt between the meditations of Aurelius and the Gospel.
To the end, Marius remains only a half-awakened soul. Even
at his death, in the midst of the ceremonies of which he is given
the benefit, his author reflects "often had he fancied of old that
not to die on a dark or rainy day might itself have a little alle-
viating grace or favour about it," recalling to our minds the
"springing of violets from the grave" in the Conclusion to *The
Renaissance*, and the death of Flavian.

I have spoken of the book as of some importance. I do not
mean that its importance is due to any influence it may have
exerted. I do not believe that Pater, in this book, has influenced
a single first-rate mind of a later generation. His view of art,
as expressed in *The Renaissance*, impressed itself upon a number of writers in the 'nineties, and propagated some confusion
between life and art which is not wholly irresponsible for some
untidy lives. The theory (if it can be called a theory) of "art
for art's sake" is still valid in so far as it can be taken as an
exhortation to the artist to stick to his job; it never was and
never can be valid for the spectator, reader or auditor. How
far *Marius the Epicurean* may have assisted a few "conversions"
in the following decade I do not know: I only feel sure that
with the direct current of religious development it has had
nothing to do at all. So far as that current—or one important
current—is concerned, *Marius* is much nearer to being merely
due to Pater's contact—a contact no more intimate than that
of Marius himself—with something which was happening and
would have happened without him.

The true importance of the book, I think, is as a document
of one moment in the history of thought and sensibility in the
nineteenth century. The dissolution of thought in that age, the

isolation of art, philosophy, religion, ethics and literature, is interrupted by various chimerical attempts to effect imperfect syntheses. Religion became morals, religion became art, religion became science or philosophy; various blundering attempts were made at alliances between various branches of thought. Each half-prophet believed that he had the whole truth. The alliances were as detrimental all round as the separations. The right practice of "art for art's sake" was the devotion of Flaubert or Henry James; Pater is not with these men, but rather with Carlyle and Ruskin and Arnold, if some distance below them. *Marius* is significant chiefly as a reminder that the religion of Carlyle or that of Ruskin or that of Arnold or that of Tennyson or that of Browning, is not enough. It represents, and Pater represents more positively than Coleridge of whom he wrote the words, "that inexhaustible discontent, languor, and homesickness . . . the chords of which ring all through our modern literature."

FRANCIS HERBERT BRADLEY

—————

IT is unusual that a book so famous and so influential should remain out of print so long as Bradley's *Ethical Studies*.[1] The one edition appeared in 1876: Bradley's refusal to reprint it never wavered. In 1893, in a footnote in *Appearance and Reality*, and in words characteristic of the man, he wrote: "I feel that the appearance of other books, as well as the decay of those superstitions against which largely it was directed, has left me free to consult my own pleasure in the matter." The dates of his three books, the *Ethical Studies* in 1876, the *Principles of Logic* in 1883, and *Appearance and Reality* in 1893, leave us in no doubt that his pleasure was the singular one of thinking rather than the common one of writing books. And Bradley always assumed, with what will remain for those who did not know him a curious blend of humility and irony, an attitude of extreme diffidence about his own work. His *Ethical Studies*, he told us (or told our fathers), did not aim at "the construction of a system of Moral Philosophy." The first words of the preface to his *Principles of Logic* are: "The following work makes no claim to supply any systematic treatment of logic." He begins the preface to *Appearance and Reality* with the words: "I have described the following work as an essay in metaphysics. Neither in form nor extent does it carry out the idea of a system." The phrase for each book is almost the same. And many readers, having in mind Bradley's polemical irony and his obvious zest in using it, his habit of discomfiting an opponent with a sudden profession of ignorance, of inability

[1] *Ethical Studies*, by F. H. Bradley, O.M., LL.D. Second Edition. (Oxford: Clarendon Press. London: Milford.)

to understand, or of incapacity for abstruse thought, have con-
cluded that this is all a mere pose—and even a somewhat un-
scrupulous one. But deeper study of Bradley's mind convinces
us that the modesty is real, and his irony the weapon of a
modest and highly sensitive man. Indeed, if this had been a
pose it would never have worn so well as it has. We have to
consider, then, what is the nature of Bradley's influence and
why his writings and his personality fascinate those whom they
do fascinate; and what are his claims to permanence.

Certainly one of the reasons for the power he still exerts,
as well as an indubitable claim to permanence, is his great gift
of style. It is for his purposes—and his purposes are more varied
than is usually supposed—a perfect style. Its perfection has prevented it from cutting any great figure in prose anthologies and
literature manuals, for it is perfectly welded with the matter.
Ruskin's works are extremely readable in snippets even for
many who take not a particle of interest in the things in which
Ruskin was so passionately interested. Hence he survives in
anthologies, while his books have fallen into undue neglect.
Bradley's books can never fall into this neglect because they will
never rise to this notoriety; they come to the hands only of
those who are qualified to treat them with respect. But perhaps
a profounder difference between a style like Bradley's and a
style like Ruskin's is a greater purity and concentration of purpose. One feels that the emotional intensity of Ruskin is partly
a deflection of something that was baffled in life, whereas Bradley, like Newman, is directly and wholly that which he is. For
the secret of Bradley's style, like that of Bergson—whom he
resembles in this if in nothing else—is the intense addiction to
an intellectual passion.

The nearest resemblance in style, however, is not Ruskin but
Matthew Arnold. It has not been sufficiently observed that
Bradley makes use of the same means as Arnold, and for similar ends. To take first the most patent resemblance, we find in
Bradley the same type of fun as that which Arnold has with his
young friend Arminius. In the *Principles of Logic* there is
a celebrated passage in which Bradley is attacking the theory
of association of ideas according to Professor Bain, and explains

how on this principle an infant comes to recognize a lump of sugar:

"A young child, or one of the lower animals, is given on Monday a round piece of sugar, eats it and finds it sweet. On Tuesday it sees a square piece of sugar, and proceeds to eat it. . . . Tuesday's sensation and Monday's image are not only separate facts, which, because alike, are therefore *not* the same; but they differ perceptibly both in quality and environment. What is to lead the mind to take one for the other?

"Sudden at this crisis, and in pity at distress, there leaves the heaven with rapid wing a goddess Primitive Credulity. Breathing in the ear of the bewildered infant she whispers, 'The thing which has happened once will happen once more. Sugar was sweet, and sugar will be sweet.' And Primitive Credulity is accepted forthwith as the mistress of our life. She leads our steps on the path of experience, until her fallacies, which cannot always be pleasant, at length become suspect. We wake up indignant at the kindly fraud by which the goddess so long has deceived us. So she shakes her wings, and flying to the stars, where there are no philosophers, leaves us here to the guidance of—I cannot think what."

This sort of solemn banter is exactly what an admirer of Arnold is ready to enjoy. But it is not only in his fun, or in his middle style, that Bradley is like Arnold; they are alike in their purple passages. The two following may be compared. By Arnold:

"And yet, steeped in sentiment as she lies, spreading her gardens to the moonlight, and whispering from her towers the last enchantments of the Middle Age, who will deny that Oxford, by her ineffable charm, keeps ever calling us nearer to the true goal of all of us, to the ideal, to perfection—to beauty, in a word, which is only truth seen from another side—nearer, perhaps, than all the science of Tübingen. Adorable dreamer, whose heart has been so romantic! who hast given thyself so prodigally, given thyself to sides and to heroes not mine, only never to the Philistines! home of lost causes, and forsaken beliefs, and unpopular names, and impossible loyalties! what example could ever so inspire us to keep down the Philistine in ourselves, what teacher could ever so save us from that bondage to which we are all prone, that bondage which Goethe, in his incomparable lines on the death of Schiller, makes it his friend's highest praise (and nobly did Schiller deserve the praise) to have left miles out of sight behind him—the bondage of 'was uns alle bändigt, *das Gemeine!*' "

The passage from the *Principles of Logic* is not so well known:

"It may come from a failure in my metaphysics, or from a weakness of the flesh which continues to blind me, but the notion that existence could be the same as understanding strikes as cold and ghost-like as the dreariest materialism. That the glory of this world in the end is appearance leaves the world more glorious, if we feel it is a show of some fuller splendour; but the sensuous curtain is a deception and a cheat, if it hides some colourless movement of atoms, some spectral woof of impalpable abstractions, or unearthly ballet of bloodless categories. Though dragged to such conclusions, we cannot embrace them. Our principles may be true, but they are not reality. They no more *make* that Whole which commands our devotion than some shredded dissection of human tatters *is* that warm and breathing beauty of flesh which our hearts found delightful."

Any one who is at all sensitive to style will recognize the similarity of tone and tension and beat. It is not altogether certain that the passage from Bradley is not the better; at any rate such a phrase as Arnold's "ineffable charm" has not worn at all well.

But if the two men fought with the same weapons—and fundamentally, in spite of Bradley's assault upon Arnold, for the same causes—the weapons of Bradley had behind them a heavier force and a closer precision. Exactly what Bradley fought for and exactly what he fought against have not been quite understood; understanding has been obscured by the dust of Bradley's logical battles. People are inclined to believe that what Bradley did was to demolish the logic of Mill and the psychology of Bain. If he had done that, it would have been a lesser service

than what he has done; and if he had done that it would have
been less of a service than people think, for there is much that
is good in the logic of Mill and the psychology of Bain. But
Bradley did not attempt to destroy Mill's logic. Any one who
reads his own *Principles* will see that his force is directed not
against Mill's logic as a whole but only against certain limitations, imperfections and abuses. He left the structure of Mill's
logic standing, and never meant to do anything else. On the
other hand, the *Ethical Studies* are not merely a demolition of
the Utilitarian theory of conduct but an attack upon the whole
Utilitarian mind. For Utilitarianism was, as every reader of
Arnold knows, a great temple in Philistia. And of this temple
Arnold hacked at the ornaments and cast down the images, and
his best phrases remain for ever gibing and scolding in our
memory. But Bradley, in his philosophical critique of Utilitarianism, undermined the foundations. The spiritual descendants
of Bentham have built anew, as they always will; but at least,
in building another temple for the same worship, they have
had to apply a different style of architecture. And this is the
social basis of Bradley's distinction, and the social basis is even
more his claim to our gratitude than the logical basis: he replaced a philosophy which was crude and raw and provincial
by one which was, in comparison, catholic, civilized, and universal. True, he was influenced by Kant and Hegel and Lotze.
But Kant and Hegel and Lotze are not so despicable as some
enthusiastic mediaevalists would have us believe, and they are,
in comparison with the school of Bentham, catholic and civilized
and universal. In fighting the battles that he fought in the
'seventies and 'eighties Bradley was fighting for a European
and ripened and wise philosophy, against an insular and immature and cranky one; the same battle that Arnold was fighting
against the *British Banner*, Judge Edmonds, Newman Weeks,
Deborah Butler, Elderess Polly, Brother Noyes, Mr. Murphy,
the Licensed Victuallers and the Commercial Travellers.

It is not to say that Arnold's work was vain if we say that
it is to be done again; for we must know in advance, if we
are prepared for that conflict, that the combat may have truces

but never a peace. If we take the widest and wisest view of a Cause, there is no such thing as a Lost Cause because there is no such thing as a Gained Cause. We fight for lost causes because we know that our defeat and dismay may be the preface to our successors' victory, though that victory itself will be temporary; we fight rather to keep something alive than in the expectation that anything will triumph. If Bradley's philosophy is today a little out of fashion, we must remark that what has superseded it, what is now in favour, is, for the most part, crude and raw and provincial (though infinitely more technical and scientific) and must perish in its turn. Arnold turned from mid-century Radicalism with the reflection "A new power has suddenly appeared." There is always a new power; but the new power destined to supersede the philosophy which has superseded Bradley will probably be something at the same time older, more patient, more supple and more wise. The chief characteristics of much contemporary philosophy are newness and crudeness, impatience, inflexibility in one respect and fluidity in another, and irresponsibility and lack of wisdom. Of wisdom Bradley had a large share; wisdom consists largely of scepticism and uncynical disillusion; and of these Bradley had a large share. And scepticism and disillusion are a useful equipment for religious understanding; and of that Bradley had a share too.

Those who have read the *Ethical Studies* will be ready with the remark that it was Bradley, in this book and in the year 1876, who knocked the bottom out of *Literature and Dogma*. But that does not mean that the two men were not on the same side; it means only that *Literature and Dogma* is irrelevant to Arnold's main position as given in the Essays and in *Culture and Anarchy*, that the greatest weakness of Arnold's culture was his weakness in philosophical training, and that in philosophical criticism Bradley exhibits the same type of culture that Arnold exhibited in political and social criticism. Arnold had made an excursion into a field for which he was not armed. Bradley's attack upon Arnold does not take up much space, but Bradley was economical of words; it is all in a few paragraphs and a few footnotes to the "Concluding Remarks":

"But here once more 'culture' has come to our aid, and has shown us how here, as everywhere, the study of polite literature, which makes for meekness, makes needless also all further education; and we felt already as if the clouds that metaphysics had wrapped about the matter were dissolving in the light of a fresh and sweet intelligence. And, as we turned towards the dawn, we sighed over poor Hegel, who had read neither Goethe nor Homer, nor the Old and New Testaments, nor any of the literature which has gone to form 'culture,' but, knowing no facts, and reading no books, nor ever asking himself 'such a tyro's question as what being really was,' sat spinning out of his head those foolish logomachies which impose on no person of refinement."

Here is the identical weapon of Arnold, sharpened to a razor edge and turned against Arnold.

"But the 'stream' and the 'tendency' having served their turn, like last week's placards, now fall into the background, and we learn at last that 'the Eternal' is not eternal at all, unless we give that name to whatever a generation sees happen, and believes both has happened and will happen—just as the habit of washing ourselves might be termed 'the Eternal not ourselves that makes for cleanliness,' or 'Early to bed and early to rise' the 'Eternal not ourselves that makes for longevity,' and so on —that 'the Eternal,' in short, is nothing in the world but a piece of literary clap-trap. The consequence is that all we are left with is the assertion that 'righteousness' is 'salvation' or welfare, and that there is a 'law' and a 'Power' which has something to do with this fact; and here again we must not be ashamed to say that we fail to understand what any one of these phrases means, and suspect ourselves once more to be on the scent of clap-trap."

A footnote continues the Arnold-baiting in a livelier style:

" 'Is there a God?' asks the reader. 'Oh, yes,' replies Mr. Arnold, 'and I can verify him in experience.' 'And what is he then?' cries the reader. 'Be virtuous, and as a rule you will be happy,' is the answer. 'Well, and God?' 'That is God,' says Mr. Arnold; 'there is no deception, and what more do you want?'

I suppose we do want a good deal more. Most of us, certainly the public which Mr. Arnold addresses, want something they can worship; and they will not find that in an hypostasised copy-book heading, which is not much more adorable than 'Honesty is the best policy,' or 'Handsome is that handsome does,' or various other edifying maxims, which have not yet come to an apotheosis."

Such criticism is final. It is patently a great triumph of wit and a great delight to watch when a man's methods, almost his tricks of speech, are thus turned against himself. But if we look more closely into these words and into the whole chapter from which they are taken, we find Bradley to have been not only triumphant in polemic but right in reason. Arnold, with all his great virtues, was not always patient enough, or solicitous enough of any but immediate effect, to avoid inconsistency—as has been painstakingly shown by Mr. J. M. Robertson. In *Culture and Anarchy*, which is probably his greatest book, we hear something said about "the will of God"; but the "will of God" seems to become superseded in importance by "our best self, or right reason, to which we want to give authority"; and this best self looks very much like Matthew Arnold slightly disguised. In our own time one of the most remarkable of our critics, one who is fundamentally on most questions in the right, and very often right quite alone, Professor Irving Babbitt, has said again and again that the old curbs of class, of authoritative government, and of religion must be supplied in our time by something he calls the "inner check." The inner check looks very much like the "best self" of Matthew Arnold; and though supported by wider erudition and closer reasoning, is perhaps open to the same objections. There are words of Bradley's, and in the chapter from which we have already quoted, that might seem at first sight to support these two eminent doctrines:

"How can the human-divine ideal ever be my will? The answer is, Your will it never can be as the will of your private self, so that your private self should become wholly good. To that self you must die, and by faith be made one with that ideal. You must resolve to give up your will, as the mere will of this or that man, and you must put your whole self, your entire will, into the will of the divine. That must be your one self, as it is your true self; that you must hold to both with thought and will, and all other you must renounce."

There is one direction in which these words—and, indeed, Bradley's philosophy as a whole—might be pushed, which would be dangerous; the direction of diminishing the value and dignity of the individual, of sacrificing him to a Church or a State. But, in any event, the words cannot be interpreted in the sense of Arnold. The distinction is not between a "private self" and a "public self" or a "higher self," it is between the individual as himself and no more, a mere numbered atom, and the individual in communion with God. The distinction is clearly drawn between man's "mere will" and "the will of the Divine." It may be noted also that Bradley is careful, in indicating the process, not to exaggerate either will or intellect at the expense of the other. And in all events it is a process which neither Arnold nor Professor Babbitt could accept. But *if* there is a "will of God," as Arnold, in a hasty moment, admits, then some doctrine of Grace must be admitted too; or else the "will of God" is just the same inoperative benevolence which we have all now and then received—and resented—from our fellow human beings. In the end it is a disappointment and a cheat.

Those who return to the reading of *Ethical Studies,* and those who now, after reading the other works of Bradley, read it for the first time, will be struck by the unity of Bradley's thought in the three books and in the collected Essays. But this unity is not the unity of mere fixity. In the *Ethical Studies,* for instance, he speaks of the awareness of the self, the knowledge of one's own existence as indubitable and identical. In *Appearance and Reality,* seventeen years later, he had seen much deeper into the matter; and had seen that no one "fact" of experience in isolation is real or is evidence of anything. The unity of Bradley's thought is not the unity attained by a man who never changes his mind. If he had so little occasion to change it, that is because he usually saw his problems from the beginning in all their complexity and connexions—saw them, in other words, with wisdom—and because he could never be deceived by his own metaphors—which, indeed, he used most sparingly—and was never tempted to make use of current nostrums.

If all of Bradley's writings are in some sense merely "essays," that is not solely a matter of modesty, or caution, and certainly not of indifference, or even of ill-health. It is that he perceived the contiguity and continuity of the various provinces of thought. "Reflection on morality," he says, "leads us beyond it. It leads us, in short, to see the necessity of a religious point of view." Morality and religion are not the same thing, but they cannot beyond a certain point be treated separately. A system of ethics, if thorough, is explicitly or implicitly a system of theology; and to attempt to erect a complete theory of ethics without a religion is none the less to adopt some particular attitude towards religion. In this book, as in his others, Bradley is thoroughly empirical, much more empirical than the philosophies that he opposed. He wished only to determine how much of morality could be founded securely without entering into the religious questions at all. As in *Appearance and Reality* he assumes that our common everyday knowledge is on the whole true so far as it goes, but that we do not know how far it does go; so in the *Ethical Studies* he starts always with the assumption that our common attitude towards duty, pleasure, or self-sacrifice is correct so far as it goes—but we do not know how far it does go. And in this he is all in the Greek tradition. It is fundamentally a philosophy of common sense.

Philosophy without wisdom is vain; and in the greater philosophers we are usually aware of that wisdom which for the sake of emphasis and in the most accurate and profound sense could be called even worldly wisdom. Common sense does not mean, of course, either the opinion of the majority or the opinion of the moment; it is not a thing to be got at without maturity and study and thought. The lack of it produces those unbalanced philosophies, such as Behaviourism, of which we hear a great deal. A purely "scientific" philosophy ends by denying what we know to be true; and, on the other hand, the great weakness of Pragmatism is that it ends by being of no *use* to anybody. Again, it is easy to underestimate Hegel, but it is easy to overestimate Bradley's debt to Hegel; in a philosophy like Bradley's the points at which he *stops* are always important points. In an unbalanced or uncultured philosophy words have a way of changing their meaning—as sometimes with Hegel; or else they are made, in a most ruthless and piratical manner, to walk the plank: such as the words which Professor J. B. Watson drops overboard, and which we know to have meaning and value. But Bradley, like Aristotle, is distinguished by his scrupulous respect for words, that their meaning should be neither vague nor exaggerated; and the tendency of his labours is to bring British philosophy closer to the Greek tradition.

MARIE LLOYD

═══

IT requires some effort to understand why one person, among many who do a thing with accomplished skill, should be greater than the others; and it is not always easy to distinguish superiority from great popularity, when the two go together. Although I have always admired the genius of Marie Lloyd I do not think that I always appreciated its uniqueness; I certainly did not realize that her death would strike me as the important event that it was. Marie Lloyd was the greatest music-hall artist of her time in England: she was also the most popular. And popularity in her case was not merely evidence of her accomplishment; it was something more than success. It is evidence of the extent to which she represented and expressed that part of the English nation which has perhaps the greatest vitality and interest.

Among all of that small number of music-hall performers, whose names are familiar to what is called the lower class, Marie Lloyd had far the strongest hold on popular affection. The attitude of audiences toward Marie Lloyd was different from their attitude toward any other of their favourites of that day, and this difference represents the difference in her art. Marie Lloyd's audiences were invariably sympathetic, and it was through this sympathy that she controlled them. Among living music-hall artists none can better control an audience than Nellie Wallace. I have seen Nellie Wallace interrupted by jeering or hostile comment from a boxful of Eastenders; I have seen her, hardly pausing in her act, make some quick retort that silenced her tormenters for the rest of the evening. But I have never known Marie Lloyd to be confronted by this kind of hostility; in any case, the feeling of the vast majority of the audience was so manifestly on her side, that no objector would have dared to lift his voice. And the difference is this: that whereas other comedians amuse their audiences as much and sometimes more than Marie Lloyd, no other comedian succeeded so well in giving expression to the life of that audience, in raising it to a kind of art. It was, I think, this capacity for expressing the soul of the people that made Marie Lloyd unique, and that made her audiences, even when they joined in the chorus, not so much hilarious as happy.

In the details of acting Marie Lloyd was perhaps the most perfect, in her own style, of British actresses. There are no cinema records of her; she never descended to this form of money-making; it is to be regretted, however, that there is no film of her to preserve for the recollection of her admirers the perfect expressiveness of her smallest gestures. But it is less in the accomplishment of her act than in what she made it, that she differed from other comedians. There was nothing about her of the grotesque; none of her comic appeal was due to exaggeration; it was all a matter of selection and concentration. The most remarkable of the survivors of the music-hall stage, to my mind, are Nellie Wallace and Little Tich; [1] but each of these is a kind of grotesque; their acts are an orgy of parody of the human race. For this reason, the appreciation of these artists requires less knowledge of the environment. To appreciate, for instance, the last turn in which Marie Lloyd appeared, one ought to know what objects a middle-aged woman of the charwoman class would carry in her bag; exactly how she would go through her bag in search of something; and exactly the tone of voice in which she would enumerate the objects she found in it. This was only part of the acting in Marie Lloyd's last song, "One of the Ruins that Cromwell Knocked Abaht a Bit."

Marie Lloyd's art will, I hope, be discussed by more competent critics of the theatre than I. My own chief point is that I consider her superiority over other performers to be in a way a moral superiority: it was her understanding of the people and

[1] Without prejudice to a younger generation.

sympathy with them, and the people's recognition of the fact
that she embodied the virtues which they genuinely most respected in private life, that raised her to the position she occupied at her death. And her death is itself a significant moment in English history. I have called her the expressive figure
of the lower classes. There is no such expressive figure for any
other class. The middle classes have no such idol: the middle
classes are morally corrupt. That is to say, their own life fails
to find a Marie Lloyd to express it; nor have they any independent virtues which might give them as a conscious class
any dignity. The middle classes, in England as elsewhere, under
democracy, are morally dependent upon the aristocracy, and the
aristocracy are subordinate to the middle class, which is gradually
absorbing and destroying them. The lower class still exists; but
perhaps it will not exist for long. In the music-hall comedians
they find the expression and dignity of their own lives; and
this is not found in the most elaborate and expensive revue.
In England, at any rate, the revue expresses almost nothing.
With the decay of the music-hall, with the encroachment of the
cheap and rapid-breeding cinema, the lower classes will tend
to drop into the same state of protoplasm as the bourgeoisie. The
working man who went to the music-hall and saw Marie Lloyd
and joined in the chorus was himself performing part of the
act; he was engaged in that collaboration of the audience with
the artist which is necessary in all art and most obviously in
dramatic art. He will now go to the cinema, where his mind
is lulled by continuous senseless music and continuous action
too rapid for the brain to act upon, and will receive, without
giving, in that same listless apathy with which the middle and
upper classes regard any entertainment of the nature of art. He
will also have lost some of his interest in life. Perhaps this will
be the only solution. In an interesting essay in the volume of
Essays on the Depopulation of Melanesia, the psychologist
W. H. R. Rivers adduced evidence which has led him to believe
that the natives of that unfortunate archipelago are dying out
principally for the reason that the "Civilization" forced upon
them has deprived them of all interest in life. They are dying
from pure boredom. When every theatre has been replaced by

100 cinemas, when every musical instrument has been replaced by 100 gramophones, when every horse has been replaced by 100 cheap motor-cars, when electrical ingenuity has made it possible for every child to hear its bedtime stories from a loud speaker, when applied science has done everything possible with the materials on this earth to make life as interesting as possible, it will not be surprising if the population of the entire civilized world rapidly follows the fate of the Melanesians.[2]

[2] These lines were written nine years ago.

WILKIE COLLINS

AND DICKENS

━━━━

IT is to be hoped that some scholarly and philosophic critic of the present generation may be inspired to write a book on the history and aesthetic of melodrama. The golden age of melodrama passed, it is true, before any person living was aware of its existence: in the very middle of the last century. But there are many living who are not too young to remember the melodramatic stage before the cinema replaced it; who have sat entranced, in the front stalls of local or provincial theatres, before some representation of *East Lynne*, or *The White Slave*, or *No Mother to Guide Her*; and who are not too old to have observed with curious interest the replacement of dramatic melodrama by cinematographic melodrama, and the dissociation of the elements of the old three-volume melodramatic novel into the various types of the modern 300-page novel. Those who have lived before such terms as "highbrow fiction," "thrillers" and "detective fiction" were invented realize that melodrama is perennial and that the craving for it is perennial and must be satisfied. If we cannot get this satisfaction out of what the publishers present as "literature," then we will read—with less and less pretence of concealment—what we call "thrillers." But in the golden age of melodramatic fiction there was no such distinction. The best novels *were* thrilling; the distinction of *genre* between such-and-such a profound "psychological" novel of today and such-and-such a masterly "detective" novel of today is greater than the distinction of *genre* between *Wuthering Heights*, or even *The Mill on the Floss*, and *East Lynne*, the last of which "achieved an enormous and instantaneous success, and was translated into every known language, including Parsee and Hindustani." We believe that several contemporary novels have been "translated into every known language"; but we are sure that they have less in common with *The Golden Bowl*, or *Ulysses*, or even *Beauchamp's Career*, than *East Lynne* has in common with *Bleak House*.

In order to enjoy and to appreciate the work of Wilkie Collins, we ought to be able to reassemble the elements which have been dissociated in the modern novel. Collins is the contemporary of Dickens, Thackeray, George Eliot; of Charles Reade and almost of Captain Marryat. He has something in common with all of these novelists; but particularly and significantly with Dickens. Collins was the friend and sometimes the collaborator of Dickens; and the work of the two men ought to be studied side by side. There is, unhappily for the literary critic, no full biography of Wilkie Collins; and Forster's *Life of Dickens* is, from this point of view, most unsatisfactory. Forster was a notable biographer; but as a critic of the work of Dickens his view was a very narrow view. To any one who knows the bare facts of Dickens's acquaintance with Collins, and who has studied the work of the two men, their relationship and their influence upon one another is an important subject of study. And a comparative study of their novels can do much to illuminate the question of the difference between the dramatic and the melodramatic in fiction.

Dickens's "best novel" is probably *Bleak House*; that is Mr. Chesterton's opinion, and there is no better critic of Dickens living than Mr. Chesterton. Collins's best novel—or, at any rate, the only one of Collins's novels which every one knows—is *The Woman in White*. Now *Bleak House* is the novel in which Dickens most closely approaches Collins (and after *Bleak House*, *Little Dorrit* and parts of *Martin Chuzzlewit*); and *The Woman in White* is the novel in which Collins most closely approaches Dickens. Dickens excelled in character; in the creation of characters of greater intensity than human beings. Collins was not usually strong in the creation of character; but he was a master of plot and situation, of those elements of drama which are most essential to melodrama. *Bleak House* is Dickens's finest piece of construction; and *The Woman in White* contains Collins's most real characterization. Every one knows Count Fosco and Marion Halcombe intimately; only the most perfect Collins reader can remember even half a dozen of his other characters by name.

Count Fosco and Marion are indeed real personages to us; as "real" as much greater characters are, as real as Becky Sharp or Emma Bovary. In comparison with the characters of Dickens they lack only that kind of reality which is almost supernatural, which hardly seems to belong to the character by natural right, but seems rather to descend upon him by a kind of inspiration or grace. Collins's best characters are fabricated, with consummate skill, before our eyes; in Dickens's greatest figures we see no process or calculation. Dickens's figures belong to poetry, like figures of Dante or Shakespeare, in that a single phrase, either by them or about them, may be enough to set them wholly before us. Collins has no phrases. Dickens can with a phrase make a character as real as flesh and blood—*"What a Life Young Bailey's Was!"*—like Farinata

Chi fur gli maggior tui?

or like Cleopatra,

I saw her once
Hop forty paces through the public street.

Dickens's characters are real because there is no one like them; Collins's because they are so painstakingly coherent and life-like. Whereas Dickens often introduces a great character carelessly, so that we do not realize, until the story is far advanced, with what a powerful personage we have to do, Collins, at least in these two figures in *The Woman in White*, employs every advantage of dramatic effect. Much of our impression of Marion is due to the words in which she is first presented:

"The instant my eyes rested on her I was struck by the rare beauty of her form, and by the unaffected grace of her attitude. Her figure was tall, yet not too tall; comely and well developed, yet not fat; her head set on her shoulders with an easy, pliant firmness; her waist, perfection in the eyes of a man, for it occupied its natural place, it filled out its natural circle, it was visibly and delightfully undeformed by stays. She had not heard my entrance into the room, and I allowed myself the luxury of admiring her for a few moments before I moved one of the chairs near me as the least embarrassing means of attracting her attention. She turned towards me immediately. The easy elegance of every movement of her limbs and body, as soon as she began to advance from the far end of the room, set me in a flutter of expectation to see her face clearly. She left the window—and I said to myself, 'The lady is dark.' She moved forward a few steps—and I said to myself, 'The lady is young.' She approached nearer, and I said to myself (with a sense of surprise which words fail me to express), 'The lady is ugly!' "

The introduction of Count Fosco—too long to quote in full— requires many more small strokes; but we should observe, Marion Halcombe being already given, that our impression of the Count is made very much stronger by being given to us as Marion's impression of him:

"There are peculiarities in his personal appearance, his habits, and his amusements, which I should blame in the boldest terms, or ridicule in the most merciless manner, if I had seen them in another man. What is it that makes me unable to blame them, or to ridicule them in *him?*"

After this who can forget the white mice or the canaries, or the way in which Count Fosco treated Sir Percival's sulky bloodhound? If *The Woman in White* is the greatest of Collins's novels, it is so because of these two characters. If we examine the book apart from Marion and Fosco, we must admit that it is not Collins's finest work of construction, and that certain of his peculiar melodramatic gifts are better displayed in other books. The book is dramatic because of two characters; it is dramatic in the way in which the dramatic differs from the melodramatic. Sir Percival Glyde is a figure of pasteboard, and the mystery and the plot of which he is the centre are almost grotesque. The one of Collins's books which is the most perfect piece of construction, and the best balanced between plot and character, is *The Moonstone;* the one which reaches the greatest melodramatic intensity is *Armadale.*

The Moonstone is the first and greatest of English detective novels. We say *English* detective novels, because there is also the work of Poe, which has a *pure* detective interest. The detective story, as created by Poe, is something as specialized and as intellectual as a chess problem; whereas the best English detective fiction has relied less on the beauty of the mathematical problem and much more on the intangible human element. In detective fiction England probably excels other countries; but in a *genre* invented by Collins and not by Poe. In *The Moonstone* the mystery is finally solved, not altogether by human ingenuity, but largely by accident. Since Collins, the best heroes of English detective fiction have been, like Sergeant Cuff, fallible; they play their part, but never the sole part, in the unravelling. Sherlock Holmes, not altogether a typical English sleuth, is a partial exception; but even Holmes exists, not solely because of his prowess, but largely because he is, in the Jonsonian sense, a humorous character, with his needle, his boxing, and his violin. But Sergeant Cuff, far more than Holmes, is the ancestor of the healthy generation of amiable, efficient, professional but fallible inspectors of fiction among whom we live today. And *The Moonstone,* a book twice the length of the "thrillers" that our contemporary masters write, maintains its interest and suspense at every moment. It does this by devices of a Dickensian type; for Collins, in addition to his particular merits, was a Dickens without genius. The book is a comedy of humours. The eccentricities of Mr. Franklin Blake, the satire on false philanthropy in the character of Mr. Godfrey Ablewhite (to say nothing of the Life, Letters and Labours of Miss Jane Ann Stamper), Betteridge with his "Robinson Crusoe," and his daughter Penelope, support the narrative. In other of Collins's novels, the trick of passing the narration from one hand to another, and employing every device of letters and diaries, becomes tedious and even unplausible (for instance, in *Armadale,* the terrific villain, Miss Gwilt, commits herself to paper far too often and far too frankly); but in *The Moonstone* these devices succeed, every time, in stimulating our interest afresh just at the moment when it was about to flag.

And in *The Moonstone* Collins succeeds in bringing into play those aids of "atmosphere" in which Dickens (and the Brontës) exhibited such genius, and in which Collins has everything except their genius. For his purpose, he does not come off badly. Compare the description of the discovery of Rosanna's death in the Shivering Sands—and notice how carefully, beforehand, the *mise-en-scène* of the Shivering Sands is prepared for us—with the shipwreck of Steerforth in *David Copperfield*. We may say, "There is no comparison!" but there *is* a comparison; and however unfavourable to Collins, it must increase our estimation of his skill.

There is another characteristic of Wilkie Collins which also brings him closer to Dickens, and it is a characteristic which has very great melodramatic value: compare the work of Collins with the work of Mrs. Henry Wood, already mentioned, and one sees how important for melodrama is the presence or absence of this. Forster, in his *Life of Dickens*, observes:

"On the coincidences, resemblances and surprises of life Dickens liked especially to dwell, and few things moved his fancy so pleasantly. The world, he would say, was so much smaller than we thought it; we were all so connected by fate without knowing it; people supposed to be far apart were so constantly elbowing each other; and tomorrow bore so close a resemblance to nothing half so much as to yesterday."

Forster mentions this peculiarity early in the life of Dickens, long before Dickens became acquainted with Collins. We may take it that this feeling was common to Dickens and Collins, and that it may have been one of the causes of their being drawn so sympathetically together, once they had become acquainted. The two men had obviously in common a passionate feeling for the drama. Each had qualities which the other lacked, and they had certain qualities in common. It is perfectly reasonable to believe that the relations of the two men—of which Forster gives us only the barest and most unsatisfactory hints—

affected profoundly the later work of each. We seem to find traces of it in *Little Dorrit* and *The Tale of Two Cities*. Collins could never have invented Durdles and Deputy; but Durdles and Deputy were obviously to play their part in a whole, *bien charpenté* as Collins's work is, and as the work of Dickens prior to *Bleak House* is not.

One of the minor works of Collins which illustrates especially this insistence upon the "coincidences, resemblances and surprises of life" is *The Frozen Deep*. The story, as we read it, was patched up from the melodrama which Collins wrote first; which was privately performed with great success on several occasions, and in which Dickens took the leading part. Collins was the cleverer at writing stage pieces; but we may imagine that Dickens was the cleverer at acting them; and Dickens may have given to the *rôle* of Richard Wardour, in acting it, an individuality which it certainly lacks in the story. This story, we may add for the benefit of those who have not read it, depends upon coincidence with a remarkably long arm; for the two men who ought not to meet—the accepted and the rejected lover—do meet, and under the most unlikely conditions they join, without knowing each other's identity, the same Polar Expedition.

In *The Frozen Deep* Collins wrote a piece of pure melodrama. That is to say, it is nothing but melodrama. We are asked to accept an improbability, simply for the sake of seeing the thrilling situation which arises in consequence. But the frontier of drama and melodrama is vague; the difference is largely a matter of emphasis; perhaps no drama has ever been greatly and permanently successful without a large melodramatic element. What is the difference between *The Frozen Deep* and *Oedipus the King?* It is the difference between coincidence, set without shame or pretence, and fate—which merges into character. It is not necessary, for high drama, that accident should be eliminated; you cannot formulate the proportion of accident that is permissible. But in great drama character is always felt to be—not more important than plot—but somehow integral with plot. At least, one is left with the conviction that if circumstances had not arranged the events to fall out in such and such a way, the personages were, after all, such that they would have ended just as badly, or just as well, and more or less similarly. And sometimes the melodramatic—the accidental—becomes for Collins the dramatic—the fatal. There is one short tale, not one of his best known, and far from being his best—a tale with an extremely improbable ghost—which nevertheless is almost dramatic. It is called *The Haunted Hotel;* what makes it better than a mere readable second-rate ghost story is the fact that fatality in this story is no longer merely a wire jerking the figures. The principal character, the fatal woman, is herself obsessed by the idea of fatality; her motives are melodramatic; she therefore compels the coincidences to occur, feeling that she is compelled to compel them. In this story, as the chief character is internally melodramatic, the story itself ceases to be merely melodramatic, and partakes of true drama.

There is another characteristic of certain tales of Collins's, which may be said to belong to melodrama, or to the melodramatic part of drama. It consists in delaying, longer than one would conceive it possible to delay, a conclusion which is inevitable and wholly foreseen. A story like *The New Magdalen* is from a certain moment merely a study in stage suspense; the *dénouement* is postponed, again and again, by every possible ingenuity; the situations are in the most effective sense theatrical, without being in the profounder sense dramatic. They are seldom, as in *The Woman in White*, situations of conflict between significant personalities; they are more often conflicts between chessmen which merely occupy hostile positions on the board. Such, for instance, is the prolonged battle between Captain Wragge and Mrs. Lecomte at Aldburgh, in *No Name*.

The one of Collins's novels which we should choose as the most typical, or as the best of the more typical, and which we should recommend as a specimen of the melodramatic fiction of the epoch, is *Armadale*. It has no merit beyond melodrama, and it has every merit that melodrama can have. If Miss Gwilt did not have to bear such a large part of the burden of revealing her own villainy, the construction would be almost perfect. Like most of Collins's novels, it has the immense—and nowadays more and more rare—merit of being never dull. It has, to a very high degree, the peculiar Collins merit above mentioned, which we might call the air of spurious fatality. The machinery of the book is operated by the Dream. The mind of the reader is very carefully prepared for acceptance of the Dream; first by the elaborately staged coincidence of the two cousins getting marooned on the wreck of the ship on which the father of the one had long before entrapped the father of the other; secondly by the way in which the Dream is explained away by the doctor. The doctor's explanation is so reasonable that the reader immediately reacts in favour of the Dream. Then, the character of the dreamer himself is made plausibly intuitive; and the stages by which the various parts of the Dream are realized are perfectly managed. Particularly is this true of the scene in which, after some excellent comedy of humours on the boating party, Miss Gwilt arrives at sunset on the desolate shore of the Norfolk Broads. By means of the Dream, we are kept in a state of tension which makes it possible to believe in characters which otherwise we should find preposterous.

The greatest novels have something in them which will ensure their being read, at least by a small number of people, even if the novel, as a literary form, ceases to be written. It is not pretended that the novels of Wilkie Collins have this permanence. They are interesting only if we enjoy "reading novels." But novels are still being written; and there is no contemporary novelist who could not learn something from Collins in the art of interesting and exciting the reader. So long as novels are written, the possibilities of melodrama must from time to time be re-explored. The contemporary "thriller" is in danger of becoming stereotyped; the conventional murder is discovered in the first chapter by the conventional butler, and the murderer is discovered in the last chapter by the conventional inspector—after having been already discovered by the reader. The resources of Wilkie Collins are, in comparison, inexhaustible.

And even if we refused to take Collins very seriously by himself, we can hardly fail to treat him with seriousness if we recognize that the art of which he was a master was an art which neither Charles Reade nor Dickens despised. You cannot

define Drama and Melodrama so that they shall be recipro-
cally exclusive; great drama has something melodramatic in
it, and the best melodrama partakes of the greatness of drama.
The Moonstone is very near to *Bleak House*. The theft of a
diamond has some of the same blighting effect on the lives
about it as the suit in Chancery; Rosanna Spearman is destroyed
by the diamond as Miss Flite is destroyed by Chancery. Collins's novels suggest questions which no student of "the art
of fiction" can afford to neglect. It is possible that the artist can
be too conscious of his "art." Perhaps Henry James—who
in his own practice could be not only "interesting," but had a
very cunning mastery of the finer melodrama—may have had
as a critic a bad influence. We cannot afford to forget that the
first—and not one of the least difficult—requirements of either
prose or verse is that it should be interesting.

THE HUMANISM

OF IRVING BABBITT

====

IT is proverbially easier to destroy than to construct; and as a corollary of this proverb, it is easier for readers to apprehend the destructive than the constructive side of an author's thought. More than this: when a writer is skilful in destructive criticism, the public is satisfied with that. If he has no constructive philosophy, it is not demanded; if he has, it is overlooked. This is especially true when we are concerned with critics of society, from Arnold to the present day. All such critics are criticized from one common standard, and that the lowest: the standard of brilliant attack upon aspects of contemporary society which we know and dislike. It is the easiest standard to take. For the criticism deals with concrete things in our world which we know, and the writer may be merely echoing, in neater phrasing, our own thoughts; whereas construction deals with things hard and unfamiliar. Hence the popularity of Mr. Mencken.

But there are more serious critics than Mr. Mencken, and of these we must ask in the end what they have to offer in place of what they denounce. M. Julien Benda, for instance, makes it a part of his deliberate programme to offer nothing; he has a romantic view of critical detachment which limits his interest. Mr. Wyndham Lewis is obviously striving courageously toward a positive theory, but in his published work has not yet reached that point. But in Professor Babbitt's latest book, *Democracy and Leadership*, the criticism is related to a positive theory and dependent upon it. This theory is not altogether ex-

pounded, but is partly assumed. What I wish to do in the present essay is to ask a few questions about Mr. Babbitt's constructive theory.

The centre of Mr. Babbitt's philosophy is the doctrine of
humanism. In his earlier books we were able to accept this idea
without analysis; but in *Democracy and Leadership*—which I
take to be at this point the summary of his theory—we are
tempted to question it. The problem of humanism is undoubtedly related to the problem of religion. Mr. Babbitt makes it
very clear, here and there throughout the book, that he is unable to take the religious view—that is to say that he cannot
accept any dogma or revelation; and that humanism is the
alternative to religion. And this brings up the question: is this
alternative any more than a *substitute?* and if a substitute, does
it not bear the same relation to religion that "humanitarianism"
bears to humanism? Is it, in the end, a view of life that will
work by itself, or is it a derivative of religion which will work
only for a short time in history, and only for a few highly
cultivated persons like Mr. Babbitt—whose ancestral traditions,
furthermore, are Christian, and who is, like many people, at the
distance of a generation or so from definite Christian belief? Is
it, in other words, durable beyond one or two generations?

Mr. Babbitt says, of the "representatives of the humanitarian
movement," that

"they wish to live on the naturalistic level, and at the same time
to enjoy the benefits that the past had hoped to achieve as a
result of some humanistic or religious discipline."

The definition is admirable, but provokes us to ask whether, by
altering a few words, we cannot arrive at the following statement about humanists:

"they wish to live on the humanistic level, and at the same time
to enjoy the benefits that the past had hoped to achieve as a
result of some religious discipline."

If this transposition is justified, it means that the difference
is only of one step: the humanitarian has suppressed the properly human, and is left with the animal; the humanist has sup-

pressed the divine, and is left with a human element which may quickly descend again to the animal from which he has sought to raise it.

Mr. Babbitt is a stout upholder of tradition and continuity, and he knows, with his immense and encyclopedic information, that the Christian religion is an essential part of the history of our race. Humanism and religion are thus, as historical facts, by no means parallel; humanism has been sporadic, but Christianity continuous. It is quite irrelevant to conjecture the possible development of the European races without Christianity— to imagine, that is, a tradition of humanism equivalent to the actual tradition of Christianity. For all we can say is that we should have been very different creatures, whether better or worse. Our problem being to form the future, we can only form it on the materials of the past; we must *use* our heredity, instead of denying it. The religious habits of the race are still very strong, in all places, at all times, and for all people. There is no humanistic habit: humanism is, I think, merely the state of mind of a few persons in a few places at a few times. To exist at all, it is dependent upon some other attitude, for it is essentially critical—I would even say parasitical. It has been, and can still be, of great value; but it will never provide showers of partridges or abundance of manna for the chosen peoples.

It is a little difficult to define humanism in Mr. Babbitt's terms, for he is very apt to line it up in battle order *with* religion *against* humanitarianism and naturalism; and what I am trying to do is to *contrast* it with religion. Mr. Babbitt is very apt to use phrases like "tradition humanistic and religious" which suggest that you could say also "tradition humanistic *or* religious." So I must make shift to define humanism as I can from a few of the examples that Mr. Babbitt seems to hold up to us.

I should say that he regarded Confucius, Buddha, Socrates, and Erasmus as humanists (I do not know whether he would include Montaigne). It may surprise some to see Confucius and Buddha, who are popularly regarded as founders of religions, in this list. But it is always the human reason, not the revelation of the supernatural, upon which Mr. Babbitt insists. Confucius

and Buddha are not in the same boat, to begin with. Mr. Babbitt of course knows infinitely more about both of these men
than I do; but even people who know even less about them
than I do, know that Confucianism endured by fitting in with
popular religion, and that Buddhism endured by becoming [1]
as distinctly a *religion* as Christianity—recognizing a dependence
of the human upon the divine.

And finally, the attitude of Socrates and that of Erasmus
toward the religion of their place and time were very different
from what I take to be the attitude of Professor Babbitt. How
much Socrates believed, and whether his legendary request of
the sacrifice of a cock was merely gentlemanly behaviour or
even irony, we cannot tell; but the equivalent would be Professor Babbitt receiving Extreme Unction, and that I cannot at
present conceive. But both Socrates and Erasmus were content
to remain critics, and to leave the religious fabric untouched. So
that I find Mr. Babbitt's humanism to be very different from
that of any of the humanists above mentioned.

This is no small point, but the question is a difficult one. It is
not at all that Mr. Babbitt has *misunderstood* any of these persons, or that he is not fully acquainted with the civilizations out
of which they sprang. On the contrary, he knows all about
them. It is rather, I think, that in his interest in the messages of
individuals—messages conveyed in books—he has tended merely
to neglect the conditions. The great men whom he holds up
for our admiration and example are torn from their contexts of
race, place, and time. And in consequence, Mr. Babbitt seems to
me to tear himself from his own context. His humanism is really
something quite different from that of his exemplars, but (to
my mind) alarmingly like very liberal Protestant theology of
the nineteenth century: it is, in fact, a product—a by-product—
of Protestant theology in its last agonies.

I admit that all humanists—as humanists—have been individualists. As humanists, they have had nothing to offer to the
mob. But they have usually left a place, not only for the mob,
but (what is more important) for the mob part of the mind in

---

[1] I wrote *becoming*, but to me it seems that Buddhism is as truly a religion
from the beginning as is Christianity.

themselves. Mr. Babbitt is too rigorous and conscientious a Protestant to do that: hence there seems to be a gap between his own individualism (and indeed intellectualism, beyond a certain point, must be individualistic) and his genuine desire to offer something which will be useful to the American nation primarily and to civilization itself. But the historical humanist, as I understand him, halts at a certain point and admits that the reason will go no farther, and that it cannot feed on honey and locusts.

Humanism is either an alternative to religion, or is ancillary to it. To my mind, it always flourishes most when religion has been strong; and if you find examples of humanism which are anti-religious, or at least in opposition to the religious faith of the place and time, then such humanism is purely destructive, for it has never found anything to replace what it destroyed. Any religion, of course, is for ever in danger of petrifaction into mere ritual and habit, though ritual and habit be essential to religion. It is only renewed and refreshed by an awakening of feeling and fresh devotion, or by the critical reason. The latter may be the part of the humanist. But if so, then the function of humanism, though necessary, is secondary. You cannot make humanism itself into a religion.

What Mr. Babbitt, on one side, seems to me to be trying to do is to make humanism—his own form of humanism—work without religion. For otherwise, I cannot see the significance of his doctrine of self-control. This doctrine runs throughout his work, and sometimes appears as the "inner check." It appears as an alternative to both political and religious anarchy. In the political form it is more easily acceptable. As forms of government become more democratic, as the outer restraints of kingship, aristocracy, and class disappear, so it becomes more and more necessary that the individual no longer controlled by authority or habitual respect should control himself. So far, the doctrine is obviously true and impregnable. But Mr. Babbitt seems to think also that the "outer" restraints of an orthodox religion, as they weaken, can be supplied by the inner restraint of the individual over himself. If I have interpreted him correctly, he is thus trying to build a Catholic platform out of Protestant planks. By tradition an individualist, and jealous of the independence of individual thought, he is struggling to make something that will be valid for the nation, the race, the world.

The sum of a population of individuals, all ideally and efficiently checking and controlling themselves, will never make a whole. And if you distinguish so sharply between "outer" and "inner" checks as Mr. Babbitt does, then there is nothing left for the individual to check himself by but his own private notions and his judgment, which is pretty precarious. As a matter of fact, when you leave the political field for the theological, the distinction between outer and inner becomes far from clear. Given the most highly organized and temporally powerful hierarchy, with all the powers of inquisition and punishment imaginable, still the idea of the religion is the *inner* control—the appeal not to a man's behaviour but to his soul. If a religion cannot touch a man's self, so that in the end he is controlling himself instead of being merely controlled by priests as he might be by policemen, then it has failed in its professed task. I suspect Mr. Babbitt at times of an instinctive dread of organized religion, a dread that it should cramp and deform the free operations of his own mind. If so, he is surely under a misapprehension.

And what, one asks, are all these millions, even these thousands, or the remnant of a few intelligent hundreds, going to control themselves *for?* Mr. Babbitt's critical judgment is exceptionally sound, and there is hardly one of his several remarks that is not, by itself, acceptable. It is the joints of his edifice, not the materials, that sometimes seem a bit weak. He says truly:

"It has been a constant experience of man in all ages that mere rationalism leaves him unsatisfied. Man craves in some sense or other of the word an enthusiasm that will lift him out of his merely rational self."

But it is not clear that Mr. Babbitt has any other enthusiasm to offer except the enthusiasm for being lifted out of one's merely rational self by some enthusiasm. Indeed, if he can infect people with enthusiasm for getting even up to the level of their rational selves, he will accomplish a good deal.

But this seems to me just the point at which "humanistic control" ends, if it gets that far. He speaks of the basis "of religion and humanistic control" in Burke, but what we should like to know is the respective parts played by religion and humanism in this basis. And with all the references that Mr. Babbitt makes to the rôle of religion in the past, and all the connexions that he perceives between the decline of theology and the growth of the modern errors that he detests, he reveals himself as uncompromisingly detached from any religious belief, even the most purely "personal":

"To be modern has meant practically to be increasingly positive and critical, to refuse to receive anything on an authority 'anterior, exterior, and superior' to the individual. With those who still cling to the principle of outer authority I have no quarrel. I am not primarily concerned with them. I am myself a thoroughgoing individualist, writing for those who are, like myself, irrevocably committed to the modern experiment. In fact, so far as I object to the moderns at all, it is because they have not been sufficiently modern, or, what amounts to the same thing, have not been sufficiently experimental."

Those of us who lay no claim to being modern may not be involved in the objection, but, as bystanders, we may be allowed to inquire whither all this modernity and experimenting is going to lead. Is everybody to spend his time experimenting? And on what, and to what end? And if the experimenting merely leads to the conclusion that self-control is good, that seems a very frosty termination to our hunt for "enthusiasm." What is the higher will to *will*, if there is nothing either "anterior, exterior, or superior" to the individual? If this will is to have anything on which to operate, it must be in relation to external objects and to objective values. Mr. Babbitt says:

"To give the first place to the higher will is only another way of declaring that life is an act of faith. One may discover on positive grounds a deep meaning in the old Christian tenet that we do not know in order that we may believe, but we believe in order that we may know."

This is quite true; but if life is an act of faith, in what is it an act of faith? The Life-Forcers, with Mr. Bernard Shaw at their head, would say I suppose "in Life itself"; but I should not accuse Mr. Babbitt of anything so silly as that. However, a few pages further on he gives something more definite to will: it is civilization.

The next idea, accordingly, to be examined is that of civilization. It seems, on the face of it, to mean something definite; it is, in fact, merely a frame to be filled with definite objects, not a definite object itself. I do not believe that I can sit down for three minutes to will civilization without my mind's wandering to something else. I do not mean that civilization is a mere word; the word means something quite real. But the minds of the individuals who can be said to "have willed civilization" are minds filled with a great variety of objects of will, according to place, time, and individual constitution; what they have in common is rather a habit in the same direction than a will to civilization. And unless by civilization you mean material progress, cleanliness, etc.—which is not what Mr. Babbitt means; if you mean a spiritual and intellectual coördination on a high level, then it is doubtful whether civilization can endure without religion, and religion without a church.

I am not here concerned with the question whether such a "humanistic" civilization as that aimed at by Professor Babbitt is or is not *desirable;* only with the question whether it is *feasible.* From this point of view the danger of such theories is, I think, the danger of collapse. For those who had not followed Mr. Babbitt very far, or who had felt his influence more remotely, the collapse would be back again into humanitarianism thinly disguised. For others who had followed him hungrily to the end and had found no hay in the stable, the collapse might well be into a Catholicism *without* the element of humanism and criticism, which would be a Catholicism of despair. There is a hint of this in Mr. Babbitt's own words:

"The choice to which the modern man will finally be reduced, it has been said, is that of being a Bolshevist or a Jesuit. In that case (assuming that by Jesuit is meant the ultramontane Catholic) there does not seem to be much room for hesitation. Ultramontane Catholicism does not, like Bolshevism, strike at the very root of civilization. In fact, under certain conditions that are already partly in sight, the Catholic Church may perhaps be the only institution left in the Occident that can be counted upon to uphold civilized standards. It may also be possible, however, to be a thoroughgoing modern and at the same time civilized. . . ."

The last sentence somehow seems to me to die away a little faintly. But the point is that Mr. Babbitt seems to be giving away to the Church in anticipation more than would many who are more concerned with it in the present than he. Mr. Babbitt is much more ultramontane than I am. One may feel a very deep respect and even love for the Catholic Church (by which I understand Mr. Babbitt means the hierarchy in communion with the Holy See); but if one studies its history and vicissitudes, its difficulties and problems past and present, one is struck with admiration and awe certainly, but is not the more tempted to place all the hopes of humanity on one institution.

But my purpose has been, not to predict a bad end for Mr. Babbitt's philosophy, but to point out the direction which I think it should follow if the obscurities of "humanism" were cleared up. It should lead, I think, to the conclusion that the humanistic point of view is auxiliary to and dependent upon the religious point of view. For us, religion is Christianity; and Christianity implies, I think, the conception of the Church. It would be not only interesting but invaluable if Professor Babbitt, with his learning, his great ability, his influence, and his interest in the most important questions of the time, could reach this point. His influence might thus join with that of another philosopher—Charles Maurras—and might, indeed, correct some of the extravagances of that writer.

Such a consummation is impossible. Professor Babbitt knows too much; and by that I do not mean merely erudition or information or scholarship. I mean that he knows too many religions and philosophies, has assimilated their spirit too thoroughly (there is probably no one in England or America who understands early Buddhism better than he) to be able to give himself to any. The result is humanism. I believe that it is better to recognize the weaknesses of humanism at once, and allow for them, so that the structure may not crash beneath an excessive weight; and so that we may arrive at an enduring recognition of its value for us, and of our obligation to its author.

SECOND THOUGHTS
ABOUT HUMANISM

═══

IN July, 1928, I published in *The Forum* the note on the Humanism of Irving Babbitt, which appears on the foregoing pages. I understand that Professor Babbitt considers that I misstated his views: but as I have not yet received detailed correction from any Humanist, I am still in the dark. It is quite likely that I am at fault, because I have meanwhile heard comments, from sympathetic friends, which indicate that they have misunderstood me. The present essay is therefore inspired rather by desire to make my own position clearer than by desire towards aggression. Here, I shall find it more useful to refer to Mr. Norman Foerster's brilliant book *American Criticism*, than to Mr. Babbitt's works. Mr. Foerster's book, as the work of a disciple, seems to give clearer hints of what Humanism is likely to become and do, than the work of Mr. Babbitt, which is more personal to himself.

My previous note has been interpreted, I am afraid, as an "attack" on humanism from a narrow sectarian point of view. It was not intended to be an attack. Having myself begun as a disciple of Mr. Babbitt, and feeling, as I do, that I have rejected nothing that seems to me positive in his teaching, I was hardly qualified to "attack" humanism. I was concerned rather to point out the weak points in its defences, before some genuine enemy took advantage of them. It can be—and is already—of immense value: but it must be subjected to criticism while there is still time.

One of the criticisms which I have heard of my criticism is

this: that my criticism is all very well from the point of view of those who "believe"; but if I succeeded in proving that humanism is insufficient without religion, what is left for those who cannot believe? Now I have no desire to undermine the humanist position. But I fear that it may take on more and more of the character of a positive philosophy—and any philosophy, in our time, is likely to take on the character of a substitute for religious dogma. It is Humanism's positivistic tendencies that are alarming. In the work of the master, and still more in that of the disciples, there is a tendency towards a positive and exclusive dogma. Conceive a Comtism from which all the absurdities had been removed—and they form, I admit, a very important part of the Comtist scheme—and you have something like what I imagine Humanism might become.

In the actual Humanist position there is, as I have tried to show, on the one hand an admission that in the past Humanism has been allied with religion, and on the other hand a faith that it can in the future afford to ignore positive religion. This curious trick of identifying humanism and religion in one context, and contrasting them in another, plays a very large part in the Humanist formulation. Mr. Foerster says (p. 244):

"This centre to which humanism refers everything, this centripetal energy which counteracts the multifarious centrifugal impulses, this magnetic will which draws the flux of our sensations toward it while itself remaining at rest, is the reality which gives rise to religion. Pure humanism is content to describe it thus in physical terms, as an observed fact of experience; it hesitates to pass beyond its experimental knowledge to the dogmatic affirmations of any of the great religions. It cannot bring itself to accept a formal theology (any more than it can accept a romantic (idealism) that has been set up in defiance of reason, for it holds that the value of supernatural intuition must be tested by the intellect. Again, it fears the asceticism to which religion tends in consequence of a too harsh dualism of the flesh and the spirit, for, as we have said, humanism calls for completeness, wishing to use and not annihilate dangerous forces. Unlike religion, it assigns an important place to the instruments of both

science and art. Nevertheless it agrees with religion in its perception of the ethical will as a power above the ordinary self, an impersonal reality in which all men may share despite the diversity
of personal temperament and towards which their attitude must
be one of subjection. This perception, immensely strengthened
for us by Christianity, was already present in the humanism of
the Greeks, who saw that the unpardonable sin is insolence or
presumption, an overweening pride of passion or reason, a failure to be mindful of the Nemesis that lies in wait for dispropor-
tionate self-assertion. Humanism, no less than religion, enjoins
the virtue of *humility*."

With all respect to Mr. Foerster's sound literary criticism, and
his usual brilliance of statement which one cannot fail to admire,
the passage I have just quoted seems to me a composition of ignorance, prejudice, confused thinking and bad writing. His first
sentence, for the meaning of which I am at a loss, is a cloudy
pseudo-scientific metaphor; and his remark that "pure humanism is content to describe it thus in physical terms" seems to give
his hand away completely to what he calls "naturism." Either
his first sentence is, as I think, merely a metaphor drawn from
nineteenth-century physics—in which case it is not a "description," and no one can be content with it—or else the author is
surrendering to the mechanistic ethics based upon old-fashioned
physics. "The reality which gives rise to religion" is a phrase
which suggests the older school of anthropology; it is a guarded
hint that religion is merely a state of feeling produced by certain
physical or quasi-physical "realities" and "facts." Mr. Foerster's
"hesitates" and "cannot bring itself" conceal dogmatism behind
apparent prudence. Here he confuses, I think, the Humanist
with Humanism. If an individual humanist hesitates or cannot
bring himself, that is a perfectly natural human attitude, with
which one has sympathy; but if the humanist affirms that *Humanism* hesitates and cannot bring itself, then he is making the
hesitation, and the inability to bring itself, into a *dogma:* the
humanist *Credo* is then a *Dubito*. He is asserting that there is a
"pure Humanism" which is *incompatible* with religious faith.
When he proceeds to distinguish Humanism from religion by

saying that Humanism "holds that the value of supernatural intuition must be tested by the intellect," one wonders with what sort of religion he is contrasting it: for this kind of test was held by the Church long before the word Humanism was coined. Next, the "fear of asceticism" is characteristic, not only of Humanism, but of liberal Protestantism, from which Humanism sometimes seems to descend. The typical humanist, I agree, is not conceived as a cenobite; but *Humanism* if it goes so far as to include in its Creed, "I fear asceticism," is merely committing itself to another anti-religious dogma. Humanism, Mr. Foerster says, "wishes to use and not annihilate dangerous forces"; but does he really believe that the Christian religion, except in several heretical varieties, has ever tried to *annihilate* those dangerous forces? And if he thinks that religion depreciates science and art, I can only suppose that his religious training took place in the mountains of Tennessee. Humanism, he says, agrees with religion in only one point: in believing in the ethical will. There was once an organization called the Ethical Culture Society, which held Sunday morning services: that seems to be the kind of liberal religion to which Mr. Foerster's Humanism comes down.

Mr. Foerster's Humanism, in fact, is too ethical to be true. Where do all these morals come from? One advantage of an orthodox religion, to my mind, is that it puts morals in their proper place. In spite of all the hard (and just) things Mr. Babbitt and Mr. More have said about Kant, the second generation of humanism seems to found its ethics on a similar basis to Kant's. Mr. Foerster finds that "the essential reality of experience is ethical." For the person with a definite religious faith, such a statement has one meaning; for the positivistic humanist, who repudiates religion, it must have another. And that meaning seems to rest upon obscurities and confusions. I can understand, though I do not approve, the naturalistic systems of morals founded upon biology and analytical psychology (what is valid in these consists largely of things that were always known); but I cannot understand a system of morals which seems to be founded on nothing but itself—which exists, I suspect, only by illicit relations with either psychology or religion or both, according to the bias of mind of the individual humanist.

Humanism depends very heavily, I believe, upon the tergiversations of the word "human"; and in general, upon implying clear and distinct philosophic ideas which are never there. My objection is that the humanist makes use, in his separation of the "human" from the "natural," of that "supernatural" which he denies. For I am convinced that if this "supernatural" is suppressed (I avoid the word "spiritual" because it can mean almost anything), the *dualism* of man and nature collapses at once. Man is man because he can recognize supernatural realities, not because he can invent them. Either everything in man can be traced as a development from below, or something must come from above. There is no avoiding that dilemma: you must be either a naturalist or a supernaturalist. If you remove from the word "human" all that the belief in the supernatural has given to man, you can view him finally as no more than an extremely clever, adaptable, and mischievous little animal. Mr. Foerster's ethics would be much more "reasonable" if they were those of Mr. Bertrand Russell; as they are, they are a form which is quite untenable and meaningless without a religious foundation.[1]

The real trouble, of course, is one of simple human fallibility. Mr. Foerster, like most humanists, was, I believe, trained as a man of letters; and Humanism bears the imprint of the academic man of letters. His approach to every other field of study is through literature. This is a perfectly proper approach; for we must all approach what we do not know with a limited equipment of the things that we do know. The trouble is that, for a modern humanist, literature thus becomes itself merely a means of approach to something else. If we try to make something do for something else, it is likely to become merely an amateur substitute for that other thing. Mr. Foerster and I would probably

---

[1] Mr. Foerster's "reason" seems to me to differ from any Greek equivalent (λόγος) by being exclusively human; whereas to the Greek there was something inexplicable about λόγος so that it was a participation of man in the divine. See the late Max Scheler's *Mensch und Geschichte* (Neue Schweizer Rundschau), p. 21.

agree about the prevalent desiccation of the study of philosophy in universities.[2] Nevertheless, there is a philosophic training, and it is not the literary training; there are rules of the philosophic game about the use and definition of terms, and they are not the literary rules. One may consider the study of philosophy vain, but then one should not philosophise. What one is likely to do is to philosophise badly, because unconsciously. My objection is not to Humanism, but to Mr. Foerster for not being humanistic enough; and for playing the games of philosophy and theology without knowing the rules.

There is another aspect to Mr. Foerster's position which might earn him the title of "The Newest Laocoön": the interesting consideration that this trick of making literature do the work of philosophy, ethics and theology tends to vitiate one's judgment and sensibility in literature; but this aspect has been so well exposed in an essay by Mr. Allen Tate that I shall not linger over it here. But I should like to mention that Mr. Foerster, in seeking, as he says, "an ethos which has never existed," looks for guidance to:

"Greek sculpture (*of what period?*), Homer, Sophocles, Plato, Aristotle, Virgil, Horace, Jesus, Paul, Augustine, Francis of Assisi, Buddha, Confucius, Shakespeare, Milton and Goethe" (p. 242).

Mr. Foerster is not quite so silly as this list makes him seem, perilously as he does approach towards Five Foot Shelf Culture; he is merely confusing two points of view. For *culture* (and Mr. Foerster's culture is a propagation of Arnold's), these

---

[2] Not, however, primarily the fault of the teachers, but of the whole educational system of which this teaching is a part. The teaching of philosophy to young men who have no background of *humanistic* education, the teaching of Plato and Aristotle to youths who know no Greek and are completely ignorant of ancient history, is one of the tragic farces of American education. We reap the whirlwind of pragmatists, behaviourists, etc. Incidentally, it is a public misfortune that Mr. Bertrand Russell did not have a classical education.

Humanism has done no greater service than in its criticism of modern education. See Mr. Babbitt's admirable essay on President Eliot in *The Forum*, several years ago.

are the sorts of authority to which we may properly look; and the man who has frequented them all will so far as that goes be a better, in the sense of being a *more cultured man*, than the man who has not. This is the best possible background. But the search for an "ethos" is a very much more serious and risky business than Mr. Foerster imagines; and Mr. Foerster is more likely to end in respectability than in perfection. Those who hunger and thirst after righteousness, and are not satisfied with a snack-at-the-bar, will want a great deal more; and if they follow any one of these leaders, will not be able to follow all the rest. Boil down Horace, the Elgin Marbles, St. Francis and Goethe, and the result will be pretty thin soup. Culture, after all, is not enough, even though nothing is enough without culture.

With these odd mixed motives, Mr. Foerster does not make very much of Shakespeare, though he gives him a patronizing word or two. Shakespeare is not a humanist. Mr. Foerster's judgment of Shakespeare is neither a literary nor a moral judgment. He seems to me to depreciate Shakespeare for the wrong reasons, just as, with all respect, Mr. Middleton Murry seems to me to extol him for the wrong reasons. If, as he says, Shakespeare was concerned "rather with mirroring life than with interpreting it," and with submitting "to actuality rather than transcending it," I should say that such a good mirror, if you call that a mirror, is worth a great many interpretations, and that such submission is worth more than most transcendence. If you stick to a literary judgment, you cannot say that Shakespeare is inferior to any poet who has ever written, unless you are prepared to substantiate your opinion by detailed analysis; and if you depreciate Shakespeare for his lower view of life, then you have issued out of literary criticism into social criticism; you are criticizing not so much the man but the age. I prefer the culture which produced Dante to the culture which produced Shakespeare; but I would not say that Dante was the greater poet, or even that he had the profounder mind; and if humanism chooses Goethe and leaves Shakespeare, then humanism is incapable of distinguishing between the chaff and the wheat.

Mr. Foerster is what I call a Heretic: that is, a person who

seizes upon a truth and pushes it to the point at which it becomes
a falsehood. In his hands, Humanism becomes something else,
something more dangerous, because much more seductive to
the best minds, than, let us say, Behaviourism. I wish to try to
distinguish the functions of true Humanism from those imposed
upon it by zealots.

I. The function of humanism is not to provide dogmas, or
philosophical theories. Humanism, because it is general culture,
is not concerned with philosophical foundations; it is concerned
less with "reason" than with common sense. When it proceeds to
exact definitions it becomes something other than itself.

II. Humanism makes for breadth, tolerance, equilibrium and
sanity. It operates against fanaticism.

III. The world cannot get on without breadth, tolerance and
sanity; any more than it can get on without narrowness, bigotry
and fanaticism.

IV. It is not the business of humanism to refute anything. Its
business is to *persuade,* according to its unformulable axioms of
culture and good sense. It does not, for instance, overthrow the
arguments or fallacies like Behaviourism: it operates by taste,
by sensibility trained by culture. It is critical rather than constructive. It is necessary for the criticism of social life and social
theories, political life and political theories.

Without humanism we could not cope with Mr. Shaw, Mr.
Wells, Earl Russell, Mr. Mencken, Mr. Sandburg, M. Claudel,
Herr Ludwig, Mrs. Macpherson, or the governments of Amer-
ica and Europe.

V. Humanism can have no positive theories about philosophy
or theology. All that it can ask, in the most tolerant spirit, is: Is
this particular philosophy or religion civilized or is it not?

VI. There is a type of person whom we call the Humanist,
for whom humanism is enough. This type is valuable.

VII. Humanism is valuable (*a*) by itself, in the "pure humanist," who will not set up humanism as a substitute for philosophy and religion, and (*b*) as a mediating and corrective ingredient in a positive civilization founded on definite belief.[3]

---

[3] An interesting infusion of humanism in a remarkable religious personality
is shown in the late Baron von Hugel's *Letters to a Niece.*

VIII. Humanism, finally, is valid for a very small minority of *individuals*. But it is culture, not any subscription to a common programme or platform, which binds these individuals together. Such an "intellectual aristocracy" has not the economic bonds which unite the individuals of an "aristocracy of birth."

Such a modest limitation of Humanism as I have tried to indicate above (the list is not exhaustive or defining, but consists merely of the qualifications which occur immediately to my mind) will seem more than unsatisfactory to the more hopeful and ambitious devotees of the world. I wish to distinguish sharply, however, between what seems to me the correct and *necessarily* vague Humanism, and what T. E. Hulme means by Humanism in his notes in *Speculations*. I agree with what Hulme says; and I am afraid that many modern Humanists are explicitly or implicitly committed to the view which Hulme denounces; and that they are, in consequence, men of the Renaissance rather than men of our own time. For instance, Hulme gives as one characteristic of the Humanist (in his sense) the "refusal to believe any longer in the radical imperfection of either Man or Nature." I cannot help feeling that Mr. Foerster and even Mr. Babbitt are nearer to the view of Rousseau than they are to the religious view. For it is not enough to chastise the romantic visions of perfectibility, as they do; the modern humanistic view implies that man is either perfectible, or capable of indefinite improvement, because from that point of view the only difference is a difference of degree—so that there is always hope of a higher degree. It is to the immense credit of Hulme that he found out for himself that there is an *absolute* to which Man can *never* attain. For the modern humanist, as for the romantic, "the problem of evil disappears, the conception of sin disappears." This is illustrated in Mr. Foerster's illusion of *the normally or typically human* (p. 241). (If Mr. Foerster met Jesus, Buddha, St. Francis or any one in the least like them, I question whether they would strike him as conforming to this ideal of 100 per cent. normalcy.) Hulme put the matter into one paragraph:

"I hold the religious conception of ultimate values to be right, the humanist wrong. From the nature of things, these categories are not inevitable, like the categories of time and space, but are *equally objective*. In speaking of religion, it is to this level of abstraction that I wish to refer. I have none of the feelings of *nostalgia*, the reverence for tradition, the desire to recapture the sentiment of Fra Angelico, which seems to animate most modern defenders of religion. All that seems to me to be bosh. What is important, is what nobody seems to realize—the dogmas like that of Original Sin, which are the closest expression of the categories of the religious attitude. That man is in no sense perfect, but a wretched creature, who can yet apprehend perfection. It is not, then, that I put up with the dogma for the sake of the sentiment, but that I may possibly swallow the sentiment for the sake of the dogma."

This is a statement which Mr. Foerster, and all liberal theologians, would do well to ponder. Most people suppose that some people, because they enjoy the luxury of Christian sentiments and the excitement of Christian ritual, swallow or pretend to swallow incredible dogma. For some the process is exactly opposite. Rational assent may arrive late, intellectual conviction may come slowly, but they come inevitably without violence to honesty and nature. To put the sentiments in order is a later and an immensely difficult task: intellectual freedom is earlier and easier than complete spiritual freedom.

There is no opposition between the religious and the *pure* humanistic attitude: they are necessary to each other. It is because Mr. Foerster's brand of humanism seems to me *impure*, that I fear the ultimate discredit of all humanism.

CHARLES WHIBLEY

═══

THERE is a peculiar difficulty, which I experience for the first time, in attempting an estimate of the literary work of a writer whom one remembers primarily as a friend. It is not so much that from a kind of reticence and fear of being uncritical one is inclined to reserve praise: it is rather that one's judgment is inevitably an amalgam of impressions of the work and impressions of the man. Any one who knew Charles Whibley, and had frequent opportunities of enjoying his conversation, will recognize the strength of the impression which his personality could produce in such intercourse, and the difficulty of valuing the writings which remain, apart from the man who is gone.

What adds to the difficulty is the fact that his true place in history is not altogether to be deduced by posterity merely from the writings he has left; and the fact that a great deal of the work into which he threw himself most zealously is of the kind which will be called ephemeral, or only to be consulted, in future, by some scholarly ferret into a past age. It was largely what is called journalism; so that I hope I shall be tolerated in a digression, which is really a preamble, on the nature of the activity which that word loosely denotes. The distinction between "journalism" and "literature" is quite futile, unless we are drawing such violent contrast as that between Gibbon's *History* and tonight's evening paper; and such a contrast itself is too violent to have meaning. You cannot, that is, draw any useful distinction between journalism and literature merely in a scale of literary values, as a difference between the well-written and the supremely well-written: a second-rate novel is not journalism, but it certainly is not literature. The term "journalism" has deteriorated in the last thirty years; and it is particularly fitting, in the present essay, to try to recall it to its more permanent sense. To my thinking, the most accurate as well as most comprehensive definition of the term is to be obtained through considering the state of mind, and the type of mind, concerned in writing what all would concede to be the *best* journalism. There is a type of mind, and I have a very close sympathy with it, which can only turn to writing, or only produce its best writing, under the pressure of an immediate occasion; and it is this type of mind which I propose to treat as the journalist's. The underlying causes may differ: the cause may be an ardent preoccupation with affairs of the day, or it may be (as with myself) inertia or laziness requiring an immediate stimulus, or a habit formed by early necessity of earning small sums quickly. It is not so much that the journalist works on different material from that of other writers, as that he works from a different, no less and often more honourable, motive.

The indignity commonly thrown at the journalist is this, that his work is said to be of only passing interest, intended to make an immediate strong impression, and destined to eternal oblivion after that instant effect has been produced. To say merely this, however, is to overlook the reasons for which writing may be "ephemeral," and the loose application of that adjective itself, as well as the curious accidents which protect a piece of writing from oblivion. Those persons who are drawn by the powerful attraction of Jonathan Swift read and re-read with enchanted delight *The Drapier's Letters;* and these letters are journalism according to my hint of a definition, if anything is. But *The Drapier's Letters* are such an important item now in English letters, so essential to any one who would be well read in the literature of England, that we ignore the accident by which we still read them. If Swift had never written *Gulliver's Travels,* and if he had not played a striking and dramatic part in political life, and if this amazing madman had not supplemented these claims to permanence by a most interesting private life, what would be the place of *The Drapier's Letters* now? They would be praised now and then by some student of Anglo-Irish history of the epoch who happened by some odd coincidence to have also an exceptional degree of literary acumen; and they would be read by nobody else. The same fate would have overcome the pamphleteering of Defoe, were he not the author of *Robinson Crusoe* and *Moll Flanders;* or the pamphleteering of Samuel Johnson, were he not the hero of Boswell. To turn to another great English writer of quite a different kind, let us suppose that John Henry Newman had not been also the great leader of the English Church whose defection Gladstone described as a "catastrophe"; that he had not played the prominent rôle in the nineteenth century that he did play; supposing also that the material of his *Apologia* was as defunct as the subject of Wood's halfpence in Ireland, who but a few discerning connoisseurs of style would ever read that book now or a century hence? And the *Apologia* of Newman is as surely journalism as is the journalism of Swift, Defoe, or Johnson.

To quote an example on the opposite side: the *Martin Marprelate* tracts are not, certainly, as fine prose as the best of Swift, Defoe, Johnson, or Newman. They belong to a cruder period. But still they contain some very fine passages indeed, and the whole controversy is on a high literary level. Who reads them now? except a very small number of people, those who interest themselves in the religious squabbles of that epoch, and those who interest themselves in the prose styles of that epoch. They are not considered a part of the necessary education of the cultivated English-speaking person. Literary style is sometimes assigned almost magical properties, or is credited with being a mysterious preservative for subject-matter which no longer interests. This is far from being absolutely true. Style alone cannot preserve; only good style in conjunction with permanently interesting content can preserve. All other preservation, such as that of Swift's or Defoe's journalism, is due to a happy accident. Even poetry is not immune, though poetry usually concerns itself with simpler and more eternal matters than anything else; for who, except scholars, and except the eccentric few who are born with a sympathy for such work, or others who have deliberately studied themselves into the right appreciation, can now read through the whole of *The Faerie Queene* with delight?

Charles Whibley, then, was a journalist in that he wrote chiefly for occasion, either in his monthly commentary on men, events, and current books; or in his essays and prefaces, or sometimes in a lecture; with the one apparent exception of that charming biographical work, *Lord John Manners and his Friends.* Had he been exactly of my generation, when the typewriter has become the direct means of transmitting even poetry to the page, I am sure that he would have employed that now indispensable engine; as it was, he used suitably a quill pen, but composed rapidly in a fine hand and made very few *ratures* or corrections. Here again, I may remark, speed and ease are no test of writing one way or the other; and some may hold that the pains of Pater produced less fine prose than the speed of Newman. As for the type of Whibley's style of writing, I think we must look, as we must always look where possible, towards the great writers of the same language in the past with whom the writer has most sympathy, and on whose thoughts his mind has been nourished. His style was fed on the great historical and political writers. Whibley's mind was not an abstract mind; rather, he saw the principle through the act. There is a paragraph beginning his essay "The Trimmer"—an essay on the Marquess of Halifax—which reveals his interest in politics, the angle from which he looked on politics, and the antecedents of his own style:

"Politics is the profession of the second-rate. The man of genius strays into it by accident. We do not need the fingers of both hands to count the statesmen who have served England since the seventeenth century. The Ministers who have served themselves are like the sands for number. And from this mob of mediocrities it is not strange that very few writers have emerged. It is not an extravagant claim that they should have some mastery of literary expression. Words are the material of their craft. They know not how to use them save in the cause of rhetoric. Charles James Fox, the world was told, was an accomplished man of letters. To hear him discourse of the Classics was almost as fine an experience as to see him take the bank at faro. And then he wrote a book, and his fame was blown away

like a bubble. Halifax and Bolingbroke, Burke and Disraeli—
these are secure of remembrance. Where shall you find a fifth?"

I regret the qualification "since the seventeenth century," only
because I should have liked a reminder of the greater name of
Clarendon, with whom, however, Whibley dealt elsewhere. But
the paragraph is most illuminating, both upon Whibley's own
style, and upon his judgments of political men. He had a particular sympathy with—and a particular gift for explaining and
making sympathetic to his readers—three classes of men of letters: statesmen, gentlemen, and ragamuffins. As for the first I
think that the paragraph I have just quoted accounts for a bias
of judgment sometimes discernible in his general opinions of
statesmen: he may, I think, have somewhat overpraised the virtues, and too much extenuated the faults, of Bolingbroke as a
statesman, because of the brilliance and vigour of Bolingbroke's
style, and the great attraction of his personality. (On the other
hand, he seems to me to have given justice to Manners and
Smythe against the more brilliant Disraeli.) However, the relation of a statesman's statesmanship to his prose style is not negligible; we can find interesting laboratory material in the writing
of Mr. MacDonald, Mr. Lloyd George, and particularly Mr.
Winston Churchill.

People sometimes talk vaguely about the *conversational style*
in writing. Still more often, they deplore the divorce between
the language as spoken and the language as written. It is true
that the spoken and the written language can drift too far apart
—with the eventual consequence of forming a new written language. But what is overlooked is that an *identical* spoken and
written language would be practically intolerable. If we spoke
as we write we should find no one to listen; and if we wrote as
we speak we should find no one to read. The spoken and the
written language must not be too near together, as they must not
be too far apart. Henry James's later style, for instance, is not
exactly a conversational style; it is the way in which the later
Henry James dictated to a secretary. The famous monologue at
the end of *Ulysses* is not the way in which persons of either sex
actually *think:* it is a very skilful attempt by a master of lan-

guage to give the illusion of mental process by a different medium, that of written words. There is, however, an essential connexion between the written and the spoken word, though it is
not to be produced by aiming at a "conversational" style in writing, or a periodic style in speech; and I have found this intimate,
though indefinable, connexion between the speech and the writing of every writer whom I have known personally who was a
good writer—even between the speech and the most recent writing of Mr. James Joyce. Now, one could not say of Whibley,
any more than of any one else, that he wrote as he talked, or
that he talked as he wrote. Nevertheless, his writings have a
quality which relates them more closely to his speech than to the
writing of any one else. I know that the word "sincerity" sounds
very vague; yet it represents that moral integrity which unites
the prose styles of speech and writing of any good writer: however the rhythm, the syntax, the vocabulary may differ. One cannot, obviously, produce negative instances; I can only repeat
that whenever I have known both the man and the work of any
writer of what seemed to me good prose, the printed word has
always reminded me of the man speaking.

One of the phrases of commendation which Whibley often
used, at least in conversation, about the style of another writer,
was (even when he had little sympathy with the matter) that
it had *life* in it; and what makes his own prose hold one's attention, in spite of, perhaps, indeed emphasized by, its relation to
remote models in the history of English literature, is that it is
charged with life. He gives always the impression of fearless sincerity, and that is more important than being always right. One
always feels that he is ready to say bluntly what every one else is
afraid to say. Thus a feeling of apprehensiveness, conducive to
attention, is aroused in the reader. And, in fact, he was, when he
chose to be, a master of invective. Now invective is a form of
writing which varies at different times and in different countries
according to the customs and laws in vogue at the time and in
the place. It is now the fashion to deplore the decay of abuse.
Certainly, the rules of the game are altered. Many years ago,
in an open letter to Lord John Russell, Disraeli addressed Lord
John as an "insignificant insect." I am not aware that a duel,

or even a solicitor's letter followed; yet when I used the same phrase about a contemporary in a letter to a journal, my letter was rejected on the ground that it might possibly be considered libellous. Well, that does not matter; for however the rules of the game might be tightened, it is all the more stimulating to the connoisseur in controversy to do what he can according to the actual rules; and once the rules are recognized, a mild statement may carry all the force of a more violent statement under laxer rules. Indeed, I think that we, looking at the daily vollies of that great French master of vituperation, Léon Daudet—who was, incidentally, a friend of Whibley—become fatigued by the very licence which this amazing journalist permits himself, and feel that a little less liberty in abuse would refine the point of sarcasm. When I add to the name of Daudet, that of a master of a very different and much more austere style, Charles Maurras, I have named with Whibley the three best writers of invective of their time. There is a great deal of fuss nowadays about freedom of speech, but very few persons nowadays care really about genuine *plain speaking*. "Free speech" has been narrowed down to speaking freely about sex, sexual irregularities and sexual perversions; it has become the peculiar privilege of World-Leaguers for Sexual Reform; but few, so far as I am aware, now claim the free speech to call a knave a knave or a fool a fool. *And knaves and fools we both abhorred alike*, says Dryden in his noble epitaph on Oldham; perhaps nowadays our abhorrence is blunted by habituation.

The "Musings Without Method" which Whibley contributed once a month to *Blackwood's* for thirty years, excepting two months, one of which was the last, are the best sustained piece of literary journalism that I know in recent times. Daudet is sometimes tiresome and Maurras sometimes dull, and both are iterative; Mr. Wyndham Lewis, the most brilliant journalist of my generation (in addition to his other gifts), often squanders his genius for invective upon objects which to every one but himself seem unworthy of his artillery, and arrays howitzers against card houses; but Whibley always had the tact to vary his objects of attack and to vary his methods according to the object. Whether he was opposing the act of a Government, or giving his opinion of Gladstone, or objecting to the insistent advertisements of what he held to be a debased *Encyclopædia Britannica,* or denouncing the project of a National Theatre, or speaking his mind about Mr. Pinero or Mr. Jones or Mr. Edmund Gosse or the Omar Khayyám Club, he modulated his thunders according to the tree, shrub, or weed to be blasted. Nor did he ever hold too long to one topic. There would be a sudden transition to something else: a book of travels that he liked, or French wines and cookery. And what excites my particular admiration is the skill of these transitions. It looks artless; as if he had exhausted the subject for the moment, and had turned quite at randon to another. But I have for some months been going slowly through these "Musings," with a view to making an anthology, primarily of those paragraphs which are concerned with literature and art. It has been like trying to carve a bird with flexible bones but no joints; you remove one paragraph from a monthly "Musing," a paragraph apparently self-contained, and unrelated to what precedes and to what follows, and something has gone out of it. The anthology will be made, but it will, I fear, have the same relation to the month's "Musing" that a falcon skilfully stuffed in the attitude of flight has to the living flash or swoop through the air. It is because the "Musings" were methodically "without method" that they were so living. Whibley followed faithfully and easily the movement of his own mind; he did not, as I and most people do, have to think up half a dozen subjects to talk about and then shuffle them into the most suitable order; the transition from one subject to the next suggested itself. Critics sometimes comment upon the sudden transitions and juxtapositions of modern poetry: that is, when right and successful, an application of somewhat the same method without method. Whether the transition is cogent or not, is merely a question of whether the mind is *serré* or *délié,* whether the whole personality is involved; and certainly, the whole personality of Whibley is present in whatever he wrote, and it is the unity of a personality which gives an indissoluble unity to his variety of subject.

In attaining such unity, and indeed in attaining a *living* style, whether in prose or in verse, the practice of conversation is invaluable. Indeed, I believe that to write well it is necessary to converse a great deal. I say "converse" instead of "talk"; because I believe that there are two types of good writers: those who talk a great deal to others, and those, perhaps less fortunate, who talk a great deal to themselves. It is two thousand and hundreds of years since, that the theory was propounded that thought is conversation with oneself; all literary creation certainly springs either from the habit of talking to oneself or from the habit of talking to others. Most people are unable to do either, and that is why they lead such active lives. But any one who would write must let himself go, in one way or the other, for there are only four ways of thinking: to talk to others, or to one other, or to talk to oneself, or to talk to God.

Whibley had another quality, not unrelated to the preceding, which is essential for the literary critic. The first requisite of literary criticism, as of every other literary or artistic activity, is that it shall be interesting. And the first condition of being interesting is to have the tact to choose only those subjects in which one is really inerested, those which are germane to one's own temper. Universality of knowledge is a less chimerical ideal than universality of taste; but there is a kind of saturation in the text of an author, more important than erudition. Whibley had this discretion, that of the *honnête homme* as critic, to select subjects suited to his own temperament. Learning he had and scholarship. He was a good Grecian, and no Hellenist. His standards of classical scholarship were acquired from such devoted scholars as R. A. Neil, but having acquired them he wore them easily. He did not, like some more pretentious and pontifical critics, occupy himself with reviewing and bluepencilling literary reputations already well established, or adding one more superfluous essay to the bibliography of some already over-criticized author. In consequence, he has added to English criticism a number of essays on subjects which have never been so well handled (if handled at all) in the past, and to his treatment of which there will be little to add in the future; and has thereby made a secure place for himself in criticism.

I have said earlier that he took a particular delight in men of letters who were gentlemen or ragamuffins; perhaps his greatest enjoyment and amusement was in men of letters who were something of both. His appreciation of Sir Thomas Urquhart, Christianus Presbyteromastix, descended from Adam the Protoplast, with his *Ekskubalauron* and his *Logopandekteison*, as well as his great translation of Rabelais, is the best possible introduction to that author. As in politics Whibley saw theory through men, so in literature he was at his best, and indeed most just in his criticism, when the author of an admired work was also a man after his own heart. Another essay which shows this delight in personality, even to the point of conjecture, is his essay on Petronius. Who else would have thought to remark of the author of the *Satyricon* that he "was a great gentleman"? but the phrase, as used here by Whibley, has its proper significance. It is not, however, true that he often distorted the literary value because of his enjoyment of the author's personality; he is able to say truly that "Petronius is as secret as Shakespeare, as impersonal as Flaubert." On the other hand, he is able to appreciate the book even when one feels that he has some dislike of the author, as with Laurence Sterne. And in the essay on Petronius his amused and Catholic delight in what he called "the underworld of letters" is as well expressed as anywhere.

"You may meet Encolpius today [he says] without surprise or misunderstanding. He haunts the bars of the Strand, or hides him in the dismal alleys of Gray's Inn Road. One there was (one of how many!) who after a brilliant career at the University, found the highway his natural home, and forthwith deserted the groves of learning for the common hedgerow of adventure. The race-course knew him, and the pavement of London; blacklegs and touts were his chosen companions; now and again he would appear among his old associates, and enjoy a taste of Trimalchio's banquet, complaining the while that the money spent on his appetite might have been better employed in the backing of horses. Though long since he forgot he was a gentleman, he always remembered that he was a scholar, and, despite his drunken blackguardism, he still took refuge in Horace from the grime and squalor of his favourite career. Not long since he was discovered in a cellar, hungry and dishevelled; a tallow candle crammed into a beer-bottle was his only light; yet so reckless was his irresponsibility that he forgot his pinched belly and his ragged coat, and sat on the stone floor, reciting Virgil to another of his profession. Thus, if you doubt the essential truth of Petronius, you may see his grim comedy enacted every day. . . ."

I would not give the impression, however, that Whibley's service to letters was simply to fish up from the bottom of the past its forgotten and outmoded cranks and whimsies, any more than it was to descant amusingly upon greater and well-known writers. His peculiar merit as a critic, I think, resided in the combination of this personal gusto and curiosity, with a faculty of just literary appreciation. If he talked of Lucian or Herondas otherwise than professors do, he did not see them out of scale with the greatest masterpieces of Greek literature, nor did he merely bring forth a pleasant chat. He was not a bookish critic in the style of James Russell Lowell. And if he talked of the minor writers and journalists of the sixteenth and seventeenth century, with whom he had so much sympathy and for whom he had so much charity, it was never to elevate them above their proper place. The history of literature, he might have said, is always being simplified into a Hall of Fame of dusty noble statues and a list of names such as are used for decorating the domes of libraries. But the *honnête homme* in literary appreciation cannot be satisfied to worship a few mummified reputations; he must have the imagination and the heart to desire to feel literature as something alive; and we can touch the life of the great works of literature of any age all the better if we know something of the less.

As I said before, Whibley had what is perhaps the first of all critical gifts, without which others are vain: the ability to detect the living style from the dead. (And I may interject parenthetically, that though he never criticized in print any of the writers of my own generation, I found in conversation that he was able to recognize vitality even in writers with whom he had little sympathy.) It is largely owing to his insight and enthusiasm, as well as to his editorial toil, that the Tudor Trans-

lators have become recognized as they deserve. In his appreciation of these humble workmen and great prose writers, he shows
the recognition of the life, not merely of men, but of speech, as
expressed in a note which he wrote many years ago on Henry
Bradley's *The Making of English* (*Blackwood's*, Aug. 1904,
p. 280):

"He, therefore, is the finest master of style who never loses
hold of the past, who feels, what he can only express to minds as
knowing as his own, that the words of his choice have each its
own pedigree and its own life. Nor will he limit himself either
to Saxon or to Latin. He will use the full resources of his
speech with a justified pride, remembering that our language
has as many colonies as our King, and that in this one respect
at least we are the resolute conquerors of the world."

It is in such ways as I have indicated, not aspiring to any
literary dictatorship or pontificate, or to academic or extra-
academic honours, and never caring to express his mind except
on what really interested him or excited his admiration or in-
dignation, that Charles Whibley made and holds his place in
literary criticism. He was too modest, and had too varied tastes
and interests in life, to care to be the monumental critic; and
indeed, the monumental and encyclopaedic critic is to be regarded with a carefully appraising eye; for the monument is
sometimes constructed either by indifference to literature or by
indifference to life. Criticism, certainly, was only a part of his
activity in life; and in being only a part, it is genuine in its
kind. I had no intention in this paper to estimate his place in
the tradition social and political which is represented by his
connexion with W. E. Henley and his early labours on the
Scots Observer and the *National Observer;* that is the subject-
matter of other chapters; I allude to them merely as a reminder of the place of his literary essays in his work.

There is a passage in one of his "Musings without Method,"
celebrating the late Professor York Powell of Oxford (*Blackwood's*, June 1904, p. 860 ff.), which I may be permitted to
transcribe with suitable excisions and slight alteration, as appli-
cable by analogy to its author:

"There was nothing that had happened in the past which was not of living interest to him. No man of his time had a deeper acquaintance with life, literature, and policy. . . . He was, for instance, the first or second expert (for he had a rival) in the history of the Prize Ring. We remember once that, the art of pantomime being mentioned in his presence, he was ready with a complete biography of Dubureau, together with an account of the pantomimes which Gautier and Charles Nodier wrote for him. This is but a single instance, taken at random, of his multifarious knowledge. . . . His knowledge of literature outstripped the common boundaries of this country or that . . . but his chief interest was perhaps in the French poetry of the newest school. He spoke French and understood it with an ease and a skill that is given to few Englishmen. . . . Like the late W. E. Henley, with whom he had many points of . . . sympathy, he was a keen upholder of some oppressed citizens, and at the same time a sturdy Jingo, where the interests of England were involved. . . . While the egoism of most men inspires them to the composition of a work which shall make them forever famous, [he] lavished his gifts in talk, and made his friend a sharer, as it were, in his own talent. . . . In conversation no subject came amiss to him, because he was familiar with all; but he was so richly endowed with humour that he regarded nothing with an overserious eye. . . . The result is that, while his contemporaries will do full justice to his temperament and omniscience, he may appear to posterity, which knew him not, as far less than he really was. . . . But he has lived his life; he has scattered his learning with a generous hand; he has bequeathed a memory of affection to all who knew him; he has set his mark on works of younger men. . . . And who shall say that this achievement is not greater than half a dozen volumes in octavo?"

MODERN EDUCATION AND
THE CLASSICS

―――

QUESTIONS of education are frequently discussed as if they bore no relation to the social system in which and for which the education is carried on. This is one of the commonest reasons for the unsatisfactoriness of the answers. It is only within a particular social system that a system of education has any meaning. If education today seems to deteriorate, if it seems to become more and more chaotic and meaningless, it is primarily because we have no settled and satisfactory arrangement of society, and because we have both vague and diverse opinions about the kind of society we want. Education is a subject which cannot be discussed in a void: our questions raise other questions, social, economic, financial, political. And the bearings are on more ultimate problems even than these: to know what we want in education we must know what we want in general, we must derive our theory of education from our philosophy of life. The problem turns out to be a religious problem.

One might almost speak of a *crisis* of education. There are particular problems for each country, for each civilization, just as there are particular problems for each parent; but there is also a general problem for the whole civilized world, and for the uncivilized so far as it is being taught by its civilized superiors; a problem which may be as acute in Japan, in China or in India as in Britain or Europe or America. The progress (I do not mean the extension) of education for several centuries has been from one aspect a drift, from another aspect a push; for it has tended to be dominated by the idea of *getting on*. The individual wants more education, not as an aid to the acquisition of

wisdom but in order to get on; the nation wants more in order
to get the better of other nations, the class wants it to get the
better of other classes, or at least to hold its own against them.
Education is associated therefore with technical efficiency on the
one hand, and with rising in society on the other. Education becomes something to which everybody has a "right," even ir-
respective of his capacity; and when everyone gets it—by that
time, of course, in a diluted and adulterated form—then we
naturally discover that education is no longer an infallible means
of getting on, and people turn to another fallacy: that of "education for leisure"—without having revised their notions of
"leisure." As soon as this precious motive of snobbery evaporates, the zest has gone out of education; if it is not going to
mean more money, or more power over others, or a better social
position, or at least a steady and respectable job, few people are
going to take the trouble to acquire education. For deteriorate
it as you may, education is still going to demand a good deal of
drudgery. And the majority of people are incapable of enjoying
leisure—that is, unemployment *plus* an income and a status of
respectability—in any but pretty simple forms—such as balls
propelled by hand, by foot, and by engines or tools of various
types; in playing cards; or in watching dogs, horses or other
men engage in feats of speed or skill. The uneducated man with
an empty mind, if he be free from financial anxiety or narrow
limitation, and can obtain access to golf-clubs, dance halls, etc.,
is, for all I can see, as well equipped to fill his leisure contentedly as is the educated man.

The inadequacy of most people's notions of education is revealed whenever there is any public discussion on the subject
of raising the school age. To dismiss as irrelevant the miserable
stop-gap idea that raising the school-leaving age will diminish
unemployment—a mere confession of inability to solve a different problem—it is assumed by most people (and there are always a great many people ready to discuss the problem) that
more education—that is to say, more years of education—would
be a good thing "if the nation could afford it." Of course the
nation could afford it, if it is such a good thing as all that. But
no one stops to consider what is this education of which no one

can have too much; or whether the society in which more of this education is a good thing is necessarily a good society. If, for instance, the "nation," or the people composing it, have only a little money, should we not assure ourselves first that our elementary education is already so good that no money could improve it, before we attempt a more ambitious programme? (Anyone who has taught children even for a few weeks knows that the size of a class makes an immense difference to the amount you can teach. Fifteen is an ideal number; twenty is the maximum; with thirty much less can be done; with more than thirty most teachers' first concern is simply to keep order, and the clever children creep at the pace of the backward.)

The first task of anyone who might be imagined as occupying a dictatorial position in the education of a country should obviously be to see that elementary education is as good as it can be made; and then proceeding forward make sure that no one received *too much* education, limiting the numbers treated to "higher education" to a third (let us say) of those receiving that treatment today. (I do not want a dictator even in education, but it is sometimes convenient to employ a hypothetical dictator in illustration.) For one of the potential causes of deterioration of the universities is the deterioration lower down. The universities have to teach what they can to the material they can get: nowadays they even teach *English* in England. American universities, ever since Charles William Eliot and his contemporary "educators," have tried to make themselves as big as possible in a mad competition for numbers: it is very much easier to turn a little university into a big one than to reduce the size of one that has grown too big. And after Eliot had taught America that a university should be as big as possible (and I have seen one that boasted an enrolment of 18,000 students—including, I must explain, evening classes) America grew very rich—that is to say, it produced a considerable number of millionaires, and the next generation set itself to an equally mad programme of building, erecting within a short time a great variety of imposing, though in some places rather hastily-built, halls and dormitories and even chapels. And when you have sunk so much money in plant and equipment, when you have a very large (though not always well-paid) staff of men who are mostly married and have a few children, when you are turning out from your graduate schools more and more men who have been trained to become teachers in other universities, and who will probably want to marry and have children too; when your whole national system of higher education is designed for an age of expansion, for a country which is going indefinitely to increase its population, grow rich, and build more universities—then you will find it very difficult to retract.

What happens in America is not so irrelevant to British affairs as it is commonly taken to be. For, as I have already said, what we have to recognize is a crisis of education not in one country but in all, a crisis which has its common features everywhere. What has happened in American universities can happen in provincial universities in England; and what happens in provincial universities exerts influence on what happens in Oxford and Cambridge. We are well advanced in an age of great social changes. I do not object to that; but I think that if we admit that social change inevitably means change in our system of education, in our conceptions of *who* should be educated, and *how*, and of the still more neglected question, *why*, we shall be better able to give intelligent direction, instead of leaving education to take care of itself.

It is against this shifting vast background, very important for my picture, that I would set the question of the place of the classics in modern education. We discern three tendencies in education as in politics, the *liberal*, the *radical*, and what I am tempted to call, perhaps simply because it is my own, the *orthodox*. In using these terms about tendencies in education I do not wish to draw any close political parallel, because in politics there is no pure breed of any kind.

The *liberal* attitude towards education is that with which we are the most familiar. It is apt to maintain the apparently unobjectionable view that education is not a mere acquisition of facts, but a training of the mind as an instrument, to deal with any class of facts, to reason, and to apply the training obtained in one department in dealing with new ones. The inference is drawn that one subject is as good, for education, as another; that the student should follow his own bent, and pursue whatever subject happens most to interest him. The student who applies himself to geology, and he who applies himself to languages, may both in the end find themselves in trade: it is assumed that if they both have made the most of their opportunities, and have equal abilities, they will both be equally fitted for their vocation, and for "life." I think that the theory that the mind can be trained equally well upon any subject, and that the choice of the class of facts to acquire is indifferent, can be pushed too far. There are two kinds of subject which, at an early stage, provide but poor training for the mind. One is the subject which is concerned more with theories, and the history of theories, than with the storing of the mind with such information and knowledge as theories are built upon: such a subject, and a very popular one, is *economics*, which consists of a number of complicated and contradictory theories, a subject by no means proved to be a science, usually based on illicit assumptions, the bastard progeny of a parent it disowns, *ethics*. Even *philosophy*, when divorced from *theology* and from the knowledge of life and of ascertainable facts, is but a famishing pabulum, or a draught stimulating for a moment, leaving behind drought and disillusion. The other kind of subject which provides indifferent training is that which is too minute and particular, the relation of which to the general business of living is not made evident. And there is a third subject, equally bad as training, which does not fall into either of these classes, but which is bad for reasons of its own: the study of *English Literature* or, to be more comprehensive, the literature of one's own language.

Another fallacy of liberal education is that the student who advances to the university should take up the study that interests him most. For a small number of students this is in the main right. Even at a very early stage of school life, we can identify a few individuals with a definite inclination towards one group of studies or another. The danger for these fortunate ones is that if left to themselves they will overspecialize, they will be wholly ignorant of the general interests of human beings. We are all in one way or another naturally lazy, and it is much easier to confine ourselves to the study of subjects in which we excel. But the great majority of the people who are to be educated have no very strong inclination to specialize, because they have no definite gifts or tastes. Those who have more lively and curious minds will tend to smatter. No one can become really educated without having pursued some study in which he took no interest —for it is a part of education to *learn to interest ourselves* in subjects for which we have no aptitude.

The doctrine of studying the subject we like (and for many youths in the process of development this is often only what they like at the moment) is most disastrous for those whose interests lie in the field of modern languages or in that of history, and worst of all for those who fancy that they will become writers. For it is these people—and there are many of them— for whom the deficiency of Latin and Greek is most unfortunate. Those who have a real genius for acquiring these dead languages are few, and they are pretty likely of their own accord to devote themselves to the Classics—if they are given the opportunity. But there are many more of us who have gifts for modern languages, or for our own language, or for history, who have only a modest capacity for mastering Latin and Greek. We can hardly be expected to realize, during adolescence, that without a foundation of Latin and Greek we remain limited in our power over these other subjects.

Now while *liberalism* committed the folly of pretending that one subject is as good as another for study, and that Latin and Greek are simply *no better* than a great many others, *radicalism* (the offspring of liberalism) discards this attitude of universal toleration and pronounces Latin and Greek to be subjects of little import. Liberalism had excited superficial curiosity. Never before had so much miscellaneous information been made available to everybody, in degrees of simplification adapted to everyone's capacity for assimilation. The entertaining epitomes of Mr. H. G. Wells bear witness in their popularity; new discoveries are made known to the whole world at once; and everyone knows that the universe is expanding or else it is contracting. In dissipated curiosity about such novelties great numbers of people, many of them poor and deserving, think that they are improving their minds, or passing their leisure in a praiseworthy occupation. Radicalism then proceeds to organize the "vital issues," and reject what is not vital. A modern literary critic, who has gained considerable publicity by Marxist criticism of literature, has told us that the real men of our time are such as the Lenins, Trotskys, Gorkys and Stalins; also the Einsteins, Plancks and Hunt Morgans. To this critic *knowledge* means "primarily scientific knowledge of the world about us and of ourselves." This statement might be given a respectable interpretation; but I am afraid that the critic meant only what the man in the street means. By "scientific knowledge of the world about us" he does *not* mean understanding of life. By scientific knowledge of ourselves he does *not* mean self-knowledge. In short, while liberalism did not know what it wanted of education, radicalism does know; and it wants the wrong thing.

Radicalism is, however, to be applauded for wanting something. It is to be applauded for wanting to select and eliminate, even if it wants to select and to eliminate the wrong things. If you have a definite ideal for society, then you are right to cultivate what is useful for the development and maintenance of that society, and discourage what is useless and distracting. And we have been too long without an ideal. It is a commonplace nowadays that Russian communism is a religion. Then its rulers must educate the young in the tenets of that religion. I am trying to indicate now the *fundamental* defence of Latin and Greek, not merely give you a collection of excellent reasons for studying them, reasons which you can think of for yourselves. There are two and only two finally tenable hypotheses about life: the Catholic and the materialistic. The defence of the study of the classical languages must ultimately rest upon their association with the former, as must the defence of the primacy of the contemplative over the active life. To associate the Classics with a sentimental Toryism, combination-rooms, classical quotations in the House of Commons, is to give them a flimsy justification, but hardly more flimsy than to defend them by a philosophy of humanism—that is, by a tardy rearguard action which attempts to arrest the progress of liberalism just before the end of its march: an action, besides, which is being fought by troops which are already half liberalized themselves. It is high time that the defence of the Classics should be dissociated from objects which, however excellent under certain conditions and in a certain environment, are of only relative importance—a traditional public-school system, a traditional university system, a decaying social order—and permanently associated where they belong, with something permanent: the historical Christian Faith.

I do not ignore the great value which negative and obstructive forces can have. The longer the better schools and the older universities in this country (for they have pretty well given up the struggle in America) can maintain some standard of classical education, the better for those who look to the future with an active desire for reform and an intelligent acceptance of change. But to expect from our educational institutions any more positive contribution to the future would be vain. As only the Catholic and the communist know, *all* education must be ultimately religious education. I do not mean that education should be confined to postulants for the priesthood or for the higher ranks of Soviet bureaucracy; I mean that the hierarchy of education should be a religious hierarchy. The universities are too far gone in secularization, they have too long lost any common fundamental assumption as to what education is for, and they are too big. It might be hoped that they would eventually follow, or else be relegated to preservation as curious architectural remains; but they cannot be expected to lead.

It is quite possible, of course, that the future may bring neither a Christian nor a materialistic civilization. It is quite possible that the future may bring nothing but chaos or torpor. In that event, I am not interested in the future; I am only interested in the two alternatives which seem to me worthy of interest. I am only here concerned with readers who are prepared to prefer a Christian civilization, if a choice is forced upon them; and it is only upon readers who wish to see a Christian civilization survive and develop that I am urging the importance of the study of Latin and Greek. If Christianity is not to survive, I shall not mind if the texts of the Latin and Greek languages became more obscure and forgotten than those of the language of the Etruscans. And the only hope that I can see for the study of

Latin and Greek, in their proper place and for the right reasons, lies in the revival and expansion of monastic teaching orders. There are other reasons, and of the greatest weight, for desiring to see a revival of the monastic life in its variety, but the maintenance of Christian education is not the least. The first educational task of the communities should be the *preservation* of education within the cloister, uncontaminated by the deluge of barbarism outside; their second, the provision of education for the laity, which should be something more than education for a place in the Civil Service, or for technical efficiency, or for social or public success. It would not be that tawdry adornment, "education for leisure." As the world at large becomes more completely secularized, the need becomes more urgent that professedly Christian people should have a Christian education, which should be an education both for this world and for the life of prayer in this world.